How to Do
Everything™

iPhone® 4S

Guy Hart-Davis

New York Chicago San Francisco Lisbon
London Madrid Mexico City Milan New Delhi
San Juan Seoul Singapore Sydney Toronto

The McGraw·Hill Companies

Library of Congress Cataloging-in-Publication Data

Hart-Davis, Guy.
  How to do everything : iPhone 4S / Guy Hart-Davis.
     p. cm.
  ISBN 978-0-07-178307-1 (alk. paper)
 1. iPhone (Smartphone) 2. Smartphones. 3. Pocket computers. I.
Title. II. Title: iPhone 4S.
  QA76.8.I64H37 2012
  004.16'7--dc23

                                                    2011050528

McGraw-Hill books are available at special quantity discounts to use as premiums and sales promotions, or for use in corporate training programs. To contact a representative, please e-mail us at bulksales@ mcgraw-hill.com.

How to Do Everything™: iPhone® 4S

23456789   DOC DOC   165432

ISBN   978-0-07-178307-1
MHID   0-07-178307-5

Sponsoring Editor Megg Morin	**Copy Editor** William McManus	**Composition** Fortuitous Publishing Services
Editorial Supervisor Janet Walden	**Proofreader** Paul Tyler	**Illustration** Fortuitous Publishing Services
Project Editor Howie Severson	**Indexer** Jack Lewis	**Art Director, Cover** Jeff Weeks
Technical Editor Dwight Spivey	**Production Supervisor** Jean Bodeaux	**Cover Designer** Jeff Weeks

Images used Courtesy of Apple, Inc.

This book is dedicated to the people who gave us the iPhone.

No iPhones were harmed during the writing of this book.

About the Author

Guy Hart-Davis is the author of more than 70 computer books, including *How to Do Everything: iPod touch*; *How to Do Everything: iPod & iTunes, Sixth Edition*; *The Healthy PC, Second Edition*; *PC QuickSteps, Second Edition*; *How to Do Everything with Microsoft Office Word 2007*; and *How to Do Everything with Microsoft Office Excel 2007*. Guy's website is at www.ghdbooks.com.

About the Technical Editor

Dwight Spivey is a technical editor and the author of all three editions of *How to Do Everything: Mac*, among many other books. He lives on the Gulf Coast of Alabama with his beautiful wife and is blessed with four amazing children.

Contents at a Glance

Contents

PART I Get Up and Running with Your iPhone

PART II   Use Your iPhone for Communications

CHAPTER 7   Make Phone Calls and Video Calls **195**

CHAPTER 8   Communicate via E-Mail and Instant Messaging **213**

PART III   Use Your iPhone for Entertainment

Acknowledgments

I'd like to thank the following people for their help with this book:

- Megg Morin for developing the book
- Dwight Spivey for reviewing the manuscript for technical accuracy and contributing many helpful suggestions
- Bill McManus for editing the manuscript with a light touch
- Janet Walden for assisting with the production of the book
- Howie Severson for coordinating the production of the book and laying out the pages
- Jack Lewis for creating the index

Introduction

The iPhone is hands-down the best cell phone you can get—but I'm sure you know that already. Small enough to fit easily into your hand or pocket but as powerful as a full-size laptop computer from a couple of years ago, your iPhone puts an incredible amount of computing power right where you need it.

Better still, your iPhone's sleek operating system, iOS, makes that computing power easy and intuitive to use. And not only does your iPhone come with a set of well-designed apps for everything from phoning and e-mailing to surfing the Web and keeping track of your commitments, but you can install third-party software that caters to almost every need imaginable.

Best of all, your iPhone has your very own personal digital assistant built in, ready to respond to the commands you speak.

What Does This Book Cover?

This book covers all you need to know to get the most out of your iPhone. The book contains 20 chapters broken up into five parts.

Part I, "Get Up and Running with Your iPhone," gets you started using your iPhone:

- Chapter 1, "Get Your iPhone and Set It Up," walks you through choosing the iPhone model that will suit you best, deciding between syncing it with your computer (PC or Mac) or with Apple's iCloud online service, and getting the iPhone set up and working. You meet your iPhone's user interface, learn how to navigate the Home screen, and discover how to launch apps. And you get to know Siri, your iPhone's voice-controlled personal assistant.

 You'll find "Tell Siri to..." sidebars throughout the book to help you learn what Siri can help you with and how you should phrase your requests.

- Chapter 2, "Load Your iPhone with Music, Videos, and Data," shows you how to start creating your iTunes library on your computer, how to choose which items to sync with your iPhone, and how to perform the sync. You also learn how to recharge your iPhone and how to eject and disconnect it from your computer.

- Chapter 3, "Connect Your iPhone to Wireless Networks and the Internet," explains how to connect your iPhone to your home wireless network, to your work wireless network, and to public wireless networks such as Wi-Fi hotspots. You learn how to make those connections safely, how to tell your iPhone which networks to prefer over others, and how to make it forget a network you no longer want to use.
- Chapter 4, "Choose Essential Settings on Your iPhone," takes you through opening the Settings app and choosing values for all the settings that aren't covered in detail elsewhere in the book. This is a long and daunting chapter, so you'll probably want to dip into it to learn about the settings for an app at a time rather than try to read through it from start to end.
- Chapter 5, "Take, Edit, and Share Photos and Videos," teaches you how to maximize your use of your iPhone's two cameras, the Cameras app, and the Photos app. Your iPhone not only can take high-quality photos and videos but can edit and share them too. You'll also learn how to use the High Dynamic Range feature to get higher-impact photos.
- Chapter 6, "Install and Manage Apps on Your iPhone," shows you how to find and install third-party apps—programs—that bring new capabilities to your iPhone. To get the apps, you use Apple's App Store, an online store that has more than half a million apps at this writing. You'll also learn how to install apps provided by your company or organization if you use your iPhone as a work tool.

Part II, "Use Your iPhone for Communications," shows you how to make phone and FaceTime calls, send and receive e-mail messages and instant messages, surf the Web, and keep your contacts and calendars with you:

- Chapter 7, "Make Phone Calls and Video Calls," shows you how to make phone calls quickly and easily—and how to set up conference calls in seconds. You also learn how to make video calls to iPhone, iPad, iPod touch, and Mac users by using FaceTime.
- Chapter 8, "Communicate via E-Mail and Instant Messaging," teaches you how to set up and use your iPhone's powerful Mail app for sending, receiving, and managing e-mail wherever you are. You also learn how to use the Messages app to send messages via Short Message Service (SMS), Multimedia Messaging Service (MMS), and Apple's iMessage service.
- Chapter 9, "Surf the Web on Your iPhone," takes you through using the Safari web browser for surfing the Web with your iPhone. Among other features, you learn how to make web pages more readable with the handy Safari Reader feature, how to open multiple web pages at the same time, and how to use the Private Browsing feature to surf secretly.
- Chapter 10, "Keep Your Calendars and Contacts Up to Date," explains how to use the Calendars app to keep tabs on your commitments and how to use the Contacts app to stay in touch with your contacts.

Part III, "Use Your iPhone for Entertainment," explains how to play music and video on your iPhone and how to use the built-in apps we don't cover in other chapters:

- Chapter 11, "Enjoy Music and Video on Your iPhone," shows you how to play music using the Music app and how to play videos using either the Videos app or the YouTube app. It also tells you how to use your iPhone as your home stereo and car stereo.
- Chapter 12, "Make the Most of the Built-in Apps," covers using the Notification Center app, the Reminders app, the Weather app, the Stocks app, the Calculator app, the Maps app, the Clock app, the Notes app, and the Voice Memos app.
- Chapter 13, "Create a Great Audio and Video Library for the iPhone and iTunes," explains how to buy and download songs online, how to manage your music and video library with iTunes, and how to create video files that work with your iPhone. You also learn how to recover your songs and videos from your iPhone if your iTunes library gets corrupted, and how to use iTunes' Home Sharing and regular sharing features.
- Chapter 14, "Use Your iPhone for File Backup, Storage, and Transfer," tells you how to use your iPhone as a highly portable external drive. This is a great way of keeping vital files with you or for moving hefty files from point A to point B. This chapter shows you how to use both the File Sharing feature in iTunes and third-party apps that give direct access to your iPhone's file system.

Part IV, "Use Your iPhone as a Work Tool," helps you use your iPhone as a corporate productivity tool:

- Chapter 15, "Connect to Your Company's Network via VPN," shows you how to use virtual private networking (VPN) to establish a secure connection to your company's network across the Internet. You can create the VPN connection either manually or by applying a configuration profile, a file an administrator provides to set up the connection automatically.
- Chapter 16, "Connect Your iPhone to Your Company's Exchange Server," explains how to set up Microsoft Exchange accounts on your iPhone. As with VPNs, you can either set up an account manually or apply a configuration profile to set it up automatically. You also learn how to troubleshoot some key problems that occur when connecting to Exchange Server.
- Chapter 17, "Create, Edit, and Share Business Documents on Your iPhone," explores your options for creating and editing word-processing documents, spreadsheets, presentations, and PDF files on your iPhone. The chapter also shows you how to share documents between your iPhone and your PC or Mac.

Part V, "Advanced Moves," teaches you advanced tricks and techniques for getting more out of your iPhone and troubleshooting problems:

- Chapter 18, "Take Your iPhone to the Limit," tells you how to use your iPhone with multiple computers rather than with a single computer, how to keep your iPhone running at full speed, and how to create custom ringtones from songs. You also learn how to share your iPhone's Internet connection with your computers or other devices by using the Personal Hotspot feature.

- Chapter 19, "Troubleshoot Your iPhone," explains what's in your iPhone, tells you how to take care of it, and then shows you essential troubleshooting moves. You learn how to troubleshoot connection issues between your iPhone and your computer; how to deal with app crashes; how to restart, reset, or erase your iPhone; and how to restore its software using iTunes.
- Chapter 20, "Troubleshoot iTunes," shows you how to sort out problems with iTunes. We'll look first at problems that occur with iTunes on Windows, then at iTunes on the Mac, and finally look at how to troubleshoot the Home Sharing feature on both operating systems.

Conventions Used in This Book

To make its meaning clear without using far more words than necessary, this book uses a number of conventions, several of which are worth mentioning here:

- Note, Tip, and Caution paragraphs highlight information to draw it to your notice.
- Sidebars provide in-depth focus on important topics.
- *Tell Siri to* sidebars show you how to give instructions effectively to your digital assistant.
- The pipe character or vertical bar denotes choosing an item from a menu. For example, "choose File | Open" means that you should click the File menu and select the Open item on it. Use the keyboard, mouse, or a combination of the two as you wish.
- The ⌘ symbol represents the COMMAND key on the Mac—the key that bears the Apple symbol and the quad-infinity mark on most Mac keyboards.
- Most check boxes have two states: *selected* (with a check mark in them) and *cleared* (without a check mark in them). This book tells you to *select* a check box or *clear* a check box rather than "click to place a check mark in the box" or "click to remove the check mark from the box." (Often, you'll be verifying the state of the check box, so it may already have the required setting—in which case, you don't need to click at all.) Some check boxes have a third state as well, in which they're selected but dimmed and unavailable. This state is usually used for options that apply to only part of the current situation.

Tip For extra information about using your iPhone and iTunes, visit my website. Point your browser at www.ghdbooks.com, and then click the picture of this book's cover to reach the pages on iOS devices and iTunes.

PART I

Get Up and Running with Your iPhone

1

Get Your iPhone and Set It Up

HOW TO...

- Get your iPhone
- Choose how you will sync your iPhone
- Get your PC or Mac ready to work with your iPhone
- Set up your iPhone using iTunes or iCloud
- Navigate the Home screen and the apps
- Greet Siri, your personal assistant

In this chapter, we'll go over how to get your iPhone and how to get it working. There are two ways to get it working. First, you can set up your iPhone using Apple's iTunes program on your PC or Mac, and then sync the iPhone using iTunes. Second, you can set up your iPhone to work without a computer by using an account on Apple's iCloud service.

We'll look at the iTunes approach first. All current Macs come with everything your iPhone needs, but you may need to add hardware to older Macs. You may also need to update iTunes to the latest version. With PCs, you will likely need to install iTunes. You may also need to add hardware. We'll make sure your PC or Mac is set up with everything the iPhone needs, and then go through the steps of connecting the iPhone to the computer and setting it up using iTunes.

After that, we'll look at the second approach, setting up your iPhone by using iCloud.

At the end of the chapter, I'll give you a quick tour of your iPhone's user interface. You'll learn how to navigate the Home screen and launch apps. Finally, I'll show you how to summon Siri, your personal assistant, and tell Siri what you want.

Get Your iPhone

The first step is to get your iPhone. If you've already gotten your hands on an iPhone, go straight ahead to the next section. Otherwise, decide which iPhone you want, choose the source and carrier, and then go get the iPhone.

Where to Get an iPhone

The following list shows the main sources of iPhones. Which options are available to you depends on which country or region you're in.

- **Apple Store (online)**   Along with Macs, iPads, and iPods, the Apple Store sells iPhones. In some countries or regions, you need to choose your carrier when buying the iPhone. For example, in the United States, the Apple Store gives you the choice among AT&T, Sprint, and Verizon. Your iPhone then comes with a SIM card in it and is locked to that carrier. In other places, you buy an unlocked iPhone without a SIM card, and then insert a suitable SIM card for your preferred carrier.
- **Apple Store (physical)**   If you have an Apple Store within striking distance, getting your iPhone from it may be a good choice, because the Apple Store lets you check out the iPhone extensively before buying and gives you a full choice of carriers for your country or region.
- **Carrier stores**   If you know which carrier you want to use, you can go to that carrier's store. For example, in the United States, you can go to an AT&T store, Sprint store, or Verizon store.
- **Third-party stores**   If you want to compare carriers and perhaps phones, go to a third-party store such as RadioShack, Best Buy, Target, or Sam's Club in the United States.
- **Other online stores**   Depending on which country you're in, you may be able to find the iPhone in online stores. Buying from these stores typically involves paying full price for an unlocked iPhone in which you can insert a SIM card for the carrier of your choice.

Choose Which iPhone to Get

The iPhone 4S comes in two colors—black and white—and three capacities: 16GB, 32GB, and 64GB. That gives you a choice of six models.

As you'd imagine, the 64GB models cost more than the 32GB models, which in turn cost more than the 16GB models. Choosing among the three capacities can be tough. 16GB is just about enough space for apps, documents, and a decent number of photos, whereas 32GB is more than enough space for those items. So usually the question is how much music and video you want to be able to take with you.

 You may also want to use some space on the iPhone as a portable drive for keeping a copy of essential files with you or for moving large files from one computer to another.

Did You Know?

How the iPhone 4 Compares to the iPhone 4S

If the iPhone 4S is too expensive, consider the iPhone 4 instead. With the introduction of the iPhone 4S, Apple has turned the iPhone 4 into the lower-cost iPhone option. (Before the iPhone 4S came out, the iPhone 4 was top dog in the pack, and the iPhone 3GS was the lower-cost option. Before the iPhone 4, the iPhone 3GS was pack leader, and the iPhone 3G was the value option.)

The iPhone 4 runs iOS5, the same operating system as the iPhone 4S, so it has access to all the same software features. The big exception is Siri, the personal assistant feature, which requires the iPhone 4S's heavier hardware. Apart from this, the differences are in the hardware.

Apart from the obvious differences in size and shape, the differences between the iPhone 4 and the iPhone 4S lie in the hardware improvements the iPhone 4S brings over the iPhone 4. These are the key differences:

Item	iPhone 4	iPhone 4S
Processor type	A4	A5
Processor speed	1 GHz	1 GHz
RAM	512MB	512MB
Storage	16GB or 32GB	16GB, 32GB, or 64GB
Camera	5 megapixels	8 megapixels

Choose Among Different Phone Plans

If you're buying an iPhone locked to a carrier, you'll need to choose the right plan for it. As normal, you must balance three things:

- **Upfront price** If you buy a locked iPhone on a long-term contract, the carrier usually subsidizes the upfront price. This makes getting the iPhone much easier, even though the final cost (at the end of the contract) is usually higher.
- **Monthly cost and what you get for it** Most carriers offer assorted packages with different numbers of call minutes, text messages, and megabytes of data. Only you can determine which package will meet your needs.
- **Number of months** The longer the contract, the lower the price per month, but the more you pay in the end.

Buy an iPhone for Less

If you'd prefer not to pay full price for an iPhone, consider these alternatives:

- **Buy a refurbished iPhone from Apple** Apple sells refurbished iPhones at a discount—sometimes up to a third off the normal price. To find them, search the Apple Store (http://store.apple.com) for **refurbished iPhone.** These iPhones have a one-year limited warranty, which you should read before buying one (look for a link to the warranty on any page that offers a refurbished iPhone). You can also buy AppleCare to extend the coverage, although this is typically worthwhile only for the most expensive models.
- **Buy a used or reconditioned iPhone from another vendor** eBay and other sites carry used or reconditioned iPhones. The prices may be attractive, but even on a reconditioned model, you will not normally get a warranty—and it may be hard to determine the quality of the reconditioning.
- **Grab an old iPhone when a relative or friend upgrades** If you know someone who simply must have the latest technology, get ready to jump in line for their existing iPhone.

Choose Which Way You Will Sync Your iPhone

Your next step is to decide whether you will sync your iPhone using your computer or using iCloud.

If you have a computer that you use most of the time, and you store your songs and video files on it, syncing with the computer is normally your best choice. The computer can be either a PC running Windows or a Mac.

> **Tip** You can sync your iPhone much more quickly with your computer than with iCloud because the USB cable (or a Wi-Fi connection) is much faster than an Internet connection. Most likely, your computer also has much more storage available than a free iCloud account, but you can pay for more iCloud storage if you want.

But if you don't have a main computer of your own, or if you are moving beyond a computer to using just your iPhone and an iPad for your computing, use iCloud to sync your iPhone instead. Using iCloud enables you to sync your songs, videos, photos, and other content seamlessly between your iPhone and your other iOS devices, such as an iPad. Using iCloud also keeps a copy of your files online, protecting you against data loss if you damage or lose your iPhone.

If you're planning to use your PC or Mac to sync your iPhone, start with the next section. If you'll be using iCloud instead, go to the section "Set Up Your iPhone."

Get Your PC or Mac Ready for Your iPhone

If you use a computer much of the time, you'll probably find it easiest to use the computer to sync your iPhone. In this section, we'll look first at what your iPhone needs your computer to provide. We'll then go through how to make sure a PC meets these requirements, adding hardware as needed and installing iTunes. After that, we'll cover checking that a Mac has everything the iPhone needs.

Know What Your iPhone Needs Your Computer to Provide

If your PC or Mac is a recent model, it probably is ready to work with whichever new iPhone you choose. If it's older, or if it's a budget model, you may need to add new components.

Here is what your iPhone needs:

- **Computer**   A PC running Windows 7 (Home Premium, Professional, Ultimate, or Enterprise Edition), Windows Vista (Home Premium, Business, Ultimate, or Enterprise Edition), or either Windows XP Home Edition or Windows XP Professional with Service Pack 3; or a Mac running Mac OS X 10.7 (Lion), 10.6 (Snow Leopard), or 10.5 (Leopard).
- **USB port**   It's best to have a high-power USB 2.0 port, although you can scrape by with a USB 1.*x* port if you're prepared to be patient. The USB port must deliver enough power to recharge the iPhone. If your keyboard has a built-in USB port (as many Apple keyboards do), it may not deliver enough power for recharging.
- **Optical drive**   You'll need a CD drive or DVD drive if you want to be able to rip songs from CDs to put in iTunes and on the iPhone.
- **Burner drive**   You'll need a CD burner if you want to burn CDs from iTunes, or a DVD burner if you want to be able to burn both DVDs and CDs. (Most modern optical drives include burning capabilities.)
- **iTunes 10.5 or a later version**   Apple provides iTunes for free. We'll look at how to install or update iTunes later in this chapter.

Get Your PC Ready to Work with Your iPhone

If you bought your PC in 2003 or later, it most likely has everything you need to start using an iPhone and iTunes:

- A USB 2.0 port.
- Windows 7 (Home Premium, Professional, Ultimate, or Enterprise Edition), Windows Vista (Home Premium, Business, Ultimate, or Enterprise Edition), or Windows XP (either Home Edition or Professional) with Service Pack 3. (If you

Did You Know?

Why USB 2.0 Makes a Huge Difference

USB 2.0 is up to 40 times faster than USB 1.x, so you'll definitely want USB 2.0 if you have the choice. USB 1.x has a top speed of 12 megabits per second (Mbps), which translates to a maximum transfer of about 1.5MB of data per second; USB 2.0 has a top speed of 400 Mbps, which gives a data transfer rate of about 60MB per second.

As a result of this difference, loading an iPhone via a USB 2.0 port will go much faster than via a USB 1.x port. The higher the iPhone's capacity, the more painful the slowness of USB 1.x is.

At this writing, the latest version of USB—USB 3.0, also called SuperSpeed USB—has been released but its use isn't yet widespread, and Apple hasn't yet used it for either iPhones or Macs. USB 3.0 provides up to 5 gigabits per second (Gbps) and is backward compatible with USB 2.0, so if your PC has a USB 3.0 port, you can plug the iPhone into that port without problems.

Instead of adding USB 3.0 to Macs, Apple still uses USB 2.0. But Apple has also added a technology called Thunderbolt, which is even faster and more capable.

don't yet have Service Pack 3, you can download it from the Microsoft website for free.)

- A 500-MHz or faster processor. You can get away with a slower processor, but it won't be much fun.
- 1GB RAM (for Windows 7), 512MB RAM (for Windows Vista), or 128MB RAM (for Windows XP). Much more RAM is much better.
- Enough hard-disk space to contain your library, on either an internal hard disk or an external hard disk.
- A CD or DVD burner if you want to rip songs from CDs or burn songs to CDs or DVDs.

If your PC can't meet those specifications, read the following sections to learn about possible upgrades.

Add USB 2.0 if Necessary

Most PCs manufactured in 2003 or later include one or more USB 2.0 ports—some have a half-dozen or more USB ports. If your PC has one or more, you're all set. If your computer has only USB 1.x, you can add USB 2.0 by installing a PCI card in a desktop PC or by inserting a PC Card in a laptop PC that has a PC Card slot.

If you don't know whether your computer's USB ports are USB 1.x or USB 2.0, simply plug in the iPhone and set it up. Either iTunes or Windows itself will warn you if the device is using a USB 1.x port rather than a USB 2.0 port. The Windows warning is usually a notification-area pop-up saying "HI-SPEED USB Device Plugged into non-

HI-SPEED USB Hub" or "This USB device can perform faster if you connect it to a Hi-Speed USB 2.0 port," while the iTunes warning is an easy-to-understand message box.

Tip If your PC has USB 2.0 but is short of ports, get a USB 2.0 hub to add extra ports. Small USB hubs have around four ports, while larger USB hubs have seven ports or more. Many larger USB hubs have their own power supplies. Plugging in an extra power brick for a USB hub can be awkward, but it makes sure that the hub has the power it needs to feed your iPhone and other USB devices.

Check Your Operating System Version

Make sure your PC is running Windows 7, Windows Vista, or Windows XP with Service Pack 2 or Service Pack 3.

If you're in doubt about which version of Windows your computer is running, press WINDOWS KEY–BREAK, and then look at the System window (on Windows 7 or Windows Vista; see Figure 1-1) or the General tab of the System Properties dialog box (on Windows XP; see Figure 1-2). If your keyboard doesn't have a BREAK key, click the Start button, right-click Computer (in Windows 7 or Windows Vista) or My Computer (in Windows XP), and then click Properties on the context menu.

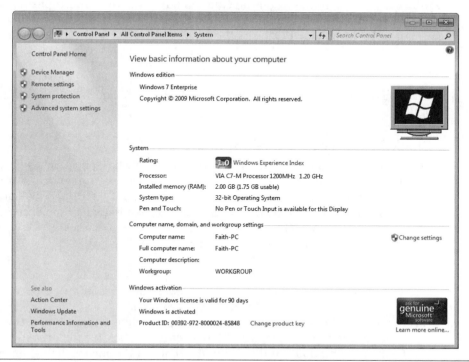

FIGURE 1-1 In Windows 7 and Windows Vista, the System window shows which version of Windows you're using, which Service Pack is installed (if any), and how much RAM the computer contains.

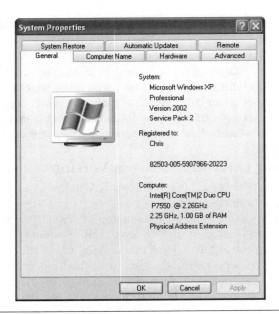

FIGURE 1-2 The readouts on the General tab of the System Properties dialog box typically include the version of Windows, the latest Service Pack installed, and the amount of RAM in your PC.

If you don't have Windows 7, Windows Vista, or Windows XP, it's well past time to upgrade to one of them.

Check Memory and Disk Space

If you don't know how much memory your computer has, check it. As in the previous section, press WINDOWS KEY–BREAK (or click the Start button, right-click Computer or My Computer, and click Properties on the context menu), and then look at the System window (on Windows 7 or Windows Vista) or the General tab of the System Properties dialog box (on Windows XP).

To check disk space, follow these steps:

1. Open a Windows Explorer window to display all the drives on your computer:
   - **Windows 7 or Windows Vista** Choose Start | Computer.
   - **Windows XP** Choose Start | My Computer.
2. Right-click the drive you want to check, and then choose Properties from the shortcut menu to display the Properties dialog box for the drive.
3. Look at the readout on the General tab of the Properties dialog box to see the amount of free space and used space on the drive. Figure 1-3 shows an example using Windows 7.
4. Click the OK button to close the Properties dialog box.

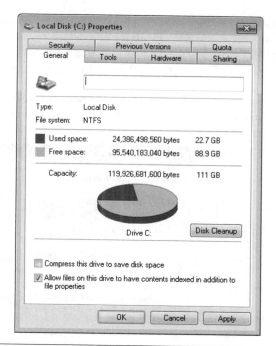

FIGURE 1-3   The General tab of the Properties dialog box for a drive shows you how much space has been used and how much remains free.

Add a Burner Drive if Necessary

If you want to be able to burn CDs or DVDs from iTunes, add a burner drive to your computer. Which drive technology is most appropriate depends on your computer type and configuration:

- For a desktop PC that has an open 5.25-inch bay and a spare internal drive connector, an internal burner drive is easiest.
- For a desktop PC that has no open 5.25-inch bay or no spare internal drive connector, or for a portable PC, get a USB 2.0 burner drive. If your PC has USB 3.0, you have the option of getting a USB 3.0 burner drive instead, but you may decide that USB 2.0 speed is adequate.

Install iTunes on Your PC

To install iTunes on your PC, follow these steps:

1. Open your browser, go to the iTunes Download page on the Apple website (www.apple.com/itunes/download/), and then download the latest version of iTunes.

The iTunes Download page encourages you to provide an e-mail address so that you can receive the New On iTunes newsletter, special iTunes offers, Apple news, and more. Unless you want to receive this information, be sure to clear the check boxes—in which case, you don't need to provide an e-mail address.

2. If Internet Explorer displays a File Download – Security Warning dialog box like the one shown here, verify that the name is iTunesSetup.exe. Then click the Run button.

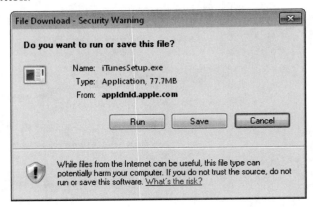

3. If Internet Explorer displays an Internet Explorer – Security Warning dialog box like the one shown here, verify that the program name is iTunes and the publisher is Apple Inc. Then click the Run button.

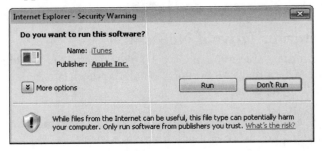

4. On the Welcome To iTunes screen, click the Next button.
5. On the License Agreement screen, read the license agreement, select the I Accept The Terms In The License Agreement option button if you want to proceed, and then click the Next button.
6. On the Installation Options screen (see Figure 1-4), choose installation options:
   - **Add iTunes And QuickTime Shortcuts To My Desktop**   Select this check box only if you need shortcuts on your desktop. The installation routine creates shortcuts on your Start menu anyway. The Start menu is usually the easiest way to launch iTunes. In Windows 7, you may want to pin iTunes to the taskbar so that you can launch it quickly.

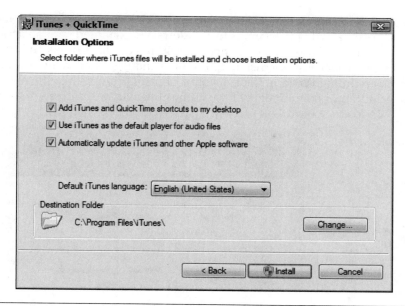

FIGURE 1-4   Choose whether to create shortcuts for iTunes and QuickTime on your desktop, use iTunes as the default audio player, and update iTunes and QuickTime automatically.

- **Use iTunes As The Default Player For Audio Files**   Select this check box if you plan to use iTunes as your main audio player. If you plan to use iTunes only for synchronizing the iPhone and use another player (for example, Windows Media Player) for music, don't make iTunes the default player. iTunes associates itself with the AAC, MP3, Apple Lossless Encoding, AIFF, and WAV file extensions.
- **Automatically Update iTunes And Other Apple Software**   Select this check box if you want to set Apple Software Update to check automatically for updates to iTunes, QuickTime, Safari, and other Apple software you install. Apple Software Update is a utility that installs in Control Panel. The automatic updating is an easy way to make sure you have the latest versions of the Apple software. The latest versions may contain bug fixes or extra features, so having them is usually helpful.
- **Default iTunes Language**   In this drop-down list, choose the language you want to use—for example, English (United States).
- **Destination Folder**   The installer installs iTunes in an iTunes folder in your Program Files folder by default. This is fine for most computers, but if you want to use a different folder, click the Change button, choose the folder, and then click the OK button.

7. Click the Install button to start the installation.

8. The installer displays the iTunes + QuickTime screen while it installs iTunes and QuickTime. On Windows XP, you need take no action until the Congratulations screen appears, telling you that iTunes and QuickTime have been successfully installed. But on Windows 7 and Windows Vista, you must go through several User Account Control prompts like the one shown here for different components of the iTunes installation (unless you've turned User Account Control off).

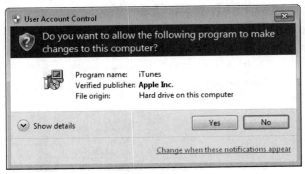

 On Windows 7 and Windows Vista, the User Account Control prompts may get stuck behind the iTunes + QuickTime screen. Look at the taskbar now and then to see if there's a flashing User Account Control prompt that you need to deal with before the installation can continue. Don't leave the installation unattended, because if you don't answer the User Account Control prompt, it times out and cancels the installation of the component.

9. When the Congratulations screen appears, leave the Open iTunes After The Installer Exits check box selected if you want to run iTunes immediately; otherwise, clear it. Then click the Finish button to close the installer.

Run iTunes for the First Time

If you allowed the installer to run iTunes, the program now opens. If not, choose Start | iTunes | iTunes when you're ready to start running iTunes.

 The first time you launch iTunes, the program displays the iTunes Tutorial window, which contains tutorial videos showing you how to get started with iTunes and your iPhone. Watch the videos that interest you, and then click the Close button (the × button) to close the iTunes Tutorial window.

You then see the iTunes window with the Music item selected in the Source list. Because you haven't yet added any music to the iTunes library, the Music item displays information on downloading music, importing your CDs, and finding the music files in your home folder.

If your computer is connected to the Internet, iTunes checks to see if an updated version of the program is available. If one is available, iTunes prompts you to download it (which may take a few minutes, depending on the speed of your Internet connection) and install it. After updating iTunes, you may need to restart your PC.

Get Your Mac Ready to Work with Your iPhone

If you bought your Mac in 2004 or later, chances are it's already all set to work with an iPhone: It has one or more USB 2.0 ports, Mac OS X (Lion, Snow Leopard, or Leopard) with iTunes, and plenty of disk space and memory. Unless it's one of Apple's new models that lack an optical disc drive, it probably has a DVD burner drive as well.

But if you have an older Mac, it may lack a USB 2.0 port; that means you'll either need to add a USB 2.0 port or suffer slow USB 1.*x* transfer speeds instead. And if your Mac doesn't have a CD or DVD burner drive, you may need to add a burner drive to get the best out of iTunes.

Add USB 2.0 if Necessary

If your Mac lacks a USB 2.0 port, add one or more USB 2.0 ports:

- **Power Mac or Mac Pro**   Insert a PCI card in a vacant slot.
- **PowerBook or MacBook**   Insert a PC Card if your Mac has a PC Card slot.

Check Your Operating System Version

Make sure your version of Mac OS is advanced enough to work with the iPhone. You need Mac OS X 10.5 (Leopard), 10.6 (Snow Leopard), or 10.7 (Lion) to use current iPhones. Upgrade if necessary, or use Software Update (choose Apple | Software Update) to download the latest point releases.

If you're not sure which version of Mac OS X you have, choose Apple | About This Mac to display the About This Mac window. Click the More Info button, then look at the Software readout on the Overview tab of the larger About This Mac window.

 Apple frequently adds new features to iTunes and the iPhone. To get the latest features and to make sure that iTunes and the iPhone work as well as possible, keep Mac OS X, iTunes, and the iPhone up to date. To check for updates, choose Apple | Software Update.

Check Disk Space and Memory

Make sure your Mac has enough disk space and memory to serve the iPhone adequately.

In most cases, memory shouldn't be an issue: If your Mac can run Mac OS X and conventional applications at a speed you can tolerate without sedation, it should be able to handle iTunes and the iPhone. Technically, Lion requires a minimum of 1GB of

How to... Check the Speed of Your Mac's USB Ports

If you're not sure of the speed of your Mac's USB ports, check them like this:

1. Choose Apple | About This Mac to display the About This Mac window.
2. Click the More Info button to display a larger version of the About This Mac window, containing six tabs of information: Overview, Displays, Storage, Memory, Support, and Service. At first, the Overview tab appears at the front.
3. On the Overview tab, click the System Report button to display the System Information window. This window shows detailed information about your Mac's hardware, software, and network connections.
4. Expand the Hardware entry in the Contents pane if it's collapsed. Then click the USB item to display its contents.
5. Select one of the USB Bus items in the USB Device Tree pane and check the Speed readout in the lower pane, as shown here. If the readout says "Up to 12 Mb/sec," it's USB 1.x. If the readout says "Up to 480 Mb/sec," it's USB 2.0.

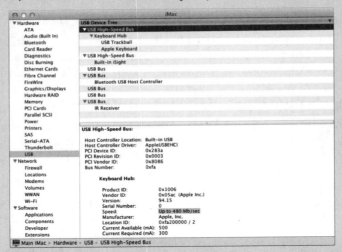

6. Press ⌘-Q or choose System Information | Quit System Information to close the System Information window.

RAM, and either Leopard or Snow Leopard requires a minimum of 512MB, but you'll get far better performance with twice those amounts—preferably four or eight times the amounts.

Disk space is more likely to be an issue if you will want to keep many thousands of songs and videos in your library. The best situation is to have enough space on your hard drive to contain your entire library, both at its current size and at whatever size you expect it to grow to within the lifetime of your Mac. That way, you can easily synchronize your entire library with the iPhone (if your library fits on it) or just whichever part of your library you want to take around with you for the time being.

If you have a Power Mac or Mac Pro, you can add another internal hard drive to provide additional storage. If you have any other Mac, you can go for an external FireWire or USB drive. If your Mac has a Thunderbolt port, you can add a Thunderbolt external drive.

Add an Optical Drive if Necessary

If your Mac doesn't have an optical drive, you may want to add one so you can rip CDs from iTunes and burn CDs or DVDs from iTunes and other applications.

If you have a Power Mac or a Mac Pro that has a full-size drive bay free, you can add an internal DVD burner drive. For any other Mac, add a USB DVD drive.

Make Sure Your Mac Has iTunes

If you have a Mac running Mac OS X, you most likely have iTunes installed already, because a default installation of Mac OS X includes iTunes.

Even if you explicitly exclude iTunes from the installation, Software Update offers you each updated version of iTunes that becomes available, so you need to refuse the updates manually or tell Software Update to ignore them. (To tell Software Update to ignore updates, select the iTunes item in the list, and then press ⌘-BACKSPACE or choose Update | Ignore Update.)

Get and Install the Latest Version of iTunes

If you've managed to refuse all these updates, the easiest way to install the latest version of iTunes is to use Software Update:

1. Choose Apple | Software Update to launch Software Update, which checks automatically for updates. (Your Mac must be connected to the Internet to use Software Update.)
2. If Software Update doesn't turn up a version of iTunes that you can install, choose Software Update | Reset Ignored Updates. Software Update then checks automatically for the latest versions of updates you've ignored and presents the list.
3. Make sure the iTunes check box is selected, and then click the Install Items button. Follow through the update process, entering your password in the authentication dialog box and accepting the license agreements.
4. Restart your Mac when Software Update prompts you to do so.

Launch iTunes

By this point, you should be ready to run iTunes on your Mac. To do so, click the iTunes icon on the Dock. If there's no iTunes icon on the Dock, click the Launchpad icon on the Dock, and then click the iTunes icon on the Launchpad screen.

If you're using a version of Mac OS X before Mac OS X Lion, you don't have Launchpad. So if the iTunes icon doesn't appear on the Dock, launch iTunes from the Applications folder. Click the Finder icon on the Dock (or simply click the desktop) to activate the Finder, choose Go | Applications or press ⌘-SHIFT-A to open your Applications folder, and then double-click the iTunes icon. You can use this method on Lion as well, but Launchpad is easier.

Set Up Your iPhone

By this point, you should be ready to set up your iPhone. You can set it up using either iTunes on your computer or using iCloud without a computer. Either way, you start setup by telling the iPhone which language you want to use and which country or region you're in.

 Using iCloud enables you to keep all your data online and sync it automatically among your iPhone, an iPad (if you have one), and your computer (likewise).

Begin Setting Up Your iPhone

To begin setting up your iPhone, follow these steps:

1. Press and hold the Power button on top of the iPhone for a couple of seconds until the Apple logo appears on screen, then release the button.
2. Wait while the iPhone starts up.
3. When the initial iPhone screen appears (shown on the left in Figure 1-5), tap the arrow button and slide it across to the right to unlock the iPhone. You then see the Language screen. If the box at the bottom shows the language you want, tap the Next button to proceed. If you need to change the language, tap the × button in the box at the bottom to display a list of languages (shown on the right in Figure 1-5), tap the correct language (putting a check mark next to it), and then tap the arrow button in the upper-right corner to move on.
4. Next, the iPhone displays the Country Or Region screen (shown on the left in Figure 1-6). If the box at the bottom shows the right country or region, tap the Next button to proceed. If not, tap the Show More button in the box at the bottom to display the Country Or Region screen shown in the right screen in Figure 1-6, tap the right country, and then tap the Next button.
5. Next, the iPhone displays the Location Services screen (shown on the left in Figure 1-7). Tap the Enable Location Services button, placing a check mark next to it, if you want to let the iPhone use Location Services to learn your approximate location. This is useful for getting maps and local information. If you don't want the iPhone to use Location Services, tap the Disable Location Services button.

FIGURE 1-5   Tap the arrow button and slide your finger to the right to unlock the iPhone (left). You can then use the list of languages to change the language the iPhone is using (right).

6. Tap the Next button to display the Wi-Fi Networks screen (shown on the right in Figure 1-7).

At this point, the setup paths diverge: You can either connect your iPhone to iTunes or connect it to a wireless network and use iCloud. The following section covers using iTunes; the section after that covers using iCloud.

Finish Setting Up Your iPhone with iTunes

Here's how to finish setting up your iPhone using iTunes:

1. On the Wi-Fi Networks screen, tap the Connect To iTunes button. The iPhone displays a screen telling you to connect it to iTunes.
2. Connect the iPhone to your PC or Mac. Connect the USB end of the iPhone's cable to your computer, and then connect the other end to the iPhone. iTunes

FIGURE 1-6 Either accept the iPhone's suggested country or region on the first Country Or Region screen (left) or tap the Show More button and then tap the correct country or region (right). Either way, tap the Next button to move on.

     recognizes the iPhone, adds it to the Devices category in the Source list, and displays the Set Up Your iPhone screen shown in Figure 1-8.

3. In the Name text box, you can change the name that iTunes has suggested for the iPhone—for example, Max's iPhone.

4. Choose what to synchronize on your iPhone:
   - Select the Automatically Sync Contacts, Calendars, Bookmarks, Notes, And Email Accounts check box if you want to sync all these items. You can also choose later to sync only specific items. We'll look at how to do this in the next chapter.
   - Select the Automatically Sync Applications check box if you want iTunes to automatically sync all apps between your computer and your iPhone. This behavior is usually helpful, but you may prefer to control app sync manually, especially if you have multiple iOS devices (for example, an iPhone and an iPad).

5. Click the Done button to apply your choices.

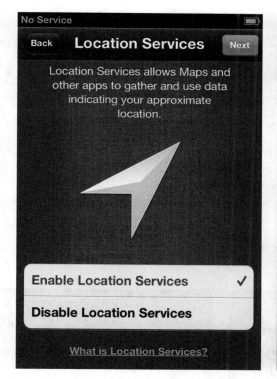

FIGURE 1-7   On the Location Services screen (left), tap the Enable Location Services button or the Disable Location Services button, as needed. On the Wi-Fi Networks screen (right), tap the wireless network you want to connect the iPhone to. The lock icons indicate networks that use security, such as a password.

Finish Setting Up Your iPhone Using iCloud

To finish setting up your iPhone using iCloud, take the following steps from the Wi-Fi Networks screen:

1. In the Choose A Network box, tap the button for the network you want to connect to. The Enter Password screen (shown on the left in Figure 1-9) appears.
2. Type the wireless network password in the Password box.
3. Tap either the upper Join button or the lower Join button. Your iPhone joins the network, and then displays the Wi-Fi Networks screen again. This time, a check mark appears next to the network you've connected to, and a Wi-Fi signal-strength indicator appears in the bar across the top of the iPhone's screen (as shown on the right in Figure 1-9).
4. Tap the Next button to move along. Your iPhone displays the Activating Your IPhone screen (shown on the left in Figure 1-10) while it contacts Apple's servers and activates service.

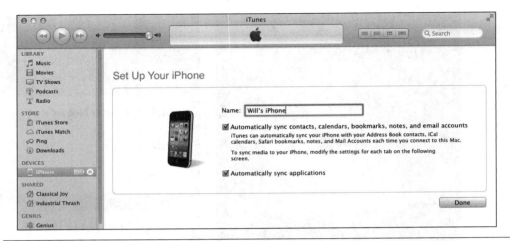

FIGURE 1-8 On the Set Up Your iPhone screen, change the name for your iPhone if necessary, and choose which items to sync with it.

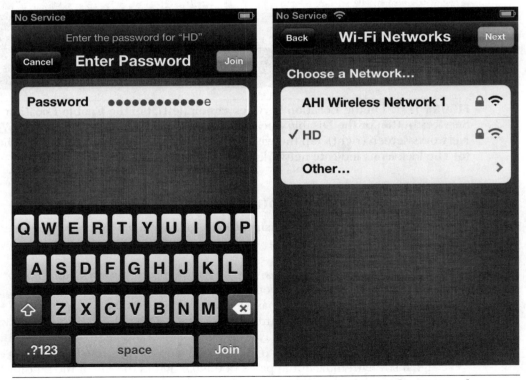

FIGURE 1-9 On the Enter Password screen (left), type the wireless network password, and then tap the Join button. A check mark then appears next to the network's name on the Wi-Fi Networks screen, and the signal-strength indicator appears in the status bar at the top of the screen (right).

FIGURE 1-10   The Activating Your iPhone screen (left) appears while your iPhone contacts Apple's servers. When your iPhone has been activated, the Set Up iPhone screen (right) appears. Tap the Set Up As New iPhone button, and then tap the Next button.

5. If activation is successful, the Set Up iPhone screen appears, as you see on the right in Figure 1-10. Tap the Set Up As New iPhone button, putting a check mark next to it, and then tap the Next button.

From the Set Up iPhone screen, you can also restore an iPhone that you have had to reset to factory settings. Tap the Restore From iCloud Backup button if you're restoring from a backup on iCloud. Tap the Restore From iTunes Backup button if the iPhone's backup is in iTunes on your computer.

6. On the Apple ID screen (shown on the left in Figure 1-11), tap the Sign In With An Apple ID button if you already have an Apple ID. If you don't have an Apple ID yet, tap the Create A Free Apple ID button, follow through the process of creating your Apple ID, and then continue with the next step.
7. On the Apple ID screen (shown on the right in Figure 1-11), type your Apple ID and password, and then tap the Next button. Your iPhone signs you into

FIGURE 1-11   On the first Apple ID screen (left), tap the Sign In With An Apple ID button or the Create A Free Apple ID button, as needed. On the second Apple ID screen (right), type your Apple ID and password.

iCloud using your Apple ID, and then displays the Terms And Conditions screen (shown on the left in Figure 1-12)

8. Read the terms and conditions to see if you can accept them. If so, tap the Agree button in the lower-right corner of the screen. Your iPhone then displays the Terms And Conditions dialog box to make sure you agree to selling your soul. Tap the Agree button in the dialog box too.

9. On the Set Up iCloud screen (shown on the right in Figure 1-12), tap the Use iCloud button (placing a check mark next to it), and then tap the Next button. If you don't want to use iCloud, tap the Don't Use iCloud button instead, and skip ahead to the last step in this list.

10. On the iCloud Backup screen (shown on the left in Figure 1-13), tap the Back Up To iCloud button (placing a check mark next to it) if you want to back your iPhone up to iCloud every day. This is usually a good idea. If you prefer to back your iPhone up to your computer, tap the Back Up To My Computer button instead, placing a check mark next to it.

FIGURE 1-12   On the Terms And Conditions screen (left), tap the Agree button in the lower-right corner, and then tap the Agree button in the Terms And Conditions dialog box. On the Set Up iCloud Screen (right), tap the Use iCloud button if you want to use iCloud.

11. Tap the Next button to display the Find My iPhone screen (shown on the right in Figure 1-13).

12. Tap the Use Find My iPhone button (placing a check mark next to it) if you want to use the Find My iPhone feature. This feature enables you to track down your iPhone's location by logging into iCloud using a web browser on another computer, and is usually helpful. If you don't want to use this feature, tap the Don't Use Find My iPhone button instead, placing a check mark next to it.

13. Tap the Next button to display the Diagnostics screen (shown on the left in Figure 1-14).

14. Tap the Automatically Send button (placing a check mark next to it) if you want your iPhone to send diagnostic data, usage data, and location data to Apple every day. This information helps Apple to improve the iPhone, the iOS operating system, and services such as iCloud. If you prefer not to let your iPhone send this information, tap the Don't Send button, placing a check mark next to it.

FIGURE 1-13   On the iCloud Backup screen (left), choose whether to back up your iPhone to iCloud every day. On the Find My iPhone screen (right), choose whether to activate the feature for finding your iPhone when you lose it.

15. Tap the Next button. Your iPhone displays the Thank You screen (shown on the right in Figure 1-14).
16. Tap the Start Using iPhone button. Your iPhone displays the Home screen, and you can start using it.

Meet the Home Screen and the Apps

Your iPhone's Home screen gives you quick access to your iPhone's apps and features. Figure 1-15 shows the Home screen with its main features labeled. To tell the truth, this isn't *the* Home screen—it's the *first* of the Home screens. There are others you'll meet shortly.

 An *app* is the short term for an application, also called a program or an application program. An app is software that has a particular purpose. For example, on your

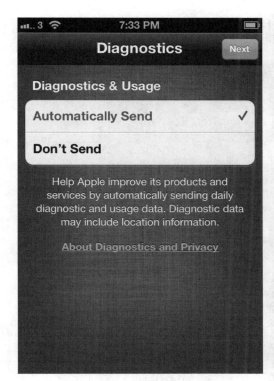

FIGURE 1-14   On the Diagnostics screen (left), choose whether to let your iPhone automatically send diagnostic, usage, and location data to Apple. On the Thank You screen (right), tap the Start Using iPhone button to start using your iPhone.

iPhone, you use the Safari app to browse the Web, the Mail app to send and receive e-mail messages, and the Camera app to take photos and videos. Each app has defined functionality—for example, you can't use the Mail app to take photos or use the Camera app to browse the Web.

Here are the essentials of the Home screen:

- **Carrier signal indicator**   This indicator shows the strength of your iPhone's connection to the cellular network, from a single tiny bar on the left indicating a 98-pound weakling connection up to a full five bars indicating a pumped-up bully connection kicking sand in its face.

- **Carrier name**   This readout shows the name of the carrier network your iPhone has connected to—for example, AT&T, Verizon, or ROGERS. Normally, you'll use the same carrier network all the time unless you go beyond your carrier's

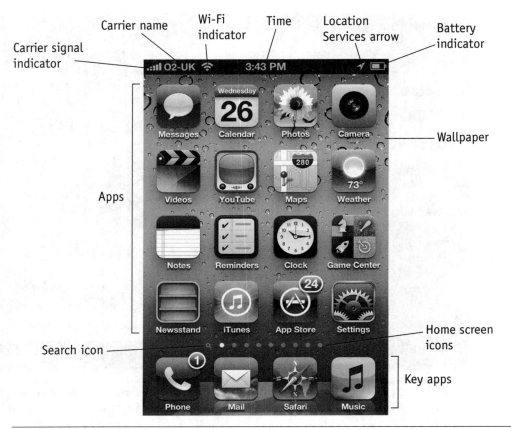

FIGURE 1-15 You can access your iPhone's apps and features from the Home screen.

range and start using roaming. Roaming can rack up charges, so it's worth paying attention if the carrier name changes unexpectedly.

- **Wi-Fi indicator** This indicator shows both that Wi-Fi is on and the strength of its connection to a network—one tiny dot for a weak connection, a dot and a short arc for a moderate connection, or a dot and two arcs for a strong connection.

- **Time** This indicator shows the current time. You can switch between 24-hour time and A.M./P.M. time on the Date & Time screen in the Settings app.

- **Location Services arrow** This arrow indicates that Location Services is on and that one or more apps are tracking your location via GPS or wireless. For example, if you use the Reminders app's feature for reminding you of tasks when you arrive at (or leave) a particular location, Reminders uses Location Services to keep tabs on where you are.

- **Battery indicator**   This indicator shows roughly how much battery power is left. When you plug your iPhone into a computer or power source, the battery indicator displays a lightning-bolt symbol to indicate that it's charging.

- **Wallpaper**   The wallpaper is the background against which the app icons appear. You can apply different wallpaper from the pictures included with the iPhone or by using your own photos.

- **Apps**   The Home screen shows an icon representing each app. Tap the icon to launch the app if it's not running, or to switch to the app if it's already running.

- **Search icon**   This icon shows a tiny magnifying glass that represents the Search feature, which lives on a screen to the left of the first Home screen. You'll meet the Search feature in a moment.

- **Home screen icons**   These dot icons represent the various Home screens. The white dot represents the current Home screen. You can move to another Home screen by swiping your finger left or right across the screen or by tapping one of the other dots.

- **Key apps**   At the bottom of the screen are key apps—by default, Phone, Mail, Safari, and Music. These apps remain in place for all the Home screens. You can customize the selection of apps here if the default ones don't suit you.

Move Among the Home Screens

When you first unbox your iPhone, you'll probably find that it has just a couple of Home screens, because all the apps will fit on two screens. But as soon as you start adding apps to your iPhone, you'll probably need a third Home screen—and then another.

Adding a Home screen couldn't be easier: As soon as you fill up one of the existing screens, the iPhone provides a new screen after whichever screen is currently last.

The line of dots at the bottom of the Home screen shows how many screens of apps you have. The leftmost dot-like icon is the tiny magnifying glass that indicates the Search screen, which appears before the first Home screen. The white dot represents the screen you're currently viewing. For example, the iPhone shown on the left in Figure 1-16 has eight screens of apps, and the fourth is currently displayed.

To display the next screen of apps, drag your finger to the left horizontally across the screen, as shown on the right in Figure 1-16. Drag to the right to display the previous screen of apps. You can also tap a dot to the right of the current dot to display the next screen or a dot to the left of the current dot to display the previous screen.

Search for an Item

To search for an item, follow these steps:

FIGURE 1-16 The dots near the bottom of the screen show how many screens of apps you have; the white dot indicates which screen is displayed. Drag to the left (as shown on the right) or to the right to change the screen of apps.

1. Drag your finger across the screen from left to right one or more times until the Search screen appears, as shown on the left in Figure 1-17. You can also tap the magnifying glass icon at the left of the dots representing the Home screens.
2. Start typing your search term. Your iPhone displays matches, as shown on the right in Figure 1-17.
3. Tap the item you want to view. Your iPhone displays it.

Launch an App

To launch an app, tap its icon on the Home screen. The app appears full screen. We'll look at many apps in the following chapters.

FIGURE 1-17 Scroll left until the Search screen (left) appears in place of the Home screen. Type your search term (right), and then tap the result you want.

Go Back to the Home Screen

To go back to the Home screen, press the Home button once.

Meet Siri, Your Personal Assistant

Your iPhone's strongest new feature is Siri, the voice-controlled personal assistant. Siri provides an easy and intuitive way to get tasks done on your iPhone without having to open apps and tap carefully at the screen. You can use Siri for everything from setting reminders and alarms to placing phone calls, taking notes, and dictating e-mail messages.

This section introduces you to Siri. We'll dig into exactly what you can do with Siri in more detail in the Siri sidebars later in this book. You'll find these sidebars in the sections that deal with particular apps and actions. For example, in Chapter 8, which shows you how to use the Mail app for e-mail, you'll find a Siri sidebar explaining how to use Siri to send an e-mail message.

Understand How Siri Works

Siri listens to your voice input through your iPhone's built-in microphones or through the headset microphone. Siri then runs your input through servers in Apple's heavy-duty data center in North Carolina to figure out what you want.

Depending on what Siri gets back from the servers, Siri either shows you the request it has understood and asks for confirmation or asks you to rephrase a request Siri has not been able to interpret.

For some tasks, if Siri can determine unambiguously what you request, and the request is pretty harmless, Siri goes ahead and performs the action without asking for confirmation. For example, if you say "Set a timer for ten minutes," Siri sets a timer and starts it, displaying it on screen.

 At this writing, Siri can use three languages: English, French, and German. For English, Siri can provide English (United States), English (United Kingdom), or English (Australia). When set for English (United States), English (Australia), or German, Siri uses a female voice. When set for English (United Kingdom) or French, Siri uses a male voice. Because of Siri's gender-switching, this book uses Siri's name rather than pronouns to refer to Siri.

Summon Siri

You can summon Siri in any of these ways:

- With the iPhone unlocked, hold it up to your face. The iPhone's accelerometer tracks the raising, and the proximity sensor notices your face is there.
- Press and hold the Home button for a couple of seconds.
- Press and hold the center button on the headset for a couple of seconds.
- Tap the Siri button (the microphone button) on the onscreen keyboard (shown on the left in Figure 1-18).

Siri appears as a microphone icon at the bottom of the screen, together with the prompt "What can I help you with?", as you see on the right in Figure 1-18.

Give Siri Commands

To give Siri commands, simply say what you want. Siri is designed to use normal language rather than formalized commands, but you will find that some phrasings work better than others.

Should You Worry About Your Privacy When Using Siri?

The way Siri works means that using Siri gives Apple a lot of data about who you are, whom you know, and what you do.

As I mentioned earlier, Siri passes all its traffic through servers in Apple's data center in North Carolina for processing. Your iPhone also sends information about itself and its location, about you, and about your contacts and your relationships with them to help the Siri service interpret your instructions. For example, once you've told Siri that the contact called Bill Smith is your dad, the Siri service retains that information so that it can interpret commands such as "Call my dad."

Apple states that it doesn't link the data you provide by using Siri with the data that Apple has about you from your use of other Apple services. For example, if you pay for extra space on your iCloud account (or if you have an account on the MobileMe service, which Apple is due to close on June 30, 2012), Apple knows your name, address, payment method, and so on. But Apple doesn't link your Siri data with your name, address, and other data.

You can turn off Location Services for Siri if you don't want Siri to pass your location to Apple's servers. If you do this, Siri can't respond helpfully to requests such as "Find the nearest Mexican restaurant," but you can still find local information by telling Siri where you are.

If you are concerned about your data footprint, you may prefer not to use Siri at all. If so, see Chapter 4 for instructions on how to turn off Siri. Even when you do this, Apple may retain your Siri commands so that it can use them to try to improve Siri. But Apple disassociates this data from you, so it shouldn't be able to come back and haunt you.

Given that the iPhone is tracking your approximate location all the time so that you can make and take calls and shunt data back and forth, the extra information that Siri gathers about you is probably not worth worrying about.

That said, there *is* a threat to your privacy from Siri and the iPhone. That threat is from law enforcement, which may be able to gather data about you from your carrier, your Internet service provider (ISP), or from Apple by using legal tools such as subpoenas. For example, the FBI can use a National Security Letter to request information from your carrier or ISP.

If Siri can't interpret what you say, Siri prompts you for more information. And if Siri gets your request wrong, you can correct it or cancel it.

 To cancel a request and hide Siri again, press the Home button.

Here are quick examples of what you can ask Siri. We'll look at other examples in more detail in Siri sidebars throughout the book.

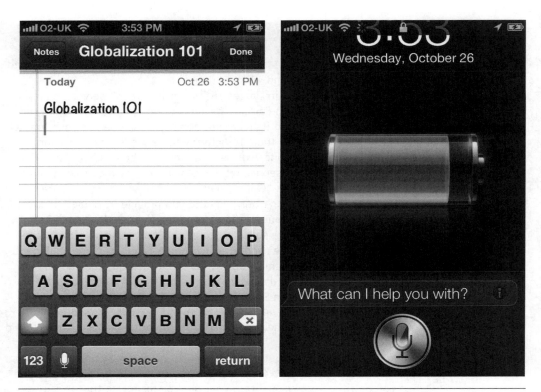

FIGURE 1-18 You can summon Siri by tapping the microphone button on the bottom row of the onscreen keyboard (left). Siri appears as a microphone icon at the bottom of the screen (right).

- **Address Book** "What's Bill Smith's address?"
- **Calendar** "Set up a meeting with Alicia Irving at noon."
- **Clock** "What time is it in Anchorage?"
- **Contacts** "Show Jane Walker."
- **Mail** "New e-mail to Shelly Ramirez."
- **Messages** "Send a message to my wife telling her I'll be late tonight."
- **Music** "Play *Rust Never Sleeps*."
- **Notes** "Note that we need to complete the relocation project by March."
- **Phone** "Call Peter Wong on his cell phone."
- **Search** "What's the average rainfall in Toronto?"
- **Timer** "Set a timer for 90 minutes."
- **Weather** "What's the forecast for Boston this evening?"

Figure 1-19 shows two screens of Siri responding to requests.

FIGURE 1-19   Siri can respond to a wide range of requests and can look up information on the Web for you.

Close Siri

To close Siri, press the Home button. Your iPhone slides the Siri screen out of view and displays the app you were using before you summoned Siri, the Home screen (if that's where you were), or the lock screen (likewise).

How to...   Deal with Siri's "Having Trouble Connecting to the Network" Messages

If Siri says "Sorry, I am having trouble connecting to the network" or "Sorry, I'm not able to connect right now," either your iPhone doesn't have an Internet connection or Siri's servers are overloaded.

First, look at the status bar at the top of the Home screen to check that your iPhone has an Internet connection, either through your carrier or through Wi-Fi.

Assuming your iPhone does have an Internet connection, the problem is likely that too many people are using Siri at once. Wait a few seconds or a few minutes, and then try again.

2

Load Your iPhone with Music, Videos, and Data

HOW TO...

- Start creating your library
- Load your iPhone with music, video, and data
- Recharge your iPhone
- Eject and disconnect your iPhone

After setting up your iPhone as explained in Chapter 1, you're ready to load it with music, video, and data using iTunes. This chapter shows you how to start creating your iTunes library, how to choose which items to sync with your iPhone, and how to perform the sync. You'll also learn how to recharge your iPhone and how to eject and disconnect it from your computer.

Start Creating Your Library

Before you can add any songs or other items to your iPhone, you must add them to your library in iTunes. This section gets you started with the basics of adding songs to your library from your home folder, from other folders, and from your CDs. Chapter 13 covers this topic in greater depth, explaining how to plan, create, and manage an effective library for iTunes, your iPhone, and your household.

Make Sure iTunes Has Suitable Settings

Before you add songs to your library, take a minute to check two important settings in iTunes. The first of these settings controls whether iTunes copies existing files into your library or adds references to their existing locations. The second controls whether iTunes automatically renames your files to match the tag information they contain.

These settings are both on the Advanced tab of the iTunes dialog box (on Windows) or the Preferences dialog box (on the Mac). Follow these steps to reach the Advanced tab:

1. Display the iTunes dialog box or the Preferences dialog box:
   - In Windows, choose Edit | Preferences or press CTRL-COMMA or CTRL-Y to display the iTunes dialog box.
   - On the Mac, choose iTunes | Preferences or press ⌘-COMMA or ⌘-Y to display the Preferences dialog box.
2. Click the Advanced tab to display its contents (see Figure 2-1).

Now choose which settings you want, as discussed in the following subsections.

Decide Whether to Copy All Song Files to Your Library

The ideal setup is to store all your songs and videos within your operating system's preferred music folder:

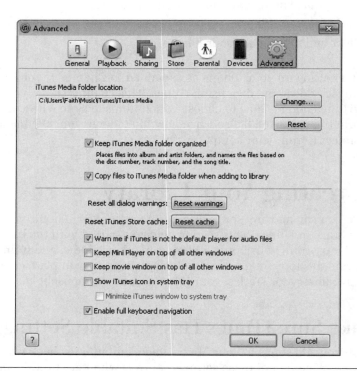

FIGURE 2-1 On the Advanced tab of the iTunes dialog box or the Preferences dialog box, choose whether to store a copy of each song file on your hard disk and whether iTunes renames your files.

- **Windows 7 or Windows Vista** The Music folder
- **Windows XP** The My Music folder
- **Mac OS X** The Music folder in your Home folder

Typically, this folder is on your computer's hard drive (or on its primary hard drive, if it has more than one hard drive) rather than on an external hard drive.

That means your hard drive must have enough space for all your songs, videos, and other items (for example, podcasts and TV shows), not to mention the operating system, your applications, and all your other files (such as documents, pictures, and video files). For a modest-sized library, this is easy enough. But for the kind of library that most music enthusiasts accumulate over the years, it means your computer must have a huge hard drive. Most modern desktop computers do, but at this writing laptop hard drives are limited to around 1TB—and most laptops have hard drives that are far smaller than this.

If your computer does have a huge hard drive, all is well. But if it doesn't, you'll have to either make do with only some of the songs and videos you want or store some of the files on other drives or other computers. You can tell iTunes to store pointers, called *references*, to where files are located rather than store a copy of each file in the library folder on your hard drive.

If you want iTunes to copy the files, select the Copy Files To iTunes Media Folder When Adding To Library check box. If you want iTunes to leave the files where they are, and simply add to your library the references to the files, clear this check box.

Storing references is great when you have too little space free on your hard disk to accommodate your colossal library. For example, if you have a laptop whose hard disk is bulging at the seams, you might choose to store in your library only references to songs located on an external hard disk rather than trying to import a copy of each song. But you won't be able to play any song stored on the external hard disk when your laptop isn't connected to it.

Did You Know?

Why You May Prefer Not to Store Your Music in the Music Folder

Even if your computer has enough hard drive space for all your songs, you may prefer not to store them in your Music folder, My Music folder, or the Music folder in your Home folder so that you can more easily share them through the file system with other members of your household.

iTunes' Sharing features (discussed in Chapter 13) enable you to share even files stored in your private folders, but they limit other users to playing the songs (rather than adding them to their music libraries) and work only when iTunes is running. For more flexibility, you may prefer to store shared songs on a server or in a folder that all members of your household can access.

Decide Whether to Let iTunes Organize Your Media Folder

Take a moment to think about the Keep iTunes Media Folder Organized setting, because it decides whether you or iTunes controls the organization of the files in your library.

If you turn this feature on, iTunes stores a song in a file named after the track number (if you choose to include it) and song name. iTunes places the song in a folder named after the album; this folder is stored within a folder named after the artist, which is placed in your iTunes Media folder.

For example, if you rip the album *Brothers* by The Black Keys, iTunes stores the first song as \The Black Keys\Brothers\01 Everlasting Light.aac on Windows or as /The Black Keys/Brothers/01 Everlasting Light.aac on Mac OS X. If you then edit the artist field in the tag to "Black Keys" instead of "The Black Keys," iTunes changes the name of the artist folder to "Black Keys" as well.

This automatic renaming is nice and logical for iTunes, but you may dislike the way folder and file names change when you edit the tags. If so, clear the Keep iTunes Media Folder Organized check box on the Advanced tab of the iTunes dialog box (in Windows) or the Preferences dialog box (on the Mac). You can change this setting at any time, but it's clearest to make a choice at the beginning and then stick with it.

Add Your Existing Song Files to Your Library

If you haven't yet added any songs to your library, the best place to start is by having iTunes add all the songs in your home folder. You can then add other folders as needed.

Make iTunes Add the MP3 and AAC Files from Your Home Folder

The quick way to start creating your library is to have iTunes add all the MP3 files and AAC files stored in your home folder. To do this, follow these steps:

1. In iTunes, click the Music item in the Library category of the Source list on the left. The Music screen appears, showing a screen of information rather than a list of songs because you haven't yet added any songs to your library.
2. Click the Find MP3 And AAC Files In My Home Folder link. iTunes automatically searches your home folder for MP3 files and AAC files, and adds all those it finds to your library. If you selected the Copy Files To iTunes Media Folder When Adding To Library check box, iTunes copies the files; if not, iTunes adds references to where they are.

Add Songs from Other Folders

To add songs to your library, follow these instructions:

- **Add a folder of songs in Windows**   Choose File | Add Folder To Library. In the Browse For Folder dialog box, navigate to and select the folder you want to add.

Click the OK button, and iTunes either copies the song files to your library (if you selected the Copy Files To iTunes Media Folder When Adding To Library check box) or adds references to the song files (if you cleared this check box).

- **Add a single file in Windows** Choose File | Add File To Library or press CTRL-O. In the Add To Library dialog box, navigate to and select the file you want to add. Click the OK button, and iTunes adds it.
- **Add a folder or file on the Mac** Choose File | Add To Library or press ⌘-O. In the Add To Library dialog box, navigate to and select the folder or the file you want to add and then click the Choose button to add the folder or file.

 On either Windows or the Mac, you can drag files to the Library section of the Source list and drop them there. On Windows, select the files on your desktop or in a Windows Explorer window first; on the Mac, select the files on your desktop or in a Finder window.

Add WMA Files on Windows

If you have files in the WMA format on your Windows PC, you can have iTunes convert them to AAC or another iTunes-friendly format for you.

To convert the WMA files, either drag them to the Library section of the Source list from a Windows Explorer window (or your desktop) or use the Add Folder To Library dialog box to pick them. When iTunes displays the dialog box shown here, warning you that it will convert the files, click the Convert button.

 WMA is the abbreviation for Windows Media Audio, Microsoft's preferred file format for audio on Windows.

Copy CDs to Your Library

The other way to add your existing digital music to your library is to copy it from CD. iTunes makes the process as straightforward as can be, but you should first verify that the iTunes settings for importing music are suitable.

Check iTunes' Settings for Importing Music

Follow these steps to check iTunes' settings for importing music:

How to... Decide Whether to Convert Your WMA Files to AAC Files

Converting your unprotected WMA files to AAC files is usually a good idea, and it's easy unless you have WMA files protected with digital rights management (DRM) restrictions that control which computers can play the files. iTunes can't convert protected WMA files to AAC files.

Technically, the AAC files you end up with contain all the flaws of the original WMA files plus any flaws that the AAC encoding introduces. This is because all "lossy" audio formats lose audio quality, introducing flaws into the resulting audio files.

But in practice, if the WMA files sound great to you, the AAC files will probably sound at least acceptable. And you can play them on your iPhone, which you cannot do with the WMA files.

In any case, the conversion process leaves the original WMA files untouched, so if you don't like the resulting AAC files, you can simply delete them. The AAC files will probably take up around the same amount of space on your computer's hard disk as the WMA files, so make sure you have plenty of free space before you convert the files.

Converting the WMA files to AAC gives you the best quality, but you can create MP3 files instead if you prefer. Before you import the files, set the file format you want. Follow the instructions in the nearby section "Check iTunes' Settings for Importing Music."

Then import the files. When iTunes warns you that it will convert the files, click the Convert button.

1. Display the iTunes dialog box or the Preferences dialog box:
   - In Windows, choose Edit | Preferences or press CTRL-COMMA or CTRL-Y to display the iTunes dialog box.
   - On the Mac, choose iTunes | Preferences or press ⌘-COMMA or ⌘-Y to display the Preferences dialog box.
2. Click the General tab if it's not already displayed.
3. In the When You Insert A CD drop-down list, choose the action you want iTunes to take when you insert a CD:
   - **Show CD**   Displays the list of songs
   - **Begin Playing**   Displays the list of songs and starts playing the first
   - **Ask To Import CD**   Displays a dialog box prompting you to import the CD
   - **Import CD**   Imports the CD without prompting you
   - **Import CD And Eject**   Imports the CD without prompting you, and then ejects it without warning

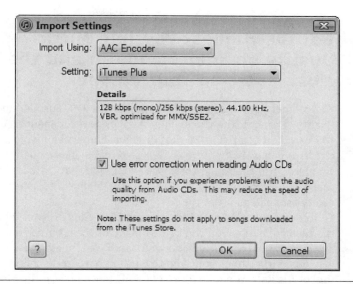

FIGURE 2-2 Before importing music, open the Import Settings dialog box and make sure that iTunes is configured with suitable settings.

When you're building your library, Show CD is usually the best choice, as it gives you the chance to scan the CD information for errors that you need to correct before you import the CD. This section assumes you're using the Show CD setting.

4. Click the Import Settings button to open the Import Settings dialog box (see Figure 2-2).
5. Verify that AAC Encoder is selected in the Import Using drop-down list.
6. In the Setting drop-down list, choose High Quality if you want good audio quality with a compact file size. Choose iTunes Plus if you're prepared to use twice as much disk space to improve the audio quality.
7. Select the Use Error Correction When Reading Audio CDs check box if you want iTunes to correct for any errors it encounters when reading the CDs.

You may not need to use error correction for many of your CDs, so you can clear the Use Error Correction When Reading Audio CDs check box if you prefer. But if any of your CDs contain defects that cause problems to the drive reading the CD, you may get interruptions or audio artifacts in the ripped files. For this reason, it's best to turn error correction on and leave it on.

8. Click the OK button to close the Import Settings dialog box.
9. Click the OK button to close the iTunes dialog box or Preferences dialog box.

Get the Highest Possible Music Quality on Your Computer and the Most Music on Your iPhone

You can get good music quality by using the AAC Encoder and either the High Quality setting or the iTunes Plus setting, as recommended in the main text. You can then use the same files on your iPhone as on your computer.

But if you want to get the highest possible music quality on your computer, use the Apple Lossless Encoding format instead. This creates files that have no loss of quality. The files are compressed somewhat, but not nearly as much as using the AAC format.

You can put the Apple Lossless Encoding files on your iPhone, but because the files are larger, you can't fit as many of them on it. To get the most music possible on your iPhone, you can have iTunes create lower-quality versions of the songs you sync to your iPhone. To do this, select the Convert Higher Bit Rate Songs To 128 Kbps AAC check box on the Summary screen in the iPhone's control screens.

Using this setting slows down syncing new music a lot, because iTunes must convert each song file to a lower-quality version before transferring it. But once iTunes has put a particular song on your iPhone, it doesn't need to convert it again unless you delete the song from your iPhone and then load it again.

iTunes can store the music extracted from CDs in several different formats, including Advanced Audio Coding (AAC, the default), MP3, and Apple Lossless Encoding. Chapter 13 discusses the pros and cons of the various formats and how to choose which will suit you best. For the moment, this book assumes that you are using AAC.

Add a CD to Your Library

To add a CD to your library, follow these steps:

1. Start iTunes if it's not already running.
2. Insert the CD in your computer's optical drive (CD drive or DVD drive). iTunes loads the CD and displays an entry for it in the Source list. If your computer is connected to the Internet, iTunes retrieves the CD's information and displays it (see Figure 2-3).

Note If you selected the Ask To Import CD item in the When You Insert A CD drop-down list, iTunes displays a dialog box asking if you want to import the CD. Click the Yes button or the No button, as needed. If you selected the Import CD item, iTunes

FIGURE 2-3   Load a CD, check that the data is correct, and then click the Import CD button to import its songs into your library.

goes ahead and imports the CD without asking you. If you selected the Import CD And Eject item, iTunes imports the CD and then spits it out.

3. Look at the CD's information and make sure that it is correct. If not, click twice (with a pause between the clicks) on the piece of information you want to change, type the correction, and then press ENTER (Windows) or RETURN (Mac).

 You can also change CD or song information in other ways. See Chapter 13 for the details.

4. Clear the check box for any song you don't want to import.
5. Click the Import CD button. iTunes extracts the audio from the CD, converts it to the format you chose, and saves the files to your library.

 If you want Windows 7 or Windows Vista to prompt you to show or import songs every time you insert an audio CD, choose Start | Control Panel, choose Large Icons in the View By drop-down list (on Windows 7) or click the Classic View button link (in Windows Vista), and then double-click the AutoPlay icon. In the Audio CD drop-down list, choose Show Songs Using iTunes or Import Songs Using iTunes (as appropriate), and then click the Save button.

How to...

Associate Your Music Files with iTunes on Windows

If iTunes notices that it's not the default player for the audio file types it normally plays, it displays the dialog box shown here telling you about the problem (as iTunes sees it). On Windows 7 or Windows Vista, iTunes prompts you to go to the Default Programs control panel to set it up, as shown on the left here. On Windows XP, iTunes simply suggests you make iTunes the default player, as shown on the right here.

 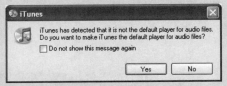

If you've set up another program to play these audio files, select the Do Not Show This Message Again check box and click the No button. Otherwise, click the Yes button. On Windows XP, iTunes simply grabs the file associations. On Windows 7 or Windows Vista, iTunes opens the Set Program Associations window, shown here.

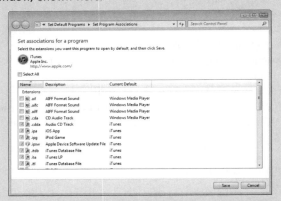

In the list box, select the check box for each of the files you want to associate with iTunes. Select the Select All check box if you're sure you want to associate all of them.

You can click the Current Default column heading to sort the list by program, which lets you quickly see which file types are assigned to other applications. Click the heading again if you need to sort in reverse order—for example, to bring the Windows Media Player–assigned file types to the top of the list.

When you've selected all the file types you want to associate, click the Save button. Windows closes the Set Program Associations window.

Check That the Songs You've Added Sound Okay

If you chose not to turn on error correction, check after adding the first CD that the songs sound okay.

Click the Music item under the Library category in the Source list, double-click the first song you imported from the CD, and listen to it to make sure there are no obvious defects (such as clicks or pauses) in the sound. If you have time, listen to several songs, or even the entire CD.

If the songs sound fine, you're probably okay without using error correction— assuming all your CDs are in at least as good shape as this first one. But if you do hear defects, or if you suspect some of your CDs contain errors, turn on error correction and copy the CD again. Here's how:

1. Display the iTunes dialog box or the Preferences dialog box:
   - In Windows, choose Edit | Preferences or press CTRL-COMMA or CTRL-Y to display the iTunes dialog box.
   - On the Mac, choose iTunes | Preferences or press ⌘-COMMA or ⌘-Y to display the Preferences dialog box.
2. Click the General tab if it's not already displayed.
3. Click the Import Settings button to open the Import Settings dialog box.
4. Select the Use Error Correction When Reading Audio CDs check box.
5. Click the OK button to close each dialog box.

If the first CD's songs contain errors, delete those songs. In your library, click the first song that you ripped from the CD, hold down SHIFT, and click the last song from the CD to select all the songs. Press DELETE or BACKSPACE on your keyboard, click the Yes button in the confirmation dialog box, and then click the Yes button in the dialog box that asks whether you want to move the files from your Music folder to the Recycle Bin (on Windows) or the Trash (on the Mac).

Click the CD's entry in the Source list, and then click the Import CD button to import the songs again. Check the results and make sure they're satisfactory before you import any more CDs.

Load Your iPhone with Music, Video, and Data

When your iTunes library is ready for syncing to your iPhone, set up syncing on your iPhone as described in this section. We'll start by choosing overall settings on the Summary screen, and then move along through the other screens—the Info screen, the Apps screen, the Ringtones screen, the Music screen, the Movies screen, the TV Shows screen, the Podcasts screen, the Books screen, and the Photos screen.

To get started, connect your iPhone to your computer via the USB cable, and then click your iPhone's entry in the Source list to display the iPhone's control screens.

Choose Settings on the Summary Screen

Click the Summary button to display the Summary screen (see Figure 2-4), and then follow these steps to choose settings:

1. In the Backup box, choose how to back up your iPhone and whether to encrypt the backup:
   - **Back Up To iCloud**   Select this option button if you want to back up your iPhone to iCloud. (See www.apple.com/icloud/ for information on iCloud.)
   - **Back Up To This Computer**   Select this option button if you prefer to back up your iPhone to your computer.
   - **Encrypt iPhone Backup**   If you select the Back Up To This Computer option button, you can select this check box to encrypt the backup and prevent other people from learning your secrets. iTunes displays the Set Password check box, shown in the next illustration. Type a password in the Password box and the Verify Password box. On the Mac, you can select the

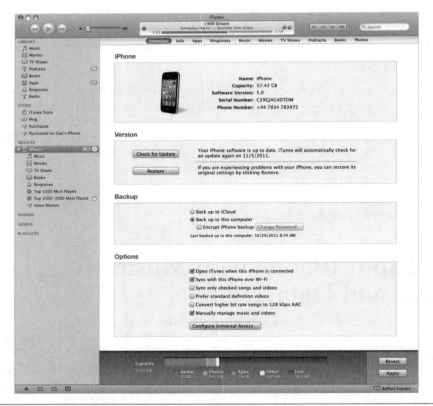

FIGURE 2-4   On the Summary screen in the iPhone's control screens, choose how to load the iPhone.

Remember This Password In My Keychain check box if you want to store the password in your Mac's keychain. Then click the Set Password button.

2. Select the Open iTunes When This iPhone Is Connected check box if you want your computer to automatically launch or activate iTunes when you connect your iPhone. This is usually handy.
3. Select the Sync With This iPhone Over Wi-Fi check box if you want your iPhone to sync automatically when it is plugged into a power source and connected to the same network as your computer.
4. Select the Sync Only Checked Songs And Videos check box if you want to prevent iTunes from putting on the iPhone any song whose check box you've cleared. This setting is usually helpful.
5. Select the Prefer Standard Definition Videos if you want to put standard-definition videos on your iPhone instead of high-definition videos when both are available.

Standard-definition videos look fine on your iPhone's screen, and you can save a lot of space by using standard-definition videos instead of high-definition videos. But if you play back your videos on a TV or an external monitor, you will get a better picture from the high-definition videos.

6. Select the Convert Higher Bit Rate Songs To 128 Kbps AAC check box if you want to get as many songs as possible on your iPhone.

Converting songs to 128 Kbps prevents iTunes from loading higher-bitrate songs on your iPhone. This setting is a great help if the songs in your library use high bitrates and your iPhone's capacity is too low to hold all the songs at that quality. The drawbacks are that the conversion slows down the loading process considerably and reduces sound quality somewhat.

7. If you want to load songs and videos manually, select the Manually Manage Music And Videos check box.

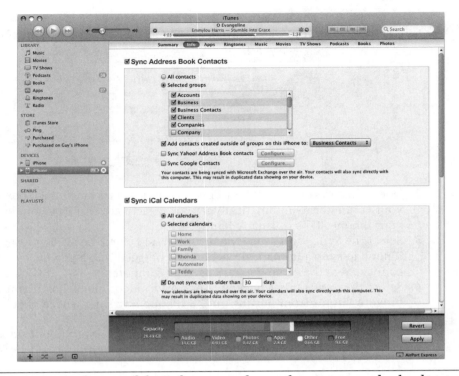

FIGURE 2-5 At the top of the Info screen, choose the contacts and calendars to sync with your iPhone.

Choose Settings on the Info Screen

On the Info screen (the top of which is shown in Figure 2-5 for Mac OS X), you can choose which contacts, calendars, e-mail accounts, bookmarks, and notes your computer syncs with your iPhone.

At the top of the screen, select the Sync Contacts From check box (on Windows) or the Sync Address Book Contacts check box (on the Mac), and then choose which contacts to sync with your iPhone. See the section "Sync Your Calendars and Contacts with Your iPhone" in Chapter 10 for details on choosing settings.

 If any of the items on the Info screen has a notice saying that it is being synced over the air, and that syncing with the computer as well may lead to duplicated data appearing on your iPhone, you probably don't want to sync the data with the computer as well.

Next, select the Sync Calendars From check box (on Window) or the Sync iCal Calendars check box (on the Mac), and choose which calendars and events you want to sync. Again, see the section "Sync Your Calendars and Contacts with Your iPhone" in Chapter 10 for details on choosing settings.

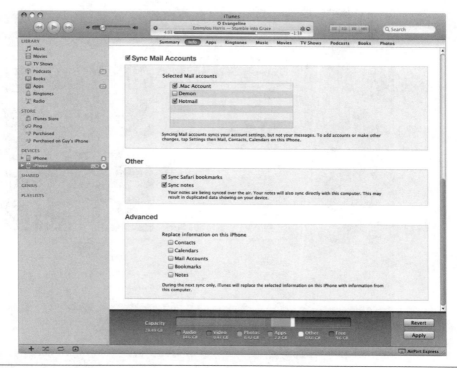

FIGURE 2-6   Farther down the Info screen, choose the e-mail accounts, bookmarks, and notes to sync with your iPhone.

To sync your e-mail accounts, scroll down the Info screen and select the Sync Mail Accounts check box (see Figure 2-6), and then select the check box for each account in the Selected Mail Accounts list box that you want to sync.

In the Other box, select the Sync Safari Bookmarks check box if you want to sync your bookmarks, which is usually helpful. Select the Sync Notes check box if you want to sync notes.

In the Advanced box at the bottom of the Info screen, you can select the Contacts check box, the Calendars check box, the Mail Accounts check box, the Bookmarks check box, or the Notes check box to overwrite the data on your iPhone with the data from your computer. Normally, you will want to do this only when the data on your iPhone has become corrupted and you need to replace it.

Choose Which Apps to Sync

On the Apps screen (see Figure 2-7), you can choose which apps to sync with your iPhone, rearrange the icons on the Home screens, rearrange the Home screens themselves, and copy documents to and from your iPhone.

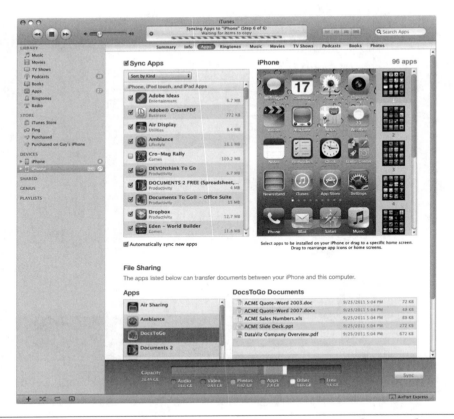

FIGURE 2-7 On the Apps screen, choose which apps to sync with your iPhone. You can also rearrange the items on the Home screens, rearrange the order of the Home screens, and use the File Sharing feature to copy documents to and from your iPhone.

Normally, you'll want to select the Sync Apps check box to turn on overall syncing of apps, and then clear the check box for any app you don't want to install. Select the Automatically Sync New Apps check box if you want to sync new apps automatically; this is usually a good idea.

 Chapter 6 shows you how to install and manage apps on your iPhone.

In the upper-right corner of the screen, you can rearrange the Home screens. We'll look at this in detail later in the book, but here are the two basic moves:

- **Move an app's icon** Drag the icon to where you want it.
- **Move a Home screen** In the panel of Home screens, click the screen you want to move, and then drag it up or down.

At the bottom of the Apps screen is the File Sharing pane, which you use to copy files to and from your iPhone. I'll show you how to do this in Chapter 14.

Choose Which Ringtones to Sync

To choose which ringtones to sync to your iPhone, click the Ringtones button to display the Ringtones screen. Select the Sync Ringtones check box, and then choose either the All Ringtones option button or the Selected Ringtones option button.

If you choose the Selected Ringtones option button, select the check box for each ringtone you want to sync.

Choose Which Music to Sync

On the Music screen (see Figure 2-8), choose whether to synchronize music and, if so, which music:

1. Select the Sync Music check box. This enables the other controls.
2. Select the Entire Music Library option button to synchronize your entire library. Select the Include Music Videos check box if you want to include

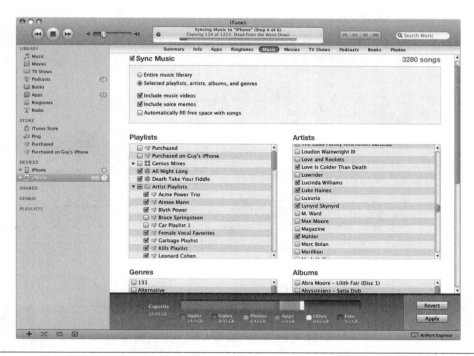

FIGURE 2-8   To choose which items iTunes syncs to your iPhone, click the Selected Playlists, Artists, Albums, And Genres option button, and then select the check box for each item you want to include.

music videos with the songs. Select the Include Voice Memos check box if you want the voice memos too.

3. Select the Selected Playlists, Artists, Albums, And Genres option button if you want to synchronize your iPhone with the items whose check boxes you select in the Playlists list box, Artists list box, Genres list box, and Albums list box that appear. This is a good choice when your iPhone doesn't have enough capacity to hold your entire library.

 When you select the Selected Playlists, Artists, Albums, And Genres option button, the Automatically Fill Free Space With Songs check box appears at the bottom of the Sync Music box. Select this check box if you want iTunes to stuff your iPhone as full of music as possible.

Choose Which Movies and TV Shows to Sync

On the Movies screen (shown in Figure 2-9) and the TV Shows screen, choose which movies and TV shows you want to synchronize with your iPhone. Select the Sync Movies check box or the Sync TV Shows check box, and then choose the details of the movies or shows to include.

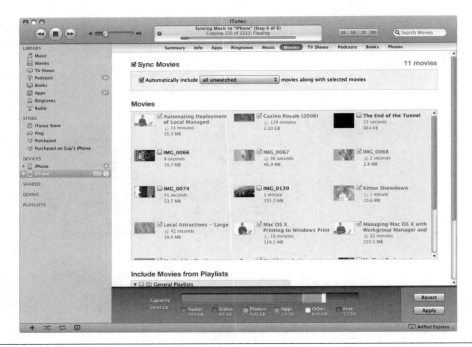

FIGURE 2-9 Use the controls on the Movies screen to specify exactly which movies you want to sync with your iPhone.

FIGURE 2-10   Use the controls on the Podcasts screen to choose which podcasts to sync to your iPhone.

Choose Which Podcasts to Sync

On the Podcasts screen (shown in Figure 2-10), select the Sync Podcasts check box, and then choose which episodes to synchronize:

- All the episodes (the simple choice)
- 1, 3, 5, or 10 of the most recent episodes
- 1, 3, 5, or 10 of the most recent unplayed episodes
- 1, 3, 5, or 10 of the least recent unplayed episodes
- All the new episodes
- 1, 3, 5, or 10 of the most recent new episodes
- 1, 3, 5, or 10 of the least recent new episodes

Then use the controls in the Podcasts list box, the Episodes list box, and the Include Episodes From Playlists list box to choose which podcasts to synchronize.

Choose Which Books to Sync

On the Books screen (see Figure 2-11), select the Sync Books check box. You can then select either the All Books option button or the Selected Books option button. If you

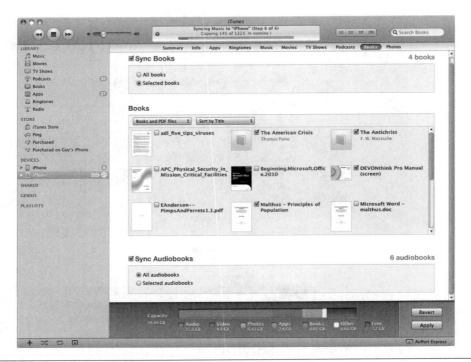

FIGURE 2-11 Use the controls on the Books screen to specify which books and audiobooks to sync to your iPhone.

choose the Selected Books option button, select the check box in the Books box of each book you want to sync.

Next, select the Sync Audiobooks check box if you want to put your audiobooks on your iPhone. Select the All Audiobooks option button if you want to load all your audiobooks. Otherwise, select the Selected Audiobooks option button, and use the Audiobooks list box, the Parts list box, and the Include Audiobooks From Playlists list box to specify which audiobooks and parts you want to sync.

Choose Which Photos to Sync

To tell iTunes which photos to put on your iPhone, display the Photos screen, select the Sync Photos From check box, and then choose the source in the drop-down list. For example, in Mac OS X, choose iPhoto (as shown in Figure 2-12) or a particular folder in the Sync Photos From drop-down list.

Once you've done that, choose which photos to include:

- **Windows** Select the All Photos option button to add all the photos. To add just some, select the Selected Folders option button, and then select the check box for each folder you want to synchronize.

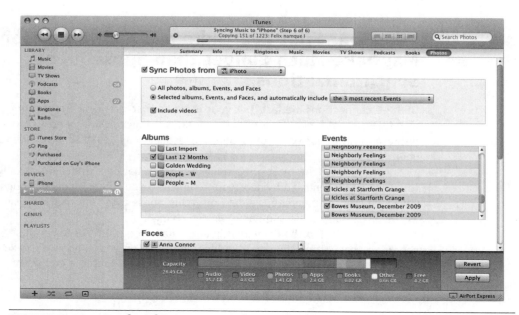

FIGURE 2-12   On the Photos screen, choose the source of the photos, and then choose between syncing all the photos or just the ones you specify.

- **Mac OS X**   Select the All Photos, Albums, Events, And Faces option button if you want to include all the photos. To choose by Events, select the Selected Albums, Events, And Faces And Automatically Include option button, and then choose which items to include:
  4. Open the Events pop-up menu and choose the appropriate item. You can choose None, All Events, an item for recent events (for example, The 3 Most Recent Events), or a time period (for example, Events From The Last 2 Months). (An *Event* is a group of photos in iPhoto that are organized by date or by topic.)
  5. In the Albums list box, select the check box for each album you want to sync.
  6. In the Events list box, select the check box for each Event you want to sync (apart from those you chose in the Events pop-up menu).
  7. In the Faces list box, select the check box for each face you want to sync.

Run the Sync

When you finish choosing settings, click the Apply button on whichever screen you're currently at. iTunes syncs the items to your iPhone.

Why Your First-Ever iPhone Synchronization May Take Much Longer than Subsequent Synchronizations

USB 2.0 connections are fast, but your iPhone's first-ever synchronization may take several hours if your library contains many songs or videos. This is because, on the first synchronization, iTunes must copy each song or video to your iPhone.

Subsequent synchronizations are much quicker, because iTunes needs only to transfer new songs and videos you've added to your library, remove songs you've deleted, and update the data on items whose tags (information such as the artist name and song name) you've changed.

If you've selected the Convert Higher Bit Rate Songs To 128 Kbps AAC check box, converting the songs and loading them on your iPhone will take longer (how much longer depends on how fast your computer is and what other tasks it's running).

Recharge Your iPhone

As with most devices, the battery icon on your iPhone's display shows you the status of the device's battery power.

The easiest way to recharge your iPhone is to plug it into a high-power USB port on a computer. If the USB port provides enough power, you will see the battery indicator add a charging symbol. (If the port doesn't provide enough power, try another port.)

Alternatively, you can use the Apple USB Power Adapter that comes with the iPhone and lets you recharge your iPhone when you are away from any computer. You can also run your iPhone from the Power Adapter even while the battery is charging.

Tip   Using the Apple USB Power Adapter to charge an iPhone is more reliable than using the USB cable, and the Power Adapter is useful for troubleshooting problems such as the iPhone becoming nonresponsive.

The iPhone's battery typically takes between three and five hours to recharge. After about half of the charging time, the battery should be at about 80 percent of its charge capacity—enough for you to use your iPhone for several hours. (This is because the battery charges quickly at first, up to around the 80 percent level, and then charges more slowly the remainder of the way so as not to overcharge.)

Eject and Disconnect Your iPhone

When iTunes has finished loading songs onto your iPhone, you can disconnect it unless you need to continue recharging its battery.

If you need to disconnect your iPhone while it's syncing, eject it first. You can use any of the following ways:

- Move the mouse pointer over the Sync button (shown on the left here) next to the iPhone's entry in the Source pane. When the button turns to an Eject icon (shown on the right here), click it.

- Right-click (or CTRL-click on the Mac) the iPhone's entry in the Source list and then click the Eject item on the shortcut menu.
- Click the iPhone's entry in the Source list and then choose Controls | Eject *device's name* or press CTRL-E (Windows) or ⌘-E (Mac).

3

Connect Your iPhone to Wireless Networks and the Internet

HOW TO...

- Connect your iPhone to your home wireless network
- Connect your iPhone to your work wireless network
- Connect your iPhone to wireless hotspots
- Manage your wireless networks
- Make your iPhone forget a wireless network
- Connect to non-secure wireless networks

To get the most out of your iPhone, you'll need to connect it to wireless networks to give yourself Internet access without chewing through your data plan. In fact, you may already have connected your iPhone to a wireless network when setting it up so that it could contact the iCloud servers across the Internet.

By connecting to your own wireless network at home, you can turn your iPhone into the ultimate Internet tablet—an always-at-hand tool for checking your mail, surfing the Web, or grabbing the latest information online. By connecting to a work network, you can use your iPhone as a work tool in your office, in meetings, or— well—in the restroom. By connecting to a public wireless network, you can stay in high-speed touch when you're out on the town, in the train, or even on a plane.

In this chapter, we'll look at how to make those connections safely, how to tell your iPhone which networks to prefer over others, and how to make it forget a network you no longer want to use.

Connect Your iPhone to Your Home Wireless Network

In this section, I'll show you how to connect your iPhone to standard wireless networks—the kind of wireless network you may well have at home. These wireless networks are secured with passwords rather than heavier-duty and more esoteric means of security. Typically, these wireless networks are *open*, which means that they broadcast their presence. But sometimes these wireless networks are *closed*, not broadcasting their presence. We'll look at how to connect to both types of network.

Get the Information You Need to Connect to the Wireless Network

To connect to a wireless network, you need to know its name and its password. You may also need to know the security type.

- **Wireless network name**   The wireless network's name is formally called the *service set identifier*, or SSID. This is the name the wireless access point has been set to call the network.
- **Wireless network password**   Most wireless networks use passwords to prevent unauthorized computers and devices from connecting to them.
- **Wireless network security type**   You can connect to many wireless networks by simply providing the correct password, but for others you need to know the security type. See the sidebar "Wireless Network Security Types" for details.

Connect to an Open Wireless Network

Armed with the name, password, and (maybe) security type of the wireless network you need to connect your iPhone to, you're ready to set up the connection. Follow these steps:

1. Press the Home button to reach the Home screen.
2. Tap the Settings icon to display the Settings screen.
3. Tap the Wi-Fi icon to display the Wi-Fi Networks screen (shown on the left in Figure 3-1). This screen shows the open wireless networks that the iPhone can detect. *Open* means that a wireless network is broadcasting its network name, not that it's unsecured.
4. Tap the button for the network you want to join. The iPhone displays the Enter Password screen for the network, as shown on the right in Figure 3-1.

 Note   If the network you want to join doesn't appear in the list on the Wi-Fi Networks screen, it's probably *closed* (not broadcasting its SSID) rather than open. See the next section for instructions. If the network *is* open, but it doesn't appear, most

FIGURE 3-1   Use the Wi-Fi Networks screen (left) to choose a network. The check mark shows the current connection (if there is one). Type the network password on the Enter Password screen.

likely it's out of range of the iPhone. If you're sure you're within range, make sure the wireless access point is powered on and the wireless network is operational.

5. Type the password. Passwords are usually case sensitive, so make sure you get it right. For security, the iPhone displays the character you just typed for a few seconds, then changes it to a security-conscious dot in case someone's peeking over your shoulder.
6. Tap the Join button—either the Join button in the upper-right corner of the screen or the one at the lower-right corner of the keyboard. The iPhone joins the network and displays the Wi-Fi Networks screen again, this time with a check mark next to the name of the connected wireless network.

 Wi-Fi network connections make the iPhone far more useful—but they use a lot of battery power. If you don't use Wi-Fi network connections, or use them only occasionally, turn Wi-Fi off to save battery life. On the Wi-Fi Networks screen,

Did You Know?

Wireless Network Security Types

Wireless networks use three main types of security:

- **WEP**   Wired Equivalent Privacy is the weakest form of protection used on wireless networks. WEP contains systemic errors that make cracking it easy for malefactors. Avoid using WEP if you have the choice. But because many Wi-Fi hotspots still use WEP, you may find yourself forced to use it.
- **WPA**   WPA is the first level of Wi-Fi Protected Access (the second is WPA2, discussed next). WPA is far more secure than WEP—some experts compare WPA to a decent safe and WEP to a brown envelope. WPA is a good choice for home use.
- **WPA2**   WPA2 is the strongest level of wireless security in widespread use. Some wireless access points do not support WPA2, but if yours does, you might as well use WPA2, because your iPhone supports it as well. There *is* such a thing as too much wireless network security, but this isn't it.

Both WPA and WPA2 also have an "Enterprise" version: WPA Enterprise and WPA2 Enterprise. These versions use a server to verify the identity of network users, whereas the regular or "Personal" versions of WPA and WPA2 use a password or passphrase. You'll find the Enterprise versions used widely in corporate networks. We'll look at how to connect to wireless networks with enterprise-type security in the section "Connect Your iPhone to Your Work Wireless Network," later in this chapter.

move the Wi-Fi switch to the Off position. When you need to join a Wi-Fi network, revisit this screen, and move the Wi-Fi switch to the On position.

Connect to a Closed Wireless Network

Closed wireless networks—ones configured not to broadcast their SSIDs, usually to deter casual attempts to connect—don't appear in the Choose A Network list on the Wi-Fi Networks screen. To join a closed wireless network, follow these steps from the Wi-Fi Networks screen:

1. Tap the Other button to display the Other Network screen (shown on the left in Figure 3-2).
2. In the Name box, type the name of the wireless network.
3. If the wireless network uses security (as most do), tap the Security button to display the Security screen (shown on the right in Figure 3-2).
4. Tap the appropriate button: WEP, WPA, WPA2, WPA Enterprise, or WPA2 Enterprise. (If you don't know which type of security the network uses, consult the network administrator.) The iPhone puts a check mark next to your choice.

FIGURE 3-2   Use the Other Network screen (left) to join a closed wireless network. Choose the security type on the Security screen (right).

5. Tap the Other Network button in the upper-left corner to go back to the Other Network screen again. This screen now shows the security type you chose on the Security line and displays a Password box under it.
6. Type the password, and then tap the Join button—again, either the Join button in the upper-right corner of the screen or the one at the lower-right corner of the keyboard. The iPhone joins the network.

Connect Your iPhone to Your Work Wireless Network

In this section, we'll look at how to connect your iPhone to a wireless network at work—for example, in a company or organization. Such wireless networks typically have tighter security than home wireless networks, so you need to provide additional information to connect to them. For example, you may need to install a digital certificate on your iPhone that will identify the iPhone to an authentication server on the network.

How to... ## Turn Off the "Ask to Join Networks" Feature When in Busy Areas

The Ask To Join Networks switch on the Wi-Fi Networks screen controls whether your iPhone, when it doesn't have a wireless network connection, offers to join other networks it finds. (As long as it has a connection, the iPhone doesn't offer to join other networks. It keeps on using that connection until it loses it.)

The Join Networks feature is useful when you want the iPhone to alert you to a wireless network you might need to join, but it can be a menace when you're somewhere in which there are many wireless networks. For example, if you wander down a business street or even a residential street, the iPhone may find dozens of wireless networks. Even at home, your neighbors may have you caged in a Wi-Fi prison, so if you wander into a dead spot for your own wireless network, your iPhone may start offering to join the network next door.

In this case, the iPhone is just wasting its battery power keeping track of the networks around. To stop it from doing so, go to the Wi-Fi Networks screen, and then move the Ask To Join Networks switch to the Off position.

  A *digital certificate* is a small chunk of encrypted code that contains information identifying a particular computer. The digital certificate is secured in such a way that its contents can't be tampered with, so you can be sure the information the certificate contains is genuine. Digital certificates come from organizations called *certificate authorities,* or CAs. The three biggest CAs are VeriSign, Comodo, and Go Daddy.

Setting your iPhone up to connect to a work wireless network can be tricky—so Apple has created a way to make the process seamless: A network administrator can give you a file called a *configuration profile* containing a *payload* (the details) for setting up the wireless network on your iPhone. To set up the wireless network on your iPhone, you simply open the configuration profile on the iPhone and follow the prompts to install it. We'll look at this method first, because it's the method you're most likely to use—if you're lucky.

If you're less lucky, you can also set up a work wireless network manually. We'll look at this method second.

Install a Wireless Network Profile on Your iPhone

The quick way to set up a work wireless network on your iPhone is by installing a configuration profile containing a payload with the wireless network's details. You'll normally get the configuration profile from a network administrator. Assuming the network administrator has set the configuration profile up correctly—and you'll have a better idea than I whether that's a reasonable assumption—this method lets you set up the wireless network in seconds with minimal effort.

For you to use a configuration profile, someone must put it on your iPhone. There are three normal ways to install a configuration profile on the iPhone:

- **Directly** The administrator connects your iPhone to the PC or Mac on which he or she is running iPhone Configuration Utility, a utility for—well—configuring the iPhone (and iPod touch and iPad). The administrator uses iPhone Configuration Utility to apply the configuration profile to the iPhone.
- **By e-mail** The administrator sends the configuration profile to your iPhone. You open the message containing the configuration profile, and then apply it to your iPhone. As long as the iPhone already has an e-mail account set up, this is easy for both the administrator and you.
- **By download** The administrator posts the configuration profile to a website you have access to. You download the configuration profile and apply it to your iPhone.

 The administrator can send you the web page's URL via e-mail or SMS or publish the address to a location where you will be able to find it. Using SMS ensures that the message reaches the right iPhone and allows the administrator to customize the URL to that iPhone if necessary.

Here's an example using a configuration profile attached to an e-mail message. The process for installing a configuration profile by download from a website is similar apart from the first step: Instead of tapping the configuration profile's button in the e-mail message, you tap the download link on a web page.

1. Open the message that contains the configuration profile.
2. Tap the button for the profile, as shown on the left in Figure 3-3. Your iPhone displays the Install Profile screen, as shown on the right in Figure 3-3.
3. Look at the information on the Install Profile screen to make sure the profile contains what you think it does. If you want to see more information about the profile, tap the More Details button to display the profile's information screen (shown on the left in Figure 3-4). Tap the Install Profile button in the upper-left corner when you're ready to return to the Install Profile screen.

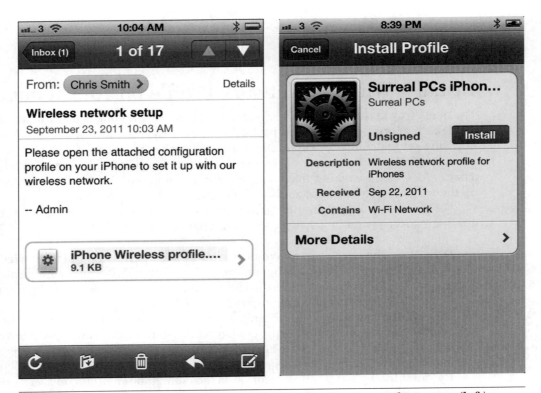

FIGURE 3-3 Tap the configuration profile's button in an e-mail message (left) to display the Install Profile screen (right).

4. Tap the Install button on the Install Profile screen. Your iPhone displays a dialog box warning you that installing the profile will change the settings on the iPhone, as shown on the right in Figure 3-4.

5. Tap the Install Now button. Your iPhone installs the profile, and then displays the Profile Installed screen telling you it has done so.

6. Tap the Done button to leave the Profile Installed screen.

You can now start using the wireless network that the profile added for you.

Set Up a Work Wireless Network Manually

In this section, we'll look at how to manually connect your iPhone to a wireless network secured with enterprise security. To connect to such a network you have to provide extra information, such as a username and password or a digital certificate that identifies your iPhone.

To set up the connection to a work wireless network, follow these steps from the Wi-Fi Networks screen:

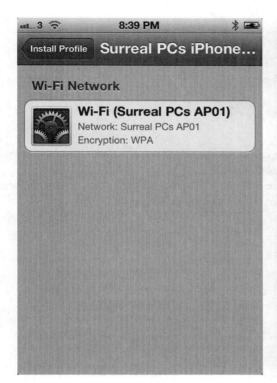

FIGURE 3-4   The profile's information screen (left) shows you the details of what the profile contains—in this case, just a Wi-Fi Network payload. When you tap the Install button on the Install Profile screen to install the profile, your iPhone makes sure you know that installing the profile will change settings on your iPhone.

1. Tap the name of the network you want to join. Your iPhone displays the Enter Password screen, as shown on the left in Figure 3-5.
2. Type your username in the Username field.
3. If the wireless network uses a password, type it in the Password field. If not, follow these steps:
   a. Tap the Mode button to display the Mode screen (shown on the right in Figure 3-5).
   b. Tap the EAP-TLS button, putting a check mark next to it.
   c. Tap the Enter Password button to go back to the Enter Password screen. You'll see that the Password field has been replaced by an Identity button, as shown on the left in Figure 3-6.
4. Tap the Identity button to display the Identity screen (shown on the right in Figure 3-6).
5. Tap the identity you want to use, placing a check mark next to it.
6. Tap the Enter Password button to return to the Enter Password screen.
7. Tap the Join button to join the network.

What the Unsigned, Not Verified, and Verified Terms on the Install Profile Screen Mean

The readout to the left of the Install button on the Install Profile screen shows the profile's status:

- **Unsigned** Whoever created the profile didn't apply a digital signature to the profile to protect it against changes.
- **Not Verified** The creator did apply a digital signature to the profile, but your iPhone can't confirm the digital signature is authentic.
- **Verified** The iPhone has confirmed the digital signature applied to the profile is authentic.

In an ideal world, you'd install only profiles that were verified as coming from whom they claim. But many companies and organizations still use unsigned profiles, so you have a fair chance of running into them. If in doubt, check with an administrator that the profile is safe to install.

Connect Your iPhone to Wireless Hotspots

These days, many public places have Wi-Fi networks that are free for their patrons to use. For example, many coffee shops and burger joints provide free Wi-Fi to tempt their customers to stay longer (and to compete with other establishments that provide free Wi-Fi), and most airports provide free Wi-Fi to make their customers' stay seem less long, let them get on with business, or enable them to e-mail their loved ones to tell them how long a delay they're facing.

Caution Wireless hotspots can be great when you need a connection—but always stay aware of the danger of connecting your iPhone to any hotspot whose operator you don't know: The hotspot can grab any data that you send to and from the Internet. Wherever possible, use hotspots provided by well-known companies or organizations rather than unknown hotspots. If in doubt about a network's benevolence, don't connect your iPhone to it.

You connect to these wireless hotspots in either of these ways:

- On the Wi-Fi Networks screen, tap the wireless network's name.
- If your iPhone displays the Select A Wireless Network dialog box, tap the network you want to join.

FIGURE 3-5   When connecting to a wireless network that uses enterprise security, you need to enter your username on the Enter Password screen (left). You also either enter your password or tap the Mode button to display the Mode screen (right), on which you can change the security mode.

 Before you connect to a wireless network in a public place, make sure it's the hotspot network. For example, at a coffee shop, check the notice on the wall or ask the barista the network's name. All too many people fail to turn off the wireless networks on their laptops, so you run the risk of connecting to one of these instead of the hotspot.

Depending on how the wireless hotspot is set up, you may need to enter a username and password at a login screen in Safari. Figure 3-7 shows an example of a login screen.

After your iPhone establishes the connection to the hotspot, you can use the Internet as usual. For example, use the Mail app to check your e-mail, or open Safari and start browsing.

FIGURE 3-6 Tap the Identity button on the Enter Password screen (left) to display the Identity screen (right). Tap the identity needed for the connection, and then tap the Enter Password button to return to the Enter Password screen.

 For security, tell the iPhone to forget any Wi-Fi hotspot you don't intend to use again. Use the technique described in the section "Make Your iPhone Forget a Wireless Network," next in this chapter.

Make Your iPhone Forget a Wireless Network

When you no longer want to use a particular wireless network, tell the iPhone to forget it. To do so, open the wireless network's configuration screen, and then tap the Forget This Network button at the top (look ahead to the left screen in Figure 3-8 to see this button). Tap the Forget Network button on the confirmation screen that the iPhone displays.

If you find you need to join the wireless network again, join it as described earlier in this chapter. You will need to type the password for the network again.

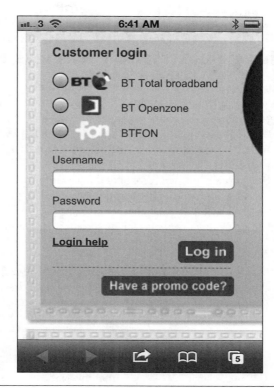

FIGURE 3-7   You may need to log in to a hotspot using a username and password.

Configure a Wireless Network Connection Manually

If you need to change the settings for the network connection, follow these steps to display the configuration screen for the wireless network:

1. Press the Home button to display the Home screen.
2. Tap the Settings icon to display the Settings screen.
3. Tap the Wi-Fi button to display the Wi-Fi Networks screen.
4. Tap the arrow button on the right side of the network you want to configure.

Your iPhone displays the configuration screen for the wireless network, which shows the network's name at the top. You can then choose settings on this screen's three tabs as described in the following sections.

Control Whether Your iPhone Automatically Joins a Subscription Wireless Network

If you use your iPhone with a subscription wireless network—a network you have to log in to and (usually) pay to use—you can control whether the iPhone automatically connects to this network or waits for you to connect manually. For example, if you connect your iPhone to the wireless network at your local coffee shop, you likely want to use that network each time you park yourself there to enjoy a quadruple espresso—but if you're just walking past the coffee shop, you probably don't want your iPhone to glom onto the wireless network like a high-tech limpet.

To control whether your iPhone automatically connects to a particular subscription wireless network, follow these steps from the Wi-Fi Networks screen:

1. In the Choose A Network list, tap the arrow button to the right of the network's name. Your iPhone displays the settings screen for the network. The following illustration shows the top part of the settings screen for the network called Lossystrata.

2. Move the Auto-Join switch to the On position or the Off position, as needed.
3. Tap the Wi-Fi Networks button to go back to the Wi-Fi Networks screen.

Note   At the bottom of each tab on the screen for a wireless network is the HTTP Proxy area. See the section "Set Up an HTTP Proxy Server," later in this chapter, for coverage of the options this area contains.

Set DHCP Information

Dynamic Host Configuration Protocol (DHCP) is an efficient way of allocating IP addresses automatically to network clients, and in many networks, it's easiest to use DHCP to provide IP addresses to the computers and devices on the network. When your iPhone connects to the network, it picks up the IP address, subnet mask, router information, and so on from the DHCP server.

If the DHCP server gives your iPhone all the information it needs, you won't need to make any changes. But if you do need to make changes, tap the DHCP tab

Did You Know?

Why You Should Never Use a Wireless Access Point's Default Name

Normally, when you buy a wireless access point, it comes with a default network name, administrator name, and password that the manufacturer has programmed into it. The idea is that you can get your wireless network up and running in short order, and then change the network name and password (and perhaps the administrator name) for security.

Most people don't change the network name. Or the password.

As you can imagine, this is grim for security, because any attacker who knows the password for one of the default network names (which are widely published on the Web) can access the network.

But it's doubly bad for the iPhone, because Apple set the iPhones up in a user-friendly but insecure way. Once you've connected to a wireless network successfully, the iPhone remembers the network and automatically connects to it again when it's within range—but without making sure that the network is the same network. So a malefactor can create a wireless network that has the same name (SSID) and password as a network you've used before, and the iPhone will happily connect to the malefactor's network. The malefactor can then attempt to grab your data off the iPhone.

For this reason, it's a good idea not to use the manufacturer's default name (SSID) for any wireless network you set up. Using a unique network name will make it harder for a casual attacker to target your iPhone. But a determined attacker who wants to target you specifically can use a "packet sniffer" program to eavesdrop on the network traffic and detect the wireless network settings you're using, after which they can implement this attack.

If you connect to a wireless network at a hotspot, you won't have the chance to change its network name or password—so be on your guard for anything unusual when connected. For example, if the iPhone can establish the connection to the wireless network, but you cannot access your e-mail as usual, you may have connected to the wrong network.

Apple may change the iPhone's firmware or software to get around this problem. But even if it does, you're better off creating a unique name for your wireless network.

on the wireless network's screen to display its contents (shown on the left in Figure 3-8). Then tap the field you need to change, and then type the information using the soft keyboard that appears automatically. You can't change the IP address, the subnet mask, or the router, but you can change these three settings:

- **DNS** If you need to point your iPhone at a different Domain Name Service (DNS) server, type in the server's address.

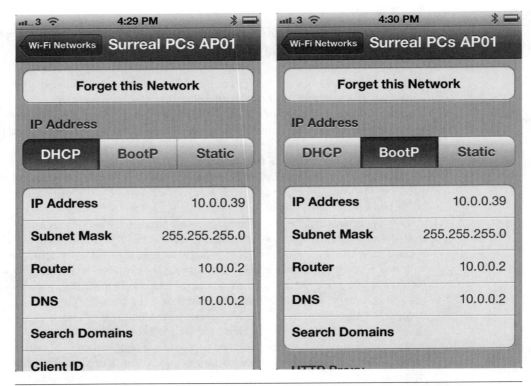

FIGURE 3-8 On the DHCP tab of the screen for the wireless network (left), you can change the DNS setting, the Search Domains setting, and the Client ID setting. On the BootP tab (right), you can change the DNS setting or the Search Domains setting.

- **Search Domains** Enter any domains that you want your iPhone to search automatically when you enter a partial address in a web browser or other Internet client. For example, if you enter **surrealpcs.com** as a search domain, you can enter simply **corp** to connect to **corp.surrealpcs.com**.
- **Client ID** If the network's administrator needs to be able to identify your iPhone by client ID, enter the name in this field. By default, your iPhone uses the name you apply during setup.

The change you're perhaps most likely to need to make here is renewing the DHCP lease to sort out network problems. To renew the lease, tap the Renew Lease button at the bottom of the DHCP tab of the screen for the wireless network.

Set BootP Information

If your network uses BootP rather than DHCP to provide network configuration information, tap the BootP tab on the screen for the wireless network to display the BootP settings (shown on the right in Figure 3-8). Then fill in the DNS setting or the Search Domains setting as needed. You can't change the IP address, the subnet mask, or the router.

Set a Static IP Address

DHCP and BootP are great for many purposes, but sometimes it's useful to set up an iPhone with a static IP address—for example, when you need to be able to always easily identify the iPhone by its IP address rather than having to dig through logs.

To set up a static IP address, tap the Static tab to display its contents (see Figure 3-9). Then tap the IP Address field and fill in the address on the soft keyboard (which the iPhone displays automatically). When you're done, tap the Return button on the keyboard to move to the next field, and continue filling in the information.

Set Up an HTTP Proxy Server

At the bottom of each of the three tabs on the screen for the wireless network, you can set up an HTTP proxy to tell Safari and other web apps where to direct their HTTP requests.

To control HTTP proxying, you tap the appropriate one of the three buttons under the HTTP Proxy heading: Off, Manual, or Auto. Normally, you'll find the Off button active until you make a change here.

To set up an HTTP proxy manually, tap the Manual button, and then enter the details in the Server field and the Port field (shown on the left in Figure 3-10). If the proxy server requires authentication, tap the left side of the Authentication switch to move it from Off to On (as in the figure), and then fill in the username and password in the fields that the iPhone displays.

To set up an HTTP proxy automatically, tap the Auto button, and then enter the server's address in the URL field (shown on the right in Figure 3-10).

Solve Connection Problems with Wireless Networks

In the early days, wireless networks were tricky to connect to, and often dropped the connection unexpectedly. These days, wireless networks are mostly pretty reliable—but you may still run into problems connecting to them.

FIGURE 3-9 If you need the iPhone to have a static IP address, fill in the details on the Static tab of the screen for the wireless network.

Solve Connection Problems on Any Wireless Network

This section shows you how to deal with a couple of problems you may experience with any wireless network, be it private or public. The next section sorts out a connection problem with public wireless networks.

Your iPhone Starts Using the Cellular Network Instead

When your iPhone is within range of a wireless network, you'll normally want to use the wireless network rather than the cellular network so that you can get the fastest possible connection and not eat up your calling plan. But you may find sometimes that, even when a wireless network icon appears on the screen, and the iPhone seems to have connected to the network, the iPhone is actually using the cellular network instead.

This usually happens when your iPhone doesn't have permission to connect to the wireless network because the wireless router is set to accept connections only

FIGURE 3-10   To set the iPhone to use an HTTP proxy server, fill in the details on the Manual tab (left) or the Auto tab (right) of the HTTP Proxy area of the screen for the wireless network.

from certain network cards. The router's owner sets the restrictions by using the Media Access Control identification number for the hardware.

The Media Access Control number is usually referred to as the MAC number (spelled in capitals to distinguish it from Apple computers), and it's an ugly string in hexadecimal (the numbers 0–9, representing themselves, and the letters A–F, representing 10 through 15).

If you find this is happening, you need to add your iPhone's MAC address to the wireless router's approved list. How you do this depends on the router, but here's how to find the MAC address:

1. Tap the Home button to reach the Home screen.
2. Tap Settings to display the Settings screen.
3. Tap General to display the General screen.
4. Tap About to display the About screen.
5. Look at the Wi-Fi Address readout. You'll see a hexadecimal number such as 00:23:6D:CD:7D:75. This is what you need to add to the wireless router's list.

Your iPhone Gives the "Could Not Connect to Server" Error

If the iPhone gives you the error "could not connect to server" when you're trying to use something on the Internet, chances are that you're right at the limit of your wireless connection, and it has become intermittent.

When this happens, you have two choices: move closer and use the wireless network (usually the better choice), or turn Wi-Fi off on the iPhone and use the cellular network instead. (You could also march briskly into the middle distance to get out of wireless range, but turning off Wi-Fi is usually smarter and easier.)

 If you know you're well within range of your wireless router, the problem may lie with the router itself. See if other computers are able to access the Internet through the router. If not, you may need to reset it.

Here's how to turn Wi-Fi off on the iPhone:

1. Press the Home button to reach the Home screen.
2. Tap Settings to display the Settings screen.
3. Tap the Wi-Fi button to display the Wireless Networks screen.
4. Tap the right half of the Wi-Fi switch to move it to the Off position.

Solve Connection Problems on Public Networks

If you're having problems connecting to the Internet through a Wi-Fi connection at a wireless hotspot, here's an easy solution: renew your DHCP lease to create a new connection to the hotspot. As previously mentioned, Dynamic Host Configuration Protocol (DHCP) is the technology used for allocating IP addresses efficiently to computers on a network.

To renew the DHCP lease, follow these steps:

1. Tap the Home button to reach the Home screen.
2. Tap Settings to display the Settings screen.
3. Tap Wi-Fi Networks to display the Wi-Fi Networks screen.
4. Tap the More Info button (the blue button with the arrow pointing to the right) next to the network's name to display the network information screen. This screen bears the network's name.
5. Make sure the DHCP button on the left is selected (if not, tap it).
6. Tap the Renew Lease button. The iPhone releases its connection with the wireless network and applies for a new connection. This gives the iPhone a different IP address (almost always; it's possible to get the same address again) and often resolves connection problems.

 You can renew the DHCP lease for any network, but if you've configured your home network so that your iPhone normally works with it, you usually won't need to renew the lease.

4

Choose Essential Settings on Your iPhone

HOW TO...

- Open the Settings app
- Use AirPlane mode
- Choose Notifications settings
- Choose Location Services settings
- Choose Carrier settings
- Choose Sounds settings
- Choose Brightness settings
- Choose your wallpaper
- Choose General settings
- Choose settings for the built-in apps
- Choose settings for third-party apps

To control its almost incredible capabilities, your iPhone has a truly terrifying number of settings. While Apple chooses sensible default values for most of these settings, you'll get more out of your iPhone by customizing many of the settings. And even those settings you don't need to change at this point, you may in the future benefit from knowing about.

This chapter walks you through choosing the most important settings. We'll start by opening the Settings app and then go through the Settings screen from top to bottom.

This chapter skips over settings covered in other chapters. For example, Chapter 3 explains how to use your iPhone's Wi-Fi settings; Chapter 8 shows you how to set Mail, Contacts, Calendars settings; Chapter 9 discusses Safari's settings; and Chapter 18 explains how to share your iPhone's Internet connection using the Personal Hotspot feature.

This chapter is long and—to be frank—repetitive, boring, and lacking a compelling plot. Unless you've blasted through the works of Proust and Tolstoy without flagging, I strongly recommend against trying to read it through in one go. Instead, skim through the chapter, identify the sections that will help you most at first, and go straight to those. Then give yourself a good recovery period before coming back for another dose.

Open the Settings App

To start, open the Settings app:

1. Press the Home button to display the Home screen.
2. Tap the Settings icon to display the Settings screen.

The Settings screen is a long screen, broken up into different boxes. Figure 4-1 shows you the main parts of the Settings screen. The upper-left screen shows the top part of the Settings screen, and the lower-left screen shows the next part, which you display by scrolling down. Scroll down farther, and you'll see the section of the Settings screen shown in the upper-right screen in the figure. Below that is the section shown in the lower-right screen. Below that appear settings for other apps.

Use Airplane Mode

Airplane mode turns off your iPhone's cellular connection, Wi-Fi, and Bluetooth completely so that the cabin crew doesn't have to evict you from the airplane during the sensitive periods around takeoff and landing. To turn on Airplane mode, tap the Airplane Mode switch at the top of the Settings screen and move it to the On position.

When you turn on Airplane mode, your iPhone displays an orange airplane symbol in the status bar, as shown here.

 Airplane mode saves a fair amount of power, so if your iPhone is running low on juice and you don't mind turning off all communications, slide the Airplane Mode switch to the On position.

While Airplane mode is on, you can't turn on the cellular connection, but you can turn on Wi-Fi or Bluetooth if necessary:

FIGURE 4-1 The Settings screen divides its many buttons into separate boxes. Here, the upper-left screen shows the top part of the Settings screen. The lower-left screen shows the second part, the upper-right screen the next part, and the lower-right screen the beginning of the final part.

- **Wi-Fi** Tap the Wi-Fi button on the Settings screen to display the Wi-Fi Networks screen (shown here), and then tap the Wi-Fi switch and move it to the On position.
- **Bluetooth** Follow these steps:
  1. Scroll down to the third box on the Settings screen.
  2. Tap the General button to display the General screen.
  3. Tap the Bluetooth button to display the Bluetooth screen (shown here).
  4. Tap the Bluetooth switch and move it to the On position.

When you're ready to stop using Airplane mode, tap the Airplane Mode switch and move it to the Off position. The orange airplane icon disappears from the status bar, and your iPhone gratefully resumes its connections.

Choose Notifications Settings

Your iPhone can display a *notification*, or alert, when you receive information you may need to act upon—for example, an incoming text message or a reminder tied to a time that has arrived or to a location that you're leaving.

To help you manage your notifications, your iPhone integrates them into the Notification Center app. Chapter 12 explains how to use Notification Center, but here's a sneak preview: Tap your finger at the top of the iPhone's screen (with any screen showing except the lock screen), and then drag it down, to open Notification Center.

To control which notifications appear in Notification Center, follow these steps:

1. Tap the Notifications button on the Settings screen to display the Notifications screen. The left screen in Figure 4-2 shows the top part of the Notifications screen. The right screen in Figure 4-2 shows the bottom part of the Notifications screen.
2. In the Sort Apps box, tap the Manually button if you want to sort the apps in Notification Center manually. Tap the By Time button if you prefer to sort the apps by time of the notifications.
3. In the In Notification Center box, you can choose which apps appear in Notification Center and (for some apps) the types of alerts they display. To choose settings, follow these steps:
   a. Tap the app to display its control screen. The left screen in Figure 4-3 shows the top of the control screen for the Messages app. The right screen in Figure 4-3 shows the bottom of the control screen for the Messages app.
   b. If you want to remove the app from Notification Center, tap the Notification Center switch at the top and move it to the Off position.

FIGURE 4-2 On the top part of the Notifications screen (left), you can choose how to sort apps and control which apps appear in Notification Center and the types of notifications they show. On the lower part of the Notifications screen (right), you can choose settings for apps that don't appear in Notification Center.

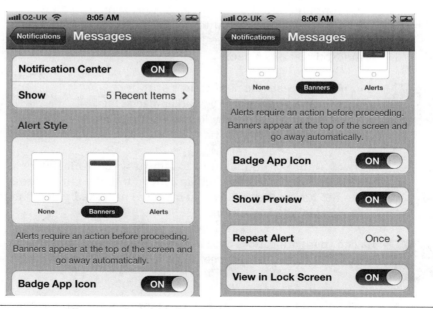

FIGURE 4-3 On the control screen for the app, choose whether to show the app in Notification Center, how many items to show, which alert style to use, and other options. The selection of options depends on the app.

c. Assuming you leave the Notification Center switch in the On position, tap the Show button to display the Show screen (illustrated here), and then tap the button for the number of items you want to show: 1 Recent Item, 5 Recent Items, or 10 Recent Items. Tap the button with the app's name (here, the Messages button) to return to the Notifications screen.

d. In the Alert Style box, tap the alert style you want: None, Banners (notification bars across the top of the screen), or alerts (dialog boxes across the middle of the screen).

e. To control whether the app displays on its Home screen icon a red badge showing the number of alerts, tap the Badge App Icon switch and move it to the On position or the Off position, as needed. Badge app icons are available only for some apps.

f. To control whether the app shows a preview of the alert in Notification Center, tap the Show Preview switch and move it to the On position or the Off position, as needed. Previews are available only for some apps.

g. To control whether and how often the app repeats the alert to draw your attention to it, tap the Repeat Alert button, and then tap the appropriate button on the Repeat Alert screen (shown here). Tap the button with the app's name (here, the Messages button) to return to the Notifications screen.

Your iPhone repeats the notifications at two-minute intervals until either you acknowledge the notifications or it reaches the Repeat Alert number you have set for the notification.

h. If you want the notifications to appear when your iPhone is locked, tap the View In Lock Screen switch and move it to the On position. If you want to see the notifications only when you've unlocked your iPhone, move this switch to the Off position.

Having your notifications appear on the lock screen is great for ones you mustn't miss, but it means that anyone who can see your iPhone can see the notifications too.

i. When you finish choosing settings for the app, tap the Notifications button in the upper-left corner of the screen to return to the Notifications screen.

If you want to customize the order in which the apps appear in Notification Center, tap the Edit button. Your iPhone displays a handle (three horizontal lines) to the right of each item in the In Notification Center box and each item in the Not In Notification Center box. Tap a handle and drag up or down to move an item. When you finish rearranging the apps, tap the Done button to turn off Edit mode.

4. In the Not In Notification Center box, you can choose settings for the apps that don't appear in Notification Center. This works in the same way as for the apps in Notification Center; see the previous step for instructions. To move an app into Notification Center, tap its Notification Center switch and move it to the On position.

5. When you finish choosing settings for notifications, tap the Settings button in the upper-left corner of the Notifications screen to return to the Settings screen.

Choose Location Services Settings

Location Services is your iPhone's feature for tracking its location and providing that information to apps and system services that need it. You can turn Location Services off altogether if you don't want to be tracked at all, or you can winnow down the list of apps and system services that use Location Services.

To choose settings for Location Services, follow these steps:

1. Tap the Location Services button on the Settings screen to display the Location Services screen. The left screen in Figure 4-4 shows the top part of the Location Services screen. The right screen in Figure 4-4 shows the bottom part of the Location Services screen.

2. If you want to turn off Location Services entirely, tap the Location Services switch and move it to the Off position.

 Normally, you'll want to keep Location Services on so that you can make the most of your iPhone's many features that use it—for example, Maps being able to determine your current location or Reminders being able to detect when you've reached your destination and barrage you with tasks that are now due.

3. In the list of apps, move the switches to the On position or the Off position to choose which apps may use Location Services and which may not. These are the apps and what they use Location Services for:
   • **Camera**   Adds the GPS location information to each photo and video you take. This information lets you use the Places feature in the Photos app (and in iPhoto on the Mac) to sort your photos. This is great for determining where that pleasant picnic spot was or where you buried your treasure chest.
   • **iMovie**   Adds the GPS location information to video clips you shoot directly

FIGURE 4-4 On the Location Services screen (left and right), choose whether to use Location Services at all. If you use it, you can narrow down the list of apps and system services permitted to access location information. A purple arrow indicates the app is using Location Services now; a gray arrow indicates the app has used Location Services in the past 24 hours.

into iMovie. If you don't have iMovie installed, Location Services doesn't offer you this option.

- **Maps** Uses Location Services to determine where you are and help you get to where you want to go. (Literally, not figuratively—for figuratively, use Reminders.)
- **Reminders** Uses Location Services to serve you with location-based subpoenas when you leave or arrive at the location you've specified for the reminders.
- **Siri** Uses Location Services to find nearby places you request. For example, if you say "find me the greasiest burger around here," Siri checks where you are and then sniffs the ether for burning fat.
- **Weather** Uses Location Services to keep tabs on weather in the current location.
- **Find My iPhone** Uses Location Services to track your iPhone. If the Find My iPhone setting shows Off, turn it on by tapping the Find My iPhone button, and then moving the Find My iPhone switch on the Find My iPhone screen (shown in the next illustration on the left) to the On position. In the information dialog box that appears (shown in the next illustration on the

right), tap the Allow button. Then tap the Status Bar Icon switch and move it to the position you want—On to display the Location Services arrow in the status bar when you're tracking this iPhone from another computer, or Off if you don't want the tracking arrow to appear.

4. At the bottom of the Location Services screen, tap the System Services button to display the System Services screen. The left screen in Figure 4-5 shows the top part of the System Services screen. The right screen in Figure 4-5 shows the bottom part of the System Services screen.

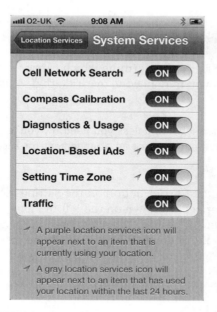 

FIGURE 4-5 On the System Services screen (left and right) choose which system services can use Location Services. A purple arrow indicates the service is using Location Services now; a gray arrow indicates the service has used Location Services in the past 24 hours.

5. In the list of system services, move the switches to the On position or the Off position to choose which services may use Location Services and which may not. These are the system services:
   - **Cell Network Search** Searches for cellular network masts.
   - **Compass Calibration** Calibrates the compass to make sure it's giving an accurate reading.
   - **Diagnostics & Usage** Uses location data to track problems that occur and to assess users' usage patterns.
   - **Location-Based iAds** Uses location data to serve up tempting ads based on where you are. This is one system service you may benefit from turning off.
   - **Setting Time Zone** Sets the time zone.
   - **Traffic** Gets traffic information for the location.
6. At the bottom of the System Services screen, tap the Status Bar Icon switch and move it to the On position or the Off position, as needed—On to display a Location Services arrow in the status bar when a system service is accessing Location Services information, or Off to not display the tracking arrow.
7. When you finish choosing System Services settings, tap the Location Services button in the upper-left corner of the screen to return to the Location Services screen.
8. Tap the Settings button in the upper-left corner of the Location Services screen to return to the Settings screen.

Choose Carrier Settings

Normally, you'll let your iPhone's SIM card determine which carrier network the iPhone connects to. But sometimes you may need to override this setting and connect to another network.

 Don't connect to another carrier network unless you need to, you're prepared to pay for the privilege, and you've put in place an arrangement for accessing that carrier's network.

To change carrier network, tap the Carrier button on the Settings screen. On the Network Selection screen that appears (shown on the left in Figure 4-6), tap the Automatic switch and move it to the Off position. Your iPhone then searches for other carriers, which may take several minutes. When your iPhone displays the list of carriers (as shown on the right in Figure 4-6), tap the carrier you want to connect to.

Choose Sounds Settings

Sounds settings let you choose everything from whether your iPhone vibrates when you've silenced it to which ringtones it plays for different types of messages.

To choose Sounds settings, follow these steps:

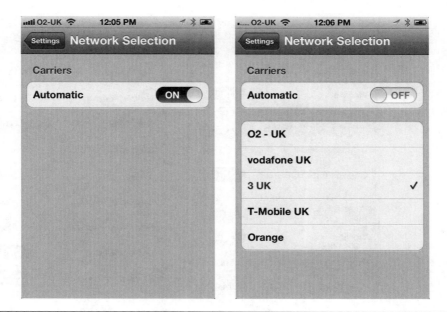

FIGURE 4-6   To change carriers, move the Automatic switch on the Network Selection screen (left) to the Off position. When the list of carriers appears (right), tap the carrier you want to use.

1. Tap the Sounds button on the Settings screen to display the Sounds screen. The left screen in Figure 4-7 shows the top of the Sounds screen, and the right screen in Figure 4-7 shows the bottom of the Sounds screen.
2. In the Silent box, tap the Vibrate switch and move it to the On position if you want your iPhone to vibrate when you've silenced it or to the Off position if you want it to play dead.
3. In the Ringer And Alerts box, tap the volume slider and drag it to a comfortable volume. If you want to be able to change the ringer and alerts volume by pressing the buttons on the left side of your iPhone, set the Change With Buttons switch to the On position; if not, set this switch to the Off position.
4. In the large box, set the Vibrate switch to the On position if you want your iPhone to vibrate when it rings. Set this switch to the Off position if you don't want to feel your calls.

 You can set your iPhone to play a specific tone for a particular contact—for example, a romantic trill when your significant other calls you, a siren for your doctor, or the sound of silence for a known telemarketer you haven't managed yet to shake. You set these tones from within the contact record for that particular contact rather than in Sounds settings.

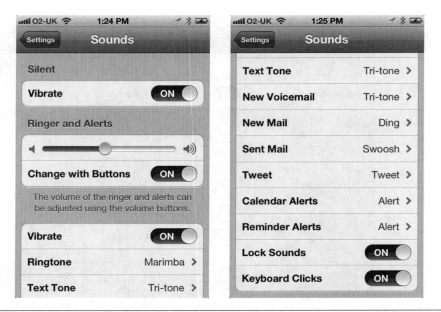

FIGURE 4-7   On the Sounds screen (left and right), you can turn vibration on and off, set the volume for the ringer and alerts, and choose the ringtones to play for particular message types.

5. Use the Ringtone button, Text Tone button, New Voicemail, New Mail button, Sent Mail button, Tweet button, Calendar Alerts button, and Reminder Alerts button to send the ringtone you want your iPhone to play for each item. Tap the button to display the screen listing the ringtones and alert tones, tap the tone you want, and then tap the Sounds button to return to the Sounds screen.
6. Move the Lock Sounds switch to the On position if you want to hear the lock and unlock sounds when you lock and unlock your iPhone. Move this switch to the Off position if you prefer not to advertise what you're doing.
7. Move the Keyboard Clicks switch to the On position if you want to hear a click when you type each character on the keyboard. Move this switch to the Off position if discretion is the better part of valor.
8. Tap the Settings button to return to the Settings screen.

Choose Brightness Settings

To control the screen's brightness and turn the Auto-Brightness setting on or off, tap the Brightness button on the Settings screen. On the Brightness screen (shown next), you can choose two settings:

- **Brightness slider** Drag this slider to set the screen to your preferred brightness.
- **Auto-Brightness** Tap this switch and move it to the On position or the Off position as needed. When you turn Auto-Brightness on, your iPhone measures the ambient light with its sensor and sets the screen brightness accordingly.

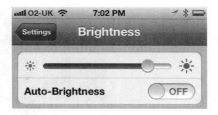

 Your iPhone's bright screen consumes a hefty proportion of its power. So if you need to get as much battery life as possible, turn the brightness down.

Choose Your Wallpaper

To choose the wallpaper your iPhone displays on the lock screen and the Home screen, tap the Wallpaper button on the Settings screen to display the Wallpaper screen (shown on the left in Figure 4-8). Then follow these steps:

1. Tap the button that shows the two screens. (This is just a single button, even though it looks as though it might be two buttons.) Your iPhone displays the screen shown on the right in Figure 4-8.

FIGURE 4-8 On the Wallpaper screen (left), tap the button that shows the two screens. You then see the list of wallpaper sources (right).

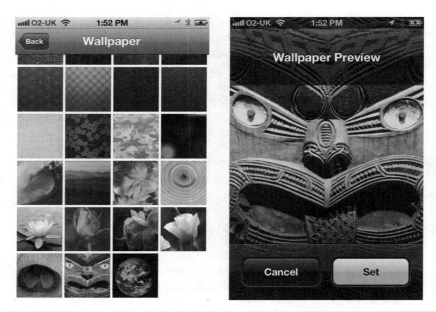

FIGURE 4-9 On the screen showing the album's contents (left), tap the photo you want to use for the wallpaper. If the Wallpaper Preview screen (right) looks good, tap the Set button.

2. Tap the Wallpaper button or the button for the photo album that contains the photo you want to use. This example uses the Wallpaper album. Your iPhone displays the album's contents. The left screen in Figure 4-9 shows the contents of the Wallpaper album.
3. Tap the photo you want to use. Your iPhone displays the Wallpaper Preview screen (shown on the right in Figure 4-9).

Note If you're using one of your own photos, you can move and scale the photo on the Wallpaper Preview screen so that it shows the part of the photo you want. Your iPhone's wallpapers are the right size, so if you use one of them, you don't need to move or scale it.

4. Tap the Set button if you want to go ahead and apply the wallpaper. (If not, tap the Cancel button, and then tap another photo.) Your iPhone displays the dialog box shown here.
5. Tap the Set Lock Screen button to use the wallpaper for the lock screen, the Set Home Screen button to use the wallpaper for the

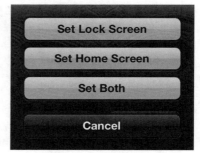

Home screen, or the Set Both button to use the wallpaper for both the lock screen and the Home screen.

Choose General Settings

Your iPhone's General screen in the Settings app contains a huge number of settings—but many of them are worth knowing about, because they'll help you get more out of your iPhone and troubleshoot problems that occur.

In this section, I'll take you through the settings on the General screen. We'll skip lightly over settings you likely won't need to change, but we'll dig in deep on the most useful settings.

Look at the About Settings

To find out your iPhone's technical details—such as its model number, serial number, Wi-Fi address, or Bluetooth address—tap the About button on the General screen, and then look at the About screen. The left screen in Figure 4-10 shows the top part of the About screen, and the right screen shows the bottom part.

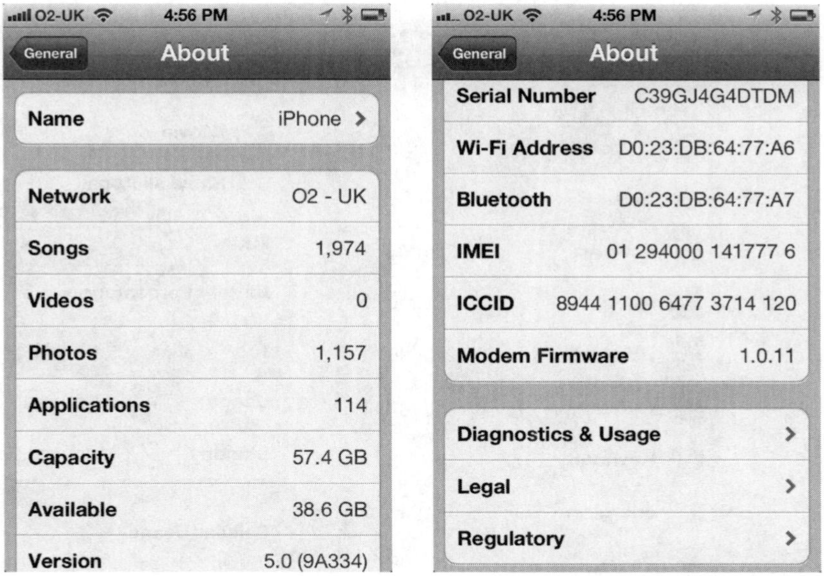

FIGURE 4-10   The About screen (left and right) is the place to find details such as your iPhone's capacity, model number, or IMEI identifying number. You can also change your iPhone's name here.

The Name button at the top of the screen shows your iPhone's name. To change the name, tap the Name button, type the new name on the Name screen, and then tap the Done button.

Run a Software Update from Your iPhone

To run a software update from your iPhone, tap the Software Update button on the General screen. The Software Update app checks for an update. If it finds one, follow the instructions for installing it.

Check Your Usage of Your iPhone's Storage, Battery, and Cellular Plan

To see how much of your iPhone's storage you've used, tap the Usage button on the General screen. You'll see the Usage screen, the top of which (shown on the left in Figure 4-11) lists the amount of space free and the amount used, and then shows a list of the apps that are taking the most space.

Lower down the Usage screen (see the right screen in Figure 4-11) is the Battery Percentage switch, which you can move to the On position to display a percentage

FIGURE 4-11 At the top of the Usage screen (left), you can see how much space is used, how much is free, and how much each large app is occupying. At the bottom of the screen (right), you can turn the battery percentage on or off, see the time since the last full charge, and reach the Cellular Usage screen.

readout of the battery's power next to the battery's icon on the status bar. You can also see how much usage time and how much standby time have elapsed since your iPhone's last full charge.

From the Usage screen, you can tap an app's button to display the app's information, as shown on the left in Figure 4-12, which shows the information for the app named "sleep." You can delete an app by tapping the Delete App button and then tapping the Delete App button in the confirmation dialog box that appears (as shown on the right in Figure 4-12).

From the Usage screen, you can also tap the Cellular Usage button to display the Cellular Usage screen, which shows the details of your call time, cellular network data sent and received, and data sent and received when your iPhone was tethered to a computer. The left screen in Figure 4-13 shows the upper part of the Cellular Usage screen, and the right screen in Figure 4-13 shows the lower part. At the bottom of the screen is the Reset Statistics button, which you can tap to reset the cellular usage statistics.

Choose Siri Settings

Siri, the voice-controlled assistant built into your iPhone, is one of the most powerful and useful features in the iPhone 4S. You can change the language Siri uses, choose

FIGURE 4-12   The app info screen (left) shows you the details of the app you tapped. To delete the app, tap the Delete App button, and then tap the Delete App button in the confirmation dialog box (right).

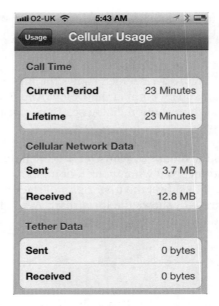

FIGURE 4-13   On the Cellular Usage screen (left and right), you can view your cellular usage statistics and reset them.

when to get voice feedback, specify which contact record contains your information, and decide whether Siri should respond when you raise your iPhone to your face.

To configure how Siri works, tap the Siri button on the General screen in the Settings app. You'll then see the Siri screen, shown on the left in Figure 4-14.

The Siri switch at the top is the master control. Make sure this switch is set to the On position if you want to use Siri. To turn Siri off altogether, move the switch to the Off position, and then tap the Disable Siri button in the dialog box that appears (shown here).

Assuming the Siri switch is in the On position, you can choose other settings:

- **Language**   This button shows the language that Siri is currently using. To change the language, tap the Language button, tap the language on the Language screen (shown on the right in Figure 4-14), and then tap the Siri button to go back to the Siri screen.

 For English (United States), English (Australia), or German, Siri uses a female voice. For English (United Kingdom) or French, Siri uses a male voice. Draw your own inferences.

FIGURE 4-14   From the Siri screen in the Settings app (left), you can display the Language screen (right) to tell Siri which language and localization to use. You can also turn off Siri altogether, and decide whether to use the Raise To Speak feature.

- **Voice Feedback**   To control when Siri gives voice feedback, tap this button. On the Voice Feedback screen (shown on the left in Figure 4-15), tap the Handsfree Only button or the Always button, as needed. Then tap the Siri button to go back to the Siri screen.
- **Raise To Speak**   Set this switch to the On position if you want to be able to activate Siri by raising your iPhone to your face. Whether you turn Raise To Speak on or off, you can always activate Siri by pressing and holding the Home button or the clicker button on the headset.

 By default, you can launch Siri from the lock screen by pressing and holding the Home button or the clicker button on the headset for a couple of seconds. If this doesn't work, someone has disabled Siri from the lock screen as a security precaution. See the section "Secure Your iPhone with Passcode Lock, Auto-Lock, and Restrictions" for details on how to re-enable Siri from the lock screen.

Choose Network Settings

To choose settings for the networks your iPhone connects to, tap the Network button on the General screen and work on the Network screen. The left screen in Figure 4-16

FIGURE 4-15 On the Voice Feedback screen (left), choose whether Siri should speak to you always or only when you're using the iPhone on hands-free. To tell Siri which contact record to use for you, tap the My Info button, and then tap the appropriate record in the Contacts list (right).

shows the top of the Network screen, and the right screen in Figure 4-16 shows the bottom of the Network screen (with lots of overlap).

Turn Cellular Data On or Off

If you need to turn off cellular data, move the Cellular Data switch at the top of the Network screen to the Off position. Normally, you'll want to leave cellular data on unless you've reached the end of your allowance and don't want to pay for more or you've connected to another carrier's network and want to use it only for voice calls.

Change Cellular Data Network Settings

If you need to change the settings your iPhone is using for connecting to the cellular data network, tap the Cellular Data Network button on the Network screen, and then work on the Cellular Data screen (shown on the left and right in Figure 4-17).

 Normally, your iPhone sets the cellular data network settings automatically. Change these settings only if you're specifically instructed to do so by a technician.

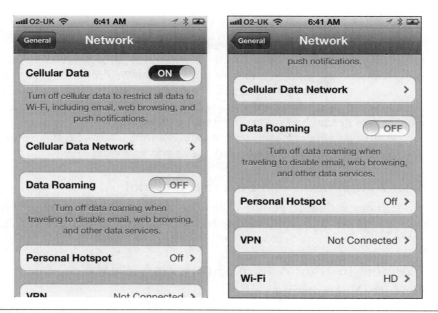

FIGURE 4-16   From the Network screen (left and right), you can turn cellular data and data roaming on and off, dig into the settings for the cellular network, turn the Personal Hotspot feature on and off, and set up virtual private network (VPN) and Wi-Fi connections.

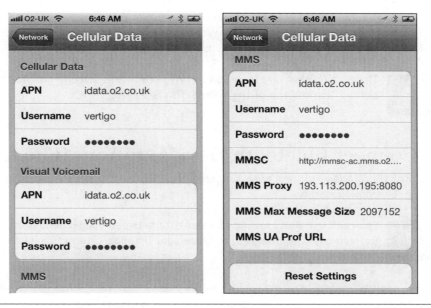

FIGURE 4-17   On the Cellular Data screen (left and right), you can change the settings for connecting to the cellular data network. Normally, you will not need to change these settings manually.

Turn Data Roaming On or Off

Data roaming is transferring data when connected to a different network than your usual carrier's network. For example, if you travel abroad and connect to a different carrier's network, sending e-mail or browsing the Web requires data roaming.

Data roaming can be inordinately expensive, so it is usually a good idea to keep data roaming turned off until you specifically need it—and then turn it on for only as long as you need it before turning it off again promptly.

To turn data roaming on, set the Data Roaming switch on the Network screen to the On position. To turn it off—okay, I see you know the drill.

Use Your iPhone as a Personal Hotspot

Your iPhone includes a feature called Personal Hotspot that enables you to connect your computers and devices to the Internet via your iPhone. See Chapter 18 for instructions on using Personal Hotspot.

Connect to Your Work Network via Virtual Private Networking (VPN)

Your iPhone can connect to your work network securely across the Internet by using a technology called virtual private networking, or VPN for short. See Chapter 15 for instructions on setting up and using a VPN connection.

Access Your iPhone's Wi-Fi Settings

You can access your iPhone's Wi-Fi settings by tapping the Wi-Fi button at the bottom of the Network screen. This takes you to the Wi-Fi Networks screen, on which you can set up and manage Wi-Fi as discussed in Chapter 3.

 There's a quicker way to get to the Wi-Fi Networks screen—just tap the Wi-Fi button near the top of the main Settings screen.

Connect Bluetooth Devices to Your iPhone

Your iPhone is equipped with Bluetooth for connecting devices such as headsets and keyboards wirelessly.

 You can't use Bluetooth to transfer data between your iPhone and your computer. But you can use Bluetooth to share your iPhone's Internet connection with your computer.

Before you can connect a Bluetooth device to your iPhone, you must do two things:

- **Turn on Bluetooth**   To save power, your iPhone keeps Bluetooth turned off until you need it.
- **Pair the device with your iPhone**   Pairing is a one-time procedure that introduces the device to your iPhone and sets them up to work together. Pairing helps ensure that only approved Bluetooth devices can connect to your iPhone.

Turn On Bluetooth

To open the Bluetooth screen in the Settings app and turn on Bluetooth, follow these steps:

1. Tap the General button on the Settings screen to display the General screen.
2. Tap the Bluetooth button to display the Bluetooth screen (shown on the left in Figure 4-18 with Bluetooth turned on).
3. Tap the Bluetooth switch and move it to the On position.

Pair a Bluetooth Device

To pair a Bluetooth device, follow these steps:

1. Turn Bluetooth on, as described in the previous section.

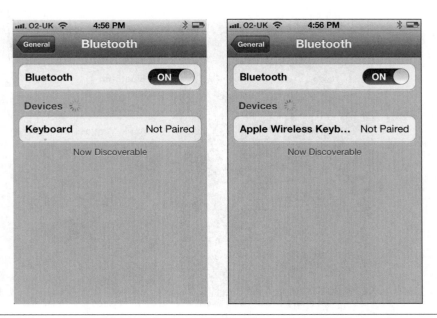

FIGURE 4-18   On the Bluetooth screen in the Settings app (left), tap the Bluetooth switch and move it to the On position. Your iPhone then detects nearby Bluetooth devices in pairing mode (right).

2. Put the Bluetooth device into Pairing mode. How you do this depends on the device, but it usually involves a magic press on the power button—for example, pressing and holding the power button until red and blue lights start flashing.
3. When the device's button appears in the Devices list, showing Not Paired (see the right screen in Figure 4-18), tap the button to connect the device.
4. When you're pairing a keyboard, your iPhone prompts you to type on the keyboard a pairing code, as shown in the left screen in Figure 4-19. Type the code and press ENTER or RETURN, and the devices establish the pairing. When you're pairing a device that doesn't have keys, such as a headset, your iPhone goes ahead and establishes the pairing without making you jump through this hoop.

After pairing the device, your iPhone connects it automatically (see the right screen in Figure 4-19), on the assumption that you want to use the device you're pairing. For subsequent use, connect the device as described in the upcoming section "Connect a Bluetooth Device Again."

Disconnect a Bluetooth Device

To disconnect a Bluetooth device from your iPhone, turn it off. Your iPhone then shows the device as Not Connected in the Devices list on the Bluetooth screen.

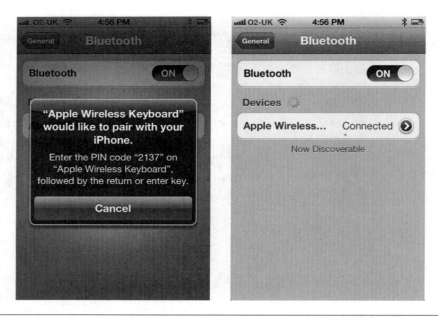

FIGURE 4-19 For a Bluetooth keyboard, your iPhone prompts you to enter a pairing code (left). After your iPhone establishes the pairing, it connects the Bluetooth device (right).

You can also disconnect a Bluetooth device by turning off Bluetooth on your iPhone.

 When you're not using Bluetooth, turn it off to save power and extend your iPhone's battery life.

Connect a Bluetooth Device Again

After you have paired a Bluetooth device, you can quickly connect it to your iPhone again by moving it within Bluetooth range of your iPhone and turning it on. As long as your iPhone's Bluetooth is turned on, the iPhone connects to the device.

Forget a Bluetooth Device

When you no longer need to use a device, you can tell your iPhone to forget it. Follow these steps:

1. On the Bluetooth screen, tap the device's > button to display the control screen for the device, as shown here.
2. Tap the Forget This Device button. Your iPhone displays a confirmation dialog box, as shown here.
3. Tap the Forget Device button. Your iPhone forgets the device, and then displays the Bluetooth screen again.

Run an iTunes Wi-Fi Sync Manually

If you sync your iPhone with your computer, you can set it to sync wirelessly by selecting the Sync With This iPhone Over Wi-Fi check box in the Options box on the Summary tab of the iPhone's control screens. After selecting this check box, click the Apply button to apply the change to your iPhone.

How to... **Change the Keyboard Layout for a Physical Keyboard**

Connecting a Bluetooth keyboard or other physical keyboard to your iPhone is a great way to enter text quickly. And if you're used to a different layout on the keyboard, such as a European layout or the optimized Dvorak layout, you can switch the keyboard to use that layout. See the section "Use International Keyboards," later in this chapter, for instructions.

Once you've set up your iPhone for Wi-Fi syncing, your iPhone syncs automatically when it's connected to power and connected to the same network as your computer.

You can also force a sync manually by tapping the iTunes Wi-Fi Sync button on the General screen and then tapping the Sync Now button on the iTunes Wi-Fi Sync screen. The left screen in Figure 4-20 shows the iTunes Wi-Fi Sync screen before starting a sync. The right screen in Figure 4-20 shows the iTunes Wi-Fi Sync screen with a sync running. The Sync symbol (a revolving circle of arrows) near the left end of the status bar indicates that the sync is running.

Configure Spotlight Search

Your iPhone uses a technology called Spotlight for searches. To get the search results you want, you can choose which items Spotlight searches and the order in which Spotlight searches them.

To customize Spotlight, follow these steps:

1. Tap the Spotlight Search button on the General screen to display the Spotlight Search screen.

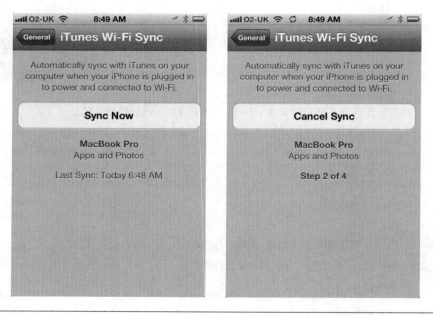

FIGURE 4-20 You can run a Wi-Fi sync manually by tapping the Sync Now button on the iTunes Wi-Fi Sync screen (left). The iTunes Wi-Fi Sync screen shows you the progress of the sync, and the Sync symbol of revolving arrows appears toward the left end of the status bar (right).

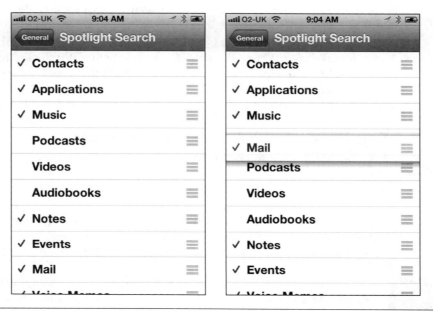

FIGURE 4-21   You can customize Spotlight Search by removing the check mark from each item you don't want to search and by dragging the items into your preferred order.

2. At first, a check mark appears on the left side of each item's button. To stop Spotlight from searching an item, tap to remove its check mark, as shown on the left in Figure 4-21.
3. Drag the items into your preferred order, putting the most important at the top. For example, if you want Spotlight to put hits in your Mail messages high on the list, tap the handle of the Mail button and drag it up the list, as shown on the right in Figure 4-21.
4. When you finish customizing the list, tap the General button to go back to the General screen.

Secure Your iPhone with Passcode Lock, Auto-Lock, and Restrictions

Packed with not only the highest technology around but also your valuable (or invaluable) private data, your iPhone is a tempting target for the light-fingered and larcenous. So no matter how firmly you grip your iPhone in public or how well you hide it at home, you need to secure it.

This section shows you three means of securing your iPhone:

- You can set your iPhone to lock itself shortly after you stop caressing it.
- You can make your iPhone demand a passcode before it unlocks. You can even set your iPhone to wipe its data if someone enters the wrong passcode too many times in succession.
- You can apply restrictions to what the iPhone's user can do with it.

Set Your iPhone to Lock Itself Automatically

First, set your iPhone's Auto-Lock feature to lock the iPhone automatically a short time after you stop using it.

Follow these steps from the General screen in the Settings app:

1. Tap the Auto-Lock button to display the Auto-Lock screen (shown in Figure 4-22).
2. Tap the button for the interval you want.
3. Tap the General button to return to the General screen.

 Tip After applying a passcode and auto-locking, try out your settings and make sure they work as you want them to. If not, go back to the appropriate screen and choose a different setting.

FIGURE 4-22 On the Auto-Lock screen, choose as short an interval as is practical for the way you use your iPhone.

Protect Your iPhone with a Passcode Lock

Next, protect your iPhone with a passcode lock. The passcode is a sequence of characters that you must type each time you unlock the iPhone from the lock screen. The nearby sidebar "Choose Between a Simple Passcode and a Complex Passcode" explains the ins and outs of passcodes.

 Note If your company or organization provides your iPhone, an administrator may apply a configuration profile that compels you to use a passcode on the iPhone. If you find you cannot change the passcode settings on your iPhone, you will know that a profile is installed.

To set your passcode lock and (if you want) automatic wiping, follow these steps from the Settings screen:

1. Tap the General button to display the General screen, and then scroll down until you see the box starting with the Auto-Lock button. The left screen in Figure 4-23 shows this section of the General screen.
2. Tap the Passcode Lock button to display the Passcode Lock screen (shown on the right in Figure 4-23).
3. If you want to use a simple passcode—a four-digit number—make sure the Simple Passcode switch is set to the On position. If you want to lock your

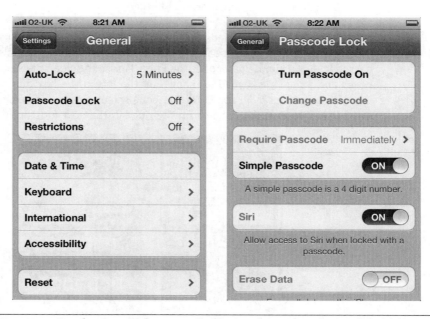

FIGURE 4-23   On the General screen (left), tap the Passcode Lock button to display the Passcode Lock screen (right).

How to... **Choose Between a Simple Passcode and a Complex Passcode**

You can protect your iPhone with either a simple passcode or a complex passcode:

- **Simple passcode**   A *simple passcode* is one that uses four digits (for example, 1924). This is what your iPhone is set to use by default.
- **Complex passcode**   A *complex passcode* is one that uses a variable number of characters and that mixes letters and other characters with digits.

A complex passcode can provide much greater security than a simple passcode in three mostly obvious ways:

- **You can set a longer passcode**   A longer passcode is harder to crack because it contains more characters (even if it consists only of numbers rather than letters and non-alphanumeric characters).
- **You can include letters**   Including letters as well as numbers greatly increases the strength of the passcode even at short lengths.
- **You can include non-alphanumeric characters**   Including non-alphanumeric characters (such as symbols—&*#$!, and other comic-book expletives) increases the strength of the passcode even further.

When your iPhone demands the passcode, the Enter Passcode screen indicates whether the device is using a simple passcode or a complex passcode. For a simple passcode, the Enter Passcode screen displays four boxes and a numeric keypad, as shown on the left in the next illustration. For a complex passcode, the Enter Passcode screen displays a text box and the QWERTY keyboard, as shown on the right in the next illustration.

(Continued)

Choosing between a simple passcode and a complex passcode can be tough, because you need to balance security against your need to be able to flourish your iPhone and get to work without flailing in frustration at the soft keyboard.

Keep these points in mind when deciding which type of passcode to use:

- **A simple passcode may be strong enough with auto-erase**   Given enough time and tries, anyone can break a simple passcode by plodding through all 10,000 possible numbers until they hit the jackpot. Your iPhone makes this harder by automatically disabling itself for increasing periods of time—1 minute, 5 minutes, 15 minutes, 60 minutes, and so on—as the wrong passcodes hit in sequence (see the next illustration). A determined attacker can keep plugging away, but if you set your iPhone to erase its data automatically after a handful of failed attempts to enter the passcode, your data should be pretty safe—unless you've chosen a personal number that the attacker can guess (for example, your birth year, which is a regrettably popular passcode).

- **With a complex passcode, you may not need auto-erase**   If you use a complex passcode of a certain length (say eight or more characters) and including both alphanumeric and non-alphanumeric characters, you may consider it strong enough that your iPhone doesn't need auto-erase. Your decision will likely depend on whether your iPhone contains nuclear launch codes, glutinous cookie recipes, or something in between.
- **A complex passcode can be simpler than a simple passcode**   Because the Enter Passcode screen for a complex passcode gives no indication of the passcode's length, you may be able to bluff an attacker by setting a short, letters-only passcode (for example, aq) rather than a mashup of the first half of *Moby Dick* and the telephone directory. A short passcode like this is easy for you to remember and type, so you can set a low number for the Maximum Number Of Failed Attempts setting as a safety net.

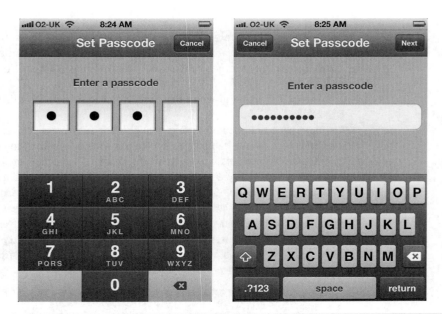

FIGURE 4-24 On the Set Passcode screen, enter either a simple four-digit passcode (left) or a complex passcode as long—or as short—as you like (right).

iPhone down more tightly by using a complex passcode, move the Simple Passcode switch to the Off position.

4. Tap the Turn Passcode On button to display the Set Passcode screen. For a simple passcode, you'll see the Set Passcode screen shown on the left in Figure 4-24; for a complex passcode, you'll see the Set Passcode screen shown on the right in Figure 4-24.

5. Tap the numbers or characters for the passcode:
   - **Simple passcode** When you've entered four numbers, your iPhone displays the Set Passcode: Re-enter Your Passcode screen automatically.
   - **Complex passcode** Tap the .?123 button when you need to reach the keyboard with numbers and some symbols. From here, you can tap the # + = button to reach the remaining symbols, punctuation characters, and currency characters. When you've finished entering the passcode, tap the Next button to display the Set Passcode: Re-enter Your Passcode screen.

6. Tap the numbers or characters for the passcode again; for a complex passcode, tap the Done button when you finish. Your iPhone displays the Passcode Lock screen again. This time, all the options are enabled, as shown in the screen on the left in Figure 4-25.

7. Look at the Require Passcode button to see how quickly the passcode requirement kicks in: Immediately, After 1 Minute, After 5 Minutes, After 15

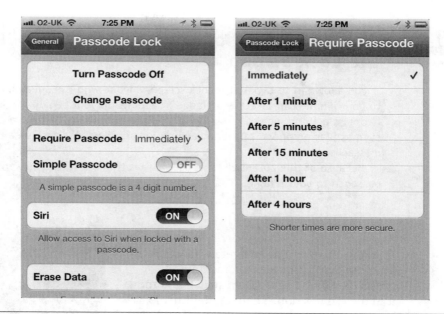

FIGURE 4-25   After you set a passcode, the remaining options on the Passcode Lock screen become available (left). Tap the Require Passcode button to display the Require Passcode screen (right), on which you can set the interval after which your iPhone requires the passcode.

Minutes, After 1 Hour, or After 4 Hours. If you need to change the setting, follow these steps:

a. Tap the Require Passcode button to display the Require Passcode screen (shown on the right in Figure 4-25).
b. Tap the button for the interval you want.
c. Tap the Passcode Lock button to return to the Passcode Lock screen.

 For the Require Passcode setting, the Immediately option is by far the most secure, because it locks your iPhone the moment you put it to sleep or the Auto-Lock feature kicks in. But if you tend to put your iPhone to sleep and then have an "and another thing" moment a few seconds later, you may find the After 1 Minute option a better choice, because it will allow you to unlock your iPhone to jot down your new item.

8. Move the Siri switch on the Passcode Lock screen to the Off position to prevent Siri from running when your iPhone is locked. See the nearby sidebar "Why You Must Not Let Siri Bypass the Lock Screen" for an explanation of why you should not let Siri run when your iPhone is locked.

Why You Must Not Let Siri Bypass the Lock Screen

If you allow Siri to bypass the lock screen, anyone who can speak intelligibly to your iPhone can take a wide range of actions on your behalf—from harmless actions such as browsing the Web to potentially harmful actions such as placing phone calls and sending instant messages and e-mail messages.

Because of this potential for abuse, always turn Siri off if you apply a passcode to your iPhone.

9. If you want your iPhone to erase its contents after ten failed attempts to crack the passcode, tap the Erase Data switch and move it to the On position. Then tap the Enable button in the confirmation dialog box (shown here) that appears.

Note   To wipe its data, your iPhone simply gets rid of the encryption key needed to decrypt the data. This happens almost instantly, and is much faster than actually overwriting all the iPhone's storage with rubbish data, which is the method early iPhones used for wiping data.

Choose Restrictions

Your iPhone includes a comprehensive set of restrictions for preventing a user from taking unwanted actions—anything from browsing the Web at all to setting up Mail accounts or watching adult movies.

You can set these restrictions for yourself if you feel the need, but normally you'll want to set these restrictions for your children and other sensitive users. You lock these restrictions with a passcode to prevent your victims from changing them.

Note   If your company or organization provides your iPhone, an administrator may use the restrictions to prevent you from taking unwanted actions on the iPhone—for example, installing games, dallying on YouTube, or disturbing the serenity of the cube-farm by barking commands at Siri.

To set restrictions, follow these steps:

1. On the General screen, tap the Restrictions button to display the Restrictions screen. The left screen in Figure 4-26 shows the top part of the Restrictions screen. It's a long screen, and you'll meet the rest of it in a minute or two.

FIGURE 4-26 On the Restrictions screen (left), tap the Enable Restrictions button. On the Set Passcode screen (right), type in a passcode to prevent anyone else from changing or removing the restrictions.

2. At first, the restrictions are all disabled, which is why they appear dull and lifeless. To reanimate them, tap the Enable Restrictions button at the top of the screen. Your iPhone then displays the Set Passcode screen, shown on the right in Figure 4-26.
3. Type a four-digit passcode, and then type it again on the Set Passcode: Re-enter Your Passcode screen. Your iPhone then returns you to the Restrictions screen, where the controls are enabled and ready for use.
4. In the Allow box, move each item's switch to the On position to allow the item or to the Off position to forbid the item. These are the items and a description of what they allow the user to do when set to the On position:
   - **Safari** Allow the user to use the Safari web browser app at all.
   - **YouTube** Allow the user to use the YouTube app.
   - **Camera** Allow the user to use the Camera app.

 Turning off the Camera app also turns off the FaceTime app, because FaceTime uses the iPhone's cameras. Even if you turn off the Camera app, the user can still capture the contents of the screen by holding down the Sleep/Wake button and pressing the Home button.

   - **FaceTime** Allow the user to use the FaceTime app for making video calls to other users of iPhones, iPads, iPod touches, and Macs.

- **iTunes**   Allow the user to use the iTunes Store.
- **Ping**   Allow the user to use the Ping social-networking feature.
- **Installing Apps**   Allow the user to install apps from the App Store.
- **Deleting Apps**   Allow the user to delete apps from the iPhone.
- **Siri**   Allow the user to use the Siri voice-controlled assistant.
- **Explicit Language**   Allow the user to access on the iTunes Store material that contains explicit language—for example, misogynistic or misanthropic rap songs.

 Setting the Explicit Language switch on the Restrictions screen to the Off position affects only the iTunes Store. The user can still get his fill of filth on the Web unless you disallow Safari.

5. In the Allow Changes box, tap the Location button to display the Location screen. The left screen in Figure 4-27 shows the top part of the Location screen, and the right screen in Figure 4-27 shows the bottom part. You can then choose the following settings:
    - **Allow Changes/Don't Allow Changes**   Tap to select the Allow Changes button, placing a check mark on it, if you want the user to be able to change the other settings on the screen. Tap to select the Don't Allow Changes button if you want to lock the other settings so that the user can't mess with them.

FIGURE 4-27   On the Location screen (left and right), you can either turn off Location Services altogether or restrict it to certain apps.

- **Location Services**   If you want to turn off Location Services entirely, tap this switch and move it to the Off position. Your iPhone displays a dialog box to warn you that turning off Location Services will prevent you from using the Find My iPhone service. Tap the Turn Off button if you're sure you want to do this.
- **Apps Using Location Services**   In the list of apps that use Location Services, tap an app's switch and move it to the Off position if you want to prevent the app from using Location Services. For example, to prevent iMovie from using Location Services, move the iMovie switch to the Off position.
- **Find My iPhone**   To control whether the Find My iPhone feature is enabled, tap the Find My iPhone button, and then work on the Find My iPhone screen (shown on the left in Figure 4-28). You can then move the Find My iPhone switch to the Off position if you want to turn off the Find My iPhone feature. You can also move the Status Bar Icon switch to the On position if you want the iPhone's status bar to display a telltale arrow showing that you're tracking this iPhone's location from another computer. When you've made your choices, tap the Location button to go back to the Location screen.
- **System Services**   Tap this button to display the System Services screen (shown on the right in Figure 4-28), and then set the switches to choose

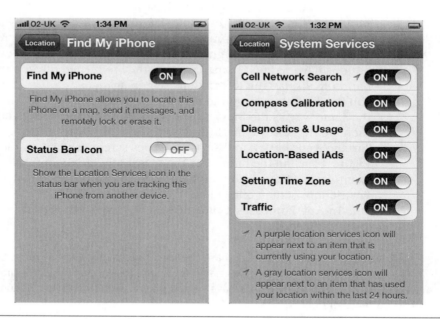

FIGURE 4-28   On the Find My iPhone screen (left), you can turn the Find My iPhone feature on or off and choose whether to display the Location Services icon when you're tracking this iPhone. On the System Services screen (right), choose which system services can use Location Services.

which system services can use Location Services. For example, move the Location-Based iAds switch to the Off position if you want to prevent your iPhone from receiving in-app ads that are based on the iPhone's location. At the bottom of the System Services screen is the Status Bar Icon switch, which you can set to the On position if you want the Location Services icon to appear in the status bar when a system service requests your location from Location Services. When you've made your choices, tap the Location button to return to the Location screen.

Tap the Restrictions button to return to the Restrictions screen.

6. In the Allowed Content box, choose which content the user may enjoy:

   a. Make sure the Ratings For button shows the right country. If not, tap the Ratings For button, tap the country on the Ratings For screen that appears, and then tap the Restrictions button to display the Restrictions screen again.

   b. Tap the Music & Podcasts button to display the Music & Podcasts screen (the top part is shown here), and then move the Explicit switch to the On position or the Off position, as needed. Tap the Restrictions button to display the Restrictions screen again.

   c. Tap the Movies button to display the Movies screen (shown on the left in Figure 4-29), and then tap the highest rating you'll permit—for example, PG-13. Your iPhone removes the check marks from the stronger-rated items and turns their buttons red. You can't see it in the book's grayscale, but the R, NC-17, and Allow All Movies buttons have red text to indicate that they're turned off. Tap the Restrictions button to display the Restrictions screen again.

   d. Tap the TV Shows button to display the TV Shows screen. This works in the same way as the Movies screen: Tap the highest rating you'll allow, and then tap the Restrictions button to display the Restrictions screen again.

   e. Tap the Apps button to display the Apps screen, shown on the right in Figure 4-29. Tap the button for the oldest app rating you'll allow (for example, tap 12+), and then tap the Restrictions button to display the Restrictions screen once more.

7. Tap the In-App Purchases switch and move it to the On position or the Off position, as needed.

An *in-app purchase* is a purchase the user can make from the iTunes Store from within an app. For example, many apps have in-app purchases for professional versions, and many games have in-app purchases for extra levels, good for wasting a few more hours.

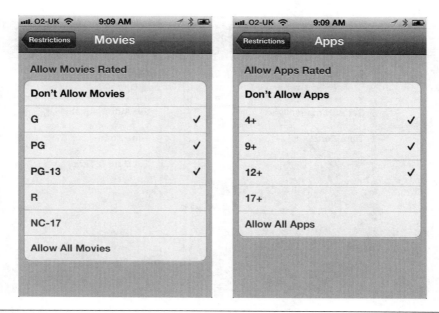

FIGURE 4-29   On the Movies screen (left), tap the highest rating you'll permit. On the Apps screen (right), tap the highest rating the user may run.

8. Tap the Require Password button to display the Require Password screen, and then tap the button for the time period after which the user must enter an Apple ID to make in-app purchases: Immediately, or 15 Minutes. Tap the Restrictions button to display the Restrictions screen again.
9. In the Game Center box at the bottom of the Restrictions screen, set the two switches to the On position or the Off position, as needed:
   - **Multiplayer Games**   This switch controls whether the user can send and receive invitations to play games.
   - **Adding Friends**   This switch controls whether the user can add friends in Game Center.
10. When you finish choosing restrictions, tap the General button to return to the General screen.

Choose Date & Time Settings

The easiest way to keep the date and time set correctly on your iPhone is to allow it to set the time automatically from time servers on the Internet. When you do this, your iPhone automatically sets the correct time zone for wherever you are.

But if you prefer, you can set the date and time manually. In this case, you can set the time zone yourself as well.

FIGURE 4-30 On the Date & Time screen (left), you can switch between 24-hour time and AM/PM time and choose whether to set the time automatically or manually. If you move the Set Automatically switch to the Off position, your iPhone displays the Set Date & Time button (right).

To choose date and time settings, follow these steps:

1. Tap the Date & Time button on the General screen to display the Date & Time screen (shown on the left in Figure 4-30 with the time being set automatically).
2. If you want to use 24-hour time, tap the 24-Hour Time switch and move it to the On position. If you prefer AM/PM time, make sure this switch is set to the Off position.
3. If you want your iPhone to set the date, time, and time zone automatically, make sure the Set Automatically switch is set to the On position. If you want to set the time manually, tap this switch and move it to the Off position. Your iPhone then displays the Set Date & Time button and enables the Time Zone button, as shown on the right in Figure 4-30.
4. To set the date and time, tap the Date & Time button, and then use the controls on the Date & Time screen (shown on the left in Figure 4-31) to choose the date and time. When you finish, tap the Date & Time button to go back to the main Date & Time screen.
5. To set the time zone, tap the Time Zone button on the main Date & Time screen. On the Time Zone screen that appears (shown on the right in Figure 4-31), start typing the name of the city or region, and then tap the matching

FIGURE 4-31   On the Date & Time screen (left), use the buttons and spin wheels to set the date and time. On the Time Zone screen (right), start typing the city's or region's name, and then tap the match in the list your iPhone displays.

name when your iPhone displays a list. Your iPhone returns you to the main Date & Time screen.

6. Tap the General button to return to the General screen.

Choose Keyboard Settings

To help you enter text quickly and accurately, your iPhone's onscreen keyboard has several clever features, including automatic capitalization, automatic correction, and spell checking.

To choose settings for the keyboard, tap the Keyboard button on the General screen, and then work on the Keyboard screen. The left screen in Figure 4-32 shows the top part of the Keyboard screen, and the right screen in Figure 4-32 shows the bottom part.

Choose Which Keyboard Features to Use

At the top of the Keyboard screen, set the five switches to the On position or the Off position to control which keyboard features you're using. These are the features:

- **Auto-Capitalization**   Automatically sets the SHIFT key on the keyboard at the beginning of a new paragraph or sentence. This is usually helpful. If you don't

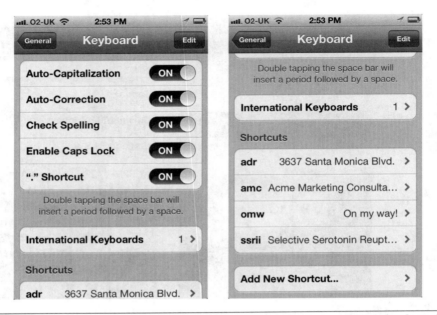

FIGURE 4-32 On the Keyboard screen (left and right), choose which keyboard features and shortcuts to use.

want a capital letter there, you can tap the SHIFT key to turn off shifting before you tap a letter key.

- **Auto-Correction** Automatically suggests a correction for a misspelling or predicts the end of the word you're typing, as shown here. You can accept the suggestion by tapping the spacebar, tapping a punctuation button (such as comma or period), or tapping the return button. You can reject the suggestion by tapping the × button at the right end of the suggestion bubble.

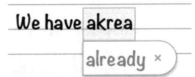

- **Check Spelling** Makes your iPhone check spelling as you type and put a dotted red underline under any word it doesn't recognize. You can then double-tap the word to display the Cut, Copy, Suggest bar shown on the left below, tap the Suggest button, and then tap the correct word on the panel that appears (as shown on the right below).

- **Enable Caps Lock** Lets you turn on Caps Lock by double-tapping a SHIFT key. (Tap the SHIFT key again when you want to turn off Caps Lock.) This feature is usually helpful unless you find yourself double-tapping the SHIFT key by mistake—in which case, set this switch to the Off position.

- **"." Shortcut** Lets you type a period by tapping the spacebar twice. This feature too is usually helpful unless you find yourself typing periods inadvertently; if so, turn this feature off.

Use International Keyboards

If you need to use a different keyboard layout than the one you currently get on either the onscreen keyboard or an external keyboard you've connected, follow these steps to change the keyboard layout:

1. Tap the International Keyboards button on the Keyboard screen to display the Keyboards screen, shown here with a single keyboard added.
2. Tap the top button. This button's name depends on which keyboard you're using—for example, English. The screen for the keyboard appears, as shown on the left in Figure 4-33.

FIGURE 4-33 On the screen for a keyboard's language (left and right), you can choose the software keyboard layout for the onscreen keyboard and the hardware keyboard layout for a physical keyboard you connect.

3. In the Software Keyboard Layout box, tap the layout you want for the onscreen keyboard—for example, QWERTY.
4. In the Hardware Keyboard Layout box, tap the button for the keyboard layout you want for your external keyboard—for example, Dvorak, as shown on the right in Figure 4-33.
5. Tap the Keyboards button to return to the Keyboards screen.
6. Tap the Keyboard button to return to the Keyboard screen.

 From the Keyboards screen, you can also add a new keyboard by tapping the Add New Keyboard button. But if you simply need to change the keyboard you're using with the iPhone, change the existing one rather than adding another keyboard.

Set Up Text Shortcuts

To make typing faster, whether you're using your iPhone's onscreen keyboard or an external keyboard, you can create text shortcuts. A *text shortcut* is a sequence of characters that you type. When your iPhone recognizes the shortcut, it displays a pop-up balloon with the replacement text, just like a spelling correction. You can type a space, type a punctuation character, or tap the return button to accept the change or tap the × button on the balloon to reject it.

 Text shortcuts are like the AutoCorrect feature in Microsoft Word and many other word-processing programs.

To create your text shortcuts, follow these steps from the Keyboard screen in the Settings app:

How to... **Switch Among Your Keyboards**

After you set your iPhone to use two or more keyboards, the onscreen keyboard displays a globe icon to the left of the Siri icon. Tap this icon to switch to the next keyboard; tap again for the next one; and so on in a circle. Alternatively, tap and hold the globe icon to display the list of keyboards, as shown here, and then tap the keyboard you want.

1. Tap the Add New Shortcut button to display the Shortcut screen (shown here).
2. Type the word or phrase in the Phrase box.
3. Type the shortcut in the Shortcut box.
4. Tap the Save button. Your shortcut appears on the Keyboard screen.

To remove a shortcut, tap the Edit button to switch the Shortcuts section of the Keyboard screen to Edit mode, as shown here. Tap the round red Delete button to the left of the shortcut you want to remove, and then tap the rectangular Delete button that appears to its right.

Choose International Settings

If you need to change the language, region formats, or calendar system your iPhone uses, tap the International button to display the International screen (shown on the left in Figure 4-34).

Change the Language for Your iPhone's User Interface

To change the language your iPhone's user interface shows, follow these steps from the International screen:

1. Tap the Language button to display the Language screen.
2. Tap the language you want, putting a check mark to its right.
3. Tap the Done button. Your iPhone restarts the user interface and displays the Home screen in the language you chose.

Note   When you change language, your iPhone automatically adds that language's keyboard to the Keyboards selection.

Change the Language Used for Voice Control

To change the language your iPhone uses for Siri and Voice Control, follow these steps:

1. Tap the Voice Control button to display the Voice Control screen (shown on the right in Figure 4-34).
2. Tap the language you want to use, putting a check mark to its right.
3. Tap the International button to return to the International screen.

FIGURE 4-34 On the International screen (left), you can change the language for the user interface and for Voice Control, set up keyboards, or change the region format or calendar system. On the Voice Control screen (right), select the language for Siri and Voice Control.

Change Your iPhone's Keyboards

To work with keyboards, tap the Keyboards button on the International screen, and then work on the Keyboards screen as described in the section "Use International Keyboards," earlier in this chapter.

Change the Region Format

The region format controls how your iPhone displays dates, times, and data such as phone numbers. For example, in the United States region format, dates, times, and phone numbers appear like this:

- **Date**   Sunday, April 1, 2012
- **Time**   10:52 AM
- **Phone number**   (707) 523-0806

To change the region format, follow these steps:

1. Tap the Region Format button to display the Region Format screen.
2. Tap the region format you want to use.
3. Tap the International button to return to the International screen.

Change the Calendar System

Your iPhone uses the standard Gregorian calendar by default, but you can switch to the Japanese calendar or the Buddhist calendar instead. To switch, follow these steps:

1. Tap the Calendar button to display the Calendar screen.
2. Tap the calendar system you want to use.
3. Tap the International button to return to the International screen.

Choose Accessibility Settings

Your iPhone includes accessibility settings to help with vision problems, hearing problems, and physical and motor problems. To choose accessibility settings, tap the Accessibility button on the General screen, and then work on the Accessibility screen. The left screen in Figure 4-35 shows the top part of the Accessibility screen, and the right screen in Figure 4-35 shows the bottom part. (To pique your interest, there's a tiny part missing in the middle.)

Here's a quick rundown on the Vision accessibility settings:

- **VoiceOver**   Your iPhone can announce the selected item out loud to help you identify it. You can also attach a Braille reader to your iPhone.

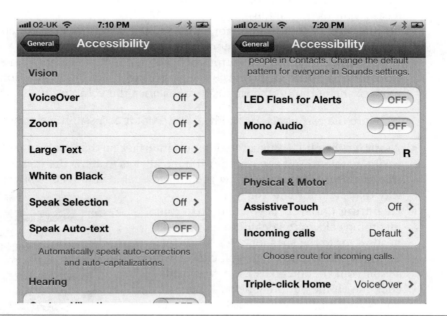

FIGURE 4-35   The Accessibility screen (left and right) provides a wide range of settings to help with vision problems, hearing problems, and physical and motor problems.

- **Zoom** After turning Zoom on, you can double-tap with three fingers on the screen to zoom in. You can then move around the screen by dragging three fingers, and change the zoom by double-tapping with three fingers and dragging up (to zoom in) or down (to zoom out).
- **Large Text** Use this setting to pump up the text in the Calendar, Contacts, Mail, Messages, and Notes apps. You can choose the text size you want—anywhere from 20-point text (moderate size) to 56-point text (huge).
- **White On Black** Move this switch to the On position to change your iPhone's display to reverse video—a black background, white text, and orange highlights.
- **Speak Selection** You can make your iPhone speak the current selection to help you identify it.
- **Speak Auto-Text** You can have your iPhone speak automatic corrections and automatic capitalizations.

Here's what you need to know about the Hearing accessibility settings:

- **Custom Vibrations** Allows you to assign a unique vibration pattern to a contact so that you can identify an incoming alert by the vibration. On the Vibration screen, you can either select a standard vibration (such as Heartbeat or S.O.S.) or record a custom vibration (for example, you tap out the beat of the opening of *Aqualung*).
- **LED Flash For Alerts** Makes the iPhone's LED flash when an alert comes in. This can be a good way of notifying you about an alert as long as you're not using a case that masks the flash.
- **Mono Audio** Makes the iPhone play mono audio instead of stereo audio. Use this setting if you're using a mono earphone or speaker.
- **L–R balance** Adjusts the output between the left and right channels. For example, if you use earphones but have stronger hearing in your left ear, move more of the output to the right side to balance the volume.

Here are the essentials of the Physical & Motor accessibility settings:

- **AssistiveTouch** Adjusts the iPhone's interface so that you can control it more easily by touch. You can set your iPhone always to show the menu, alter the tracking speed, and create new gestures to enable you to control your iPhone in a way that's comfortable for you.
- **Incoming Calls** Lets you choose to route incoming calls to the default device, to the headset, or to the speaker.
- **Triple-Click Home** Lets you choose which action your iPhone takes when you triple-click the Home button: Off (no action), Toggle VoiceOver, Toggle White On Black, Toggle Zoom, Toggle AssistiveTouch, or Ask (display a dialog box asking you what you want to do, as shown here).

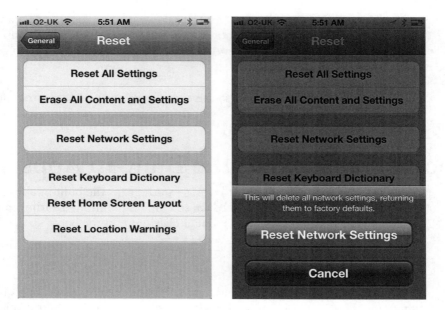

FIGURE 4-36   From the Reset screen (left), you can reset a particular type of setting, reset all settings, or erase your iPhone completely. Whichever action you take, your iPhone asks you to confirm it (right).

Reset Your iPhone's Settings

If you mess up your iPhone's settings, or if your iPhone gets confused and messes them up for you, you can reset the settings by tapping the Reset button at the very bottom of the General screen and then tapping the appropriate button on the Reset screen (shown on the left in Figure 4-36). Your iPhone prompts you to confirm the action (as shown on the right in Figure 4-36).

Here's what the buttons on the Reset screen do:

- **Reset All Settings**   Resets all your iPhone's settings to their default values but doesn't delete your content from the iPhone.
- **Erase All Content And Settings**   Deletes all your content from your iPhone and resets all the settings to their default values. You then have to set up your iPhone from scratch again. Normally, you'd use this command before giving your iPhone to someone else.
- **Reset Network Settings**   Resets all network settings to their default values. You can use this command if your iPhone's network settings get messed up.
- **Reset Keyboard Dictionary**   Deletes your custom words from the keyboard dictionary.
- **Reset Home Screen Layout**   Moves all the app icons and folders on the Home screen back to their default positions.

- **Reset Location Warnings**   Resets all the warnings about apps using Location Services. This makes your iPhone display a warning when each app requests information from Location Services. You can then allow the app to get the information or refuse to allow it.

Chapter 19 explains how to use the commands on the Reset screen to troubleshoot your iPhone.

Choose Settings for the Built-In Apps

In this section, we'll look at how to choose settings for the built-in apps that appear in the list on the lower part of the Settings screen. As mentioned earlier in the chapter, we'll skip the apps that we cover in detail elsewhere in the book.

Set Up iCloud

If you haven't already set up iCloud on your iPhone, you can set it up quickly by tapping the iCloud button on the Settings screen, entering your Apple ID and password on the iCloud screen (shown on the left in Figure 4-37), and then tapping the Sign In button.

FIGURE 4-37   On the iCloud screen (left), enter your Apple ID and password, and then tap the Sign In button. If you need to create an Apple ID, tap the Get A Free Apple ID button, and then work through the Create An Apple ID screens (right).

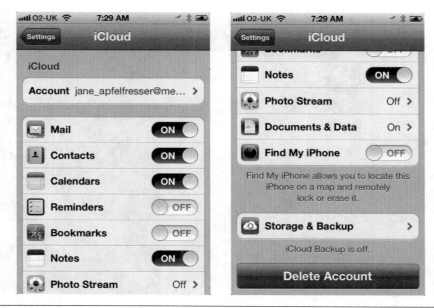

FIGURE 4-38 On the iCloud settings screen (left and right), choose which iCloud features to use on your iPhone.

If you don't yet have an Apple ID, tap the Get A Free Apple ID button at the bottom of the iCloud screen to start the process of applying for one (see the right screen in Figure 4-37).

After you set up your iCloud account on your iPhone, you can choose settings on the iCloud screen (shown on the left and right in Figure 4-38) to control which iCloud features your iPhone uses.

Set Up Twitter

If you use Twitter, you can quickly set it up on your iPhone so that you can tweet bite-size wisdom and photos from anywhere. Tap the Twitter button on the Settings screen to display the Twitter screen (shown on the left in Figure 4-39), type your username and password, and then tap the Sign In button.

 If you don't have a Twitter account, tap the Create New Account button to start the signup process.

From the Twitter screen in Settings, you can also install the Twitter app by tapping the Install button. Your iPhone then downloads the Twitter app from the App Store, installs it, and displays the Home screen containing it. Tap the Twitter icon to launch Twitter, and you'll be in business (see the right screen in Figure 4-39).

FIGURE 4-39   On the Twitter screen (left), type your username and password, and then tap the Sign In button. You can also install the Twitter app (right).

Choose Phone Settings

To set up phone services such as call forwarding and call waiting, tap the Phone button in the Settings app and work on the Phone screen. The left screen in Figure 4-40 shows the top part of the Phone screen. The right screen in Figure 4-40 shows the bottom part of the Phone screen.

On the Phone screen, you can choose the following settings:

- **My Number**   This button shows your phone number—handy if you haven't memorized it. You can change the number by tapping the button, entering the new number on the My Number screen, and then tapping the Save button.
- **Call Forwarding**   To turn call forwarding on or off, tap the Call Forwarding button. On the Call Forwarding screen, tap the Call Forwarding switch and move it to the On position or the Off position. If you turn call forwarding on, tap the Forward To button, type the number on the Forwarding To screen, and then tap the Call Forwarding button to return to the Call Forwarding screen. Tap the Phone button to get back to the Phone screen.
- **Call Waiting**   To turn call waiting on or off, tap the Call Waiting button. On the Call Waiting screen, tap the Call Waiting switch and move it to the On position or the Off position. Tap the Phone button to return to the Phone screen.

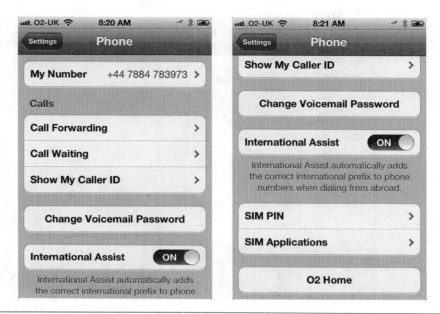

FIGURE 4-40   On the Phone screen (left and right), you can view or change your phone number; set up call forwarding, call waiting, or caller ID; and control other phone features such as International Assist.

- **Show My Caller ID**   To control whether your iPhone shows your caller ID when you call others, tap the Show My Caller ID button. On the Show My Caller ID screen, tap the Show My Caller ID switch and move it to the On position or the Off position. Tap the Phone button to return to the Phone screen.
- **Change Voicemail Password**   To change your voicemail password, tap this button, type the new password on the Password screen, and then tap the Done button.
- **International Assist**   This switch controls whether your iPhone automatically adds the right international prefix to phone numbers you dial from abroad. This feature is usually helpful.
- **SIM PIN**   To set a personal identification number (PIN) for your iPhone's SIM card, tap this button. On the SIM PIN screen, tap the SIM PIN switch and move it to the On position, type the PIN, and then tap the Done button.
- **SIM Applications**   If this button appears, tap it to display the SIM Applications screen. You can then tap the Get Settings button to show the details of SIM applications available.
- **Carrier button**   Tap the button at the bottom of the Phone screen to open your carrier's web page in Safari. (The button's name varies depending on your carrier.)

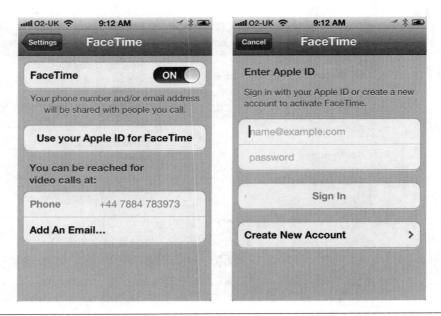

FIGURE 4-41 On the FaceTime screen (left), you can turn FaceTime on and off. To add an e-mail address, tap the Add An Email button, and then enter your Apple ID on the resulting screen (right).

Choose FaceTime Settings

To make sure you can receive FaceTime calls, take a minute to choose settings for FaceTime. Tap the FaceTime button on the Settings screen to display the FaceTime screen (shown on the left in Figure 4-41). You can then choose these settings:

- **FaceTime** Tap this switch and move it to the Off position if you don't want to use FaceTime. Otherwise, make sure it's in the On position.
- **Use Your Apple ID For FaceTime** To set up FaceTime to use your Apple ID, tap this button, type your Apple ID and password on the FaceTime screen shown on the right in Figure 4-41, and then tap the Sign In button.
- **Phone** This button shows the phone number you're using for FaceTime.
- **Add An Email** To add an e-mail address to FaceTime, tap this button, enter the details on the FaceTime screen shown on the right in Figure 4-41, and then tap the Sign In button.

Choose Messages Settings

To make the most of the Messages app, check that its settings are set the way you want them. To access the settings, tap the Messages button on the Settings screen, and

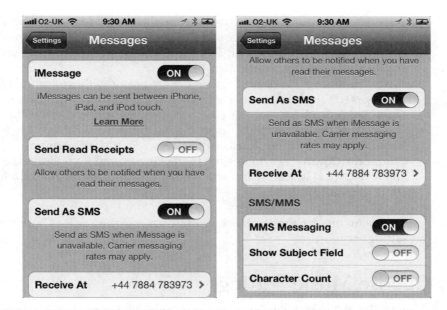

FIGURE 4-42   On the Messages screen (left and right), you can turn iMessage on and off, choose whether to send read receipts, and choose whether to display the Subject field.

then work on the Messages screen. The left screen in Figure 4-42 shows the top part of the Messages screen, and the right screen in Figure 4-42 shows the bottom part.

These are the settings you can choose on the Messages screen:

- **iMessage**   Make sure this switch is set to the On position if you want to use iMessage.

 iMessage enables you to send messages via Wi-Fi networks to other users of iPhones, iPod touches, and iPads.

- **Send Read Receipts**   Tap this switch and move it to the On position if you want your iPhone to send read receipts to messages. Set this switch to the Off position if you don't want your iPhone to confirm automatically that you've read a message. Receiving read receipts is handy for the sender, but you may prefer not to send them automatically to everyone who sends you messages.
- **Send As SMS**   Set this switch to the On position if you want your iPhone to send messages via SMS when iMessage isn't available. This feature helps make sure your message gets sent; the only downside is that you may get through your text allowance faster.

- **Receive At**   This button shows the phone number or e-mail address at which you are receiving messages. You can add an e-mail address by tapping the Receive button, tapping the Add An Email button, entering your Apple ID on the iMessage screen, and then tapping the Sign In button.
- **MMS Messaging**   Set this switch to the On position if you want to receive MMS messages. If you don't want to receive them, set it to the Off position.
- **Show Subject Field**   Set this switch to the On position if you want the Messages app to show the Subject field, in which you can enter a subject line for a message. If you don't need subject lines, set this switch to the Off position.
- **Character Count**   Set this switch to the On position if you want the Messages app to show a character count when your message goes to its second line. This count is usually helpful.

When you finish choosing Messages settings, tap the Settings button to return to the Settings screen.

Choose Music Settings

To make the Music app play songs the way you prefer, tap the Music button on the Settings screen, and then choose settings on the Music screen (shown on the left in Figure 4-43).

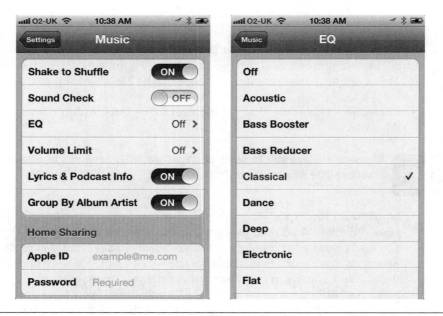

FIGURE 4-43 On the Music screen (left), choose settings for playback, shuffling, and Home Sharing. On the EQ screen (right), choose the equalization to use, or choose Off to turn equalization off.

These are the settings you can choose on the Music screen:

- **iTunes Match**   If you have subscribed to iTunes Match using iTunes on your computer, make sure this switch is set to the On position to use iTunes Match.

 iTunes Match enables you to quickly store a version of your music library online so that you can play your song from iTunes or any device running iOS 5. At this writing, iTunes Match is available only in some countries. If it's not available where you are, the iTunes Match switch doesn't appear.

- **Shake To Shuffle**   Tap this switch and move it to the On position if you want to be able to shuffle the current playlist by giving your iPhone a quick shake. Set this switch to the Off position if you find yourself shuffling your songs inadvertently.
- **Sound Check**   Tap this switch and set it to the On position if you want your iPhone to try to equalize the volume of songs as it plays them back. If you prefer not to have your iPhone mess with the dynamic range of the music, set this switch firmly to the Off position.
- **EQ**   To apply an equalization to songs that don't have one set, tap this button. On the EQ screen (shown on the right in Figure 4-43), tap the equalization to use, and then tap the Music button to return to the Music screen.
- **Volume Limit**   To help prevent the user from damaging his or her ears, you can limit the iPhone's maximum volume. Follow these steps:
    1. Tap the Volume Limit button to display the Volume Limit screen (shown on the left in Figure 4-44).
    2. Tap the slider and drag it to a less-than-shattering volume.
    3. Tap the Lock Volume Limit button. The iPhone displays the Set Code screen (shown on the right in Figure 4-44).
    4. Type a four-digit code. The iPhone prompts you to re-enter the code.
    5. Type the code again. The iPhone sets the code and displays the Volume Limit screen again.
    6. Tap the Music button to return to the Music screen.
- **Lyrics & Podcast Info**   Tap this switch and set it to the On position if you want your iPhone to display song lyrics and podcast info on top of the album art. Set this switch to the Off position if you don't want to see this text.
- **Group By Album Artist**   Tap this switch and set it to the On position if you want the Music app to group songs by the Album Artist field when this field contains data. Set this switch to the Off position if you want the Music app to ignore the contents of the Album Artist field.
- **Home Sharing**   To use Home Sharing on your iPhone, type your Apple ID in the Apple ID box and your password in the Password box, and then tap the Done button on the keyboard.

When you finish choosing Music settings, tap the Settings button to return to the main Settings screen.

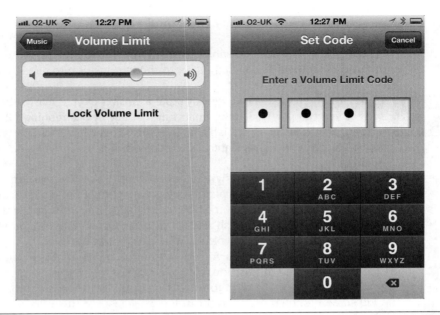

FIGURE 4-44   To help prevent the iPhone's user from playing music too loud, set the maximum volume on the Volume Limit screen (left). Tap the Lock Volume Limit button, and type a lock code on the Set Code screen (right).

Choose Video Settings

Your iPhone has only a few settings for video playback, so it takes just a minute to set them. Tap the Video button on the Settings screen to display the Video screen, shown on the left in Figure 4-45.

You can then set these settings:

- **Start Playing**   To control whether the Video app restarts playing a video at the beginning or where you stopped watching, tap the Start Playing button. On the Start Playing screen (shown on the right in Figure 4-45), tap the From Beginning button or the Where Left Off button, as needed. Tap the Video button to return to the Video screen.
- **Closed Captioning**   If you want to view closed captions, tap this switch and move it to the On position.
- **Home Sharing**   To use Home Sharing on your iPhone, type your Apple ID in the Apple ID box and your password in the Password box, and then tap the Done button on the keyboard.

FIGURE 4-45   On the Video screen (left), you can turn on closed captioning and set up Home Sharing. On the Start Playing screen (right), choose whether to start playing at the beginning or where you stopped watching.

Choose Photos Settings

The Photos app has only a few settings, but they make a big difference—so you should take the time to set them. Tap the Photos button on the Settings screen to display the Photos screen (shown on the left and right in Figure 4-46).

Turn Photo Stream On or Off

Photo Stream is an iCloud feature that automatically shares your latest photos among your iOS devices and computers. Photo Stream shares up to 1000 photos in your Camera Roll album.

   To use Photo Stream, set the Photo Stream switch on the Photos screen to the On position. If you don't want to use Photo Stream, set this switch to the Off position.

Choose Slideshow Settings

To control how slideshows you play on your iPhone appear, choose settings in the Slideshow area of the Photos screen:

- **Play Each Slide For**   Tap this button to display the Play Each Slide For screen. Tap the appropriate button—2 Seconds, 3 Seconds, 5 Seconds, 10 Seconds, or 20 Seconds. Then tap the Photos button to go back to the Photos screen.

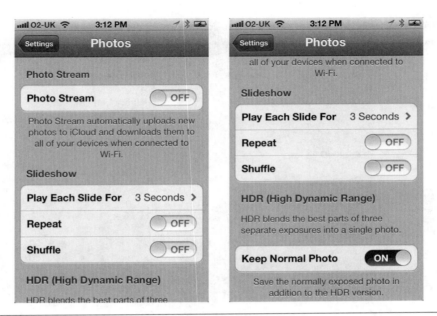

FIGURE 4-46 On the Photos screen (left and right), you can turn on Photo Stream, set up slideshows, and choose whether to keep a normal photo when shooting High Dynamic Range photos.

- **Repeat** Move this switch to the On position if you want the slideshow to repeat until you stop it.
- **Shuffle** Move this switch to the On position if you want to play the slides in a random order.

Choose Whether to Keep the Normal Photo with the HDR Photo

When you take High Dynamic Range (HDR) photos with your iPhone's rear-facing camera, the camera can also take a normal photo at the same time. Saving this photo takes a moment longer, but it gives you an alternative version of the photo, so it's usually a good idea.

To make the Camera app keep this normal photo, set the Keep Normal Photo switch on the Photos screen to the On position. If you don't want the normal photo, set this switch to the Off position.

Choose Store Settings

To control how the iTunes Store app downloads items to your iPhone, tap the Store button on the Settings screen and choose settings on the Store screen.

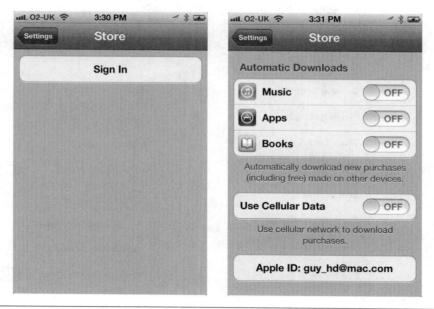

FIGURE 4-47   If the Store screen shows the Sign In button (left), tap the button and sign in to display the full Store screen (right).

If the Store screen contains only a Sign In button, as shown on the left in Figure 4-47, tap the Sign In button, and then follow through the procedure for signing in. You'll then see the full Store screen, as shown on the right in Figure 4-47.

In the Automatic Downloads area, set the Music switch, the Apps switch, and the Books switch to the On position or the Off position as needed. These switches control whether your iPhone automatically downloads items you've bought using other devices (for example, an iPad).

If you want to download your purchases over the cellular network rather than waiting until a Wi-Fi connection is available, tap the Use Cellular Data switch and move it to the On position. Usually, you'll want to keep this switch set to the Off position to avoid caning your data plan.

You can tap the Apple ID button at the bottom of the Store screen to display a dialog box that enables you to view your Apple ID details, sign out, or recover a forgotten password.

Choose Settings for Third-Party Apps

The final section of the Settings screen contains a button for each app that you can configure through the Settings app. Other apps have settings that you can access

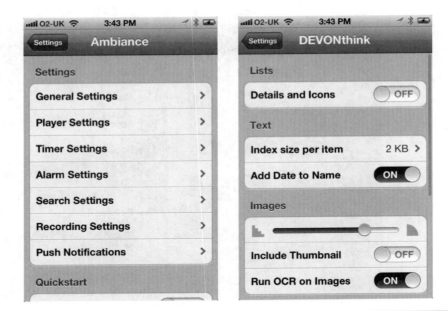

FIGURE 4-48 Some third-party apps have only a few settings, but others have many. To get the most out of an app, be prepared to spend some time customizing its settings.

from within the app itself—for example, because you may need to change the settings frequently without leaving the app.

To choose settings for an app, tap its button, and then work on the resulting screen. Figure 4-48 shows a couple of examples of these screens.

5

Take, Edit, and Share Photos and Videos

HOW TO...

- Take photos with the Camera app
- Take videos with the Camera app
- View your photos in the Photos app

Your iPhone includes not one but two cameras—one on the front and one on the back—that can each manage both photos and video. The back camera can take high-resolution photos (3264 × 2448 pixels), while the front camera is lower resolution, being mainly for self-portraits and video calls using FaceTime.

Having a camera with you wherever you go, available at the touch of a couple of buttons, means you're ready to take photos and videos of anything, anywhere (apart from in the water).

This chapter shows you how to take, edit, and share photos and videos using your iPhone. We'll start with the Camera app and then move along to the Photos app, which you use for viewing and sharing your photos.

Take Photos with the Camera App

With its eight-megapixel resolution, your iPhone's main camera can take high-quality photos of whatever you point the iPhone at. In this section, I'll take you through opening the Camera app, taking straightforward photos, and using features such as the flash, zooming, the grid, and High Dynamic Range. You'll also learn how to switch between your iPhone's two cameras, edit your photos, and share your photos with others.

Open the Camera App

To open the Camera app, press the Home button to display the Home screen (unless you're already there), and then tap the Camera icon.

 To open the Camera app when your iPhone is locked, press the Home button twice in quick succession, and then tap the Camera icon that appears to the right of the Unlock slider.

With the Camera app open, the screen shows whatever the camera on the back of the iPhone is pointing at. Figure 5-1 shows the features of the Camera app's screen with labels.

FIGURE 5-1   Your iPhone's Camera app enables you to take high-quality photos quickly and easily.

Here are the essentials of what these items do. In the following sections, we'll look at how to use the features they control.

- **Flash button** Switches the flash among its three settings: Auto, On, and Off.
- **Options button** Displays a control panel that lets you turn the grid feature on and off and the High Dynamic Range (HDR) feature on and off. We'll look at these features in a minute.
- **Switch Cameras button** Switches between the rear camera and the front camera.
- **Camera Roll button** Displays the Camera Roll, your current album. The button shows the most recent picture you've taken.

 The Camera Roll album contains not only the photos you've taken in the Camera app—as you'd expect—but also screens you capture using the Screen Capture feature and images you save from web pages, from e-mail messages, or from multimedia messages.

- **Shutter button** Takes a photo of whatever the current camera is viewing.
- **Camera/Video switch** Switches from Camera mode to Video mode.
- **Focus and exposure area** This square (not shown in the figure) indicates where the Camera app is focusing and metering for exposure. You can move the focus to a different part of the screen by tapping the target. For example, if you're taking a photo of your favorite person in front of a beautiful landscape, and you compose the photo with the person's face on the left of the screen, tap the person's face (on the screen) to bring the focus there rather than in the middle distance.

Take a Photo

To take a photo, aim your iPhone so that your subject appears on the screen the way you want him or her to be in the photo. Then tap the Shutter button on the screen in the Camera app or press the Volume Up button on the side of the iPhone.

 Taking a photo by pressing the Volume Up button is handy when you have only one hand free to operate your iPhone or when you can't see the Shutter button on the screen because of glare.

Use the Flash

Until you change the setting, the Camera app's flash is set to Auto. This makes the iPhone use the flash when the light is too poor to take a photo at a shutter speed fast enough to help eliminate camera movement. Your iPhone uses its light sensor to detect the light level and decide whether or not to use the flash.

How to... Capture What's on Screen Using the Screen Capture Feature

Your iPhone has a built-in way of capturing whatever's currently shown on the screen. All you need to do is hold down the Sleep/Wake button on the top of the iPhone while you press the Home button. This is great for capturing any strange error messages you want to be able to look up or for grabbing a picture of something you want to share with someone else. (Or if you're writing a book about the iPhone.)

When you take a screen capture, you'll see the screen flash briefly, and you'll hear a shutter sound if sound is on.

Your iPhone puts the screen captures in the Camera Roll folder, where you can view them using the same techniques as you use for viewing your photos.

Your iPhone has an LED flash that works well at short range but is pretty puny by the standards of regular cameras. When shooting with flash, keep your subjects within spitting distance to get good results.

The Auto setting works well for general use, but at other times you may need to either turn the flash off or force the iPhone to use it even when there is technically enough light to take a photo.

Turn your iPhone's flash on when you need flash to fill in light on your subject even though there is otherwise enough light. For example, when your subjects have the light behind them, the iPhone's light sensor may detect plenty of light to take a photo without flash—but the light won't be where you need it. By turning the flash on, you can use it to fill in the light on your subjects' faces, which would otherwise be in shadow.

To make your iPhone use the flash for all photos, tap the Flash button, and then tap the On button on the control bar that appears.

To prevent your iPhone from using the flash even when the light is low, tap the Flash button, and then tap the Off button on the control bar. Turning the flash off is helpful for social situations when you need to take photos without the flash distracting those around you.

You can find various flashlight apps on the App Store that use the rear camera's flash as a flashlight or strobe. Many of these apps are free. It's well worth putting one of these apps on your iPhone to enable you to use it as a flashlight when you find yourself in the dark. The LED beam can't compete with heavy-duty flashlights, but it's good enough to get you through the dark, and it has them beat hands-down for convenience.

Zoom In and Out

To make the photo show only the part of your subject or scene that you want to capture, you can zoom in or out as far as necessary.

 Only the rear camera has zoom. The front camera doesn't zoom.

To zoom in, place two fingers on the middle of the target area and then pinch them outward. Your iPhone zooms in and displays the zoom slider, as you see here. You can then adjust the zoom in three ways:

- Pinch farther outward, or pinch back in.
- Tap the + button or the – button on the zoom slider.
- Tap the circle on the zoom slider and drag it to the left or the right.

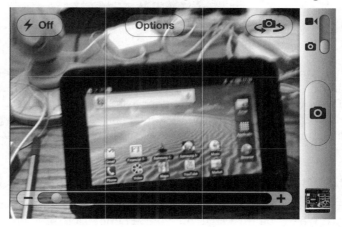

 Your iPhone's camera uses digital zoom rather than optical zoom. In optical zoom, the camera moves lenses to zoom in, giving full quality even when zoomed in all the way. But in digital zoom, the camera increases the size of the pixels (dots) to make the zoomed area fill the entire picture. So the more you zoom in, the worse the picture quality gets.

Your iPhone hides the zoom slider automatically after you've left it alone for a few seconds.

To start zooming out when the zoom slider is not displayed, place two fingers apart on the screen, and then pinch them together. The zoom slider appears, and you can use it as described above to adjust the zoom further.

Use the Grid to Compose a Photo

Your iPhone's camera is easy to use, but it's also easy to take pictures at an angle that makes them look as though you were riding out an earthquake while shooting. To help you get your uprights vertical and your horizons horizontal, the Camera app can display a grid across the screen. The grid is great for getting alignment right, but it can also help you to compose your photos—for example, by putting your subjects bang in the middle of the frame.

To turn the grid on, tap the Options button to display the Options dialog box, shown here.

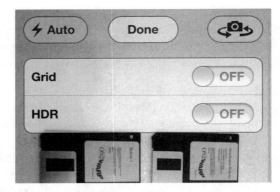

Then tap the Grid switch and move it to the On position. You can then tap the Done button to close the Options dialog box, leaving the grid displayed (see Figure 5-2). If you want to use the grid only for a single photo, you may prefer to leave the Options dialog box displayed, so that you can move the Grid switch back to the Off position before you tap the Done button to close the Options dialog box.

Use the High Dynamic Range (HDR) Feature

Your iPhone's Camera app includes a feature called High Dynamic Range, or HDR for short. When you turn HDR on, your iPhone takes three photos in immediate succession instead of a single photo. The iPhone merges these three photos into a single photo, which is the HDR version of the photos.

Because having the three photos enables the iPhone to average out the differences in exposure and coloring, the HDR photo should look better than a normal photo, or at least truer to life. HDR is well worth using when you have plenty of time to take a photo and you want its colors to look as good as possible.

 You can make the Camera app take a normal photo at the same time as each HDR photo. To do so, set the Keep Normal Photo switch in the HDR (High Dynamic Range) area of the Photos screen in the Settings app to the On position.

FIGURE 5-2 Use the grid feature in the Camera app to help orientate your iPhone for good results and compose your pictures with your subjects in suitable positions.

Taking three exposures takes longer than taking a single exposure, so don't use HDR when you need to take photos in a hurry.

To turn HDR on or off, tap the Options button to display the Options dialog box. Then tap the HDR switch and move it to the On position or the Off position, as needed.

 HDR works best when both you and your subject are stationary. For example, if you're taking a photo of a rainbow or a beautiful landscape (or—bonus points!—both), turning on HDR is a great idea. Don't try to take HDR photos when you yourself are moving or when you're shooting action—for example, sports, or children doing anything except sleep. If you do, the HDR photos will merge information that doesn't quite fit together, giving a blurry result.

Move the Area for Focusing and for Metering the Light

By default, the Camera app focuses on whatever's in the middle of the picture, because that's where most people put their subjects. The Camera app also uses the focus area to meter the light for the photos.

If your subject is in the middle of the picture, the automatic focus and light metering works well. But if your subject is outside the default focus area, you can move the focus area by tapping the middle of the area you want to focus on. The Camera app momentarily displays a square where you tap, so you can see it has registered the change.

Camera Roll
button

Edit
button

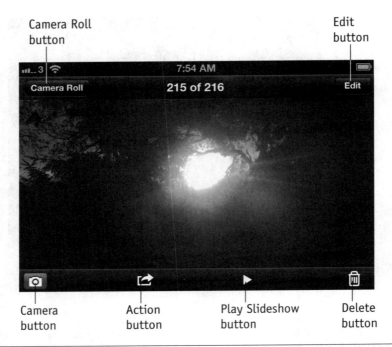

Camera
button

Action
button

Play Slideshow
button

Delete
button

FIGURE 5-3 Use the control buttons to work with the photos in the Camera Roll or to return to the Camera app.

Look at the Photos You've Taken

To look at the photos you've taken, tap the Camera Roll button. Your iPhone displays the most recent photo first. You can then swipe your finger from left to right across the screen to display the previous picture.

 You use the same techniques to navigate and view photos in the Photos app, which you'll meet at the end of this chapter.

At first, when you display the contents of the Camera Roll, your iPhone displays control buttons on screen, as shown in Figure 5-3.

These buttons are straightforward to use:

- **Camera Roll button** Tap this button to display the Camera Roll album showing thumbnails of photos and videos, as shown next. You can then tap the item you want to view. Tap the three tab buttons—the All button, the Photos button, and the Videos button—at the top of the screen to switch the display among displaying all photos and videos, displaying just photos, and displaying just videos.

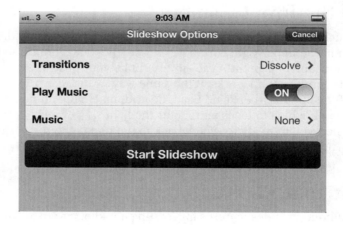

- **Edit button**   Tap this button to start editing the current photo. I'll show you how to edit photos in the next section.
- **Camera button**   Tap this button to return from the Camera Roll to the Camera so that you can take photos or videos.
- **Action button**   Tap this button to use or share the photo. We'll look at the actions you can take with photos later in this chapter.
- **Play Slideshow button**   Tap this button to display the Slideshow Options screen (shown here). You can then choose which transition to use between photos, choose whether (and if so, which) music to play, and then tap the Start Slideshow button.

- **Delete button** Tap this button to display the Delete Photo dialog box (shown here), and then tap the Delete Photo button.

Switch Between the Rear Camera and the Front Camera

To switch between the rear camera and the front camera, tap the Switch Cameras button in the upper-right corner of the screen. Your iPhone's screen shows whatever the front camera is pointing at—for example, your nostrils.

The front camera works in the same way as the rear camera, but it doesn't have any of the options: there's no flash, no grid, no HDR, and no zoom. You can still tap the area on which to focus and meter the light.

When you're ready to switch back to the rear camera, tap the Switch Cameras button again.

Edit Your Photos

Your iPhone includes features for rotating a photo, automatically enhancing its colors, removing red-eye from eyes, and cropping the photo to just the parts you want to keep.

Rotate a Photo

To rotate a photo, follow these steps:

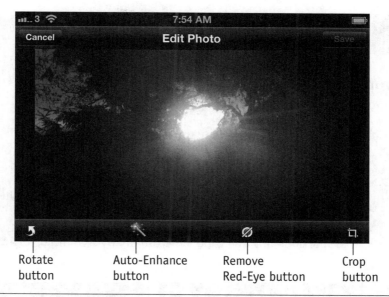

Rotate   Auto-Enhance   Remove   Crop
button   button   Red-Eye button   button

FIGURE 5-4   From the Edit Photo screen, you can rotate a photo, enhance it automatically, remove red-eye, or crop it.

1. Tap the Edit button to display the Edit Photo screen (see Figure 5-4).
2. Tap the Rotate button to rotate the photo 90 degrees counterclockwise. Tap again if you need to rotate the photo again.
3. Tap the Save button if you want to save the rotated photo. To revert to the unrotated photo, tap the Cancel button.

Enhance a Photo

To enhance a photo, follow these steps:

1. Tap the Edit button to display the Edit Photo screen.
2. Tap the Auto-Enhance button. Your iPhone enhances the colors in the photo.
3. Tap the Save button if you want to save the enhanced photo. To revert to how the photo was before, tap the Cancel button.

Remove Red-Eye from a Photo

To remove red-eye from a photo, follow these steps:

1. Tap the Edit button to display the Edit Photo screen.
2. Tap the Remove Red-Eye button.
3. Tap each feral eye in turn.
4. Tap the Apply button to apply the change. To go back to wild eyes, tap the Cancel button.

The iPhone's Remove Red-Eye feature works only for human eyes, not for animal eyes.

Crop a Photo

To crop a photo, follow these steps:

1. Tap the Edit button to display the Edit Photo screen.
2. Tap the Crop icon in the lower-right corner to display the Crop Photo screen (shown on the left in Figure 5-5).
3. If you want to constrain the cropping to specific dimensions, tap the Constrain button to display the Constrain dialog box, shown on the right in Figure 5-5. Then tap the button for the appropriate constraint. For example, tap the Square button to keep the cropping grid square, or tap the 3 × 5 button to make it keep the proportions of three units horizontally by five units vertically.

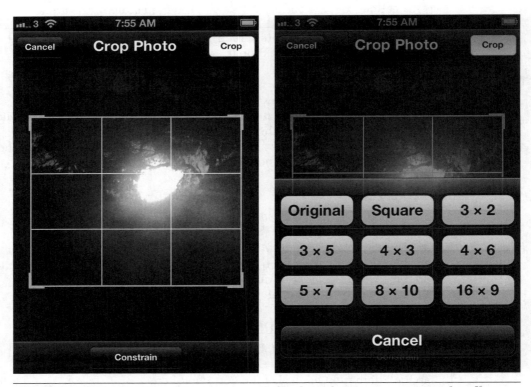

FIGURE 5-5   On the Crop Photo screen (left), drag the corner cropping handles or the outside edges of the cropping grid to select the area. To constrain the cropping to specific dimensions, tap the Constrain button, and then tap the constraint in the Constraint dialog box (right).

4. Select the area of the photo you want to keep. Tap and drag the corner cropping handles to where you need them. You can also tap and drag the outside border.
5. Tap the Crop button. Your iPhone applies the cropping
6. Tap the Save button if you want to save the cropped photo. If the cropped photo doesn't look right, tap the Cancel button to undo the cropping.

Share Your Photos

Your iPhone makes it easy to share your photos via e-mail, instant messaging, or tweeting. You can also add a photo to a contact's record, use a photo as your iPhone's wallpaper, or simply print it.

Share One or More Photos via E-Mail

To share the open photo via e-mail, tap the Action button at the bottom of the screen, then tap the Email Photo button in the Action dialog box.

To share multiple photos via e-mail, tap the Action button. On the Select Photos screen, tap each photo you want to include, putting a check mark on it. Then tap the Action button to display the Action dialog box.

Next, tap the Email Photo button in the Action dialog box. Your iPhone causes the Mail app to create a new e-mail message containing the photo or photos. You can then address the message, type any text needed, and send the message.

If the Mail app displays the dialog box shown here offering to resize the photo or photos, tap the Small button, the Medium button, the Large button (not shown here), or the Actual Size button, as needed.

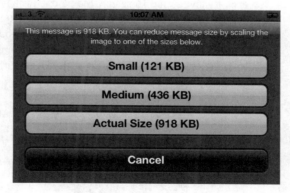

Tip Send your photos at actual size if the recipient will need to work with them. Otherwise, send the Small size for use as contact photos or at other small sizes, the Medium size for viewing on screen, and the Large size for printing at a reasonable size and acceptable quality.

How to... **Select Multiple Photos for Printing or for Sharing via E-Mail or Instant Messaging**

You can print multiple photos at once from the Camera app or from the Photos app. You can also share two photos at once via instant message or up to five photos at once via e-mail.

To choose which photos to print or share, follow these steps:

1. Tap the Camera Roll button to display the Camera Roll screen. In the Photos app, tap the button with the name of the current album to display that album.

2. Tap the Action button in the upper-right corner of the screen. Your iPhone displays the Select Items screen, shown here with two photos selected.

3. Tap each item you want to select. The iPhone displays a red circle containing a white check mark on each selected item.

4. Tap the Action button to display the Action dialog box, shown here. If you've selected more than two photos, the Message button doesn't appear. Similarly, if you've selected more than five photos, the Email button doesn't appear either.

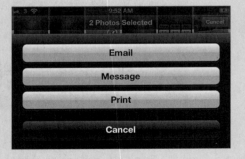

5. Tap the Email button, the Message button, or the Print button, as needed, and then follow through the steps of creating and sending the message or selecting the printer, as discussed later in this chapter.

Share a Photo via Instant Messaging

To share one or two photos via instant messaging, tap the Message button in the Action dialog box. Your iPhone makes the Messages app create a new multimedia message containing the photo or photos. You can then choose the recipient for the message, enter any text needed, and then tap the Send button to set it winging on its way.

Tweet a Photo on Twitter

If you've set up your Twitter account on your iPhone, you can quickly tweet a photo by tapping the Tweet button in the Action dialog box. Your iPhone creates a tweet and displays it on the Tweet screen. Type any explanatory text, tap the Add Location button if you want to add the location, and then tap the Send button.

 If you tap the Tweet button before setting up your Twitter account, your iPhone displays the No Twitter Accounts dialog box, which points out the problem. Tap the Settings button in the No Twitter Accounts dialog box to go directly to the Twitter screen in the Settings app. You can then set up your existing account or create a new account.

Assign a Photo to a Contact Record

When you've taken a photo that'll work well on a contact record, assign it to the contact record by tapping the Assign To Contact button in the Action dialog box. Tap the contact in the Contacts list your iPhone displays, and then use the Move And Scale screen (shown here) to position the face in the center and resize it to fit the unshaded area. Then tap the Set Photo button to finish assigning the photo to the contact record.

Use a Photo as Your iPhone's Wallpaper

To use a photo as your iPhone's wallpaper, tap the Use As Wallpaper button in the Action dialog box. Use the Move And Scale screen to position and scale the photo so that it looks good, and then tap the Set button.

Print One or More Photos

To print one or more photos, tap the Print button in the Action dialog box. Select the printer and the number of copies on the Printer Options screen, and then tap the Print button.

 Your printer must have the AirPrint feature for your iPhone to be able to print on it.

Take Videos with the Camera App

Your iPhone's built-in rear camera can take videos in full 1080p high definition at 30 frames per second (fps)—so if your subject matter and composition are good enough, you can use your iPhone to create videos worth showing on high-definition TVs or video projectors.

In this section, I'll show you how to take videos, view the videos you've taken, and trim them down to the parts you want, and how to share videos. I'll also tell you how to create movies on your iPhone from your video clips.

 Whereas a full-scale video camera uses a mechanical shutter to create separate video frames, for video, your iPhone uses a *rolling shutter*, which takes several milliseconds to create each frame. The rolling shutter is not good at capturing movement, because a fast-moving subject can move while a frame is being captured. This results in blurred video. If you (the cameraperson) are moving at the same time, the blur is much worse.

Take Videos

To take a video, open the Camera app by tapping the Camera icon on the Home screen, and then move the Camera/Video switch to the Video position. The camera displays the video controls, which you see in Figure 5-6.

Tap the Flash button if you want to switch the flash on, or tap the Switch Cameras button if you want to switch from the rear camera to the front camera, or vice versa.

When you're ready to start taking a video clip, tap the Record button or press the Volume Up button on the left side of your iPhone.

To stop recording, tap the Record button or press the Volume Up button again.

Flash
button

Switch Cameras
button

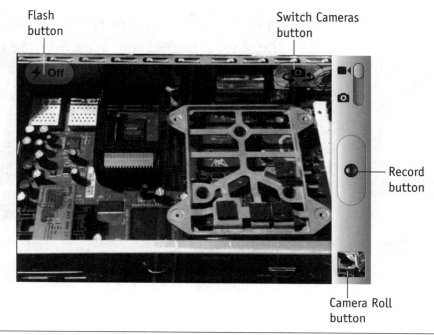

Record
button

Camera Roll
button

FIGURE 5-6   The video controls are straightforward to use.

View the Videos You've Taken

Your iPhone puts the videos you've taken in the Camera Roll along with your photos, so you can view the videos by tapping the Camera Roll button.

Tap the video you want to view, and you'll see the video's opening frame with control buttons, as shown in Figure 5-7.

Trim a Video Down to Size

You can trim a video by cutting off the beginning, the end, or both. You can save the trimmed video either in its original file, deleting the parts you've trimmed off, or to a new file that contains only the trimmed section, leaving the original file untouched.

To trim a video, follow these steps:

1. Open the video for viewing.
2. Tap the left trim handle and drag it inward to the point at which you want the video to start.
3. Tap the right trim handle and drag it inward to where you want the video to end, as shown next.

4. Play the video through and make sure you've got the trim handles where you need them.

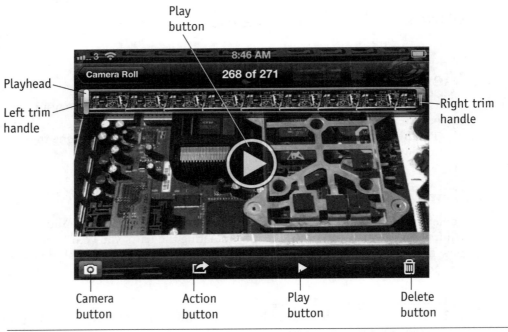

FIGURE 5-7 The video screen contains controls for playing back, trimming, sharing, and deleting the video.

How to...   # Avoid the Curse of Handheld Video

Handheld video can be great, because it enables you to capture footage anywhere you go. But the results are often hard to watch because of camera shake.

An easy way to make your videos look better is to use a tripod to hold your iPhone steady while shooting.

You can get tripods especially designed for the iPhone, but the affordable ones are small, and the full-size ones tend to be expensive. If you already have a tripod for a regular camera, all you need is an iPhone holder that will mount on the tripod's screw thread. You'll find plenty of iPhone tripod holders on sites such as Amazon.com and eBay.

If you keep your iPhone in a case that you don't want to remove, make sure the holder you get is big enough to accommodate the case. This may mean buying a tripod holder for a larger phone rather than one designed to hold the iPhone itself snugly. Measure your iPhone with its case on, and then look for a tripod whose holder's dimensions are big enough.

If you need to shoot steadily while you're moving, you can put your iPhone on a Steadicam, a rig for damping movement and vibration. Here you have a similar choice as with the tripod: you can either buy a Steadicam designed for the iPhone or get a holder that will enable you to mount your iPhone on a regular Steadicam.

As I mentioned earlier in this chapter, the rolling shutter on the iPhone's video camera means it's not great for shooting while moving. But if you must shoot while moving, a Steadicam can make your video much more watchable.

5. Tap the Trim button. Your iPhone displays the Trim dialog box (shown here).

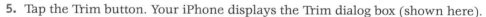

6. Tap the appropriate button:
- **Trim Original**   Tap this button to delete the trimmed-off parts from the original file.

- **Save As New Clip**   Tap this button to create a new clip containing only the trimmed section. Creating new clips like this enables you to trim the same video clip to different lengths for different uses.

Your iPhone then trims the video and either saves the existing file or creates a new file, depending on your choice.

Share Your Videos

You can share a video by attaching it to an e-mail message, by including it in an instant message, or by uploading it to your account on YouTube. To get started on each of these actions, follow these steps:

1. Open the video file.
2. Tap the Action button at the bottom of the screen to display the Action dialog box (shown here).

3. Tap the Email Video button, the Message button, or the Send To YouTube button, as appropriate.

Did You Know?

You Can Create Movies on Your iPhone Using iMovie

Being able to trim your video clips in the Camera app is great, but it only scratches the surface of what you can do with your videos on your iPhone.

If you buy and install Apple's iMovie app for iPhone from the App Store, you can turn your video clips into full-scale movies right on your iPhone. Using iMovie, you can trim your video clips, assemble them into the right order, and add music to them. You can also record video clips directly into iMovie from your iPhone's camera or add narration to your movie.

When you finish a movie, you can share it to online sites such as YouTube, Facebook, or Vimeo.

Because video files are large, your iPhone creates smaller versions of videos for sending via e-mail and instant messaging. For e-mail, this helps you to avoid having servers bounce your messages back to you because they are too big. For instant messaging, this helps you to avoid taking large bites out of your data plan.

Send a Video via E-Mail

To send a video via e-mail, tap the Email Video button in the Action dialog box. Your iPhone creates a smaller version of the video and attaches it to a new e-mail message in the Mail app. You can then address the message, type its subject and any explanation needed, and then tap the Send button to send it.

Send a Video via Instant Messaging

To send a video via instant messaging, tap the Message button in the Action dialog box. Your iPhone creates a smaller version of the video and attaches it to a new MMS message in the Messages app. You can then address the message, type its subject and any comments it needs, and then tap the Send button.

Upload a Video to YouTube

If you have an account on YouTube, you can quickly upload a video by tapping the Send To YouTube button in the Action dialog box.

 The first time you try to publish a video to YouTube, your iPhone prompts you to enter your YouTube username and password. Type them, and then tap the Sign In button.

Your iPhone then displays the Publish Video screen. The left screen in Figure 5-8 shows the top part of the Publish Video screen; the right screen in Figure 5-8 shows the rest of the Publish Video screen.

Fill in the information for the video you're uploading:

- **Title**   Make the title as catchy and descriptive as possible.
- **Description**   Enter a description that will help anybody browsing through videos to understand what the video is about and why they might want to view it.
- **Definition**   Tap the Standard Definition button, placing a check mark next to it, if you want to upload the video in standard definition. This is usually the best choice, but if you need to upload the file in high definition, tap the HD button instead.
- **Tags**   Tap this button, and then type in each tag you want to associate with the video. Using tags effectively helps your video show up when people search for videos.
- **Category**   Tap this button to display a spin wheel of categories at the bottom of the screen, and then tap the right category—for example, Comedy, Education, or Nonprofits & Activism.
- **Scope**   In the box at the bottom of the Publish Video screen, tap the Public button, the Unlisted button, or the Private button, as needed.

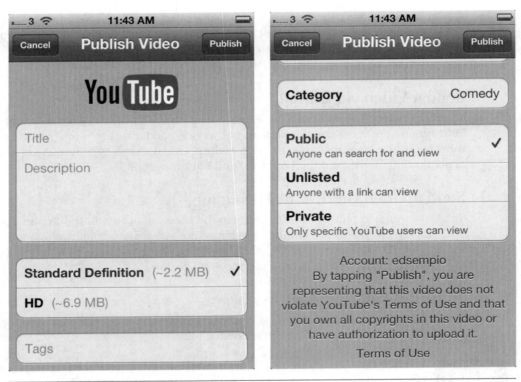

FIGURE 5-8 Fill in the information for the video on the Publish Video screen, and then tap the Publish button.

 Tip When you give a video Unlisted scope, the video doesn't appear to anyone browsing or searching. But you can send links to the video to anyone you want to be able to view it.

After you finish filling in the information on the Publish Video screen, tap the Publish button. Your iPhone creates the standard-definition version (if you chose that option), uploads the video, and then displays the Published dialog box shown here.

Tap the View On YouTube button if you want to view the video on YouTube (bear in mind that the video may take a few minutes to become available). Tap the Tell A Friend button if you want to send your friends an e-mail message containing a link to the video. Or tap the Close button to simply close the Published dialog box

View Your Photos in the Photos App

As you saw earlier in this chapter, tapping the Camera Roll button in the Camera app takes you straight to the Camera Roll, the album of photos that you've taken using the iPhone's camera; captured on screen; or saved from web pages, e-mail messages, or instant messages.

To access the photos in other albums on your iPhone, you use the Photos app. In this section, I'll show you how to use the Photos app. Many of these capabilities overlap with those in the Camera app, so I'll refer you back to earlier in the chapter rather than covering the same material again. For example, both the Photos app and the Camera app use the same iOS technologies to share photos with others, so the sharing process works in the same way no matter which app you use.

 If you sync your iPhone with your computer, you use iTunes to control which photos your iPhone syncs with your computer. See Chapter 2 for instructions on syncing photos with your iPhone.

Open the Photos App

First, open the Photos app by tapping the Photos icon on the Home screen. If you're not already at the Home screen, press the Home button to display the Home screen first.

Navigate the Photos App

With the Photos app open, you'll see its interface, which is easy to navigate. Your first step is to tap the appropriate button on the toolbar across the bottom of the screen. This bar contains up to four buttons, depending on which photos you've synced with your iPhone:

- **Albums**   Tap this button to view the list of albums, as shown on the left in Figure 5-9. The Albums list normally opens by default. This button always appears on the toolbar. Tap an album to display its contents. You can then tap a photo to display it.
- **Events**   Tap this button to view the list of Events, as shown on the right in Figure 5-9. By default, an Event is photos grouped based on the time they were taken—for example, photos you took on a particular day, or within a particular two-hour period—but you can also add photos to Events manually in iPhoto on the Mac. Tap an Event to view the photos it contains. You can then tap a photo to display it full screen.

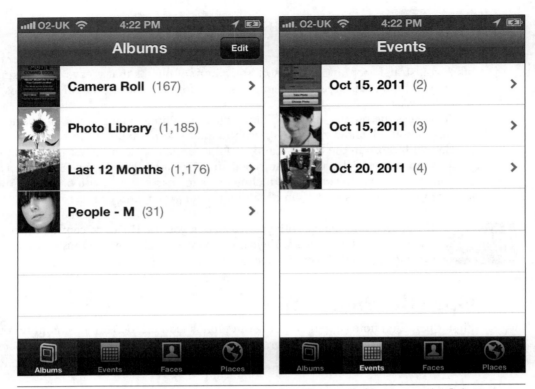

FIGURE 5-9 You can navigate your photos by Albums (left), Events (right), Faces, or Places by tapping the buttons on the toolbar at the bottom of the Photos screen.

 Note If your iPhone contains no list of events, the Events button doesn't appear on the toolbar. Similarly, if there's no list of faces on your iPhone, the Faces button doesn't appear. And if there's no list of places, the Places button doesn't appear either.

- **Faces** Tap this button to view the list of faces, as shown on the left in Figure 5-10. These faces are ones you've identified in iPhoto on the Mac. You can then tap a face to display the photos it appears on, and then tap a photo to open it for viewing.
- **Places** Tap this button to view a map showing the photos' places—the geographical locations either recorded by the iPhone's GPS system or which you've added to your photos manually. You can then tap a place's pin to display the number of photos for that place, as shown on the right in Figure 5-10. Tap the > button to display the photos, and then tap a photo to open it for viewing.

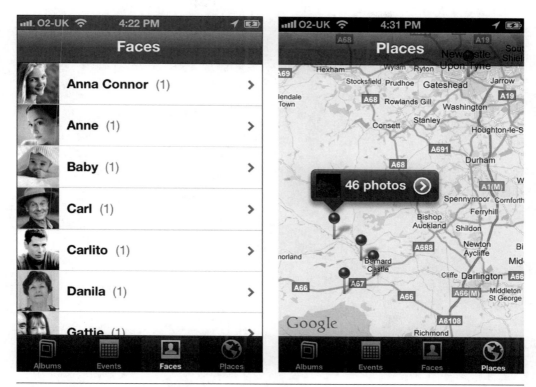

FIGURE 5-10   Tap the Faces button on the toolbar to see a list of the faces you've identified (left). Tap the Places button to view the locations at which your photos were taken (right).

Edit or Share Your Photos

The Photos app has the same capabilities for editing and sharing photos as the Camera app, discussed earlier in this chapter. See the sections "Edit Your Photos" and "Share Your Photos," both earlier in this chapter, for information.

6

Install and Manage Apps on Your iPhone

HOW TO...

- Find, download, and install apps for your iPhone
- Install custom apps provided by your company or organization
- Sync your apps with iTunes
- Configure an app
- Update an app on your iPhone
- Navigate, rearrange, and delete apps
- Jailbreak your iPhone and install non-approved apps

Perhaps the greatest thing about the iPhone is that it can run third-party software as well as the software Apple provides. Apple provides a wide selection of third-party software in its App Store, which is a division of the iTunes Store.

At this writing, the App Store has more than half a million apps. Even if you ignore the 90 percent that are either worthless or so specialized that few people need them, that leaves over 50,000 apps—far more than you can comfortably buy (unless you enjoy banker-size bonuses) or sensibly install on your iPhone. I can't guess which apps you'll need, but I will point you to some of the best productivity apps around.

If you work for a corporation or organization that arms you with an iPhone, you may need to install apps provided by that corporation or organization. I'll show you how to do this along the way.

If the App Store can't provide what you're looking for, you can "jailbreak" your iPhone's bonds so that you can install unapproved software. You'll learn about this drastic step toward the end of this chapter.

Find, Download, and Install Apps for the iPhone

For the iPhone, Apple provides a single source of software, the App Store. The App Store provides only apps that Apple has checked and approved for quality, content, and suitability, so that you can be sure not only that they'll run properly on the iPhone but also that you can download, install, and update them easily—and that they don't contain any unpleasant surprises (such as viruses or hidden adult content).

You can access the App Store either through iTunes or directly from your iPhone. If you sync your iPhone with a computer, using iTunes is easier, because you have more space for browsing and reading reviews. But browsing the App Store on the iPhone works fine too.

 Many developers provide free but limited versions of their apps in the hope of selling more copies of the paid and more powerful versions. If you're thinking of buying a paid app, always look to see if there's a free version that you can try first.

Browse the App Store Using iTunes

To browse the App Store using iTunes, follow these steps:

1. Display the iTunes Store in one of these ways:
   - Click the iTunes Store item in the Source list to display the iTunes Store in the main iTunes window.
   - Double-click the iTunes Store item if you want to open a separate window. Using a separate window is useful if you want to be able to keep playing music or videos in the main window.

 Here's another way to jump to the App Store: If the Apps item appears in the Source list, click it, and then click Get More Apps.

2. In the bar across the top of the window, click App Store to display the contents of the App Store. Figure 6-1 shows an example.
3. Click the iPhone button in the bar at the top of the main pane. The App Store displays iPhone apps rather than iPad apps.
4. Follow links, categories, or recommendations to find an app that interests you. Click the app's icon to display full information about it. Figure 6-2 shows an example of such information.
5. If you decide to get an app, click the Free App button (for a free app) or the price button (for a paid app).

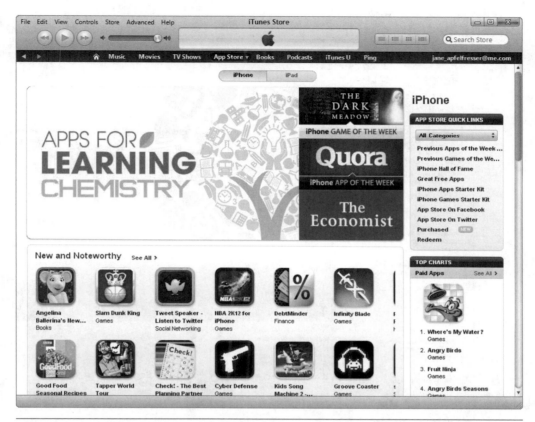

FIGURE 6-1 The App Store includes various categories and lists of apps that you can browse using the same techniques as you use for the other items in the iTunes Store.

6. Follow through the process of signing in to the App Store (if you're not already signed in) and confirming the purchase (even if the app is free). iTunes then starts downloading the app. You can see the progress of the download by clicking the Downloads item in the Store category of the Source list.

After the download finishes, connect your iPhone to your computer, and then sync the apps to install the new apps on your iPhone.

 If you want iTunes to sync new apps automatically to your iPhone, select the Automatically Sync New Apps check box on the Apps screen in the iPhone's control screens in iTunes.

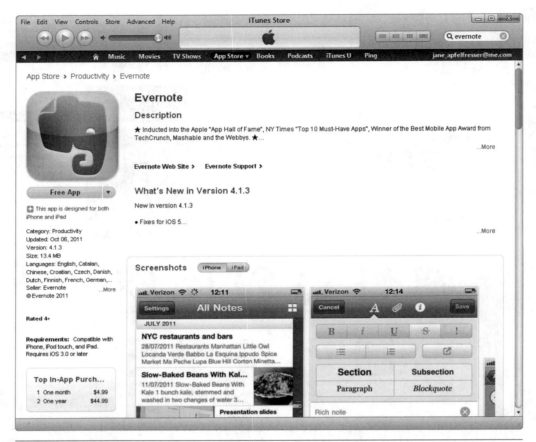

FIGURE 6-2   Each app includes a detailed description. Most apps worth using include customer ratings and comments; these appear further down the screen.

Browse the App Store Using Your iPhone

When you're using your iPhone, you can browse the App Store like this:

1. Press the Home button to go to the Home screen unless you're already there.
2. Tap the App Store icon to display the App Store screen.
3. Tap one of the buttons at the bottom of the screen to see the screen of apps you want to view:
   - **Featured**   This screen contains a New list (of the latest apps), a What's Hot list (showing the apps that are currently most popular), and a Genius app that suggests new apps based on the apps you already have. The left screen in Figure 6-3 shows an example of the Featured screen.
   - **Categories**   This screen lets you browse the apps by different categories: Games, Entertainment, Utilities, Social Networking, Music, Productivity,

How to... Find Useful Productivity Apps

Developers are adding thousands of apps per month to the App Store, so it's almost impossible to provide solid recommendations. But here are ten productivity apps—all available from the App Store—that you may benefit from knowing about:

- **Todo** Todo is a task-management tool that follows productivity guru David Allen's widely acclaimed Getting Things Done principles. Todo can sync with various online task-management services.
- **OmniFocus** OmniFocus is a task-management tool that follows the Getting Things Done principles. OmniFocus on the iPhone syncs with OmniFocus on the Mac (www.omnigroup.com/products/omnifocus-iphone).
- **Things** Things is a simple but powerful task-management tool that syncs with Things on the Mac.
- **WriteRoom** WriteRoom provides a "clean-room" screen for writing without distractions. You can turn on document sharing, connect to your iPhone via a web browser, and type documents directly from a computer.
- **iTeleport** iTeleport lets you take control of your Windows PC or Mac remotely from your iPhone. This app is relatively expensive, and you need to configure your PC or Mac for remote sharing before it will work.
- **Mocha VNC** Mocha VNC lets you take control of your Windows PC or Mac remotely from your iPhone. As with iTeleport, you will need to configure your PC or Mac for remote sharing. Start with Mocha VNC Lite, which has fewer features but is free.
- **Pennies** Pennies is an expense-tracking app that will help you whip your budget into shape.
- **Air Sharing** Air Sharing lets you mount your iPhone as a wireless drive on a Windows PC or Mac so that you can transfer files to and from it or view documents stored on it.
- **Evernote** Evernote is a powerful note-taking app that can store your notes on the Internet, where you can access and update them from all your computers and devices as well as your iPhone.
- **Dropbox** Dropbox is a utility for storing your essential files in an online locker, in which you can access them using your iPhone, any computer, or most any device. Go to www.dropbox.com to get the companion app for your PC or Mac.

Lifestyle, and so on. The right screen in Figure 6-3 shows an example of the Categories screen.

- **Top 25** This screen contains lists of the top 25 paid apps and the top 25 free apps. The masses aren't always right, but they'll often point you to the most useful or most amusing apps.
- **Search** This screen lets you search by using keywords.
- **Updates** This screen lets you quickly find updates for apps that are already installed on your iPhone.

FIGURE 6-3 On the iPhone, you can browse the App Store using the Featured list (left) or the Categories list (right). You can also visit the Top 25 screen, search for apps, or update your existing apps.

4. When you've found an app that looks promising, tap its icon to display the Info screen. The left screen in Figure 6-4 shows an example of the Info screen for a free app.
5. To get the app, tap the price button (for a pay app) or the Free button (for a free app), and then tap the Install button that replaces this button.
6. Enter your password when the iPhone prompts you for it. The iPhone then displays the Home screen, which shows you a progress readout as the app loads and installs (see the third icon at the top of the right screen in Figure 6-4).

Once the app has finished installing, tap the icon to launch it.

The next time you sync your iPhone with your computer, iTunes copies the app from the iPhone to the computer. If you sync your iPhone via iCloud rather than with a computer, your other i-devices—for example, your iPad—that you also sync with the same account automatically pick up the app.

FIGURE 6-4   Check the Info screen (left) for details and reviews before buying or downloading an app. As the app installs and downloads, the Home screen shows you what's happening (right).

Most apps are licensed per computer rather than per device. So if you buy an app for your iPhone and sync it back to iTunes, you can load the app on your iPod touch and iPad at their next sync. iCloud can handle this syncing automatically for you.

Sync Your Apps with iTunes

If you sync your iPhone with your computer, you'll probably want to sync with iTunes all the apps you buy or get for free—at least at first. This will let you see how well the apps work on the iPhone and decide whether you want to keep them.

Once you've done that, you may then want to prevent iTunes from loading an app onto a particular device. For example, if you sync both an iPhone and an iPod touch with the same computer, you may want to load some productivity apps on the iPhone and some games on the iPod touch, but not everything on both. Or you may want to load only some apps on your iPhone at a time, either to save space or to prevent the Home screens from becoming too cluttered and unwieldy.

How to... Install Custom Apps Provided by Your Company or Organization

If your company or organization provides custom apps for your iPhone, an administrator may either install them for you directly (using a tool called iPhone Configuration Utility) or provide them to you to install.

An administrator normally provides a custom app by first having you install a *provisioning profile*, a file that contains details of the app and gives your iPhone permission to install it. (For security, your iPhone won't install any unapproved apps.) The administrator gets the provisioning profile to your iPhone either by sending it via e-mail or by having you download it from a website (for example, your company's or organization's internal website). Either way, you go through a short and straightforward installation routine.

Once the provisioning profile is installed on your iPhone, you can install the custom app using iTunes on your computer. The administrator gets the file containing the custom app to you in one of these ways:

- **E-mail** You receive the custom app file as an attachment to an e-mail message. You then save the file to a convenient temporary location—for example, your desktop.
- **Network drive** You copy the file from a shared drive on the network.
- **Website** You download the file from a website—again, usually an internal website rather than a public one.

You then add the app to iTunes in one of these ways:

- Drag the custom app's file to the Library section of the Source list in iTunes.
- In iTunes, choose File | Add To Library to display the Add To Library dialog box. Select the custom app's file, and then click the Open button.
- On Mac OS X, drag the custom app's file to the iTunes icon on the Dock.

You can now sync your iPhone with your computer to install the app.

Note You can rearrange the apps on the Home screens into your preferred order, and create folders to put apps and other items in. I'll show you how to do this in the "Navigate, Rearrange, and Delete Apps" section later in this chapter.

To control how iTunes handles syncing, follow these steps:

1. Connect your iPhone to your computer as usual.
2. Click the iPhone's entry in the Source list to display its control screens.
3. Click the Apps tab to display the settings for syncing apps (see Figure 6-5).
4. Select the Sync Apps check box if you want to sync apps, as usually you will.

FIGURE 6-5   On the Apps screen in the iPhone's control screens, choose whether to sync all apps or just some of them.

5. Select the check box for each app you want to sync.

 You can select or clear all the check boxes by holding down CTRL (on Windows) or ⌘ (on the Mac) as you click a check box to change its state. For example, CTRL-click a cleared check box to select all the check boxes.

6. Click the Apply button to run the sync.

Choose Settings for an App

Many apps for the iPhone come set up to run straight out of the virtual box, but most have settings that you can configure to make the apps run the way you want them to and give you the best results.

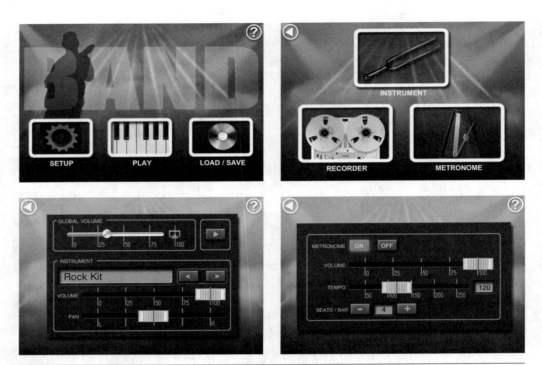

FIGURE 6-6   Many apps have their own setup screens that you access directly from the app.

Many apps have Setup screens that are built directly into the app and intended for you to run through when you start to use the app. For example, Figure 6-6 shows the Setup arrangements for the Band app, which lets you play and record music directly on your iPhone. From the main screen (shown at the top left), tap the Setup button to reach the Setup screen (top right). You can then tap the Instrument button, the Recorder button, or the Metronome button to display the configuration screen for that item (see the bottom two screens).

Some apps also add one or more screens of settings to the iPhone's settings area. You can reach these settings from the iPhone's Settings screen:

1. Press the Home button to reach the Home screen (unless you're already there).
2. Tap the Settings icon to display the Settings screen.
3. Scroll down to find the third-party apps (shown on the left in Figure 6-7), and then tap the app you want.
4. Choose settings on the resulting screen. The right screen in Figure 6-7 shows an example.
5. Tap the Settings button in the upper-left corner of the screen when you're ready to return to the Settings screen.

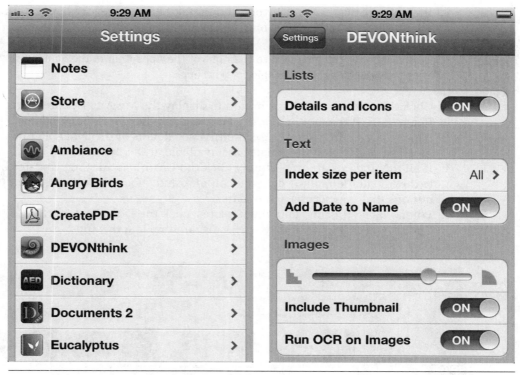

FIGURE 6-7   You can also find settings for some third-party apps on the iPhone's main Settings screen (left). Tap the app's name to display its settings (right).

Update the Apps on Your iPhone

You can update the apps on your iPhone either by using the iPhone itself or—if you sync your iPhone with your computer—by using iTunes. In most cases, using iTunes is faster and easier, so we'll look at that first.

 Many updates to apps are free—especially updates that fix bugs with the app—but major updates and new versions tend to require payment. Check whether you'll need to pay for an upgrade before you install it.

Update an App Using iTunes

If you sync your iPhone with your computer, the best way to update an app is by using iTunes. As before, this is because you can more easily see what you're doing, and you can access the Internet at the full speed of your Internet connection.

To update an app, follow these steps:

1. In the Source list, click the Apps item in the Library category. iTunes displays a screen showing all the apps on your iPhone. Figure 6-8 shows an example.

The number in the gray oval to the right of the Apps item in the Source list shows how many updates are available for your apps.

2. Click the Updates Available button to display the My App Updates screen (see Figure 6-9). If this button doesn't appear, click the Check For Updates button, which appears in its place. You'll either see details of the available updates or a message saying that no updates are available at the moment.
3. If all the updates are free, simply click the Download All Free Updates button to download them all. If not, you can pick and choose by using the Get Update buttons that appear on each update.
4. When you've finished applying updates, click the Done button.
5. Connect your iPhone and sync it as usual to update the apps.

FIGURE 6-8 The Apps screen lists the number of available updates that iTunes knows about. If none is available, click the Check For Updates button, which appears in place of the Updates Available button shown here.

FIGURE 6-9   From the My App Updates screen, you can either update all your apps in one fell swoop or get updates for individual apps.

After you update an app from the App Store, you'll find an .ipa (iOS app) file in the Recycle Bin on a Windows PC or in the Trash on the Mac. For example, if you update the Stanza e-book app, you'll find a file with a name such as Stanza 1.4.ipa in the Trash afterward. This file is the old version of the app, and you can safely get rid of it.

Update an App Directly on Your iPhone

If you sync your iPhone using iCloud, or if you're not at your computer and you need to get the latest update, you can update an app directly on your iPhone. If you do sync with a computer, your iPhone then syncs the changes back to iTunes, making it ready to apply the updates to another iPhone, iPod touch, or iPad you sync with the same computer.

To update the apps on your iPhone, follow these steps:

1. Press the Home button to reach the Home screen (unless you're there already). If updates are available, a red badge appears on the App Store icon, as shown on the left in Figure 6-10.

FIGURE 6-10 The number in the red badge on the App Store icon shows how many app updates are available. Tap the App Store icon and then tap the Updates icon to see which apps the updates are for.

 The App Store automatically checks for updates to apps and displays the results on the telltale badge on its icon. But you will often find that there are more updates than the badge shows, so it's worth checking even if no badge appears—especially if you've learned that an app's developer has released a new version that fixes bugs or adds features.

2. Tap the App Store icon to display the App Store screen.
3. Tap the Updates icon at the bottom of the screen to display the Updates screen. This screen (shown on the right in Figure 6-10) lists the apps for which updates are available.
4. Tap the Update All button if you want to update all the apps at once. Otherwise, tap an app to display the details of the update (the left screen in Figure 6-11 shows an example), and then tap the button to update it. Your iPhone displays the Home screen as it downloads and installs the updates. The right screen in Figure 6-11 shows an app being updated (the app whose name appears to be Waiting).

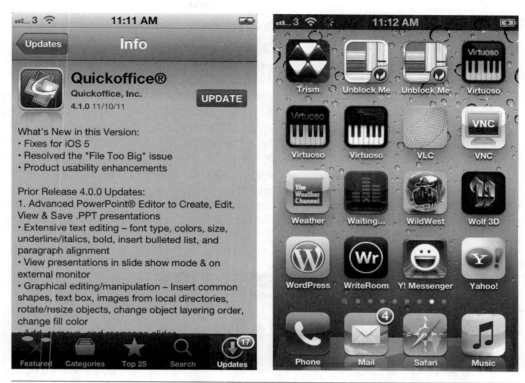

FIGURE 6-11   You can view the details of an update (left) to help decide whether you want to install it. The Home screen (right) shows how the downloads and installations are progressing. The app we're updating here is marked Waiting.

Navigate, Rearrange, and Delete Apps

When you add an app, the iPhone automatically puts its icon in the first available space on one of the Home screens. For example, if the first Home screen is full, and the second is only partly full, the iPhone puts the app's icon in the first empty space on the second screen. If there are several screens of apps, but there's an empty space on the first Home screen, the iPhone puts the app's icon in that space.

This automatic placement works fine and is easy enough to grasp, but you'll almost certainly be able to work (or play) faster if you rearrange the icons for the apps on the Home screens so that they're where you want them. You can also create folders as needed to group related items and reduce the number of Home screens you need.

You can rearrange the apps and create folders either in iTunes when the iPhone is connected to your computer (either via USB or wirelessly) or on the iPhone itself. Both ways of rearranging the apps are simple enough, but most people find making extensive changes easier in iTunes.

Navigate the Home Screens

Depending on what's installed on your iPhone, it may have only a couple of Home screens at first. But as soon as you fill up one of the existing screens, the iPhone provides a new screen—a third, a fourth, a fifth, and so on.

The iPhone displays a line of dots toward the bottom of the Home screen to show how many screens of apps you have. The leftmost dot-like icon is actually not a dot but a tiny magnifying glass that indicates the Search screen. The white dot represents the screen you're currently viewing. For example, the iPhone shown on the left in Figure 6-12 has eight screens of apps, and the fourth is currently displayed.

To display the next screen of apps, drag your finger to the left horizontally across the screen, as shown on the right in Figure 6-12. Drag to the right to display the previous screen of apps. You can also tap a dot to the right of the current dot to display the next screen or a dot to the left of the current dot to display the previous screen.

FIGURE 6-12 The dots toward the bottom of the screen show how many screens of apps you have and which screen is displayed. Drag to the left (as shown on the right) or to the right to change the screen of apps.

Rearrange the Apps on the Home Screens Using iTunes

To use iTunes to rearrange the apps on your iPhone, first display the Home screen containing the icons to rearrange. Follow these steps:

1. Connect your iPhone to the computer.
2. If iTunes doesn't launch or activate automatically when your computer detects your iPhone, launch or switch to iTunes manually.
3. In the Devices category in the Source list, click the entry for your iPhone to display its control screens.
4. Click the Apps tab to display its contents.
5. In the scrolling list of Home screens, click the Home screen that contains the icons you want to rearrange.
6. Make the changes as discussed in the following sections, and then click the Apply button to apply them to your iPhone.

Move an App to a New Position on the Same Home Screen Using iTunes

To move an app to a new position on the same Home screen, click the app and drag it to where you want it to appear. The other apps move out of the way to make room for the app you're moving.

Move an App to a Different Home Screen Using iTunes

To move an app to a different Home screen, follow these steps:

1. Click the app and drag it to the list of Home screens and hold it over the small version of the Home screen to which you want to move it. iTunes displays the larger version of that Home screen.
2. Drag the app to where you want it to appear, and then drop it. The other apps move out of the way to make space for the app. If the Home screen is full, the last app gets bumped off it. If the next Home screen has a free space, the app lands on that Home screen; if the next Home screen is full, the iPhone creates a new Home screen and puts the app there all on its lonesome (until you rearrange the apps further).

You can customize the main apps at the bottom of the Home screens. Click one of the main apps and drag it off the bar at the bottom of the screen. Then click and drag there the app or folder you want instead.

FIGURE 6-13 When you create a new folder, iTunes darkens the other apps and displays a box for naming the folder.

Add an App to a Folder Using iTunes

To create a folder, follow these steps:

1. Identify the apps you want to put in a folder. You may prefer to put all the apps on the same Home screen as a preliminary move to make things easier.
2. Drag one of the apps that you want to put into a folder to the app in whose position you want to create a folder. The iPhone creates a folder, puts both apps into it, and displays a text box with a suggested name, as shown in Figure 6-13. iTunes darkens the other icons to make it clear that you're working with the folder.
3. To change the suggested name, edit it as needed, or click the × button to delete the suggested name, and then type the name you want.
4. Click the folder's icon (or anywhere on the darkened area of the screen) to display the rest of the icons again.

You can now drag other apps to the folder and drop them there.

 You can't nest one folder inside another. If you try to drag one folder to another folder, the iPhone moves the other folder smartly out of the way.

Remove an App from a Folder Using iTunes

To remove an app from a folder, double-click the folder to open it, then click the app and drag it up to the top of the screen. When the remaining icons appear, drag the app to where you want it.

Change the Order of the Home Screens Using iTunes

In iTunes, you can quickly change the order of the Home screens by dragging them up and down the list of Home screens.

You can't change the order of the Home screens on your iPhone itself—you have to move the apps from screen to screen instead.

Rearrange the Apps Directly on Your iPhone

Instead of using iTunes to rearrange the apps on your iPhone, you can work directly on the iPhone. The following sections give you the details.

Move an App to a New Position on the Same Home Screen Using the iPhone

To move an app to a new position on the same Home screen, follow these steps:

1. Display the Home screen that contains the app.
2. Tap any app and keep holding it until the app icons start to jiggle (see Figure 6-14).
3. Tap the app you want to move, and then drag it to where you want it to appear. The other apps make room for it.
4. Move other apps as needed, and then press the Home button when you're ready to stop customizing.

Move an App to a Different Home Screen Using the iPhone

To move an app to a different Home screen, follow these steps:

1. Display the Home screen that contains the app.
2. Tap any app and keep holding it until the app icons start to jiggle.
3. Tap the app you want to move, then drag it off the left side of the screen (to get to the previous Home screen) or the right side of the screen (to get to the next Home screen). You can then drag to the left or right again if necessary to reach another Home screen.

The screens don't have to be full of apps. You can create a new screen by dragging an app to it.

4. Drag the app to where you want it to appear, and then drop it. The other apps move out of the way to make space for the app. If the Home screen is full, the last app gets bumped off it. If the next Home screen is full, its last icon gets bumped to the following Home screen, and so on until you hit a Home screen that has a free parking space.

FIGURE 6-14 To move apps, tap and hold an app until the app icons start to jiggle. The × marks indicate apps you can delete.

 You can customize the main apps at the bottom of the Home screens. Tap and hold an app until the icons start jiggling, then drag one of the main apps off the bar at the bottom of the screen. Then drag there the app or folder you want instead. Or simply drag the main apps at the bottom of the Home screen into a different order if you prefer.

Add an App to a Folder Using the iPhone

To reduce the number of icons on your Home screens, you can create folders containing related apps. (Or unrelated apps if you prefer—for example, you could create a Seldom Useful folder for the apps you rarely use but can't yet bring yourself to part with.)

To create a folder, follow these steps:

1. Decide which apps you'll put in the folder. To make the process easier, first put them on the same Home screen.

2. Tap any app and keep holding it until the app icons start to jiggle.
3. Drag one of the apps that you want to put into a folder to the app in whose position you want to create a folder. For example, the left screen in Figure 6-15 shows me dragging the Pages icon onto the Numbers icon, which will create a folder containing those two apps. Your iPhone creates a folder, puts both apps into it, and displays a text box with a suggested name, as shown in the right screen in Figure 6-15. The iPhone darkens the other icons to make it clear that you're working with the folder.
4. To change the suggested name, edit it as needed, or click the × button to delete the suggested name, and then use the onscreen keyboard to type the name you want.
5. Tap the folder's icon (or anywhere outside the folder) to display the rest of the icons again.

You can now drag other apps to the folder and drop them there.

FIGURE 6-15   You can create a new folder on the iPhone by dragging one app on top of another (left). Your iPhone creates a new folder (right), which you can rename as needed.

You can't nest one folder inside another. If you try to drag one folder to another folder, the iPhone moves the other folder, as it assumes you're rearranging the icons.

Open an App in a Folder on the iPhone

To open an app that you've stored in a folder, tap the folder to open it, and then tap the app's icon.

Remove an App from a Folder Using the iPhone

To remove an app from a folder, tap the folder to open it, then tap the app and drag it up to the top of the screen. When the remaining icons appear, drag the app to where you want it, and then set it free.

Delete an App

As soon as you've synced an app after installing it, the app is installed both on your iPhone and on your computer. If you don't want to keep the app on your iPhone, you can delete it from there without affecting the copy in iTunes. And if you really don't want to keep the app at all, you can delete it from iTunes and remove it from your iPhone as well.

Delete an App from the iPhone

You can delete an app from your iPhone in moments:

1. Tap the app's icon and hold it down until the icons start jiggling.
2. Tap the circle with the × at the upper-left corner. The iPhone displays a confirmation dialog box, as shown here.

3. Tap Delete. The iPhone deletes the app.

Delete an App from iTunes and from the iPhone

When you want to get rid of an app completely, delete it from iTunes as follows. iTunes then removes it from your iPhone at the next sync.

1. Click the Apps item in the Source list to display the iPhone Apps screen.
2. Click the app to select it.
3. Press DELETE. iTunes displays a confirmation dialog box, as shown here.

4. Click the Remove button. iTunes removes the app.

Switch Quickly Among Apps

When you want to switch from one app to another, you can press the Home button to display the Home screen, and then tap the icon for the app you want. But your iPhone also gives you a quicker way of switching from one running app to another:

1. In the running app, press the Home button twice in quick succession to display the app-switching bar, shown here.

2. Scroll left or right until you find the icon for the app you want.
3. Tap the app's icon. Your iPhone displays the app as you left it.

Jailbreak Your iPhone and Install Non-Approved Apps

If you'll forgive a technical term, your iPhone's operating system (iOS) is a "locked" platform for apps. Any developer who wants to provide an app for the iPhone must submit it to Apple for approval. If Apple approves the app, up it goes on the App Store, and anyone who has an iPhone can buy it, download it, and use it.

Before Apple unleashed the App Store on a deeply suspecting world, enterprising hackers had "jailbroken" the iPhone's virtual shackles so that they could install non-approved software on the iPhone. Even with the App Store up and active, some developers prefer not to go through the approval process, some on general principles and others secure in the knowledge that their apps offend enough of Apple's guidelines that approval isn't even a pipe dream.

If you want to install non-approved apps on the iPhone, you'll find plenty of tools and instructions online for jailbreaking the iPhone. As usual with the Internet, these tools and instructions are only a quick search away.

But before you take this step, make sure you understand the potential downside. Apple doesn't support jailbroken iPhones, and in fact plays Whac-a-Mole with the jailbreaking teams: Each update Apple releases to the iPhone software stands a good chance of putting a jailbroken iPhone back in jail. If the update doesn't do that, it may even "brick" the iPhone—knocking its functionality on the head, so that the iPhone is useful only as a brick. The jailbreaking process itself isn't always successful, and it too can stop an iPhone from working.

"Bricking" is an evocative term, but an iPhone is actually of little use as a brick. Still, an iPhone works well as a desk paperweight—if you still allow paper on your desk.

PART II

Use Your iPhone for Communications

7

Make Phone Calls and Video Calls

HOW TO...

- Make phone calls with your iPhone
- Receive phone calls on your iPhone
- Make conference calls with your iPhone
- Get your messages with Visual Voicemail
- Make and receive video calls using FaceTime

We're already one-third of the way through the book, and we haven't even touched on the functionality that gives the iPhone most of its name. It's time to fix that—so in this chapter, I'll show you how to make phone calls on your iPhone. As a bonus, you can make video calls as well using Apple's FaceTime technology; we'll go through how to do this at the end of the chapter.

We'll start with making and taking regular phone calls—the kind with only one other participant. We'll then move along to making conference calls on your iPhone and getting your messages using Visual Voicemail. Finally, we'll use FaceTime.

Make and Receive Phone Calls

Making phone calls with the iPhone is about as easy as it possibly could be—provided that you have a signal. If in doubt, look at the signal-strength icon at the left end of the status bar at the top of the screen. As long as there's at least one bar, you should be good to go. If you see the dreaded No Service status, you'll need to shift yourself to somewhere your carrier's cell towers have colonized more of the landscape.

 If you get the No Service status somewhere you know there is service, you'll know your iPhone is lying to you. To fix this, first tap the Settings icon on the Home screen, and then turn Airplane mode on for a minute before turning it off again.

This should restart your cellular connection and enable you to get service. If that doesn't work, restart your iPhone.

Make a Phone Call

To make a phone call, follow these steps:

1. If you're planning to use the headset and its microphone rather than the iPhone's built-in speaker and microphone, plug in the headset and plant the ear-buds in your ears. Or if you're using a Bluetooth headset, make sure it's connected to your iPhone via Bluetooth and clipped firmly to your skull or ear.
2. Press the Home button to go to the Home screen unless you're already there.
3. Tap the Phone button at the bottom of the screen to display whichever of the five Phone screens you were using last:
   - **Favorites** Displays a list of up to 20 favorite numbers you designate. This is handy for making quick calls to those numbers.
   - **Recents** Shows a list of calls you've made, received, and missed. The missed calls appear in red. Tap the Missed button at the top of the screen to see the list of missed calls so that you can easily return them. Tap the All button at the top of the screen to restore the full list. Tap the Clear button if you want to get rid of all the recents (for example, because you've dealt with all the missed calls).
   - **Contacts** Shows a list of your contacts, as on the left in Figure 7-1. You can display either all your contacts or just a group, such as your personal contacts or business contacts. To choose a group, tap the Groups button at the upper-left corner of the Contacts screen, and then tap the group on the Groups screen.
   - **Keypad** Displays a keypad so that you can dial a call, as shown on the right in Figure 7-1. Dialing with the keypad is good for numbers you'll never need to dial again. For all other numbers, it's usually a good idea to create a contact so that you can call the number again easily in the future.
   - **Voicemail** Tap the message to which you want to reply, and then tap the Call Back button.
4. Choose the number you want to dial, either from the Phone screen you're on, or by tapping the button for the Phone screen you want to access.

Receive a Phone Call

Receiving a phone call is almost as easy as picking up the phone. Follow these steps:

1. When a call comes in, your iPhone rings—as you'd expect. Your iPhone also switches to Phone mode and displays information on the call—the caller's name (if it's in your Contacts) or the phone number (if it's available). The left screen in Figure 7-2 shows what you'll see when your iPhone is locked. The right

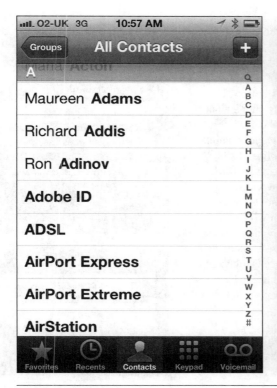 

FIGURE 7-1   The most convenient way to call a contact is by choosing their entry on the Contacts screen (left). You can also do things the hard way by using the keypad (right).

How to...   ## Make Calls Quickly and Easily by Using Your Favorites List Fully

If you have a small group of people you telephone most frequently, you can save a lot of time by putting them on your Favorites list. You can add a number to the Favorites list either from the Contacts list or from the Favorites list itself.

To add a number to the Favorites list from the Contacts list, follow these steps:

1. Open the Contacts list from either the Phone app or the Contacts app:
   - **Phone app**   Tap the Phone button at the bottom of the Home screen, and then tap the Contacts button at the bottom of the Phone screen.

(Continued)

- **Contacts app** Tap the Utilities folder on the Home screen, and then tap the Contacts icon.

2. Tap the name of the contact you want to add to the Favorites list. The iPhone displays the Info screen for the contact.

3. Tap the Add To Favorites button. If the contact has only a single phone number, your iPhone adds it. If the contact has two or more numbers, your iPhone displays the Add To Favorites dialog box, shown here, to let you choose which number to add to the Favorites.

4. Tap the number you want to add.

5. If you tap a number that is accessible via FaceTime, your iPhone displays the Add *Number* To Favorites As dialog box, shown here. Tap the Voice Call button or the FaceTime button, as needed.

6. Tap the All Contacts button to return to the Contacts list.

To add a number to the Favorites list starting from the Favorites list itself, follow these steps:

1. Tap the + button in the upper-left corner to display the list of contacts.
2. Find the contact you want. If necessary, change the group of contacts displayed—for example, choose a group such as Business Contacts if you want to pick from just that group of contacts rather than from your full list.
3. Tap the contact's name to add them to your contacts.
   - As before, if the contact has two or more numbers, your iPhone displays the Add To Favorites dialog box to let you choose which number to use.
   - Also as before, your iPhone may display the Add *Number* To Favorites As dialog box to prompt you whether to add the favorite as a Voice Call favorite or as a FaceTime favorite.

To change the order of the Favorites list, follow these steps:

1. Tap the Favorites button to display the Favorites screen.
2. Tap the Edit button in the upper-left corner to switch the Favorites list into editing mode.
3. Tap and hold the three bars at the right end of the contact you want to move, and then drag the contact up or down the screen.
4. When you've finished changing the order, tap the Done button.

(Continued)

To remove a favorite from the Favorites list, follow these steps:

1. Tap the Favorites button to display the Favorites screen.
2. Tap the Edit button in the upper-left corner to switch the Favorites list into editing mode.
3. Tap the round red Delete button at the left of the favorite you want to remove. Your iPhone displays a rectangular red Delete button to the right of the favorite.
4. Tap the Delete button.
5. When you've finished removing favorites, tap the Done button.

 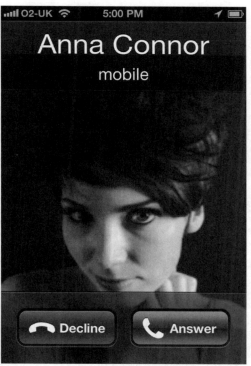

FIGURE 7-2   From the lock screen (left), you can accept an incoming phone call by moving the slider to the right. When your iPhone is unlocked, tap the Answer button or the Decline button to deal with the call. You can also accept the call by clicking the headphone clicker button once or decline the call by holding it down.

Make Phone Calls for You

Siri is a great way of making phone calls without muss or fuss, especially when you're out and about and you have the headset connected.

Here's how to get Siri to make a phone call for you:

- "Call Anna Connor."
- "Call Helen Hochwasser on her mobile."
- "Call my wife on her iPhone."
- "Siri, phone home."
- "Phone 707 555 1234."

Navigate Quickly Through Your Contacts

You can navigate through the Contacts list in three ways:

- Tap a letter in the column on the right to jump to the first name starting with that letter.
- Tap in the column on the right, and then drag your finger up or down to scroll down or up rapidly.
- Tap in the list of contacts, and then drag your finger up or down to scroll down or up more slowly—for example, when you've reached almost the right point in the Contacts list.

screen in Figure 7-2 shows what you'll see when your iPhone is unlocked. If you're listening to music, the iPhone fades the music, and then pauses it.

Note If you've set the iPhone to vibrate, it vibrates as well. To turn vibration on or off, press the Home button, tap the Settings icon, and then tap the Sounds button. On the Sounds screen, set the Vibrate switch in the Silent box to the On position or the Off position to control whether your iPhone vibrates when you've silenced the ringer. Set the Vibrate switch in the third box to the On position or the Off position to control whether your iPhone vibrates when the ringer is on.

2. Tap the Answer button if you want to take the call. If you're using the iPhone's headset, click the button on the cord. If you want to send the call to voicemail, tap the Decline button, hold down the clicker on the headset cord, or simply don't answer for the set number of rings (the default is four rings). If you accept the call, your iPhone displays the control buttons shown in the left screen in Figure 7-3.

Control How Your iPhone Sorts Your Contacts List

Your iPhone can sort your Contacts list into either "first, last" order (for example, "Jan Weiss") or "last, first" order (for example, "Weiss, Jan"). And your iPhone can also display the contacts in the same order as the sort order or in the other order.

To choose the sort order, follow these steps:

1. Press the Home button to go to the Home screen unless you're already there.
2. Tap the Settings icon to display the Settings screen.
3. Tap the Mail, Contacts, Calendars button to display the Mail, Contacts, Calendars screen.
4. Scroll down to the Contacts area and look at the Sort Order readout. It'll say either "Last, First" or "First, Last." To change the order, tap the Sort Order item, tap the other item on the Sort Order screen, and then tap the Phone button to return to the Phone screen.
5. Still in the Contacts area, look at the Display Order readout. This too will say either "Last, First" or "First, Last." To change the order, tap the Display Order item, tap the other item on the Display Order screen, and then tap the Settings button to return to the Settings screen.

Tip   You can press either volume key or the Sleep/Wake button on the top of the iPhone to turn off the ringing before you answer the call—for example, because the phone ringing will disturb other people while you're trying to put your headset on. You can also turn the iPhone's ringer off completely by moving the Silencer switch on the left side of the iPhone toward the back, so that the orange dot appears.

3. During the call, you can use your iPhone's other features freely, except for playing music or video. For example, if you need to take a note during the call, press the Home button, tap the Notes icon, and work on the Notes screen as usual.
4. To end the call, tap the End button. If you're using the iPhone's headset, click the button on the cord. If you were listening to music when the call came in, the iPhone restarts the music automatically for you.

Use the Onscreen Icons During Calls

When you make a call, your iPhone displays the icons shown on the left in Figure 7-3. Here's what you can do with them:

FIGURE 7-3 When you're on a call, your iPhone displays a panel of control buttons (left) for muting the call, displaying the keypad (right), switching to the speaker, adding a call, switching to FaceTime, or displaying your contacts.

- **Mute**   Tap this icon to mute the iPhone's microphone—for example, so that you can confer with someone near you without the person at the other end of the phone call being able to hear. Tap this icon again to remove the muting. You can still hear the person at the other end when your microphone is muted. If you need to put the call on hold, tap and hold the Mute button until the button turns blue and the Hold symbol appears, as shown here. Hold interrupts the entire call, so neither end hears anything from the other. Tap the Hold icon again to remove the hold.

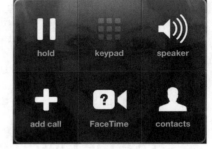

- **Keypad**   Tap this icon to bring up the iPhone's keypad—for example, so that you can navigate your way through the voicemail hell that pretends to be customer service for all too many companies these days. The right screen in Figure 7-3 shows the keypad. Tap the Hide Keypad button when you're finished with the keypad. (Alternatively, tap the End button to end the call.)

- **Speaker** Tap this icon to switch from the earpiece to the speaker at the bottom of the iPhone. The speaker works only when you don't have the headset connected. Tap the Speaker icon again if you want to stop using the speaker.
- **Add Call** Tap this icon to make a conference call or to make another call while putting the current call on hold. See the next two sections for details.
- **FaceTime** Tap this icon to switch to a video call with the contact. This icon is available only if FaceTime is available for the contact. If the FaceTime icon bears a question mark, your iPhone can't tell if FaceTime is available.
- **Contacts** Tap this icon to display the Contacts list.

Put the Current Call on Hold and Make Another Call

If you make and receive many calls, you probably use call waiting to let you interrupt an existing call to take an incoming call. If so, you'll love the iPhone's Add Call feature, as it not only lets you do this (see the next section) but also lets you make an outgoing call while putting the current call on hold.

To put the current call on hold and make another call, follow these steps:

1. In your current call, tap the Add Call button. iPhone puts the current call on hold and displays whichever Phone screen you were using last—for example, Contacts.
2. Dial the second call as usual. For example, tap the Favorites icon, and then tap the favorite you want to call.
3. Make the call as usual. The only difference is that the name or number of the first call appears at the top of the screen, and two icons change, as shown here.
4. To switch to the caller who's on hold, tap the Swap button. You can also tap the caller's name or number at the top of the screen.
5. Tap the End button when you want to hang up the current call. You then go back to the call that's on hold.

Receive an Incoming Call During an Existing Call

If you receive an incoming call during an existing call, you have three choices (see Figure 7-4):

FIGURE 7-4 You can put an existing call on hold to take an incoming call.

- **Send the call to voicemail**   Tap the Ignore button.
- **Put the current call on hold, and take the call**   Tap the Hold Call + Answer button.
- **End the current call, and take the call**   Tap the End Call + Answer button.

 If you've turned off call waiting on the Phone screen in the Settings app, any call made to your phone while you're already on a call goes directly to voicemail.

Make Conference Calls

One of the iPhone's great features is that it enables you to make conference calls easily. Here's all you need to do to establish a conference call to two people:

1. Call the first person.
2. Put the first person on hold.
3. Call the second person, as described in the section "Put the Current Call on Hold and Make Another Call," earlier in this chapter.

FIGURE 7-5 After calling the second person with the first on hold, tap the Merge Calls button (left) to merge the calls into a conference call. The button at the top of the screen (right) then indicates that the call has multiple participants.

4. Tap the Merge Calls button (see the left screen in Figure 7-5). You're then speaking to both people.
5. To add another person to the conference call, you can dial another number, and then tap the Merge Calls button to add that person to the conference call.
6. To hang up on one of the participants, tap the > button near the upper-right corner of the screen to display the Conference screen (shown in Figure 7-6), and then tap the red button to the left of the participant's name.
7. To speak privately to one of the participants, tap the > button to display the Conference screen, and then tap the Private button to the right of the participant's name.

Use Visual Voicemail

When you send a message to voicemail, your iPhone records it directly on the phone, so you can access it at any time.

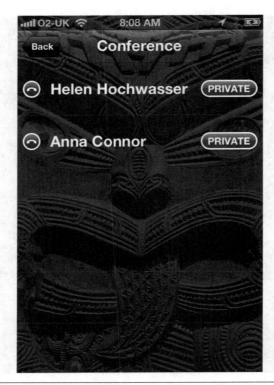

FIGURE 7-6 From the Conference screen, you can hang up on a participant or tap a participant's Private button to speak privately.

First, though, you must set up your outgoing message. Follow these steps:

1. Press the Home button to go to the Home screen unless you're already there.
2. Tap the Phone button to display whichever Phone screen you were using last.
3. Tap the Voicemail button. Your iPhone displays the initial Voicemail screen, shown on the left in Figure 7-7.
4. Tap the Set Up Now button. Your iPhone displays the Password screen, shown on the right in Figure 7-7.
5. Tap a four-digit password, and then tap the Save button. Your iPhone displays the Greeting screen (shown on the left in Figure 7-8).
6. If you want to keep the default voicemail greeting, leave the Default button selected. Otherwise, tap the Custom button to reveal the recording controls (shown on the right in Figure 7-8).

 The default greeting depends on your carrier, but it is often a simple announcement of the phone number followed by an invitation to leave a message.

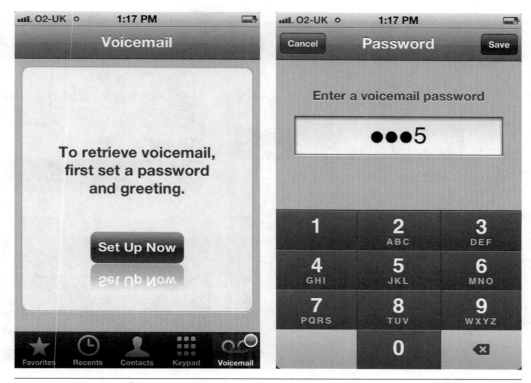

FIGURE 7-7 Tap the Set Up Now button on the initial Voicemail screen (left) to start setting up your voicemail, then enter a password on the Password screen (right).

7. Tap the Record button, and then speak your greeting. Tap the Stop button to stop recording.
8. Tap the Play button to play back the greeting to check that it sounds the way you want. If necessary, tap the Record button to record the greeting again.
9. When you are satisfied with the greeting, tap the Save button to save it.

To listen to your messages, follow these steps:

1. Press the Home button to go to the Home screen unless you're already there.
2. Tap the Phone button to display whichever Phone screen you were using last.
3. Tap the Voicemail button. The iPhone displays the Voicemail screen, shown in Figure 7-9. The blue dots show the messages you haven't listened to yet.
4. Connect the headset or tap the Speaker button to switch the speaker on.
5. To listen to a message, tap it twice in quick succession.
6. To delete the current message, tap the Delete button. The iPhone doesn't ask you to confirm the deletion.

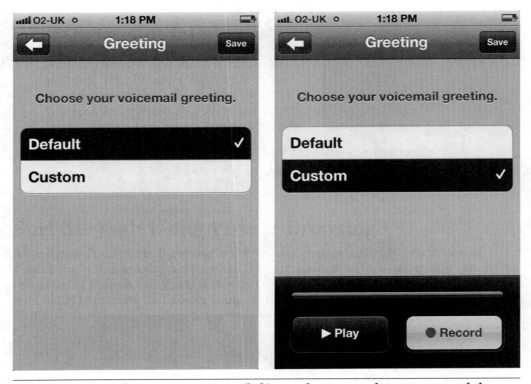

FIGURE 7-8 On the Greeting screen (left), tap the Custom button to reveal the recording controls (right), then record your message.

7. To call the person who left a message, tap the message, and then tap the Call Back button.

Make Video Calls with FaceTime

FaceTime is Apple's technology for making video calls quickly and easily to users of the iPhone, iPad, iPod touch, and Mac. At this writing, there's no Windows version of FaceTime.

Before you can use FaceTime on your iPhone, you need to set it up as explained in the section "Choose FaceTime Settings" in Chapter 4. You'll find setup quick and easy.

Make a FaceTime Call

To make a FaceTime call, follow these steps:

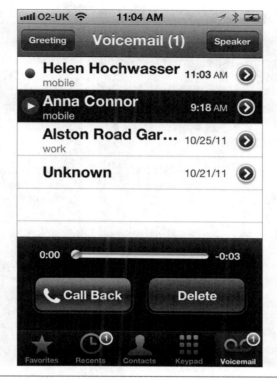

FIGURE 7-9 On the Voicemail screen, tap the message you want to hear. You can then tap the Call Back button to return the call or tap the Delete button to delete the message.

1. Open the Phone app if it's not already open.
2. Open the contact record for the contact you want to call. For example, tap the Contacts button at the bottom of the screen, and then tap the contact's button.
3. On the Info screen, tap the FaceTime button.
4. If your iPhone displays the FaceTime dialog box (shown here) prompting you to choose which number or e-mail address to use, tap the appropriate button.
5. Your iPhone then places a FaceTime call to the contact. While your iPhone sets up the call, you see your preview (see the left screen in Figure 7-10) so that you can check your teeth for spinach.
6. If the contact accepts the call, you see the contact's face—or, more accurately, whatever the contact's camera is seeing. Your contact sees whatever is in front of your iPhone's front-facing camera. A

FIGURE 7-10 Your iPhone displays your video preview (left) as it sets up the FaceTime call. When your contact accepts the call, the contact's video takes over the screen, with your video preview appearing inset.

thumbnail of this image appears superimposed on your contact's video so that you can see your progress with the toothpick. The right screen in Figure 7-10 shows a FaceTime call in progress.

 Tip You can reposition your video preview by tapping it and dragging it.

7. If necessary, mute the call by tapping the Mute button (the microphone icon with a diagonal slash) in the lower-left corner of the screen.
8. If you want to switch to your iPhone's rear-facing camera, tap the Switch Cameras button in the lower-right corner of the screen. Tap this button again to switch back to the front-facing camera.
9. When you're ready to end the call, tap the End button.

FaceTime Someone

To get Siri to place a FaceTime call to someone, just say "FaceTime" and their name—for example, "FaceTime Patty."

Receive a FaceTime Call

When someone calls you via FaceTime, your iPhone displays your video preview (so that you can compose your features in a smile) along with a Decline button and an Accept button. Tap the Accept button, and your iPhone sets up the FaceTime call. You can then control and end the call as described in the previous section.

8

Communicate via E-Mail and Instant Messaging

HOW TO...

- Send and receive e-mail
- Communicate via instant messaging

Your iPhone is great for keeping in touch wherever you go—by voice call, by video call, by e-mail, and by instant messaging. In this chapter, we'll look at how to make the most of the iPhone's powerful features for e-mail and instant messaging.

We'll start with the basics: setting up your e-mail accounts and configuring Mail's settings so that it works the way you prefer. We'll then move on to sending e-mail and sending photographs, notes, and other files. After that, we'll look at how to receive e-mail messages and attachments; how to get through your Inbox quickly by using batch editing; and how to create, change, and delete mail folders.

In the second part of the chapter, we'll dig into instant messaging. First, you need to understand how SMS and MMS differ, and what Apple's iMessage service is. From there, we'll move on to sending text messages and MMS messages and then cover receiving messages, editing or clearing conversations, and deleting messages from the message list. Finally, I'll show you how to choose settings for the Messages app if you find the default settings don't suit you.

Send and Receive E-Mail

Your iPhone can send and receive e-mail messages that include attachments, so you can receive files while out and about, view them immediately, and then share them with others if necessary.

Your iPhone supports various widely used file formats for attachments, including:

- **Word documents**   Word 2010 and Word 2007 format (DOCX) or Word 97–2003 format (DOC).
- **Excel workbooks**   Excel 2010 and Excel 2007 format (XLSX) or Excel 97–2003 format (XLS).
- **Portable Document Format**   PDF files, such as those produced by Adobe Acrobat or any program running on Mac OS X.
- **Text files**   Plain text files, in the TXT format. The iPhone can't display Rich Text Files (RTF format).

First, you need to set up your iPhone to use your e-mail accounts. You may have set up one or more accounts when setting up your iPhone at first, but we'll look at the process of adding accounts in case you need to set up others. Once your accounts are set up, you can start sending and receiving messages and attachments.

Set Up Your E-Mail Accounts

You can set up an e-mail account on your iPhone either by having iTunes transfer the details from your computer's e-mail program or by entering the necessary information directly on your iPhone.

Transferring the details from your e-mail program saves you from having to retype your username, password, mail servers, and so forth. But even when you set up an account using your iPhone, Apple has streamlined the process as much as possible, so in many cases you need to type only your e-mail address and password rather than the details of the mail servers the account uses.

These are the Windows mail programs that iTunes supports at this writing:

- **Outlook**   Outlook 2010, Outlook 2007, and Outlook 2003.
- **Outlook Express**   The free e-mail program included with Windows XP and other versions of Windows before Windows Vista.
- **Windows Mail**   The free e-mail program included with Windows Vista. (Windows Mail is an updated and renamed version of Outlook Express.)

 At this writing, iTunes doesn't support Windows Live Mail.

These are the Mac mail programs that iTunes supports at this writing:

- **Mail**   The mail program included with Mac OS X.
- **Entourage**   The e-mail (and much more) program included in Office for the Mac in Office 2004 and Office 2008. (In Office 2011, Microsoft replaced Entourage with a Mac version of Outlook.)

If you have another type of e-mail account, you can set it up manually on your iPhone. The iPhone provides help for setting up widely used web-mail accounts, such as Gmail, AOL, Yahoo! Mail, and Apple's own iCloud service and the MobileMe service

How to...   **Connect Your iPhone to Exchange Server**

If you use your iPhone at a workplace that has a Microsoft Windows network, you may well need to connect it to Exchange Server, the Microsoft messaging server software.

Normally, you connect to Exchange Server by using a configuration profile supplied by a network administrator at your workplace, but you can also set up the Exchange account manually. See Chapter 16 for instructions on setting up Exchange accounts.

that Apple will terminate in June 2012. Even if you have a different type of account, the iPhone usually makes it pretty easy to set up.

Set Up E-Mail Accounts from Your Computer

To set up one or more e-mail accounts from your computer, follow these steps:

1. Connect your iPhone to your computer, and allow synchronization to take place.
2. In iTunes, click your iPhone's entry in the Source list to display the iPhone's control screens.
3. Click the Info tab, and then scroll down to the Mail Accounts area.
4. Select the Sync Mail Accounts check box.
5. In the Selected Mail Accounts list box, select the check box for each account you want to put on your iPhone. If the e-mail account doesn't appear there, chances are that iTunes doesn't support it.
6. Click the Apply button. iTunes passes the details of the account or accounts to your iPhone.

Set Up an E-Mail Account Manually on Your iPhone

If iTunes can't copy the details of the e-mail account you want to use with your iPhone, you'll need to set up the account manually on your iPhone. Follow these steps:

1. Press the Home button to go to the Home screen unless you're already there.
2. Tap the Settings icon to display the Settings screen.
3. Scroll down to the third box, and then tap the Mail, Contacts, Calendars button to display the Mail, Contacts, Calendars screen, shown on the left in Figure 8-1.
4. Tap the Add Account button to display the Add Account screen, shown on the right in Figure 8-1.
5. If the Add Account screen shows your e-mail provider, touch its button. Otherwise, tap the Other button. You can't see the Other button in Figure 8-1, but you'll find it at the bottom of your screen.

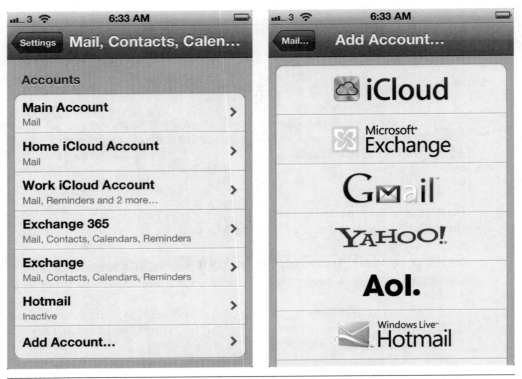

FIGURE 8-1 From the Mail, Contacts, Calendars screen (left), tap the Add Account button to reach the Add Account screen (right). If your e-mail provider is listed here, touch it; if not, tap the Other button.

6. On the resulting screen, enter the details for the connection. Most of the mail screens look like the Gmail screen shown on the left in Figure 8-2, and you enter the following information:
   - **Name** This is the name that your e-mail messages will be sent from—for example, your real name, or a variation of it.
   - **Address** This is the e-mail address for the account.
   - **Password** This is the password for the e-mail account.
   - **Description** This is the name under which the account appears on the iPhone. The more e-mail accounts you have on your iPhone, the more helpful an explicit description is.
7. Tap the Next button. The iPhone verifies the account information.
8. If the account offers different features—for example, contacts, calendars, or notes—the iPhone displays a screen with switches for choosing which you want to use, as shown on the right in Figure 8-2.
9. Move each switch to the On position or the Off position, as needed.

FIGURE 8-2   On the screen for setting up your e-mail account (left), enter your name, address, and other required information. When the iPhone has set up the account (right), move the switches to choose which services to use.

10. If your iPhone prompts you to decide whether to keep your existing local calendars (as shown here) or contacts when you move a switch to the On position, tap the Keep On My iPhone button or the Delete button, as appropriate.

11. When you finish setting up the account, tap the Save button to save your settings. The e-mail account then appears on the Mail, Contacts, Calendars screen.

 When you set up an account using the Other screen, your iPhone tries to automatically detect the names of the mail servers and the settings required to access them. If your iPhone prompts you for additional information to set up the account, provide it. If you don't already have the information, you'll need to ask your e-mail provider.

You're now ready to send and receive e-mail using this e-mail account. But while you're at the Mail, Contacts, Calendars screen, let's look quickly at some of the configuration options you may want to set.

Configure Mail Settings

When you set up an e-mail account, your iPhone automatically applies standard settings to it. These settings work fine for many people, but you may want to change some of them. These settings apply to all the e-mail accounts you've set up on your iPhone: You can't apply them to one account but not to another.

These settings appear on the Mail, Contacts, Calendars screen below the list of your e-mail accounts. The left screen in Figure 8-3 shows the first section of settings. The right screen in Figure 8-3 shows the second section.

FIGURE 8-3 It's worth spending a few minutes examining the mail settings on the Mail, Contacts, Calendars screen (both left and right) in case the defaults cause you grief.

How to...

Control When and How Your iPhone Gets New Data

Your iPhone can receive e-mail and other updated data in two ways:

- **Push** The server "pushes" out the data to your iPhone as soon as the data becomes available.
- **Fetch** Your iPhone checks in with the server for new data, either at specified intervals or whenever you choose to check manually.

If you need to receive your e-mail urgently, and your e-mail provider offers Push, you'll probably want to use Push. Otherwise, you can use Fetch and set a short interval. Your iPhone falls back on Fetch if you've set it to use Push but Push isn't available.

To control how and when your iPhone gets new data, follow these steps:

1. On the Mail, Contacts, Calendars screen, tap the Fetch New Data button to display the Fetch New Data screen, shown on the left in the next illustration.

2. To use Push, tap the Push switch and move it to the On position. If you don't want to use Push, make sure the Push switch is in the Off position.
3. In the Fetch box, tap the timing you want: Every 15 Minutes, Every 30 Minutes, Hourly, or Manually. The only disadvantage to checking frequently is that it uses battery power.
4. If you want to use Push for some accounts and Fetch for others, tap the Advanced button at the bottom of the screen to display the Advanced screen (shown on the right in the first illustration in this sidebar). From here, tap the

(Continued)

account you want to configure to display its settings screen (shown here), and then tap the Push button, the Fetch button, or the Manual button, as needed.

Tap the Advanced button to return to the Advanced screen, tap the Fetch New Data button to go back to the Fetch New Data screen, and then tap the Mail, Contacts, Calendars button to reach the Mail, Contacts, Calendars screen.

Here's what you need to know about the Mail settings:

- **Show**   Controls how many recent messages Mail shows. Your choices are 50 Recent Messages, 100 Recent Messages, 200 Recent Messages, 500 Recent Messages, or 1,000 Recent Messages.
- **Preview**   Controls how many lines of the message Mail shows as a preview. Your choices are None, 1 Line, 2 Lines, 3 Lines, 4 Lines, or 5 Lines.
- **Minimum Font Size**   Controls the smallest font size used. Your choices are Small, Medium (the default), Large, Extra Large, or Giant.
- **Show To/Cc Label**   Controls whether Mail automatically shows the To label for a message (and the Cc label, if there is one) when you open the message. Move the switch to the On position or the Off position, as appropriate. You can display these labels manually by tapping the Details button to the right of the sender's name. Hiding the labels lets you see more of the message onscreen at once.
- **Ask Before Deleting**   Controls whether Mail prompts you to confirm each deletion of an e-mail message. Some people find the confirmation handy, while others find it irritating. Again, move the switch to the On position or the Off position, as appropriate.

If you delete a message and then wish you hadn't, you can usually retrieve it from the Trash and move it back to your Inbox or another folder. Open the Trash folder and tap the Move button (the button with the folder on it) to display the list of folders for the mail account. Tap the destination folder.

- **Load Remote Images** Controls whether Mail automatically loads images stored on remote servers. The problem with remote images is that the technically savvy can use them to learn not only when you open the message that requests the remote image but also your IP address and approximate geographical location.

If you choose not to load remote images, the missing images appear as placeholders in your messages. You can tap a placeholder to display its image— preferably after checking that the message is wholesome.

- **Organize By Thread** Controls whether Mail organizes your messages into threads, which are also called *conversations*. For example, if you send a message to Bill, and he replies, you reply, he replies, and so forth, those messages are a single thread or conversation. When you move the Organize By Thread switch to the On position, Mail displays the thread as a single item in your Inbox with a number showing how many messages the thread contains, as shown on the left in Figure 8-4. You then tap the thread to display a screen showing its messages, as shown on the right in Figure 8-4. From there, you tap the message you want to open.
- **Always Bcc Myself** Controls whether Mail automatically sends a blind carbon copy (one that the other recipients of the message can't see) to your e-mail address. On some e-mail systems, this is a convenient way of keeping copies of messages you send. Other e-mail systems provide a more sensible way of keeping copies, such as a Sent Items folder.
- **Increase Quote Level** Controls whether Mail automatically indents the content of replies and forwarded messages further to indicate its status. This behavior is usually helpful, and this setting is on by default. To turn it off, tap the Increase Quote Level button, then move the Increase Quote Level switch on the Increase Quote Level screen to the Off position. Tap the Mail, Contacts, Calendars button to return to the Mail, Contacts, Calendars screen.
- **Signature** Lets you set up text that Mail adds automatically to each new message you create. The iPhone's default signature is "Sent from my iPhone." This is cute for the first couple of messages but not great for long-term use. (For example, you may not want your colleagues to know that you're actually working from the beach today.) To change the signature, tap the Signature bar, and then use the Signature screen (shown on the left in Figure 8-5) to compose a signature; alternatively, simply tap the Clear button to clear the current signature so that you can type whatever sign-off you want to use. Tap the Mail, Contacts, Calendars button when you've finished.
- **Default Account** Controls which e-mail account Mail uses when you send a photo or a note (both discussed later in this chapter). If you've set up only one account, that will be the default account. If you've set up two or more, check the

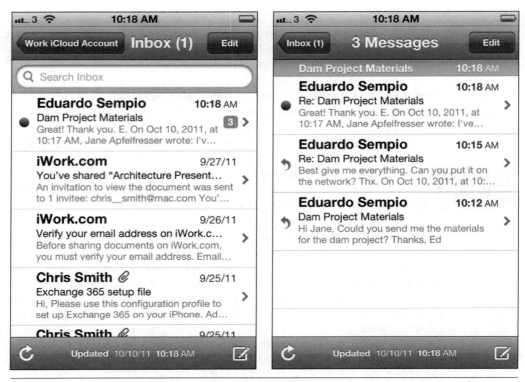

FIGURE 8-4 When you turn on the Organize By Thread switch, each thread or conversation appears as a single item in your Inbox, with a number showing how many messages it contains (left). Tap the thread to display its messages (right).

readout. If it shows the wrong account, tap the Default Account bar to display the Default Account screen (shown on the right in Figure 8-5), tap the account you want to use as the default, and then tap the Mail, Contacts, Calendars button.

When you've finished choosing mail settings, tap the Settings button to return to the Settings screen.

Send E-Mail

To send e-mail, follow these steps:

1. Press the Home button to go to the Home screen unless you're already there.
2. Tap the Mail icon to display the Mail app.
3. If Mail displays the Mailboxes screen, tap the account you want to use.
4. Tap the Compose button in the lower-right corner of the window (see the left screen in Figure 8-6). Mail starts a new message from this account (see the

FIGURE 8-5   You'll almost certainly want to customize your e-mail signature (left). And if you set up two or more e-mail accounts on your iPhone, it's vital to make sure the correct one is set as the default.

right screen in Figure 8-6). If you chose in the settings to use a signature, Mail adds it to the end of the message for you.

5. Address the message:
   - If the recipient is in your Contacts list, tap the + button at the right end of the To line to display the Contacts screen. Tap the contact to add them to the To line.
   - Otherwise, type the e-mail address. If Mail finds matches for what you type, it displays a menu showing them. You can then tap the entry you want.

To remove one of the recipients you've added, backspace over the name. The first backspace selects the address, and the second deletes it.

6. If you need to add Cc recipients, tap the "Cc/Bcc, From" to display the Cc and Bcc lines, as shown here. Then add the address or addresses using the same techniques as in the previous step.

Stop Your iPhone from Checking a Particular E-Mail Account

Sometimes you may need to prevent your iPhone from checking a particular e-mail account—for example, when you go on vacation and can leave your business e-mail to pile up for a few days. To do so, follow these steps:

1. Press the Home button to go to the Home screen unless you're already there.
2. Tap the Settings icon to display the Settings screen.
3. Scroll down, and then tap the Mail, Contacts, Calendars button to display the Mail, Contacts, Calendars screen.
4. Tap the name of the e-mail account you want to switch off. The contents of the screen that appears depend on the type of account, but the next illustration shows a couple of examples.

5. Tap the Mail switch or the Account switch and move it to the Off position.
6. Tap the Mail, Contacts, Calendars button in the upper-left corner to go back to the Mail, Contacts, Calendars screen.

When you want to start checking your e-mail again, repeat these steps, but move the switch to the On position.

7. Add the subject line. Tap the Subject field, and then type the text.
8. Add the message content. Tap in the text area, and then type the text.

If you realize that you've started the e-mail message from the wrong e-mail account, don't worry—all is not yet lost. Tap the From field to display a spin wheel of your e-mail accounts, tap the account you want to use, and then tap elsewhere in the message to apply the change.

9. Tap the Send button.

Compose
button

FIGURE 8-6   Tap the Compose button (left) to start a new message (right) from the e-mail account you've selected.

Send Photographs via E-Mail

You can send a photo that you've either taken on your iPhone or loaded onto your iPhone. Follow these steps:

1. Press the Home button to go to the Home screen unless you're already there.
2. Tap the Photos icon to display the Albums screen.

 If you're taking photos with the camera, you can start directly from there. Open the Camera Roll album, and then open the photo.

3. Tap the album that contains the photo, and then tap the photo to open it.
4. Tap the Actions button in the lower-left corner of the screen, and then tap the Email Photo button in the Actions dialog box that opens (shown on the left in

How to... Save a Draft Message

Sometimes you may need to stop writing a message for now, and then complete it later. When this happens, you can save a message as a draft. To save a message as a draft, follow these steps:

1. Tap the Cancel button. Your iPhone displays the dialog box shown here.
2. Tap the Save Draft button. Mail saves the message in your Drafts folder. (If the Drafts folder doesn't yet exist, Mail creates it.)

You can quickly reopen the last draft message you were working on by simply tapping and holding the Compose button in Mail. To open an older draft message, go to the Drafts mailbox for the account, and then tap the message:

1. Tap the Mailboxes button in the upper-left corner of the screen to display the Mailboxes screen.
2. In the Accounts box, tap the account you were using when you created the draft. The list of folders for that account appears.
3. Tap the Drafts button. The Drafts folder opens, showing the list of draft messages.
4. Tap the message you want to open.

Figure 8-7). Mail starts a new message including the photo, as shown on the right in Figure 8-7.

5. Address the message, type the subject line, type any text that's needed, and then tap the Send button.
6. If Mail displays a dialog box suggesting you may want to send a smaller version of the photo, as shown here, tap the button for the size you want.

When sending a photo, use the Small size only when you expect the recipient to view or use the picture at a small size—for example, if you're sending a headshot for use as a contact photo. Use

FIGURE 8-7 You can send a photo from the Photos app or the Camera app by tapping the Actions button and then tapping the Email Photo button in the Actions dialog box (left). Mail creates a new message containing the photo (right).

the Medium size for photos you expect the recipient to view in e-mail or use on a web page. Use the Large size when the recipient needs to use the picture at a larger size—for example, printing it. Use the Actual Size option when the recipient will work with the photo—for example, editing it.

Send a Note via E-Mail

If you create notes in your iPhone's Notes app, you can quickly share them via e-mail. To share a note, follow these steps:

1. In the Notes app, open the note you want to share.
2. Tap the Actions button to display the Actions dialog box.
3. Tap the Email button. Notes causes Mail to create an e-mail message

Tell Siri to...

Send E-mail Messages for You

When you need to write and send an e-mail message using only the power of your lungs, tell Siri to create the message for you.

Here are examples of what you can say to create an e-mail message:

- "E-mail Bill about the missing chapter."
- "New e-mail to Ricki Mason."
- "Mail my wife about picking up the kids from camp."
- "Mail Dave about the meeting and say both Jane and I will be there."

How Siri responds depends on what you've said (and how Siri has interpreted it). For example, if you give only the addressee, Siri asks you for the message's subject and then the message's content. If you give the addressee and the subject, Siri asks you for the content. And if you manage to give addressee, subject, and content (as in the "Mail Dave..." example above), Siri provides you with a message ready for sending. You can then send it by saying "Send" or tapping the Send button.

When you've opened a message, you can compose a reply quickly. For example:

- "Reply Dear Bill comma new line thanks for the project documentation period new line best comma Ed."
- "Call Donna on her mobile."
- "Send Crisis Cars a text saying we need the van at noon."

containing the text of the note. Mail enters the note's name (the first line) in the subject line.

4. Address the message, amend the subject line as needed, type any explanation the recipient will benefit from, and then tap the Send button.

Send Other Files via E-Mail

You can also send other files via e-mail by using the same general technique:

1. Open the file in an app that can handle it.
2. Tap the Tools button, Actions button, or Share button.
3. Tap the button for e-mailing the document.

The specifics vary depending on the app. Here are two examples:

- **Pages**   In Apple's Pages app, you can send a file via e-mail like this:
    1. Tap the Tools button to display the Tools screen.
    2. Tap the Share And Print button to display the Share And Print screen.
    3. Tap the Email Document button to display the Email Document screen.
    4. Tap the button for the file format you want to send: Pages, PDF, or Word. Pages then transfers the appropriate file to a new message in Mail.

- **FileApp Pro**   In the third-party app FileApp Pro, you can send a file via e-mail like this:
    1. Tap the Actions button in the lower-left corner to display the Actions dialog box.
    2. Tap the Email Document button. FileApp causes Mail to create a new message with the file attached.

Receive E-Mails and Attachments

Sending e-mail is only half the fun. You'll almost certainly receive it as well. To check, review, and deal with e-mail, follow these steps:

1. Press the Home button to go to the Home screen unless you're already there.
2. Tap the Mail icon to go to Mail. The Mailboxes screen shows how many new messages each Inbox contains, as shown on the left in Figure 8-8.
3. In the Inboxes box, tap the All Inboxes button if you want to view all your Inboxes together. If you prefer to deal with your messages by accounts, tap the Inbox you want to display. Mail displays the Inbox or Inboxes. The right screen in Figure 8-8 shows an individual Inbox open.
4. Tap the message you want to view. Your iPhone displays its contents. The left screen in Figure 8-9 shows a message. The right screen in Figure 8-9 shows an example of a message with attachments.

 To open an attached file, tap its button. At first, Mail opens it in one of the iPhone's built-in file viewers, which lets you see the file's contents. To open the file in another app, tap the Action button in the upper-right corner, and then tap the app in the dialog box that opens. To return from the viewer to the message, tap the Message button in the upper-left corner of the screen.

5. To reply to the message or forward it, tap the button with the left-pointing arrow at the bottom of the screen, and then tap the Reply button or the Forward button in the dialog box that opens. Write the required text, address the message if you're forwarding it, and then tap the Send button.
6. To delete the message, tap the Delete button in the middle of the row at the bottom of the screen.

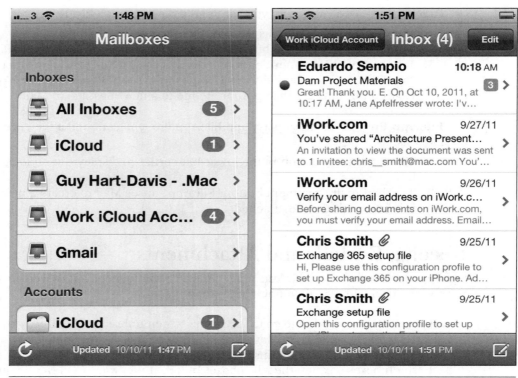

FIGURE 8-8 Mail lets you see at a glance how many messages are in each account (left). Tap the button in the lower-left corner to check for new messages. Tap the All Inboxes button to view all your Inboxes together, or tap an individual mailbox to display its contents (right).

Tell Siri to...

Check Your E-mail Messages for You

You can have Siri check your e-mail messages for you and even ask for messages from particular contacts. Here are examples:

- "Check my e-mail."
- "Show me yesterday's e-mail from Howie."
- "Any new messages from Janet today?"

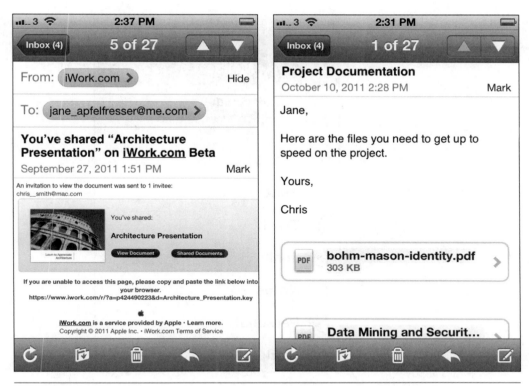

FIGURE 8-9   Tap the message you want to open. If the message contains attachments, they appear as buttons in the message text (right).

7. To file the message, tap the Move button, the button with the folder on it. Mail displays the list of folders for the mail account, as shown in Figure 8-10. Tap the destination folder. Mail moves the message there, and then displays the next message in the Inbox (if there is one).

8. To move through the messages, tap the Up button or the Down button in the upper-right corner of the screen.

9. To return to your Inbox, tap the Inbox button or the All Inboxes button in the upper-left corner of the screen.

Get Through Your Inbox Quickly by Using Batch Editing

So far, we've looked at dealing with individual messages. But if you get a lot of e-mail, you can save time by using Mail's batch-editing feature. This works much like batch

FIGURE 8-10 To remove a message from your Inbox without deleting it, file it in one of the folders for the mail account.

editing in e-mail programs on Windows or the Mac: You select the messages you want to affect, and then take a single action on all of them.

To use batch editing, follow these steps:

1. Open the folder that contains the messages you want to manipulate. For example, open an Inbox.
2. Tap the Edit button in the upper-right corner to turn on Edit mode. An empty selection button appears to the left of each message, and three buttons—the Delete button, the Move button, and the Mark button—appear across the bottom of the screen. The left screen in Figure 8-11 shows an Inbox in normal mode. The right screen in Figure 8-11 shows the Inbox in Edit mode.
3. Tap the selection button to the left of each message you want to work with. Mail displays a red circle containing a white check mark in the selection button. Mail also updates the three buttons across the bottom of the screen with the total number of messages selected—for example, the Delete button shows "Delete (2)."

How to...

Mark an E-Mail Message as Unread, or Flag a Message

When you receive an e-mail message, it is marked as Unread and appears with a blue dot to its left. When you display the message, Mail marks it as Read, so you can easily see which messages you've read and which you haven't.

Sometimes it's handy to mark a message as Unread even though you've already opened it. To mark a message as Unread, follow these steps:

1. Open the message.
2. On the right side of the From line, tap the Details link to display the Details area.
3. On the right side of the subject line, tap the Mark link to display the dialog box shown here.
4. Tap the Mark As Unread button.

From this dialog box, you can also flag a message by tapping the Flag button. For example, you might flag the messages you need to deal with most urgently.

After you flag a message, you can unflag it by tapping the Mark link, and then tapping the Unflag button in the dialog box.

Similarly, you can mark a message as Read by tapping the Mark link, and then tapping the Mark As Read button in the dialog box. But often it's easier simply to open the message and have Mail mark the message as Read for you automatically as usual.

4. Perform the operation you want. For example, tap the Move button to display the Mailboxes screen, and then tap the mailbox you want to put the selected messages in.

Organize Your Mail Folders

For most e-mail accounts, you can create new mail folders and delete existing ones as needed.

To work with folders, first open the account whose folders you want to change. Follow these steps:

1. Go to the Mailboxes screen. For example, if you're working in an Inbox, tap the Mailboxes button in the upper-right corner.
2. In the Accounts box, tap the account. The list of folders appears.

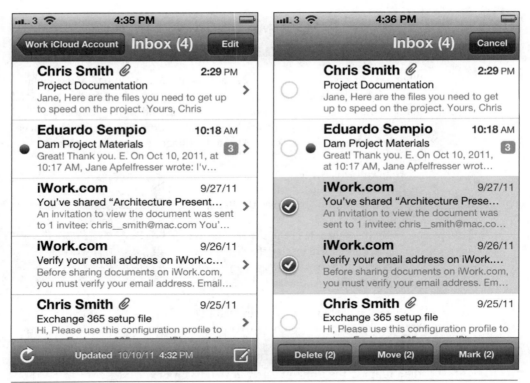

FIGURE 8-11 Tap the Edit button in the upper-right corner of the screen (left) to turn on Edit mode (right).

Create a New Folder

To create a new folder, follow these steps from the list of folders:

1. Tap the Edit button in the upper-right corner to turn on Edit mode. The left screen in Figure 8-12 shows a folder in Edit mode.
2. Tap the New Mailbox button to display the Edit Mailbox screen (shown on the right in Figure 8-12).
3. Type the name for the new folder.
4. If the Mailbox Location button shows the folder you want to put the new folder in, you're set. Otherwise, tap the Mailbox Location button to display the Mailbox Location screen, tap the folder you want to put the new folder in, and then tap the Edit Mailbox button to go back to the Edit Mailbox screen.
5. Tap the Save button. Mail saves the new folder.

Change or Delete an Existing Folder

To change or delete an existing folder, follow these steps from the list of folders:

How to... Avoid Dangerous Links in E-Mail Messages

Spam and phishing e-mail messages often contain links that go to different websites than the messages claim. For example, in a phishing message that claims to come from eBay, a Sign In link might appear to go to eBay, but in fact would steer your browser to a copycat attack site on the lawless side of the virtual tracks.

One way to avoid following a dangerous link in an e-mail message is simply not to tap *any* link in an e-mail message. But if you use your iPhone for genuine e-mail rather than solely for enjoying spam, phishing, and other malevolent e-mail, you probably won't find this practical.

To see the URL to which a link in an e-mail message points, tap and hold the link until Mail displays the Actions dialog box (shown here) with a button for each action you can take with the link. The URL appears at the top. You can then tap the Open button if it's safe to open the link, tap the Copy button if you want to store the URL or share it with someone, or tap the Cancel button to stop opening it.

1. Tap the Edit button in the upper-right corner to turn on Edit mode.
2. Tap the folder to display the Edit Mailbox screen, the top half of which is shown here.
3. Change the folder as needed:

   - If you want to change the folder's name, edit it on the name button at the top of the screen.
   - To change the folder that holds this folder, tap the Mailbox Location button to display the Mailbox Location screen, tap the folder you want to put this folder in, and then tap the Edit Mailbox button to go back to the Edit Mailbox screen.
   - To delete the folder, tap the Delete Mailbox button, and then tap the Delete Mailbox button in the confirmation dialog box that opens.
4. If you changed the folder's name, location, or both, tap the Save button to save your changes.
5. Tap the Done button to turn off Edit mode.

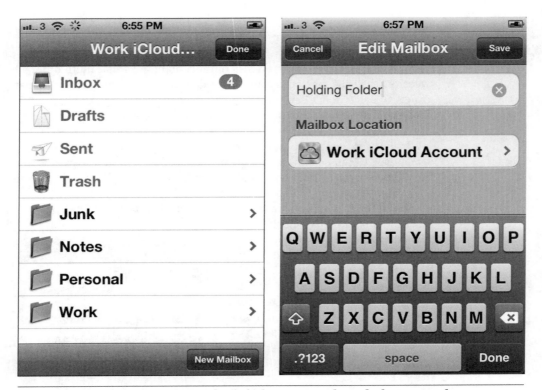

FIGURE 8-12 Turn on Edit mode (left) by tapping the Edit button in the upper-right corner of the screen. Then tap the New Mailbox button and use the Edit Mailbox screen (right) to name and locate the new folder.

Communicate via Instant Messaging

When you need to communicate instantly with a contact, you can send an instant message. This section shows you how to use your iPhone's capabilities to send either text messages or multimedia messages.

Understand SMS, MMS, and iMessage

Your iPhone can send either text-only messages (SMS, or Short Message Service) or MMS (Multimedia Messaging Service). For text messages, it can use either the cellular service or Apple's iMessage service.

- **SMS** An SMS message can contain up to 160 characters. Your iPhone can display the current character count to help you avoid running long.
- **MMS** An MMS message can contain a picture or video as well as text. You can start an MMS message from an existing photo or video, or you can start a message

and then add a photo or video to it. You can add either an existing photo or video or one that you capture on the spot.

 Sending MMS messages containing large photos or videos can chew through your data plan very quickly.

- **iMessage**   iMessage is a text-messaging service available to anyone using an iPhone running iOS 5, the latest version of the iPhone, iPad, and iPod touch operating system. iMessage is free when your iPhone is using a Wi-Fi network, so you can send text messages to any iPhone, iPad, or iPod touch user without eating away at your data plan.

Send a Text Message

To send a text message, follow these steps:

1. Press the Home button to display the Home screen.
2. Tap the Messages icon to display the Messages app. At first, you see a list of messages you've received, as shown in the left screen in Figure 8-13.

FIGURE 8-13   Tap the Compose Message button in the upper-right corner of the Messages screen (left) to start a new instant message (right).

3. Tap the Compose Message button in the upper-right corner to start a new message, as shown in the right screen in Figure 8-13.

4. Address the message:
   - If the recipient is in your Contacts list, tap the + button at the right end of the To line to display the Contacts screen. Tap the contact to add them to the To line.
   - Otherwise, type the contact's name, phone number, or e-mail address. If Messages finds matches for what you type, it displays a menu showing them. You can then tap the entry you want.

5. Tap in the Text Message box, and then type the message. If you turned on the Character Count feature, Messages shows the number of characters as soon as the text wraps to a second line, as shown here.

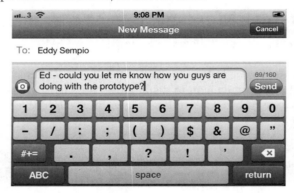

6. When you finish writing the message, tap the Send button to send it.

Tell Siri to...

Send, Read, and Reply to Texts for You

Siri is great for handling your text messages. Here are examples of asking Siri to send text messages:

- "Tell the big boss I'll be there by noon."
- "Send a text to Paula on her iPhone saying the keys are in the safe."
- "Tell Lex that our team did great at the meeting."
- "Send a text message to Pete saying get your six to the conference room."

You can also ask Siri to check your texts for you and quickly reply to them:

- "Check my messages."
- "Siri, what new messages have I got?"
- "Read my messages."
- "Read it again."
- "Reply you need to keep your head down."
- "Tell her there's a hundred bucks in the emergency drawer."

Send a Picture or Video in a Message

You can send a picture or video in either an MMS message or an iMessage message. To send a picture or video, follow these steps:

1. Start and address the text message as described in the previous section.
2. When you're ready to add the picture or video, tap the Camera button to the left of the text box. Messages displays the dialog box shown here.
3. Tap the appropriate button, and then take or select the photo or video:
   - **Take Photo Or Video**   Tap this button to launch the Camera app. You can then take a photograph or video using the camera as normal. After you take it, the Camera app displays a Preview screen. Tap the Retake button if you want to try to improve the photo or video, or tap the Use button to add the photo or video to the message.

 After adding a photo or video to the message, you can delete the photo or video by backspacing over it.

   - **Choose Existing**   Tap this button to display the Photos app. You can then tap the photo or video you want. After you choose it, the Photos app displays a Preview screen. Tap the Cancel button if you want to pick another photo or video, or tap the Choose button to use the photo or video you've chosen.

4. Add any text needed to the message, and then tap the Send button to send it.

Send a Location in a Text Message

After finding a location in the Maps app, you can share it with others by using a text message. To do so, follow these steps:

1. Tap and hold to drop a pin on the location.
2. Tap the > button on the pin to display the Info screen.
3. Tap the Share Location button to display the Share Location Using dialog box.
4. Tap the Message button to start a text message containing the location.
5. Address the message, add any text needed, and then tap the Send button to send it.

Receive an Instant Message

When you receive an instant message, your iPhone plays the ringtone set for texts or vibrates if you've turned off sound. The text appears in a dialog box on the lock screen if the iPhone is locked, as shown on the left in Figure 8-14. If you're on the Home screen or working in an app, the text appears on a notification bar across the top of the screen, as shown in the next illustration.

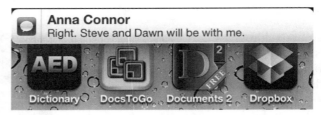

When you open the Messages app, the messages between you and your contact appear as a conversation, as shown on the right in Figure 8-14.

 To change the ringtone your iPhone plays when you receive a text message, choose Settings | Sounds to display the Sounds screen. Tap the Text Tone button to display the Text Tone screen, and then tap the alert tone or ringtone you want.

FIGURE 8-14 Your iPhone displays incoming text messages on the lock screen (left). In the Messages app, the text messages between you and your contact appear as a conversation (right).

Messages sent over the cellular network appear in green balloons in the conversation. Messages sent via iMessage appear in blue balloons.

If you receive a message that contains a picture or a video, tap the picture or video to open it for viewing. If you want to keep the picture or video, tap the Action button in the lower-left corner, and then tap the Save Image button or the Save Video button in the Actions dialog box.

Edit or Clear a Conversation

Sometimes you may want to keep some of the messages in a conversation but get rid of others. To do this, open the conversation, and then tap the Edit button. Messages displays a selection button to the left of each message and displays the Delete button and the Forward button across the bottom of the screen. You can then tap the selection buttons to select the message or messages you want (see the left screen in Figure 8-15), and then tap the Delete button to delete them or the Forward button to forward them.

To clear the whole conversation, open the conversation, tap the Edit button, tap the Clear All button, and then tap the Clear Conversation button in the dialog box that opens (see the right screen in Figure 8-15).

Delete Messages from the Messages List

To delete one or more messages from the Messages list, follow these steps:

1. On the Messages screen, tap the Edit button. Messages displays a round Delete button (a red circle with a white horizontal bar across it) to the left of each message.
2. Tap the round Delete button for the message you want to delete. Messages displays a rectangular Delete button to the right of the message, as shown here.
3. Tap the rectangular Delete button. Messages deletes the message.
4. Delete other messages as needed.
5. Tap the Done button to turn off Edit mode.

 You can quickly delete a single message from the Messages list without turning on Edit mode. Swipe your finger across the message from left to right to display the rectangular Delete button, and then tap that button.

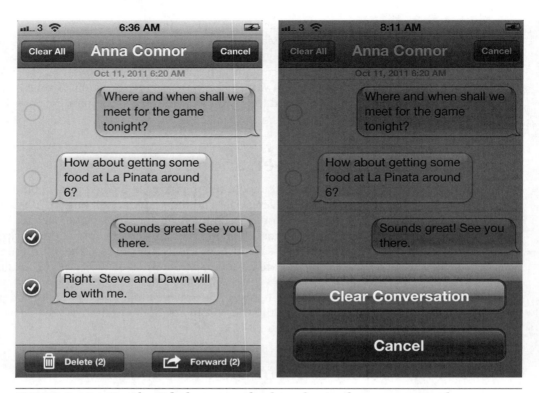

FIGURE 8-15 Tap the Edit button to display selection buttons next to the messages. You can then choose messages to delete or forward (left). To get rid of the whole conversation, tap the Clear All button, and then tap the Clear Conversation button (right).

Choose Settings for Messages

Your iPhone comes with default settings for messaging that work pretty well for many people. But if you use messaging extensively, you'll probably want to set the settings the way you prefer.

To choose settings for Messages, first open the Messages settings screen like this:

1. Press the Home button to display the Home screen unless you're already there.
2. Tap the Settings icon to display the Settings screen.
3. Scroll down to the third box, and then tap the Messages button to display the Messages settings screen. The left screen in Figure 8-16 shows the upper part of the Messages settings screen. The right screen in Figure 8-16 shows the lower part of the Messages settings screen.

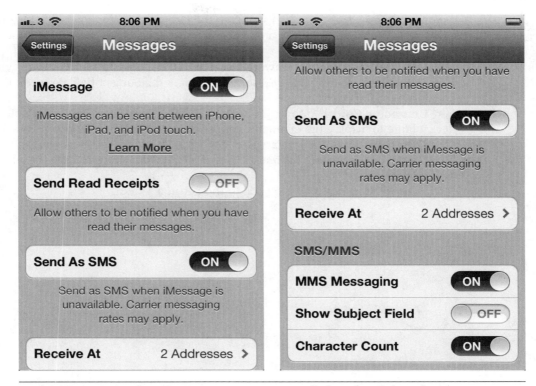

FIGURE 8-16   On the Messages settings screen (left and right), make sure iMessage is turned on, and then choose settings for sending instant messages.

4. Tap the iMessage switch and move it to the Off position if you don't want to use iMessage. For most people, iMessage is helpful, so you'll probably want to leave it on.

5. If you want people who send you instant messages to receive notifications when you read their messages, tap the Send Read Receipts switch and move it to the On position. This switch is set to Off by default to protect your privacy.

6. If you want your iPhone to send SMS messages automatically when iMessage is unavailable, make sure the Send As SMS switch is set to the On position. Turning this feature on makes sure that your messages will go through even if iMessage is unavailable (at least, assuming that your iPhone can get cellular service), but it will eat up your text allowance.

7. To choose which addresses your iPhone receives iMessage instant messages at, tap the Receive At button, and then work on the iMessage screen that appears. You can add other e-mail addresses by tapping the Add Another Email button.

8. In the SMS/MMS box, choose suitable settings for your needs:

- **MMS Messaging**   Set this switch to the On position if you want to be able to use MMS messaging. If you want to use only SMS messaging, set this switch to the Off position.
- **Show Subject Field**   Move this switch to the On position if you want your SMS messages and MMS messages to display the Subject field. You can then enter a subject line in this field.
- **Character Count**   Move this switch to the On position if you want your iPhone to display the character count while you're writing a text message. The character count appears above the Send button as soon as your message starts a second line. This feature helps you avoid writing messages that are too long.

9. Tap the Settings button to go back to the Settings screen.

9

Surf the Web on Your iPhone

HOW TO...

- Launch the Safari app
- Go to a web page by typing or pasting its address
- Follow links and return to web pages you've visited before
- Search for information
- Use bookmarks to store addresses and navigate quickly
- Read web pages more easily with Safari Reader
- Open multiple web pages at the same time
- Configure how you want Safari to work
- Surf secretly with Private Browsing

In this chapter, you'll learn how to surf the Web using the Safari browser app that comes with your iPhone. If you take your iPhone with you (as seems likely), it'll be always at hand when you need to look up information on the Web, connecting either through a wireless network or through the cellular network. And although the iPhone's screen is too small to display much of a web page at a time, Apple has built into Safari various features and tricks that make it easy to view, zoom, scroll, and navigate web pages.

We'll start by launching the Safari app and meeting its user interface. After that, we'll move on to getting to a web page first the hard way—by typing in its address—and then by using the easier ways that Safari offers. You'll learn how to return to web pages you've visited before, use the handy Safari Reader feature to make web pages more readable, and open multiple web pages at the same time and navigate among them. I'll also show you how to configure Safari so that it works the way you prefer and how to turn on the Private Browsing feature so that you can surf the Web without Safari recording the pages you visit.

Launch the Safari App

First, launch the Safari app. Follow these steps:

1. Press the Home button to go to the Home screen unless you're already there.
2. Tap the Safari icon at the bottom of the screen.

Safari opens. If this is the first time you've run Safari, it displays the Bookmarks screen (shown on the left in Figure 9-1) so that you can quickly go to a web page. For example, tap the News button on the Bookmarks screen to display the News screen (shown on the right in Figure 9-1), and then tap the New York Times button to display the *New York Times* website.

If you've run Safari before, it automatically loads the last web page you had open.

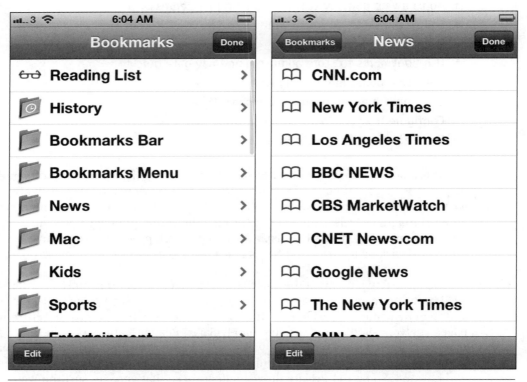

FIGURE 9-1 From the Bookmarks screen (left), you can tap a Bookmarks category to display the bookmarks it contains—for example, the News category (right). Then tap the bookmark for the web page you want to open.

FIGURE 9-2   The Safari browser with a web page open.

Meet the Safari Interface

When you have opened a web page, you'll see the elements of the Safari interface. Figure 9-2 shows these items with labels.

Here's what you need to know about the items shown in Figure 9-2:

- **Web page title**   This bar shows the title of the web page. The title is the name or other descriptive text that whoever created the web page added to identify it.
- **Address box**   This box shows the address, or URL, of the current web page. When you're holding your iPhone in portrait (vertical) orientation, there often isn't space for the whole URL in the Address box. When the iPhone is in landscape (horizontal) orientation, the Address box is wider, and the URL has a better chance of fitting in it.
- **Refresh button**   This button appears at the right end of the Address box. You can tap this button to refresh the information on the current web page—for example, to update the prices on the sports betting site you're using in defiance of your company, your spouse, the laws of probability, and your common sense.

While a web page is loading, a Stop (×) button takes the place of the Refresh button. You can tap this button to stop the web page from loading—for example, because it has gotten stuck halfway.

- **Search box**   Tap in this box and type one or more terms for which you want to search. We'll look at how to search for information in the section "Search for Information," later in this chapter.
- **Web page**   This area displays the contents of the web page.
- **Back button**   Tap this button to display the previous web page that was open on this particular page. You can tap multiple times to move back along the chain of web pages that you've browsed on this Safari page. (Other Safari pages you open have their own chain of web pages as well.)
- **Forward button**   Tap this button to display the previous web page from which you went back to a previous page by tapping the Back button. Until you've used the Back button to go back, this button is unavailable.
- **Action button**   Tap this button to display a dialog box showing commands you can take with this web page or the current item. You'll see this dialog box in action later in this chapter.
- **Bookmarks button**   Tap this button to display the Bookmarks screen. You'll learn how to work with the Bookmarks screen later in this chapter.
- **Pages button**   Tap this button to display each open page as a thumbnail, so that you can see how many pages you have open, close any pages you no longer need, and display the page you want to view. You'll learn how to work with pages later in this chapter.

Learn How to Zoom and Scroll

As you can see in Figure 9-2, a full-size web page tends to be too small to read on the iPhone's screen. To view it, you need to zoom and scroll.

- **Zoom**   Either pinch out with your fingers (or a finger and thumb) on the area you want to zoom in on, or double-tap a point to zoom in quickly on it. Pinch back in or double-tap again to zoom back out.
- **Scroll**   Flick your finger in the direction in which you want to move the page— up, down, left, right, or diagonally. For example, if you want to view part of the page that's further down, flick your finger up the screen to move the page up.

 Depending on their layout, some web pages are easier to read in landscape orientation, while others are easier to read in portrait orientation. If the page is hard to read in whichever orientation you're using, try turning your iPhone to see if it looks better the other way around.

Go to a Website by Typing or Pasting Its Address

As you saw a moment ago, you can use the Bookmarks screen to navigate quickly to a web page. We'll look at how to create and manage your bookmarks later in this chapter.

You can also go to a website by typing or pasting its URL into the Address box like this:

1. Tap in the Address box. Safari displays the onscreen keyboard and places an × button at the right end of the Address box.
2. If you want to delete the current URL, tap the × button. Otherwise, tap where you want to start editing the current URL. Safari displays a pop-up bar containing the Select button, Select All button, and Paste button, as shown here.

3. Change the URL as needed. For example, tap the Backspace key to delete part of the URL, and then type the new URL.

 As you type, Safari suggests matching addresses. If Safari suggests the correct address, tap the address's entry to display that web page.

4. If you need to add the .com domain to the end of the URL, tap the .com button on the onscreen keyboard. If you need to add another widely used domain, tap and hold the .com button, and then tap the appropriate button on the pop-up panel (shown here).

Share a Web Page's Address via E-Mail

When you find a web page that you want to share with someone else via e-mail, follow these steps:

1. Tap the Action button on the toolbar. Your iPhone displays the Share dialog box (shown here).
2. Tap the Mail Link To This Page button. Safari makes Mail create a new e-mail message with the web page's title as its subject line and a link to the web page's address in the body of the message.
3. Address the message.
4. Change the subject line as needed.
5. Add any explanatory text to help the recipient.
6. Tap the Send button to send the message.

5. Tap the Go button to display the web page.

Tip If you find it hard to type a long URL accurately on the iPhone's keyboard, rotate the iPhone to landscape view to display the keyboard at a larger size.

Follow Links and Return to Web Pages You've Visited Before

When browsing, you'll often want to follow links from one web page to another. Most likely, you'll also want to return to web pages you've visited earlier in your browsing session. Safari makes both of these easy to do.

Follow Links Using the Same Page or a Different Page

The quickest way to follow a link is to tap it on the web page that contains it. Safari opens the destination web page in place of the web page you were viewing.

Often, it's helpful to open the destination web page in a separate page from the web page you're viewing. To do this, tap and hold the link for a moment instead of just tapping it. When Safari displays the dialog box shown next, tap the Open In New Page button. Safari then opens the destination web page in a different page and displays that page.

 From this dialog box, you can also check the URL of the linked web page. This information can be useful for avoiding potentially dangerous websites. If you want to open the web page in the same page, tap the Open button. If you want to add the page to your Reading List, tap the Add To Reading List button. And if you decide not to open the web page, tap the Cancel button.

To navigate among the web pages you've visited before in this session, tap the Back button or the Forward button at the lower-left corner of the screen.

Navigate Back and Forth

The Back button is available as soon as you've navigated from one web page to another. The Forward button becomes available when you use the Back button to go back to a web page you've visited earlier.

 Swipe your finger up the screen to scroll down; swipe your finger down the screen to scroll up. To move down by a small amount, double-tap near the bottom of the screen; to move up by a small amount, double-tap near the top. Double-tapping makes Safari center the web page on where you tap. To scroll quickly all the way to the top of a web page, tap the status bar at the top of the screen.

Search for Information

To search for information, follow these steps:

1. Tap in the Search box.
2. Start typing your search terms. Safari displays matching terms as you type, as shown on the left in Figure 9-3.
3. Tap a search term to display a page of results, as shown on the right in Figure 9-3.
4. Tap a result to display its web page. Alternatively, tap and hold a result to display the Action dialog box, and then tap Open In New Page to open the web page in a new page in Safari.

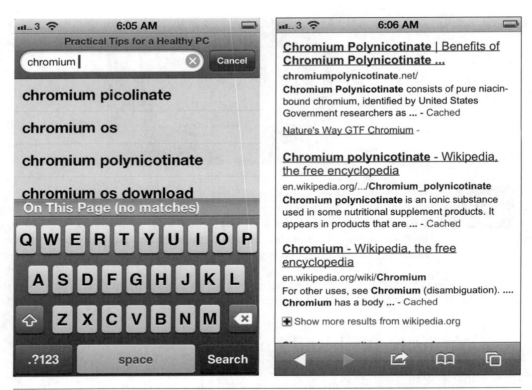

FIGURE 9-3 To search for information, tap in the Search box and start typing your search terms. Tap a suggestion (left) to display a page of results (right), and then tap the result you want to see.

 You can change the search engine your iPhone uses. See the section "Choose Your iPhone's Default Search Engine," later in this chapter.

Use Bookmarks to Store Addresses and Navigate Quickly

Typing URLs into a web browser is a chore even on a full-sized keyboard. Typing URLs on the onscreen keyboard is slow and awkward, even though the iPhone does its best to help by putting essential keys such as /, ., and .com on Safari's onscreen keyboard.

In this section, I'll show you how to use bookmarks to store addresses easily and navigate to them quickly. You can either import bookmarks from your computer using iTunes or create bookmarks directly on your iPhone.

Get Your Bookmarks into Safari

If you browse extensively, you'll need to type some URLs on the onscreen keyboard sooner or later. But what you should do instead is create a bookmark in your computer's web browser for each website you'll want to access frequently using your iPhone, and then synchronize those bookmarks with the iPhone.

To synchronize your bookmarks with the iPhone, follow these steps:

1. Connect the iPhone to your computer, and allow synchronization to take place.
2. Click the iPhone's entry in the Source pane to display its control screens.
3. Click the Info button, and then scroll down to the Web Browser area.
4. Select the check box for synchronizing the bookmarks:
   - **Windows** Select the Sync Bookmarks From check box, and then choose the browser in the drop-down list. If the browser doesn't appear there, chances are that iTunes doesn't support it.
   - **Mac** Select the Sync Safari Bookmarks check box.

Tip If iTunes can't import the bookmarks from your favorite browser, there is a workaround—even if it's an ugly one. Export the bookmarks from the browser, import them into Internet Explorer or Safari, and then synchronize the iPhone with Internet Explorer or Safari. You will not be able to keep your bookmarks synchronized with your preferred browser, but at least this gives you a way of getting your bookmarks from that browser onto the iPhone.

5. Click the Apply button. iTunes copies the bookmarks to the iPhone.

Go to a Bookmark

To go to a bookmark on the iPhone, follow these steps:

1. Tap the Bookmarks button at the bottom of the screen, as shown on the left in Figure 9-4.
2. The iPhone displays the Bookmarks screen you were using last. The first time, you will usually see the main Bookmarks screen, as shown on the right in Figure 9-4.
3. Tap the category of bookmarks you want to view. For example, tap the Bookmarks Menu button to display the Bookmarks Menu screen, as shown on the left in Figure 9-5.
4. Tap the bookmark for the web page you want to display, as shown on the right in Figure 9-5. Safari opens the web page.

Add a Bookmark on Your iPhone

If you browse on the iPhone, you'll probably run into web pages that you want to bookmark for later reference. Not only can you do this, but iTunes syncs your

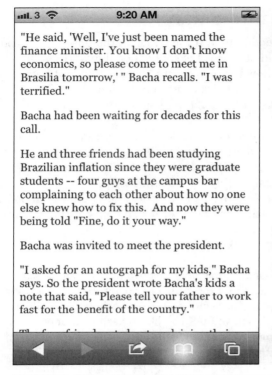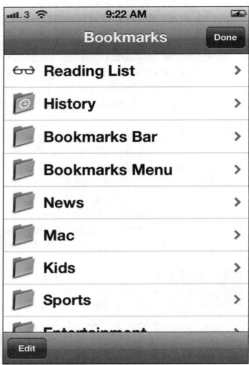

FIGURE 9-4 The easiest way of getting to a website on the iPhone is to use a bookmark.

Did You Know?

Why the iPhone Can't Show Flash Websites

If you've spent any time browsing the Web, you're probably familiar with Adobe Flash, a technology for adding multimedia, animations, and animated graphics to websites. Nearly as many people consider Flash a bane (because it creates large and unwieldy sites) as consider it a boon—but love it or hate it, Flash is very widely used.

Unfortunately for you and me, the iPhone doesn't support Flash, so if you browse to a website that uses Flash, Safari won't be able to display it properly.

Adobe is apparently working on a version of Flash for iOS, but the main problem is that Flash appears to contravene Apple's guidelines for applications that run on the iPhone. This is because developers would be able to create applications in Flash and install them on the iPhone from web pages rather than having to get the applications approved by Apple and then sell or distribute them via the App Store.

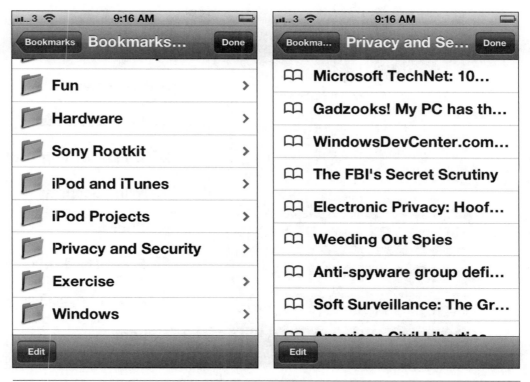

FIGURE 9-5 Tap the bookmark category you want (left), and then tap the bookmark to display the web page it marks (right).

bookmarks back to your browser, so you can use the bookmark on your computer as well.

To add a bookmark, follow these steps:

1. On the iPhone, browse to a web page that deserves a bookmark.
2. Tap the Action button at the bottom of the screen, and then tap the Add Bookmark button in the dialog box that opens (shown here).
3. Your iPhone displays the Add Bookmark screen, shown on the left in Figure 9-6.
4. Your iPhone displays the web page's title in the top text box. You can either accept this as the name for the bookmark, edit it by using the keyboard, or clear the name (tap the × button) and then type a new name.

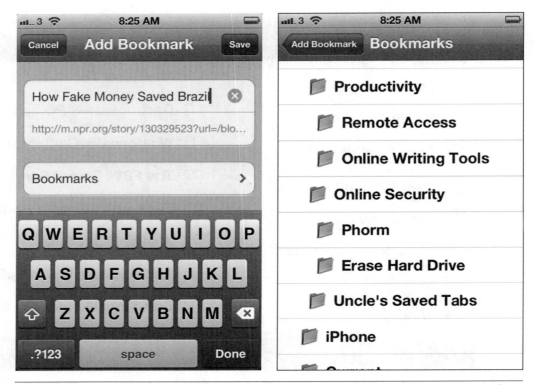

FIGURE 9-6   You can add a bookmark on the iPhone and have it be synchronized back to your computer.

5. To change the location in which your iPhone stores the bookmark, tap the button indicating the current location (in the example, this is Bookmarks). On the resulting screen, shown on the right in Figure 9-6, tap the location you want. Your iPhone displays the Add Bookmark screen again, with the bar now showing the location you chose.

6. Tap the Save button to save the bookmark. Your iPhone then returns you to the web page from which you started the bookmarking process.

Organize the Bookmarks on Your iPhone

No matter how carefully you name and file the bookmarks you create, you'll probably need to reorganize them now and then to make them easy to navigate. Most likely, you'll also want to get rid of old bookmarks you no longer need.

Open a Bookmarks Screen for Editing

To organize your bookmarks, open the appropriate Bookmarks screen for editing:

FIGURE 9-7   Tap the Edit button in the lower-left corner of the Bookmarks screen to turn on editing mode (left). You can then take various actions—for example, tap the round Delete button to the left of a bookmark or folder, and then tap the Delete button that appears to the right of the name (right).

1. Tap the Bookmarks button on the Safari toolbar to display the Bookmarks screen.
2. If you want to work with a particular bookmarks folder, tap it to display its contents.
3. Tap the Edit button in the lower-left corner to turn on editing mode. In editing mode, shown on the left in Figure 9-7, a round Delete button appears to the left of each item, and a handle of three horizontal lines appears to its right.

Delete a Bookmark Folder or a Bookmark

To delete a bookmark folder or a bookmark, follow these steps:

1. Tap the round Delete button to the left of the bookmark folder's name or bookmark's name. Safari displays a rectangular Delete button to the right of the name, as shown on the right in Figure 9-7.
2. Tap the rectangular Delete button. Safari deletes the bookmark.

FIGURE 9-8 You can move a bookmark folder or bookmark up or down the list by tapping its handle and dragging (left). To rename a bookmark folder or a bookmark, tap the main part of its button, and then work on the Edit Folder screen (right) or the Edit Bookmark screen.

Move a Bookmark Folder or Bookmark Up or Down

To move a bookmark folder or a bookmark up or down the list, tap its handle and drag it to where you want, as shown on the left in Figure 9-8.

Edit the Name of a Bookmark Folder or Bookmark

To edit the name of a bookmark folder or a bookmark, tap the main part of its button, and then work on the Edit Folder screen (shown on the right in Figure 9-8) or the Edit Bookmark screen.

Move a Bookmark to a Different Folder

To move a bookmark to a different folder, follow these steps:

1. With editing mode turned on, tap the bookmark's button to display the Edit Bookmark screen (shown on the left in Figure 9-9).

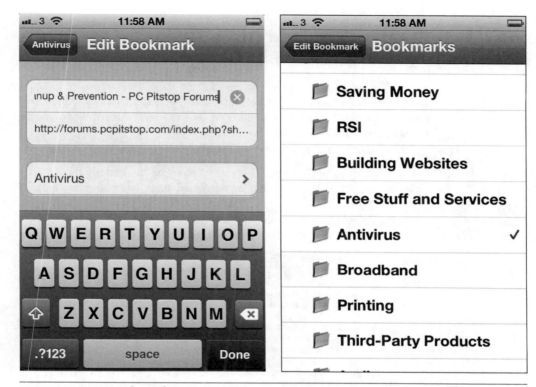

FIGURE 9-9   On the Edit Bookmark screen (left), tap the current folder button (here, Antivirus) to display the Bookmarks screen (right). Then tap the folder you want to move the bookmark to.

2. Tap the current folder button (here, it's called Antivirus) to display the Bookmarks screen (shown on the right in Figure 9-9).
3. Tap the bookmark folder you want to put the bookmark in. Safari displays the Edit Bookmark screen again, now with the folder's name on the current folder button.
4. Tap the Done button.

 You can use this same technique to move a subfolder from one folder to another.

Keep Web Pages to Read with the Reading List

Safari includes a special type of bookmark called the Reading List that you can use to store web pages you want to read later (or read again).

How to... Create Web Clips to Go Instantly to Your Favorite Web Pages

Safari's bookmarks are an easy way of getting to web pages you use regularly. But your iPhone gives you an even quicker way to get to a web page: You can create a shortcut called a web clip right on the Home screen. When you tap the web clip, Safari opens the web page.

To create a web clip, follow these steps:

1. In Safari, go to the web page you want to create the web clip for.
2. Tap the Action button to display the Action dialog box, shown on the left in the next illustration.
3. Tap the Add To Home Screen button. Your iPhone displays the Add To Home screen, shown on the right in the next illustration.

4. Improve the suggested name for the web clip, or type a new name.
5. Tap the Add button. Safari creates the web clip, adds it to the first Home screen that has space for it, and displays that Home screen.
6. If necessary, move the web clip to a different Home screen:
   • Tap and hold the web clip's icon until all the icons start to jiggle.
   • Drag the web clip's icon to where you want it.
   • Press the Home button to lock the Home screens again.

You can now tap the web clip to open that web page in Safari.

If an administrator manages your iPhone, he may install web clips for you to reach important web pages—for example, a company announcements web page or a campus directory. The administrator can either install web clips while setting up the iPhone for you or install them as part of the contents of a configuration profile that he sends to your iPhone via e-mail or that you download from a web page.

To add a web page to the Reading List, tap the Action button, and then tap the Add To Reading List button in the Action dialog box.

To view the Reading List, tap the Bookmarks button, and then tap the Reading List bookmark at the top of the Bookmarks screen, shown on the left in Figure 9-10. (If Safari displays a folder of bookmarks rather than the Bookmarks screen, tap the button in the upper-left corner of the screen one or more times until the Bookmarks screen appears.)

As you can see on the right in Figure 9-10, the Reading List screen has two tabs:

- **All**   Tap this tab to display the list of all the pages you've added to the Reading List.
- **Unread**   Tap this tab to display the list of all the pages you haven't read yet.

You can then tap the web page you want to display.

To return from the Reading List to the web page you were viewing last, tap the Done button.

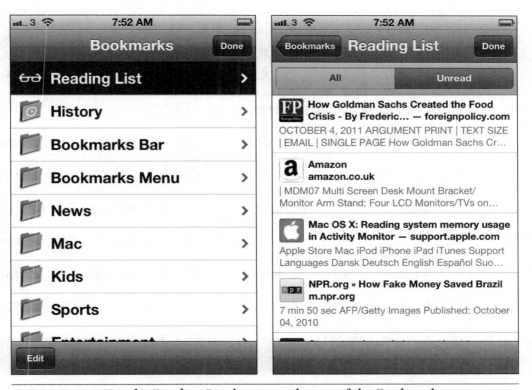

FIGURE 9-10   Tap the Reading List button at the top of the Bookmarks screen (left) to display the Reading List (right). Tap the All tab or the Unread tab, as needed, and then tap the web page you want to read.

Go Back to a Web Page in Your History

Like most web browsers, Safari includes a History feature that keeps a list of the web pages you visit so that you can easily go back to them.

 Tip If you don't want Safari to record your browsing in the History, turn on Private Browsing. See the section "Surf Secretly with Private Browsing," later in this chapter.

To view your History and display a web page from it, follow these steps:

1. Tap the Bookmarks button to display the Bookmarks screen. If Safari displays a folder of bookmarks rather than the Bookmarks screen, tap the button in the upper-left corner of the screen one or more times until the Bookmarks screen appears.
2. Tap the History button near the top of the screen to display the History screen (shown on the left in Figure 9-11).

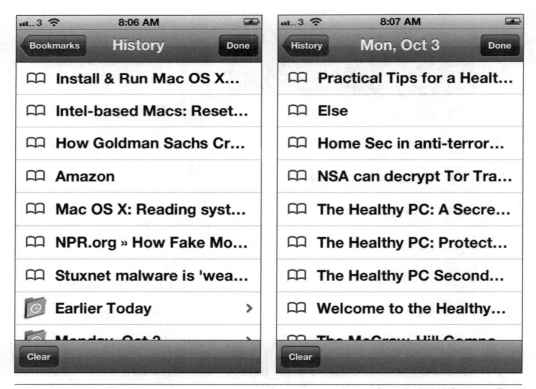

FIGURE 9-11 Your History gives you quick access to the web pages you browsed recently. If the web page you want doesn't appear on the first History screen (left), tap the button for the appropriate day to display its list of web pages (right).

3. Tap the button for the appropriate day to display the web pages it contains. For example, tap the Earlier Today button to display the Earlier Today screen (shown on the right in Figure 9-11). Then tap the web page you want to view.

To return from your History to the web page you were viewing last, tap the Done button.

Read Web Pages More Easily with Safari Reader

Safari Reader is a special view that hides ads, navigation boxes, and other peripheral content from web pages so that you can read the main text more easily. Safari Reader is available only for some web pages, not for all web pages.

When Safari Reader is available for a web page, a Reader button appears at the right side of the Address box, as shown on the left in Figure 9-12. Tap this button to switch to Safari Reader, shown on the right in Figure 9-12, and you see the article's text and pictures in an easy-to-read format.

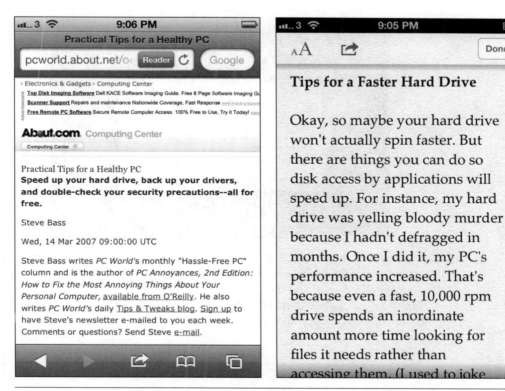

FIGURE 9-12   Tap the Reader button in the Address box (left) to switch a web page to Safari Reader (right), which eliminates distractions such as ads.

Note Safari Reader also hides most of Safari's controls. Tap the ᴀA button on the toolbar to choose between Normal font size and Large font size. Tap the Action button to display the Action dialog box for adding a bookmark, adding the web page to your Reading List, and so on.

When you've finished using Safari Reader, tap the Done button in the upper-right corner of the screen to return the web page to normal view.

Open Multiple Web Pages at the Same Time

Safari lets you open multiple pages at the same time, and then switch among them. This is handy when you want to view another web page without closing the web page you're currently viewing.

To open a new page in Safari, follow these steps:

1. Tap the Pages button, the button in the lower-right corner of the screen. Safari shrinks the current page and displays a New Page button and a Done button, as shown here.

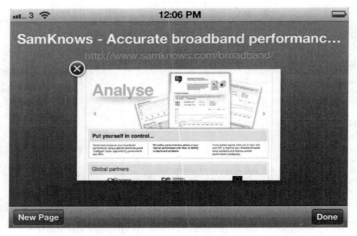

2. Tap the New Page button. Safari displays a blank new page. The button in the lower-right corner of the screen shows the number of pages you have open.
3. Go to a URL in one of the usual ways:
   • Tap the Address box to display the keyboard, type the URL, and then tap the Go button, as shown next.

- Tap the Bookmarks button to display your list of bookmarks, and then choose the bookmark you want.

To navigate from one open page to another, tap the Pages button in the lower-right corner of the screen to shrink the current page and display the control buttons, as shown here. The dots below the page show you how many pages you have open, with the white dot showing which of the pages you're looking at.

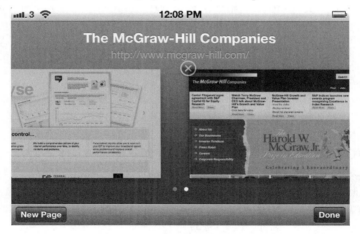

To close a page, tap the × button that appears in its upper-left corner. Otherwise, scroll left or right to reach the page you want to view, and then tap it to display it.

Configure How You Want Safari to Work

To make Safari work your way, you can configure its options. You'll find these on the Safari settings screen in the Settings app. To display the Safari settings screen, follow these steps:

How to... # Save a Picture from a Web Page—or Send It to Someone

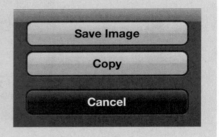

When you're browsing the Web, you'll often run into pictures that you want to keep for reference or share with someone else.

To keep or share a picture, tap and hold the picture on the web page for a moment. When Safari displays the dialog box shown here, tap the Save Image button if you want to save the picture to your Camera Roll. Tap the Copy button if you want to copy the picture so that you can paste it into an e-mail message or an MMS message.

1. Press the Home button to display the Home screen.
2. Tap the Settings icon to display the Settings screen.
3. Scroll down to the third box, and then tap the Safari button to display the Safari settings screen. The left screen in Figure 9-13 shows the top of the Safari settings screen; the right screen in Figure 9-13 shows the bottom of the Safari settings screen.

Now you can choose General settings, Privacy settings, and Security settings, as discussed in the following subsections. You can also use the Advanced settings to delete the data that websites have stored on your iPhone.

Choose General Settings for Safari

In the General box on the Safari settings screen, you can choose your iPhone's default search engine, specify which information AutoFill provides (if any), and control whether Safari opens each link in a new page or in the background.

Choose Your iPhone's Default Search Engine

To change your iPhone's default search engine, tap the Search Engine button. On the Search Engine screen that appears, tap the search engine you want to use, placing a check mark next to it. At this writing, your choices are Google, Yahoo!, or Bing (Microsoft's search engine). Tap the Safari button to go back to the Safari settings screen.

Control Which Information AutoFill Fills in Automatically for You

AutoFill is a feature that can automatically fill in standard information for you in web pages to save your having to type it. You specify which contact record contains your

FIGURE 9-13 On Safari's settings screen, you can choose General settings, Privacy settings, and Security settings.

information, and AutoFill can then fill in information such as your name and address. AutoFill can also fill in usernames and passwords for you, but you may prefer to keep this more sensitive information under your own control.

 Before choosing AutoFill settings, open the Contacts app and set up a card that contains exactly the information you want AutoFill to have. For example, give the card the standard form of your name, your address spelled in exactly the way your credit-card companies prefer, and your public e-mail address.

To set up AutoFill to provide only the information you want, follow these steps:

1. On the Safari settings screen, tap the AutoFill button to display the AutoFill screen (shown on the left in Figure 9-14).
2. Tap the Use Contact Info switch and move it to the On position if you want to use AutoFill or to the Off position if you want to prevent AutoFill from providing information from a contact record.
3. If the My Info button shows the contact record that contains the contact information you want to use, you're set. Otherwise, tap the My Info button

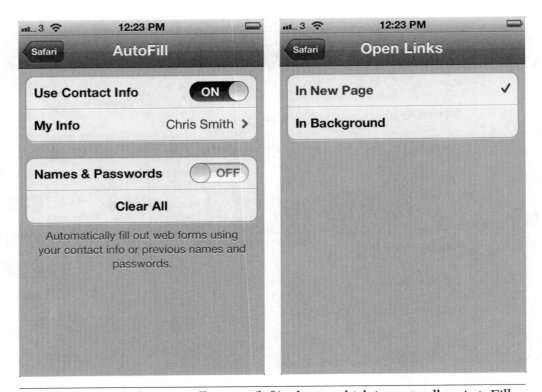

FIGURE 9-14 On the AutoFill screen (left), choose which items to allow AutoFill to complete, and specify which contact record contains your information. On the Open Links page (right), choose whether to open each link on a new page or in the background.

to display the list of contacts, and then tap the contact record you set up for AutoFill.

4. Tap the Names & Passwords switch and move it to the On position if you want AutoFill to fill in names and passwords for you. Otherwise, move the switch to the Off position.

 If you want to delete all your stored names and passwords from AutoFill, tap the Clear All button, and then tap the Clear AutoFill Data button in the confirmation dialog box that appears.

5. Tap the Safari button in the upper-left corner to go back to the Safari settings screen.

Choose Whether to Open Links in a New Page or in the Background

As you saw earlier in this chapter, you can tap and hold a link to display the Action dialog box, then tap the Open In New Page button to open the link's destination page in a new page rather than in the current page. The new page comes to the front in Safari, taking the place of the current page.

Instead of opening the new page at the front, you may prefer to open the new page in the background, so that you keep viewing the current page and can switch to the new page when it suits you. To do this, you can replace the Open In New Page button in the Action dialog box with the Open In Background button.

To replace the button, tap the Open Links button on the Safari Settings screen. On the Open Links screen (shown on the right in Figure 9-14), tap the In Background button, placing a check mark next to it. Then tap the Safari button in the upper-left corner to return to the Safari settings screen.

Choose Privacy Settings for Safari

In the Privacy area on the Safari settings screen, you can choose these settings:

- **Private Browsing** Tap this switch and move it to the On position to turn on Private Browsing mode. In this mode, Safari tracks your movements as little as possible while still enabling web pages to work.
- **Accept Cookies** A *cookie* is a small text file that a website uses to track your movements and choices. Cookies are necessary for features such as shopping carts and "you recently found these items fascinating" features, but it is normally a good idea to accept cookies only from sites you visit, refusing cookies from third-party sites associated with those sites. To choose which cookies Safari accepts, follow these steps:
    1. Tap the Accept Cookies button on the Safari settings screen. The Accept Cookies screen appears.
    2. Tap the appropriate item: Never, From Visited, or Always. From Visited is the best choice, because Always makes Safari accept potentially dangerous third-party cookies, and Never prevents some websites from working correctly.
    3. Tap the Safari button in the upper-left corner to return to the Safari settings screen.
- **Clear History** To clear your browsing history, tap this button, and then tap the Clear History button in the confirmation dialog box (shown here).

- **Clear Cookies And Data**   To clear out your cookies and other stored data, tap this button, and then tap the Clear Cookies And Data button in the confirmation dialog box (shown here).

Choose Security Settings for Safari

In the Security area on the Safari settings screen, you can choose these settings:

- **Fraud Warning**   Make sure this switch is in the On position to use Safari's feature for alerting you to websites suspected of being fraudulent. This is almost always a good idea.
- **JavaScript**   Tap this switch and move it to the Off position if you want to turn JavaScript off. JavaScript is a potential threat to your iPhone, because it can be used to create malevolent scripts as well as helpful scripts. But so many web pages use JavaScript to provide functionality that turning it off may prevent pages you need to see from loading.
- **Block Pop-Ups**   Make sure this switch is in the On position if you want to use Safari's feature for blocking pop-up windows. Pop-up windows are often used to display unwanted content—anything from ads to smut—so you'll normally want to keep this feature on.

Surf Secretly with Private Browsing

When you need to browse the Web without leaving traces of what you're doing, use Safari's Private Browsing feature. First, you turn on Private Browsing in the Settings app. Then you browse in Safari as normal. Finally, you turn off Private Browsing in the Settings app.

Turn On Private Browsing

To turn on Private Browsing, follow these steps:

1. Press the Home button to display the Home screen.
2. Tap the Settings icon to display the Settings screen.

How to...   # Clear Out the Data a Website Is Storing About You

To see which websites are storing data about you, and to clear out the data from a site that you don't want to store it, follow these steps:

1. On the Safari settings screen, tap the Advanced button at the bottom to display the Advanced screen (the top part of which is shown here).

2. Tap the Website Data button to display the Website Data screen (shown on the left in the following illustration). The list shows each website that has stored data on your iPhone, and how much data each has stored. You can see that the amounts of data are minute—a kilobyte or two. The concern is that the data is sensitive, not that it's hogging your iPhone's memory.

3. To delete a website's data, tap the Edit button, displaying a round red Delete button to the left of each website. You can then tap the round Delete button to display a rectangular Delete button to the right of the website (as shown on the right in the illustration), which you then tap to delete the data. Tap the Done button when you finish wiping websites.

4. If you want to remove the data for all the sites, tap the Remove All Website Data button at the bottom, and then tap the Remove Now button in the confirmation dialog that appears.

5. When you have finished clearing data, tap the Advanced button to return to the Advanced screen, and then tap the Safari button to go back to the Safari screen.

3. Scroll down to the third box, and then tap the Safari button to display the Safari settings screen.

4. In the Privacy box, tap the Private Browsing switch, and move it to the On position. Your iPhone displays the Close All Tabs? dialog box, shown here, which prompts you to close all your existing tabs (pages) before turning on Private Browsing.

5. Tap the Close All button if you want to close all the pages, which is good for security. Tap the Keep All button if you want to start your browsing from the pages.

Surf the Web Using Private Browsing

After turning on Private Browsing in the Settings app, press the Home button to display the Home screen, and then tap the Safari icon to launch Safari. You can then use Safari as normal, but you'll notice that the title bar and window frame are darker than usual to indicate that you're using Private Browsing.

Turn Off Private Browsing

When you finish using Private Browsing, turn it off. Follow these steps:

1. Press the Home button to display the Home screen.
2. Tap the Settings icon to display the Settings screen.

Did You Know?

Other Web Browsers Are Available for Your iPhone

Safari comes built into your iPhone's operating system, so it's the web browser you'll probably want to use. But if you decide you don't like Safari, there's plenty of competition for it.

Here are the three top competitors for Safari. You'll find them all on the App Store:

- **Opera Mini** Opera Mini is the iPhone version of the Opera browser, which runs on Windows, Mac OS X, Linux, and other platforms.
- **Mercury Web Browser** Mercury's features include ad-blocking and integration with Dropbox, Twitter, and Facebook.
- **Private Browser With Fullscreen And Multi-Tabs** If you find Safari's Private Browsing feature useful, you may want to try Private Browser With Fullscreen And Multi-Tabs, which keeps all your browsing in a private state.

3. Scroll down to the third box, and then tap the Safari button to display the Safari settings screen.

4. Tap the Private Browsing switch and move it to the Off position. Your iPhone displays the Close All Tabs? dialog box, shown here, which prompts you to close all your existing tabs (pages) before turning off Private Browsing

5. Tap the Close All button if you want to close the pages you were browsing privately. This is what you should do for security purposes. If you need to keep the pages open, tap the Keep All button instead.

10

Keep Your Calendars and Contacts Up to Date

HOW TO...

- Sync your calendars and contacts with your iPhone
- Work with your calendars on your iPhone
- Work with contacts on your iPhone
- Choose settings for working with calendars and contacts

Your iPhone is the perfect device for keeping your calendars and contacts on, because it not only is always with you but also can use or update any of your calendar events or contact records at a moment's notice.

In this chapter, we'll look at how to keep your calendars and contacts up to date using your iPhone. We'll start by going through the process of syncing your computer's calendars and contacts with your iPhone, and then we'll move along to working first with calendars and then with contacts. Toward the end of the chapter, I'll walk you through choosing settings for calendars and contacts, because you'll probably find you do better with custom settings than with the default settings.

Sync Your Calendars and Contacts with Your iPhone

You can create calendar entries and contact records directly on your iPhone, but you'll probably want to pick up as many as possible from your computer. If you sync your iPhone with your computer, you can quickly sync your contacts and calendars by using the controls in the Info screen of the iPhone's control screens in iTunes.

Open the Info Screen in the iPhone's Control Screens in iTunes

To control which contacts and calendars iTunes syncs with your iPhone, first open the Info screen. Follow these steps:

1. Connect your iPhone to your computer, either via the USB cable or via Wi-Fi (if you've selected the Sync With This iPhone Over Wi-Fi check box on the Summary screen).
2. Click the iPhone's entry in the Source list to display the iPhone's control screens.
3. Click the Info tab to display the Info screen.

Choose Sync Settings for Contacts

To choose which contacts iTunes syncs to your iPhone, follow these steps:

1. At the top of the Info screen (shown in Figure 10-1 on the Mac), choose which contacts to sync:
   - **Windows** Select the Sync Contacts With check box and choose the source in the drop-down list: Yahoo! Address Book, Windows Address Book or Windows Contacts, Google Contacts, or Outlook.
   - **Mac OS X** Select the Sync Address Book Contacts check box at the top of the Info screen.

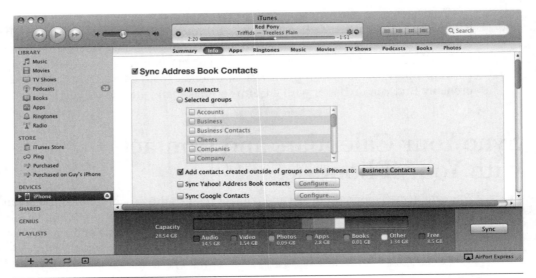

FIGURE 10-1 In the Contacts box at the top of the Info screen, choose which contacts to sync with your iPhone.

2. At the top of the Contacts box, choose which contacts to sync:
   - **All Contacts**   Select this option button to sync all your contacts.
   - **Selected Groups**   Select this option button to sync just the contacts in the groups whose check boxes you select in the list box.
3. To control which group receives any contacts you create on the iPhone without assigning to groups, select the Add Contacts Created Outside Of Groups On This iPhone To check box, and then choose the appropriate group in the drop-down list.
4. If you want to sync your Yahoo! Address Book contacts to your iPhone, follow these steps:
   a. Select the Sync Yahoo! Address Book Contacts check box. iTunes displays the Yahoo! Address Book dialog box shown here.

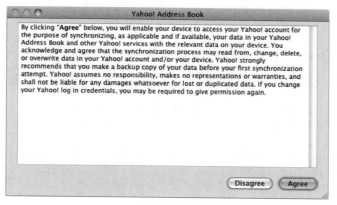

   b. Follow the warnings to back up your data, and then click the Agree button if you want to go ahead and set up the sync. iTunes displays the Yahoo! Address Book dialog box shown here, asking for your Yahoo! ID and password.

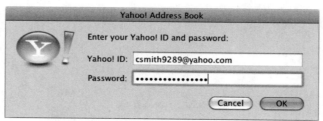

   c. Type your Yahoo! ID and password, and then click the OK button. iTunes connects to Yahoo! and gets the contact data.
5. If you want to sync your Google Contacts with your iPhone, follow these steps:
   a. Select the Sync Google Contacts check box. iTunes displays the Google Contacts dialog box shown next.

b. Type your Google ID and password, and then click the OK button. iTunes connects to Google and gets the contact data.

6. If you're ready to sync at this point, click the Apply button; if you've already applied the changes, click the Sync button. Otherwise, choose sync settings for calendars as described in the following section.

Choose Sync Settings for Calendars

To choose which calendars iTunes syncs to your iPhone, follow these steps:

1. Select the check box for syncing calendars, partway down the Info tab on the iPhone's control screens in iTunes. Figure 10-2 shows the Calendars box in iTunes on the Mac.
   - **Windows** Select the Sync Calendars With check box, and the choose the program in the drop-down list. For example, choose Outlook.
   - **Mac** Select the Sync iCal Calendars check box.

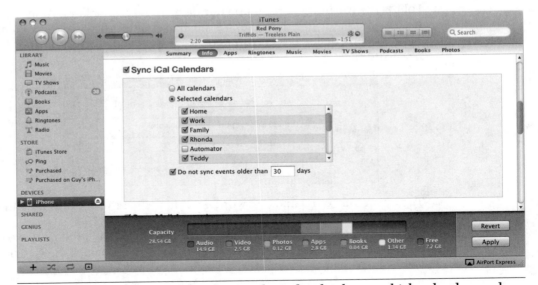

FIGURE 10-2 In the Calendars box on the Info tab, choose which calendars and events to sync with your iPhone.

2. At the top of the Calendars box, choose which calendars to sync:
   - **All Calendars**   Select this option button to sync all your calendars. Usually, this is the best option.
   - **Selected Calendars**   Select this option button to sync just the calendars whose check boxes you select in the list box.
3. If you want to save space and time by syncing only recent events, select the Do Not Sync Events Older Than *N* Days check box, and then enter a suitable figure in the text box. The default number is 30 days, which you may want to try to start with.
4. If you're ready to sync now, click the Apply button; if you've already applied the changes, click the Sync button. Otherwise, choose further sync settings, and then click the Sync button when you finish.

Work with Your Calendars on Your iPhone

To work with your calendars on your iPhone, you use the Calendar app. Launch the Calendar app by tapping the Calendar icon on the Home screen. The first time you launch Calendar, it normally displays the All Calendars view for the current month, as shown in Figure 10-3.

These are the main elements of the Calendar screen in Month view:

- **New button**   Tap this button to start creating a new event.
- **Selected day**   The blue square shows the selected day. Tap a day to select it.
- **Events for selected day**   The events for the selected day appear in a list below the calendar grid. Only a couple of events fit here, so you may need to scroll down to see other events.
- **Calendar indicator**   Each event in the list of events for the selected day has a color-coded dot to indicate which calendar it belongs to.
- **Previous button**   Tap this button to display the previous month in Month view or the previous day in Day view.
- **Next button**   Tap this button to display the next month in Month view or the next day in Day view.
- **Invitations button**   Tap this button to display the Invitations screen, on which you can review the invitations you've received via Mail.
- **Events indicator**   The grid displays a dot in the square for each day that has one or more events.
- **View buttons**   Tap the button for the view you want. Month view, which you've met already, shows the whole month, with a box for each day. List view (shown on the left in Figure 10-4) shows your upcoming events as a list with a heading for each day that has events, so you can quickly see what's coming up. Day view (shown on the right in Figure 10-4) shows a timeline for the day you choose, so you can see exactly what's due to happen when.
- **Today button**   Tap this button to display the current day in whichever view you're using. For example, in Month view, tapping the Today button selects the square for the current day.

FIGURE 10-3 Calendar usually first displays the All Calendars view for the current month.

Manage Your Calendars

If you've synced your calendars from your computer to your iPhone, you may have all the calendars you need at this point. If needed, you can create new calendars and delete existing calendars directly on your iPhone.

You can also choose which of the calendars on your iPhone to display and which to hide. We'll start there.

Choose Which Calendars to Display

Often, you'll find it useful to display only some of your calendars on your iPhone. For example, if you're assessing your work schedule, you may not need to see your Little League commitments at the same time.

To control which calendars your iPhone displays, follow these steps:

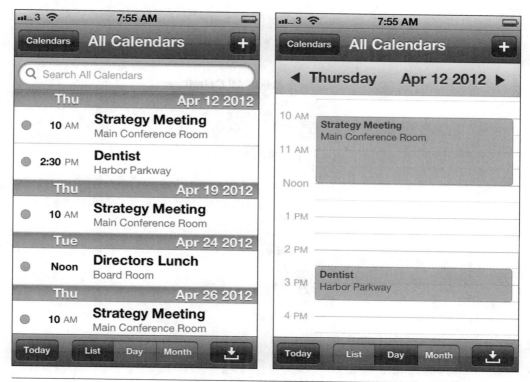

FIGURE 10-4   Use List view (left) to get a picture of your upcoming events, even if they're spread out over several weeks. Use Day view (right) to zero in on your events for a particular day.

1. Tap the Calendars button in the upper-left corner of whichever calendar you're using to display the Calendars screen (shown in Figure 10-5). Each calendar that has a check mark to its right is set for display in the Calendar app.

The calendars on the Calendars screen appear in different category boxes. For example, if you have synced calendars from your Mac, they appear in the From My Mac box. Which boxes you see depends on which calendars you have synced with your iPhone.

2. Tap to remove a check mark from each displayed calendar you want to hide, or tap to place a check mark next to each hidden calendar you want to display.

If you need to hide most of your calendars, tap the Hide All Calendars button at the top of the Calendars screen. You can then tap to place a check mark next to each calendar you want to display. To select all the calendars quickly, tap the Show All Calendars button that appears when one or more calendars are hidden.

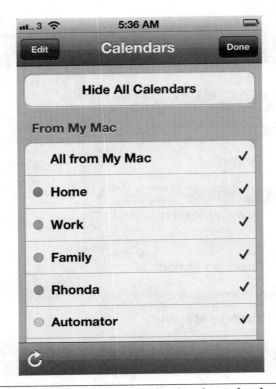

FIGURE 10-5 Tap the Calendars button to display the Calendars screen, on which you can choose which calendars to show and which to hide.

3. Tap the Done button when you're ready to return to viewing your calendars.

Change the Name or Color Displayed for a Calendar

Each calendar has the name you gave it and a color that your iPhone automatically assigned to it. You can change the name and color to suit you. For example, if you sync two calendars that have the same name, you can change the name of one of them to make them easier to distinguish.

To change the name or color your iPhone displays for a calendar, follow these steps:

1. Tap the Calendars button in the upper-left corner of the screen to display the Calendars screen (unless you're already there).
2. Tap the Edit button in the upper-left corner of the screen to switch to the Edit Calendars screen (shown on the left in Figure 10-6).
3. Tap the calendar you want to change. Your iPhone displays the Edit Calendar screen for that calendar, as shown on the right in Figure 10-6.

FIGURE 10-6   On the Edit Calendars screen (left), tap the calendar you want to edit or delete. Your iPhone displays the calendar's details on the Edit Calendar screen (right).

4. To change the name, tap in the Name box at the top, and then use the onscreen keyboard to type the new name. Tap the × button if you want to wipe out the existing name rather than merely edit it.
5. To change the color, tap the color you want to use, placing a check mark to its right.
6. Tap the Done button to return to the Edit Calendars screen.
7. Tap the Done button to return to the Calendars screen.

Create a New Calendar

To create a new calendar by working on your iPhone, follow these steps:

1. Tap the Calendars button in the upper-left corner of the screen to display the Calendars screen (unless you're already there).
2. Tap the Edit button in the upper-left corner of the screen to switch to the Edit Calendars screen.

3. Scroll down to the bottom of the category in which you want to create a new calendar. For example, if you sync calendars from your Mac, scroll down to the bottom of the From My Mac category.
4. Tap the Add Calendar button at the bottom of the category box (see the left screen in Figure 10-7). Your iPhone displays the Add Calendar screen (shown on the right in Figure 10-7).
5. In the Name box at the top, type the name for the calendar. Tap the × button if you want to delete the default name rather than edit it.
6. In the Color box, tap the color you want to give the calendar.
7. Tap the Done button. Your iPhone displays the Edit Calendars screen, now showing the calendar you added.
8. Tap the Done button when you finish adding calendars.

Delete a Calendar

To delete a calendar, follow these steps:

FIGURE 10-7 Tap the Add Calendar button in the appropriate box on the Edit Calendars screen (left) to display the Add Calendar screen (right). Then name your calendar and choose its color.

1. Tap the Calendars button in the upper-left corner of the screen to display the Calendars screen (unless you're already there).
2. Tap the Edit button in the upper-left corner of the screen to switch to the Edit Calendars screen.
3. Tap your victim calendar to display the Edit Calendar screen.
4. Scroll all the way down to the bottom.
5. Tap the Delete Calendar button. Your iPhone displays a confirmation dialog box, as shown here.
6. Tap the Delete Calendar button. Your iPhone deletes the calendar.

Work with Events and Invitations

After you've put your calendars on your iPhone and chosen which calendars to display, you're ready to work with events. Your iPhone will already contain all the events you synced in your calendars, but you can create, modify, and delete events as needed on your iPhone.

Create an Event

To create an event, follow these steps:

1. If you're using Month view, tap the date on which you want to add the new event. This step is optional, but it often saves time.
2. Tap the New (+) button in the upper-right corner of the screen to display the Add Event screen (shown on the left in Figure 10-8).
3. Tap the Title field and type the event's title—the name it displays in the Calendar.
4. Tap the "Starts, Ends" button to display the Start & End screen (shown on the right in Figure 10-8).
5. With the Starts button selected (as it is by default), spin the date dial and the time dials to set the start date and time. If you selected the date in the first step, you shouldn't need to change it at this point. Your iPhone automatically sets the Ends time to one hour after the Starts time.

 If the event is an all-day one, tap the All-Day switch and move it to the On position.

6. Tap the Ends button, and then spin the time dials to set the end time as needed.

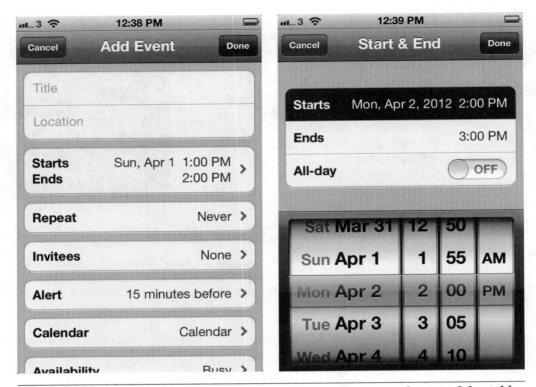

FIGURE 10-8 Enter the title and location of your new event at the top of the Add Event screen (left), then tap the "Starts, Ends" button to display the Start & End screen (right) so that you can set the start and end times.

Note If you have turned on Time Zone Support, the Start & End screen includes a Time Zone button that shows the time zone for which you're setting the event. If you need to change the time zone, tap the Time Zone button, and then use the resulting screen to set the time zone. See the sidebar "When You Should Use Time Zone Support—and When You Shouldn't," later in this chapter, for an explanation of Time Zone Support.

7. When you have set the date and time for the event, tap the Done button to return from the Start & End screen to the Add Event screen.
8. If the event will repeat, tap the Repeat button, tap the appropriate button on the Repeat screen (shown on the left in Figure 10-9), and then tap the Done button.
9. If the event will be a meeting that requires invitees, follow these steps to add them:
   a. Tap the Invitees button to display the Add Invitees screen (shown on the right in Figure 10-9).

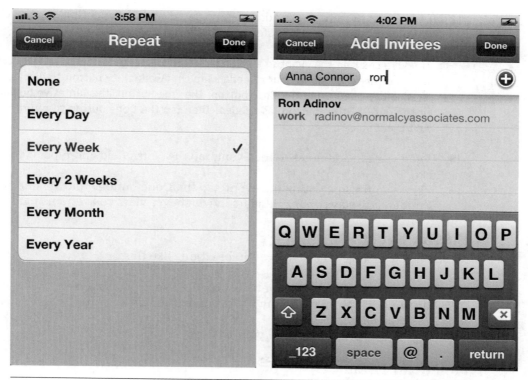

FIGURE 10-9   Use the Repeat screen (left) to set up a repeating schedule for the event. Use the Add Invitees screen (right) to add invitees, either by tapping the + button and picking them from your Contacts list or by typing a name or address and tapping any match.

b. Either type the first invitee's e-mail address, or tap the + button to display the list of contacts, and then tap the name.

c. Add other invitees by repeating the previous step.

d. When you finish building the list of invitees, tap the Done button.

10. To set an alert for the event, tap the Alert button, tap the appropriate interval button (for example, 15 Minutes Before) on the Event Alert screen, and then tap the Done button.

 After setting an alert, you can set a second alert by tapping the Second Alert button. For example, if you're facing a make-or-break meeting, you might want both a two-hour alert and a 15-minute alert.

11. To specify the calendar you're adding the event to, tap the Calendar button. On the Calendar screen, tap the calendar, and then tap the Done button.

12. If you want to store a web address associated with the meeting, tap the URL button, and then type or paste the URL.

Note If you're creating the event in a calendar on an Exchange account, you can control how the time appears in your calendar. Tap the Availability button to display the Availability screen. Tap the Busy button, the Free button, the Tentative button, or the Out Of Office button, as needed. Then tap the Done button to return to the Add Event screen.

13. If you want to add notes to the event, tap the Notes field and type or paste in text.
14. When you finish creating the event, tap the Done button. Your iPhone adds the event and displays your calendars in whichever view you were using.

Edit an Event

If you need to change an event, open it for editing like this:

1. Tap the event in the calendar to display the Event Details screen.
2. Tap the Edit button to display the event on the Edit screen.
3. Make the edits you need.
4. Tap the Done button to save your changes.

Delete an Event

To delete an event, follow these steps:

Tell Siri to...

Create Calendar Events for You

Siri is great for creating calendar events, especially when you're not in a position to type in the details yourself. Here are examples of what you can say:

- "Schedule a meeting with Dawn Johnson at nine tomorrow morning."
- "New appointment with Dr. Newman at five P.M. on Friday."
- "Meet Bill for lunch at one today."

You can also ask Siri which events you've got scheduled. Here are examples:

- "What does tomorrow's schedule look like?"
- "What time am I meeting with Janet today?"
- "Where is my next appointment?"
- "What's happening this weekend?"

Tell Siri to...

Edit or Change an Event

You can tell Siri to edit an event or delete it completely. Here are examples of what you can say:

- "Move my twelve thirty lunch to one o'clock."
- "Add Don to tomorrow's planning meeting."
- "Cancel my dentist appointment on Friday."

As usual, if Siri requires more information than you've given, Siri asks you for the details.

1. Tap the event in the calendar to display the Event Details screen.
2. Tap the Edit button to display the event on the Edit screen.
3. Scroll all the way down to the bottom.
4. Tap the Delete Event button. Your iPhone displays the confirmation dialog box shown here.
5. Tap the Delete Event button. Your iPhone removes the event and then returns you to the calendar.

Deal with Invitations

When people send you invitations to events via e-mail, Mail automatically passes the events to the Calendar app. You can then tap the Invitations button in the Calendar app to see a list of pending invitations, as shown in the left screen in Figure 10-10. Tap an invitation to open its Event Details screen (as shown in the right screen in Figure 10-10), and then tap the Accept button, the Maybe button, or the Decline button, as needed.

From the Event Details screen, you can also take the following actions:

- **Check the sender's information**   Tap the Invitation From button to see the Info screen for the invitation's sender. Seeing the information helps you distinguish between contacts with similar names and decide which meetings require your brilliance and which you can safely skip.
- **Check other participants**   Tap the No Reply button, the Accepted button, the Declined button, or the Tentative button to see the details of the other people. On the Invitees screen, tap the button for a contact whose information you want to view. From the Info screen, you can get in touch with the contact using any of your iPhone's means of communication—for example, e-mail, text message,

FaceTime, or good old-fashioned voice call. Communicating with your contacts should help you decide which meetings to attend.

- **Set an alert for the meeting** Tap the Alert button to display the Event Alert screen, and then set an alert for the interval you want—for example, 15 Minutes Before.
- **Change your availability** Tap the Availability button to display the Availability screen, and then tap the Busy button or the Free button as appropriate, putting a check mark next to it.

 If the Calendar app doesn't automatically pick up your invitations from Mail, check that the New Invitation Alerts switch in Calendars settings is set to On. Press the Home button to display the Home screen, tap the Settings icon to display the Settings screen, and then tap the Mail, Contacts, Calendars button to display the Mail, Contacts, Calendars screen. Scroll down to the Calendars box, and then move the New Invitation Alerts switch to the On position.

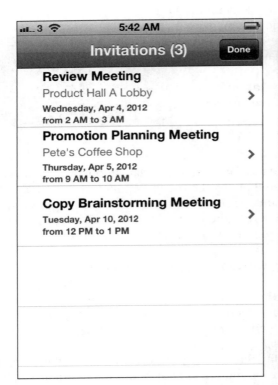

FIGURE 10-10 On the Invitations screen (left), tap the invitation you want to open. On the Event Details screen (right), choose whether to accept the invitation, decline it, or give it a decisive "maybe."

Work with Contacts on the iPhone

Normally, you'll add your contacts to the iPhone by synchronizing them from your address book, as described in Chapter 2. But sometimes you may want to create a contact directly on your iPhone—or perhaps edit a contact record when you learn a new detail about the contact that you want to keep or when you meet a contact and have a chance to take his photo. You can also share your contacts with others rather than jealously hoarding them.

Add a New Contact on Your iPhone

If you carry your iPhone with you all the time, you can add a contact immediately. This is great when you need to capture information that may otherwise slip away or when you have a chance to add a contact and snap her photo at the same time. If you don't want to type all the contact's details on the iPhone, you can just start the record, and then add to it later.

Start a New Contact Record on the iPhone

To create a new contact record on your iPhone, follow these steps:

1. Press the Home button to display the Home screen.
2. Open the Contacts app in one of these ways:
   - Tap the Phone icon to launch the Phone app, and then tap the Contacts button on the button bar at the bottom of the screen.
   - Tap the Utilities folder to open it, and then tap the Contacts icon.
3. Tap the New (+) button in the upper-right corner of the Contacts screen to display the New Contact screen, shown in Figure 10-11.
4. Tap in the First field, and then type the contact's first name. Tap the Return button to move to the next field, the Last field.
5. Type the contact's last name, and then tap the Return button to move to the next field, the Company field.
6. Type the contact's company name (if there is one).

Add the Contact's Photo to the Record

To make the contact's record easy to recognize, you can add a photo to it. You can add the photo either by taking a photo on the spot or by picking an existing photo from those on your iPhone.

To add a photo in either way, tap the Add Photo button on the New Contact screen. Your iPhone then displays the Photo dialog box, shown on the left in Figure 10-12.

To use one of your existing photos, follow these steps from the Photo dialog box:

1. Tap the Choose Photo button. Your iPhone displays the Photos screen.

What a Unified Contact Is

When you open a contact record to see its details, you may see Unified Info at the top of the screen (as shown on the left in the following illustration) rather than Info (as shown on the right). Unified Info means that your Contacts list has two or more entries for the same name, and the Contacts app has assembled the information from all those entries into a single entry for you.

Normally, the way you get multiple contact records for the same person is by using multiple sources of contacts—for example, getting some contacts from your computer and others from an Exchange account, or getting some contacts from iCloud and the rest from a campus directory. But you can also create multiple contact records manually. When you do so, the Contacts app automatically displays the Unified Info screen for the contact, as long as the names in each contact record are exactly the same.

(Continued)

2. Navigate to the photo you want to use, and then tap it. Your iPhone displays the photo on the Move And Scale screen, shown on the right in Figure 10-12.
3. Move the photo so that the face is in the middle of the unshaded area, and then pinch in or pinch out as needed to make the face smaller or larger.
4. When you've got the face fitting, tap the Choose button. Your iPhone applies the photo to the contact.

To take a photo of a contact, follow these steps from the Photo dialog box:

1. Tap the Take Photo button. Your iPhone displays the Take Picture screen, shown on the left in Figure 10-13.
2. Line up your subject's face, demand a smile or the ritual announcement of "Cheese!", and then tap the Take Photo button (the button with the camera

If the names aren't exactly the same, you can link contact records manually. To link records, follow these steps:

1. In the Contacts app, open one of the records.
2. Tap the Edit button in the upper-right corner to open the record for editing.
3. Scroll down to the bottom, where you'll find the Linked Cards area, as shown on the left in the following illustration.

4. Tap the Link Contact button. The list of contacts appears. The current record appears in gray to help you avoid selecting the same one again.
5. Tap the contact record you want to link. The Contacts app displays the Info screen for that contact record (or the Unified Info screen, if the record is already linked). The right screen in the nearby illustration shows the Info screen.
6. Tap the Link button. The Contacts app displays the Unified Info screen for the contact so that you can review the information and add any other data.
7. Tap the Done button.

icon). Your iPhone takes the photo and then displays the Move And Scale screen (shown on the right in Figure 10-13).

3. Move the photo so that the face is in the middle of the unshaded area, and then pinch in or pinch out as needed to make the face smaller or larger.

 If the photo isn't good enough, tap the Retake button on the Move And Scale screen.

4. When you've got the face fitting, tap the Choose button. Your iPhone applies the photo to the contact.

FIGURE 10-11 Creating a new contact on the iPhone is easy enough, but it can mean a whole bunch of one-fingered typing.

Add Further Information to the Contact Record

You can now continue adding information to the fields of the New Contact screen, such as the Mobile field, Home field, Ringtone field, Text Tone field, and Home Page field. Either tap the Return button to move to the next field or—if you want to jump several fields—simply tap in the field you want to move to.

Save the Contact Record

When you've finished adding the contact's details, tap the Done button. The iPhone displays the Info screen for the contact.

Tap the All Contacts button to return to the All Contacts screen. If you started adding the contact from within a group, tap the button to return to that group instead.

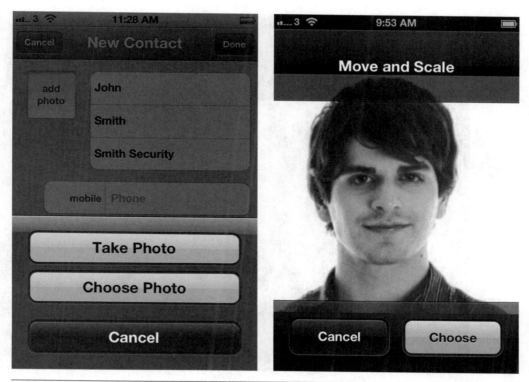

FIGURE 10-12   In the Photo dialog box (left), tap the Take Photo button or the Choose Photo as needed. If you tap the Choose Photo button, tap the picture you want, choose the appropriate part of it on the Move And Scale screen (right), and then tap the Choose button.

Create a New Contact from a Text, Phone Call, E-Mail Message, or vCard File

Creating a new contact manually, as explained in the previous section, tends to be hard work—so any way of creating a contact more quickly is welcome. The iPhone provides several ways, which we'll look at in this section. We'll start with the easiest way: using a vCard file.

Create a New Contact from a vCard File

The easiest way to create a new contact is by using a vCard file. vCard is a standard format for exchanging virtual business cards—tiny files containing the information that you'd normally find on a business card. So when someone sends you a vCard file via e-mail or instant messaging, you can open the file and add the contact's details to your Contacts list.

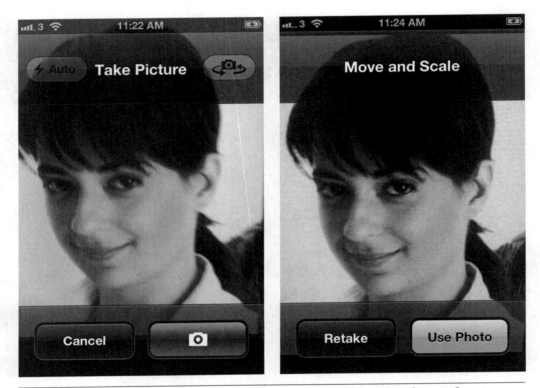

FIGURE 10-13   On the Take Picture screen (left), line up your subject's face in the unshaded area, and then tap the Take Photo button. On the Move And Scale screen (right), move and scale the photo to show the face, and then tap the Use Photo button.

Tap the vCard file's button in the e-mail message (the left screen in Figure 10-14 shows an example) or in the instant message. Your iPhone opens the file so that you can see its contents (the right screen in Figure 10-14 shows an example). From here, tap the Create New Contact button, add any extra information you have, and then tap the Done button.

 If the vCard file provides extra information for one of your existing contacts, tap the Add To Existing Contact button, and then tap the appropriate contact.

Create a New Contact from an E-Mail Message

When you receive an e-mail message from someone you want to add to your Contacts list, follow these steps to create a new contact using the name and e-mail address:

How to...   # Change, Edit, or Remove a Contact's Photo

You can quickly change or remove a contact's photo.

Tap the contact in the Contacts list to open it, and then tap the Edit button to start editing the contact. You can then tap the photo to display the Photo dialog box shown here, from which you can take the following actions:

- **Take Photo**   Tap this button to take a new photo of the contact, as discussed earlier in this chapter.
- **Choose Photo**   Tap this button to choose a different photo from your iPhone's selection. Use the techniques you learned earlier in this chapter.
- **Edit Photo**   Tap this button to display the Move And Scale screen, on which you can reposition or resize the photo.
- **Delete Photo**   Tap this button to delete the photo. You'll need to tap the Delete Photo button in the confirmation dialog box to get rid of the photo.

1. Tap the message to open it (if it's not open already). The left screen in Figure 10-15 shows a message open.
2. Tap the sender's name button on the From line to display the Sender screen (shown on the right in Figure 10-15).
3. Tap the Create New Contact button to create a new contact containing the sender's name and e-mail address.

Note   If the sender of the e-mail message is already one of your contacts, but the e-mail address isn't in your Contacts list, tap the Add To Existing Contact button on the Sender screen. On the screen that opens, tap the contact to which you want to add the e-mail address.

Create a New Contact from a Text Message

When you receive a text message from someone who's not in your Contacts list, you can quickly add the phone number to a new contact and then type in the name. To add the number to a new contact, follow these steps:

1. On the Messages screen, tap the message to display its screen. The left screen in Figure 10-16 shows an example.

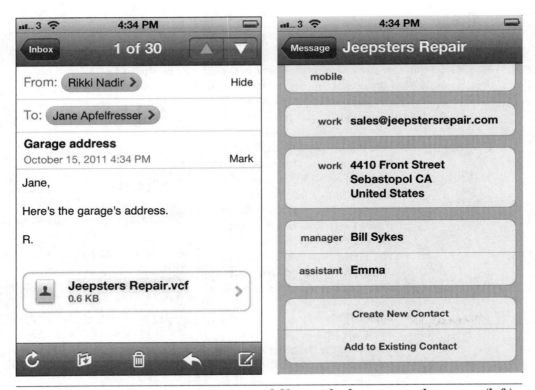

FIGURE 10-14 When you receive a vCard file attached to an e-mail message (left) or an instant message, tap the card's button to display its contents (right). You can then start a new contact record by tapping the Create New Contact button.

2. Tap the Add Contact button in the upper-right corner. Messages displays the Contact dialog box, shown on the right in Figure 10-16.
3. Tap the Create New Contact button. Your iPhone creates a new contact record and enters the phone number. You can then type in the name and any other data.

> **Tip** If the text message is from one of your existing contacts, but the phone number isn't in the contact record, tap the Add To Existing Contact button in the Contact dialog box, and then tap the appropriate contact in the list.

Create a New Contact from a Phone Call

Similarly, when you receive a phone call from someone who's not in your Contacts list, you can add the phone number to a new contact record and then enter the name. To start a new contact record, follow these steps:

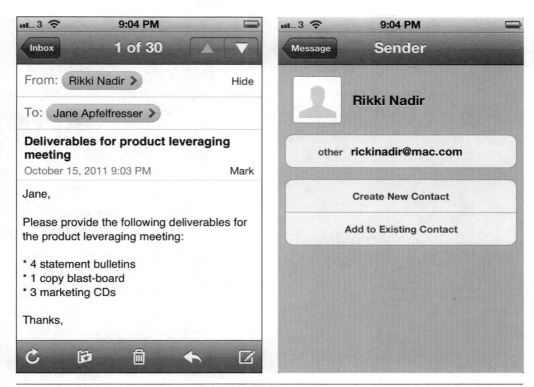

FIGURE 10-15   In an e-mail message (left), tap the sender's name button on the From line to display the Sender screen (right). You can then tap the Create New Contact button to create a new contact based on the sender's name and e-mail address.

1. Open the Phone app if it's not already open.
2. Tap the Recents button at the bottom to display the Recents screen (shown on the left in Figure 10-17).
3. Tap the > button to the right of the number you want to create the contact from. The Phone app displays the Info screen for the call (shown on the right in Figure 10-17).
4. Scroll down a little way, and then tap the Create New Contact button. Your iPhone creates a new contact record and enters the phone number. You can then type in the name and any other data.

 Tip   If the phone number is a new number for an existing contact, tap the Add To Existing Contact button on the Info screen, and then tap the appropriate contact in the list.

FIGURE 10-16 Tap the Add Contact button on the message screen (left) to start creating a new contact and add the phone number automatically. In the Contact dialog box that opens (right), tap the Create New Contact button.

Add Data to an Existing Contact

Rather than add a whole new contact on the iPhone, you may want to add data to an existing contact. To do so, tap the contact's name on the All Contacts screen or the screen for a group, and then tap the Edit button on the Info screen for the contact.

 If you meet with a contact in person and have your iPhone handy, you have a great opportunity to add a new photo for the contact if the contact record doesn't have one yet. Tap the contact's name to display the Info screen, tap the Edit button, and then tap the Add Photo button. In the dialog box that opens, tap the Take Photo button, line the contact up against some attractive scenery, and then tap the Take Photo button (the button with the camera icon). On the Move And Scale screen, move or scale the photo as needed, and then tap the Use Photo button to apply it to the contact.

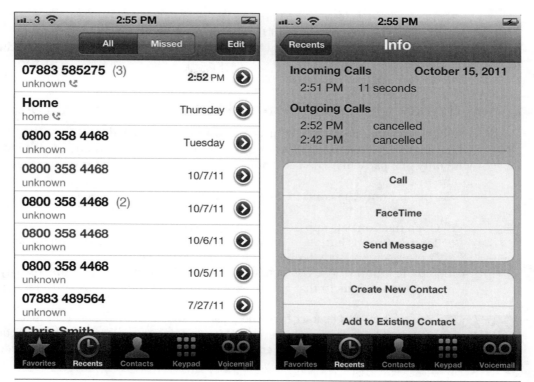

FIGURE 10-17 On the Recents screen (left), tap the > button to the right of a number to display the Info screen (right), and then tap the Create New Contact button.

Share a Contact

No matter how good your contacts are, you probably can't afford to keep them strictly to yourself—and your iPhone makes sharing your contacts with others as easy as possible.

To share a contact, open the contact's record, and then tap the Share Contact button. In the Share Contact Using dialog box that opens, tap the Email button or the Message button, complete the message your iPhone creates, and then send it.

Delete a Contact

In business as in love, not all relationships work out—and you may sometimes need to delete a contact from your iPhone. To do so, follow these steps:

1. On the Contacts screen or a group screen, tap the contact's name to display the Info screen.

2. Tap the Edit button to start editing the record.
3. Scroll down to the bottom of the screen, tap the Delete Contact button, and then tap the Delete Contact button on the confirmation dialog box that appears.

Display Only the Contacts in a Particular Group

Usually, when you open the Contacts app at first, it displays the All Contacts list, which shows the contacts in all your separate contact groups. When you need to work with only one particular contact group, you can display only the contacts in that group.

To display only the contacts in a particular group, follow these steps:

1. Open the Contacts app if it isn't already open.
2. Tap the Groups button in the upper-left corner. The Contacts app displays the Groups screen (shown on the left in Figure 10-18).
3. Tap the group whose contacts you want to view. The Contacts app displays only the contacts in that group, as shown on the right in Figure 10-18.

 You can't move a contact from one group to another on the iPhone. Instead, you need to do this in whichever tool you're using to manage contacts on your computer—for example, Address Book on the Mac, Windows Contacts on Windows, or Google Contacts on the Web.

Search for a Contact

To search for a contact, tap the magnifying-glass icon at the top of the navigation column of letters on the right of the Contacts screen. Your iPhone displays the Search box at the top of the screen.

Tell Siri to...

Remember Who's Who in Your World

To help Siri figure out what you want, tell Siri the names of your family members, boss, and other contacts. Here are examples of what you can say:

- "My wife is Anna Connor."
- "My boss is Phil Ramirez."
- "My mom is Shelly White."

Siri confirms each relationship before noting it. After you've told Siri the relationship, you can tell Siri to call your mom, insult your boss, and so on.

FIGURE 10-18   Use the Groups screen (left) to set up the contact groups you want to use on your iPhone. Tap a contact group to display the list of contacts that group contains (right).

Type your search term. Your iPhone displays matching results as you type. Tap the result you want to see.

Choose Settings for Working with Contacts and Calendars

So far in this chapter, we've assumed you're working with default settings for contacts and calendars. The default settings work pretty well, so this may be a fair assumption—but chances are that sooner or later you'll want to customize the settings to suit your needs. This section explains the settings and their effects.

You'll find the settings for controlling how your iPhone handles your contacts in the Contacts box on the Mail, Contacts, Calendars screen in the Settings app. Similarly, the settings in the Calendars box on the Mail, Contacts, Calendars screen control how the Calendar app works.

Tell Siri
to...
Find a Contact for You

To have Siri find a contact or a contact's details, say something like this:

- "Show contacts named David."
- "Show me the phone number for Anna Connor."
- "What is Bill Robinson's address?"

Display the Mail, Contacts, Calendars Screen

To display the Mail, Contacts, Calendars screen, follow these steps:

1. Press the Home button to display the Home screen.
2. Tap the Settings icon to display the Settings screen.
3. Scroll down to the third box, and then tap the Mail, Contacts, Calendars button to display the Mail, Contacts, Calendars screen.
4. Scroll down to the Contacts box, shown on the left in Figure 10-19, or (farther down) the Calendars box, shown on the right in Figure 10-19.

Choose Settings for Working with Contacts

These are the settings you can choose for the Contacts app:

- **Sort Order**   You can sort your contacts by "First, Last" order or by "Last, First" order. "First, Last" order sorts the contacts alphabetically by their first name and then by their last name: Andrew Jones, Andrew Smith, Anna Connor, Brian Dowell, and so on. "Last, First" order sorts the contacts alphabetically by their last name: Anna Connor, Brian Dowell, Andrew Jones, Andrew Smith. Use whichever you find most helpful. To change the order, tap the Sort Order button, make your choice on the Sort Order screen, and then tap the Mail, Contacts, Calendars button to return to the Mail, Contacts, Calendars screen.
- **Display Order**   You can display your contacts by "First, Last" order or by "Last, First" order. "First, Last" order puts the first name first, as is usual—for example, Anna Connor. "Last, First" order puts the last name first—for example, "Connor, Anna." Use whichever order you find easiest. To change the order, tap the Display Order button, make your choice on the Display Order screen, and then tap the Mail, Contacts, Calendars button to return to the Mail, Contacts, Calendars screen.
- **My Info**   To tell your iPhone which contact record contains your information, tap this button, and then tap the appropriate contact record in the list that appears.

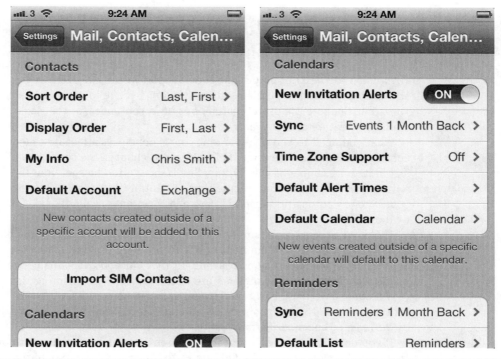

FIGURE 10-19   Use the Contacts box (left) on the Mail, Contacts, Calendars screen in the Settings app to control how your iPhone handles contacts. Use the Calendars box (right), farther down the Mail, Contacts, Calendars screen, to configure the Calendar app.

How to...   Import Contacts from an Existing SIM Card

If you have contacts stored on a micro-SIM card from another iPhone, you can import those contacts to your iPhone. Follow these steps:

1. Replace your existing SIM card with the other phone's SIM card. Use the SIM-eject tool to open the SIM card tray on the right side of your iPhone. Remove your iPhone's SIM, and put the other phone's SIM in its place. Then slide the tray back in.
2. Open the Mail, Contacts, Calendars screen by displaying the Home screen, tapping the Settings icon, and then tapping the Mail, Contacts, Calendars icon.
3. Tap the Import SIM Contacts button.

After the import, put your iPhone's SIM card back in again.

If the other phone uses a larger SIM, export the contacts from it on that phone, and then transfer them to your iPhone.

When You Should Use Time Zone Support— and When You Shouldn't

If you read the description of Time Zone Support in the main text and scratched your head in puzzlement, don't worry—you're in good company. Time Zone Support is a useful feature, but it's a contender for the Most Confusing Feature of iOS Award.

What you need to know first is that your iPhone uses a feature called Location Services to determine its location and changes the time zone to match it. For example, if you fly from San Francisco to Chicago, your iPhone switches automatically from Pacific time to Central time. (You can turn off your iPhone's automatic setting of date and time, but usually it's helpful, so we'll assume it's on.)

The point of Time Zone Support is to enable you to create appointments in a different time zone than the one you're currently in. With Time Zone Support off, if you create appointments for that Chicago trip while you're still in San Francisco, the appointments use Pacific time. So when you retrieve your luggage at O'Hare, Location Services will change your iPhone's time to Central time—but your appointments will still be on Pacific time, so they'll be a couple of hours adrift from reality.

If you don't want to be fashionably late for those appointments, turn on Time Zone Support and specify Chicago as the time zone before entering the appointments on your iPhone. While you're in San Francisco and your iPhone is on Pacific time, the Calendar app still displays the appointments at their correct time—even though that time is in a different time zone. And when you're in Chicago, and your iPhone has switched to Central time, the appointments are still at their correct times.

When you create the event for an appointment, the Start & End screen includes the Time Zone button, which shows the time zone you've set on the Time Zone Support screen. You can change the time zone for a particular appointment if necessary—for example, if you need to set up an appointment in Albuquerque using Mountain time rather than in Chicago using Central time.

If you need this capability, make sure Time Zone Support is turned on. Depending on who set up your iPhone, you may find Time Zone Support turned on by default.

Caution Make sure that the contact record you set as your My Info record contains not only correct information but also only information you want to share. If you use Safari's AutoFill feature, Safari can enter information such as your name and address automatically in forms on web pages to save you time.

- **Default Account**   Make sure this button shows the account to which you want to add contacts you create outside any specific account. If the wrong account appears on the button, tap the Default Account button, tap the right account on the Default Account screen, and then tap the Mail, Contacts, Calendars button to return to the Mail, Contacts, Calendars screen.

Choose Settings for Working with Calendars

These are the settings you can choose for the Calendars app:

- **New Invitation Alerts**   Make sure this switch is in the On position if you want your iPhone to alert you to new invitations when you receive them. If you don't want alerts, move this switch to the Off position.
- **Sync**   Tap this button to display the Sync screen (shown on the left in Figure 10-20), and then tap the button for the period of calendar events

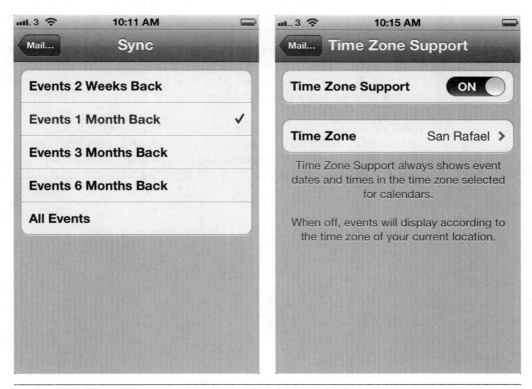

FIGURE 10-20   On the Sync screen (left), choose which events to sync to your iPhone. On the Time Zone Support screen (right), choose whether to use Time Zone Support and which time zone to use.

you want to sync: Events 2 Weeks Back, Events 1 Month Back, Events 3 Months Back, Events 6 Months Back, or All Events. Tap the Mail, Contacts, Calendars button to return to the Mail, Contacts, Calendars screen.

 To keep down sync time, sync only the calendar events you need to carry with you on your iPhone. Syncing All Events is usually overkill.

- **Time Zone Support**   Tap this button to display the Time Zone Support screen (shown on the right in Figure 10-20), and then decide whether to turn on Time Zone Support. Turning on Time Zone Support by moving the Time Zone Support switch to the On position makes your iPhone always display event dates and times in whichever time zone you select by tapping the Time Zone button and choosing your time zone on the Time Zone screen. Leaving Time Zone Support turned off makes your iPhone display event times and dates in your current time zone.
- **Default Alert Times**   This button lets you set the default alert times to use for birthdays, events, and all-day events. Tap this button to display the Default Alert Times screen (shown on the left in Figure 10-21), and then tap the button for the event type whose default alert time you want to set: Birthdays, Events, or All-Day Events. The right screen in Figure 10-21 shows the Events screen, on which you set the default alert time for regular events (ones that aren't all-day events or birthdays). Tap the button for the amount of warning you want—for example, 15 Minutes Before—and then tap the Default Alert Times button to go back to the Default Alert Times screen.
- **Default Calendar**   This button lets you specify the calendar to use for new events you create outside any specific calendar. Tap the Default Calendar button to display the Default Calendar screen, tap the calendar, and then tap the Mail, Contacts, Calendars button to return to the Mail, Contacts, Calendars screen.

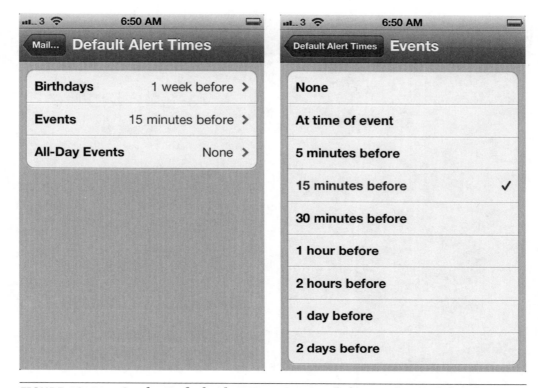

FIGURE 10-21   On the Default Alert Times screen (left), tap the Birthdays button, the Events button, or the All-Day Events button. On the resulting screen, such as the Events screen shown here, choose the amount of warning.

PART III

Use Your iPhone for Entertainment

11

Enjoy Music and Video on Your iPhone

HOW TO...

- Choose among the different ways of outputting your music
- Play music
- Play videos
- Play videos from your iPhone on your TV
- Find and watch videos on YouTube
- Use your iPhone as your home stereo
- Use your iPhone as your car stereo

In this chapter, we'll look at how to play music and video on your iPhone. We'll start by recapping the four different ways of playing music, from using the built-in speaker to using AirPlay. We'll then go through the mechanics of playing music and playing video, and consider how to find and watch videos on the built-in YouTube app. Finally, I'll tell you how to use your iPhone as your home stereo or your car stereo.

Choose How to Output the Music

There are four main ways to get music out of your iPhone:

- **Use the built-in speakers** This is fine for listening at low volumes in quiet places.
- **Use earphones or headphones** The earphone headset that comes with the iPhone includes not just ear-buds but also built-in controls for playing back audio, taking phone calls, and summoning Siri—so it's hard to beat for effectiveness. But you can also use any third-party headphones you want with your iPhone.

Earphones and headphones are the best solution when you're out and about or when you want privacy.

- **Plug in a pair of external speakers** When you need to fill a room with sound, plug in a pair of external speakers. You can use either the headphone socket or the Dock Connector port. We'll look at your options in the section "Use Your iPhone as Your Home Stereo," later in this chapter.
- **Use AirPlay to play through speakers connected to an AirPort Express** If you have an AirPort Express, you can connect speakers to it and play music to them wirelessly using AirPlay.

Play Music

This section shows you how to play music on your iPhone. As you'd imagine, you use the Music app.

Launch or Switch to the Music App

To play a song, first launch the Music app by tapping its button at the bottom of any Home screen. (If you've customized your iPhone's Home screens and removed the Music app from the row of key apps at the bottom, tap the Music app on whichever screen you've placed it.)

Switch to the Category You Want

In the Music app, four buttons appear at the bottom of the screen: Playlists, Artists, Songs, and Albums, together with a More button. Tap the button by which you want to browse. For example, tap the Songs button to browse by song name, as shown on the left in Figure 11-1, or tap the Artists button to browse by artist name, as shown on the right in Figure 11-1.

The Playlists list contains playlists you create on your iPhone, plus any Genius playlists you've created on your iPhone or in iTunes, together with any other playlists you've created in iTunes.

 Note The Songs list has a Shuffle item at the top that you can tap to play the songs in random order.

To browse by audiobooks, compilations, composers, genres, iTunes U items, or podcasts, tap the More button. Your iPhone displays the More screen (shown on the left in Figure 11-2). From here, you can tap one of the browse categories to browse by that category. For example, tap the Genres category to browse by genre name, as shown on the right in Figure 11-2.

FIGURE 11-1   Use the browse buttons at the bottom of the Music screen to switch among playlists, artists, songs, albums, and other items (tap the More button).

Find the Song or Other Item You Want to Play

To move down one of the lists, either drag your finger up the screen to pull the list upward, or tap one of the letters on the right to jump to that letter's section of the list. Once you find the song, playlist, album, artist, or other item you want to play, tap it. If the item is a song, video, or podcast, your iPhone starts playing it. If the item contains other items (such as songs), your iPhone displays a list of the contents. Tap the item you want to start playing.

Play a Song or Other Item

When you start a song or other item playing, your iPhone displays any available art for it, together with play controls. The left screen in Figure 11-3 shows an example of a song playing.

How to... **Change the Buttons at the Bottom of the Music Screen**

To change the buttons at the bottom of the Music screen, follow these steps:

1. Tap the More button to display the More screen.
2. Tap the Edit button to display the Configure screen, shown here with the Genres icon being moved.
3. Drag the icon from the main part of the screen to the browse button whose current icon you want to replace. (You can't replace the More button.)
4. Change other buttons as needed, and then tap the Done button.

The icon you removed from the button appears on the More screen, so you can easily restore it if you want to.

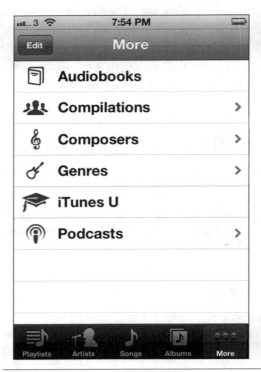
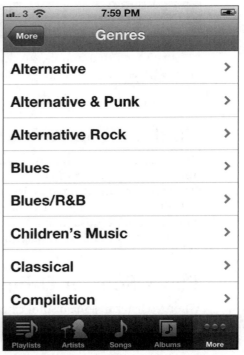

FIGURE 11-2   The More screen lets you browse by audiobooks, compilations, composers, genres, iTunes U items, or podcasts.

Back
button

Artist, Song Name, and
Album Name readout

Track List
button

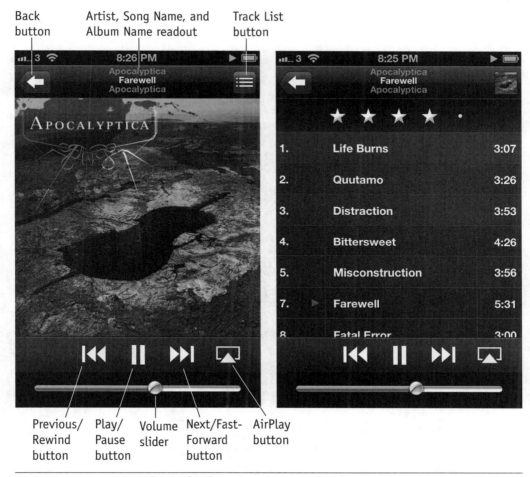

Previous/
Rewind
button

Play/
Pause
button

Volume
slider

Next/Fast-
Forward
button

AirPlay
button

FIGURE 11-3   Your iPhone displays the cover art for the item you're playing (left).
The Track List screen (right) lets you rate the playing item or go to another item on
the album or playlist.

Tap the Track List button to display the list of tracks from the album, as shown on
the right in Figure 11-3. You can tap a track to play it, or tap a star on the row of five
stars to apply a rating to the song. Your iPhone synchronizes this rating back to iTunes
the next time you synchronize the iPhone. Tap the Track List button again to return to
the album art.

Tap the Back button to go back to the screen from which you started the song or
other item playing.

Tap the cover art to display the additional play controls (see Figure 11-4). You can
then:

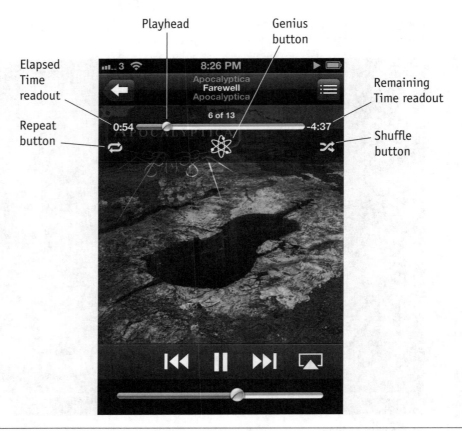

FIGURE 11-4 Display the additional play controls if you want to change the position of the Playhead or turn repeating or shuffle on or off.

- **Play a different part of the song**   Drag the Playhead (the dot that shows the current playing position in the song) back or forward.
- **Turn repeat on or off**   Tap the Repeat button once to repeat the album or playlist, a second time to repeat the playing item, and a third time to turn off repeating.
- **Turn shuffle on or off**   Tap the Shuffle button to toggle shuffle on or off.
- **Create a Genius playlist based on this song**   Tap the Genius button.

Tap the cover art again when you want to hide the additional play controls.

Use Cover Flow View

Once you've started a song or other audio item playing, you can turn your iPhone to landscape orientation to switch to Cover Flow view (see Figure 11-5). You can then

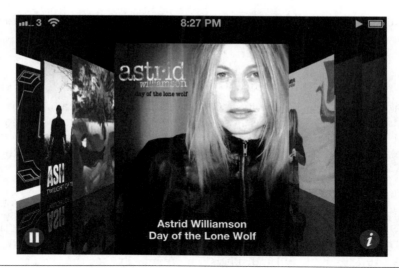

FIGURE 11-5 Cover Flow view lets you browse through songs or other items by their covers.

How to...

Apply an Equalization to the Music You Play

Your iPhone includes a couple of dozen built-in equalizations that you can apply—one at a time—to make the music sound the way you want it. For example, you can apply the Classical equalization that's designed to make classical music sound better.

The best way to set the equalization for a particular song is to set it in the song file using iTunes. You can set the equalization for a single song by using the Item Information dialog box (right-click or CTRL-click the song, and then click Get Info) or the Multiple Item Information dialog box (select the songs, right-click or CTRL-click, and then click Get Info). Then choose the equalization in the Equalizer Preset drop-down list on the Options tab.

When you set an equalization in a song file like this, the equalization setting carries through to your iPhone as long as the equalization you applied is one of the built-in ones rather than a custom equalization you've created.

You can also apply an equalization directly on your iPhone if necessary. You may want to do this when you've connected your iPhone to speakers or you're using different headphones than usual.

To apply an equalization on the iPhone, open the Settings app, tap the Music button, tap the EQ button, and then tap the equalization on the EQ screen.

browse through songs by tapping the cover whose songs you want to view. Drag your finger left or right to scroll through the covers more quickly.

Create a Genius Playlist

Like iTunes, your iPhone has a Genius feature that automatically creates a playlist based on a song you choose, drawing from the songs on your iPhone at the time. Genius can be a great way of digging out an interesting list of songs that have some relationship to each other but that you yourself wouldn't have put together.

To create a Genius playlist on your iPhone, follow these steps:

1. Tap the Playlists button to display the Playlists screen.
2. At the top of the list, tap Genius Playlist to display the Choose A Song To Create A Genius Playlist screen (shown on the left in Figure 11-6).
3. Tap the song on which you want to base the Genius playlist. Genius puts together a playlist, displays it momentarily (see the right screen in Figure 11-6), and starts playing the first song (the song you chose).

FIGURE 11-6   You can quickly put together a Genius playlist on your iPhone. If you don't like the result, tap the Refresh button.

4. To check or change the playlist, tap the Back button in the upper-left corner to go back to the Genius playlist. You can then take one of these actions:
   - **Play another song**   Tap the song you want to play.
   - **Refresh the playlist**   Tap the Refresh button to tell Genius to try again, still basing the list on the song you chose.
   - **Save the playlist**   Tap the Save button. Your iPhone saves the playlist under the name of the first song. (You can change this later in iTunes after you sync your iPhone.)
   - **Create a new playlist**   Tap the New button to go back to the Choose A Song To Create A Genius Playlist screen.

Create a New Playlist on Your iPhone

If none of your existing playlists appeals to you, and if even Genius can't dredge up a stimulating mix, you can create a new playlist directly on your iPhone. Follow these steps:

1. Tap the Playlists button to display the Playlists screen.
2. Near the top of the list, tap the Add Playlist button to display the New Playlist dialog box, shown here.
3. Type the name for the new playlist, and then tap the Save button. Your iPhone displays the Add Songs To *Playlist* screen (shown on the left in Figure 11-7).

4. Tap the first song you want to add to the playlist. Your iPhone turns the song's listing gray instead of black to show that you've added it to the playlist. This helps you avoid getting duplicates on the playlist.

 While adding to your new playlist, you can switch to another browse category. For example, tap the Artists button to view songs by artist.

5. Tap additional songs in the order in which you want to add them. You can also change the order later, as you'll see in a moment.
6. When your playlist is complete, tap the Done button. Your iPhone displays the playlist, as shown on the right in Figure 11-7. From here, you can start the playlist playing (by tapping a song or the Shuffle button), clear the playlist by tapping the Clear button, delete the playlist by tapping the Delete button, or tap the Edit button to edit it further:
   - **Delete a song from the playlist**   Tap the red button on the left, and then tap the Delete button that appears (see the left screen in Figure 11-8).
   - **Add songs to the playlist**   Tap the + button in the upper-left corner, and then work as described in step 4 above. Tap the Done button when you've finished adding songs.

FIGURE 11-7 You can quickly create a new playlist on your iPhone.

- **Move a song up or down the playlist** Tap the three-bar handle on the right, and then drag the song to where you want it (see the right screen in Figure 11-8).

Control Your Music While You're Using Another Application

When you're listening to music on your iPhone but you've switched to another application (for example, Safari), you can control the Music app from the app-switching bar.

Press the Home button twice in quick succession to display the app-switching bar (shown in the next illustration on the left) below the app you're using. Then scroll to the left to display the Music controls (shown in the next illustration on the right). You can then pause the music, rewind or go to the previous track, fast-forward or go to the next track, or tap the Music icon to open the Music app.

When you finish using the play controls, tap in the app you were using to hide the app-switching bar again.

Play Videos

Playing videos on your iPhone could hardly be easier. Tap the Videos button on the Home screen, and you'll see the Videos screen. This screen lists the movies at the top

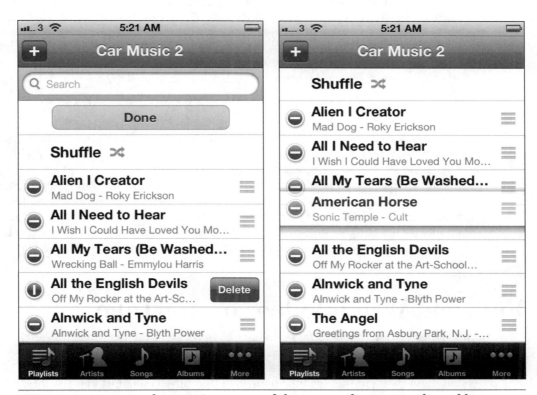

FIGURE 11-8   From this screen, you can delete a song by tapping the red button on the left or drag a song to a different position by using the three-bar handle on the right.

Tell Siri to...

Control Music Playback for You

You can tell Siri to control music playback for you. This is especially helpful when you're using the headset, because you don't need to touch your iPhone to control or change the music.

Here are examples of the commands you can give:

- **Play an artist** "Play Bruce Springsteen."
- **Play an album** "Play the album *Wrecking Ball*."
- **Play a song** "Play 'Mirrorball.'"
- **Play a playlist** "Play Road to Bataan."
- **Play a genre** "Play me some classical music."
- **Pause playback** "Pause the music" *or* "Pause playback."
- **Play the next song** "Next song" or "Skip."
- **Play the previous song** "Previous song."
- **Stop playback** "Stop the music."
- **Create a Genius playlist** "Make a Genius playlist from this song."

As you can see, Siri can understand a wide range of requests—so you'll probably want to experiment further. If Siri doesn't understand what you want, Siri will either start playing some music in the hope it's right or will prompt you to sort out your request.

(as you can see on the left in Figure 11-9) and the video podcasts below them (as you can see on the right in Figure 11-9).

Find the video you want, and then tap it to start it playing. Your iPhone switches automatically to landscape orientation if you're holding it in portrait orientation.

If you need to display the playback controls (shown in Figure 11-10), tap the screen. You can then pause, fast-forward, or rewind the video; move the Playhead manually by dragging its dot; control the volume; or zoom the video to fill as much of the screen as possible. Tap the screen again when you're ready to hide the playback controls.

Find and Watch Videos on YouTube

Your iPhone's YouTube app makes it easy to find videos on YouTube and watch them (I was going to say "enjoy them," but that part is harder).

To get started with the YouTube app, press the Home button to display the Home screen, and then tap the YouTube icon. The first time you run it, the YouTube app displays the Featured screen, as shown on the left in Figure 11-11. If you've run the app before, it displays whichever screen you used last; you can display the Featured screen by tapping the Featured button at the bottom of the screen.

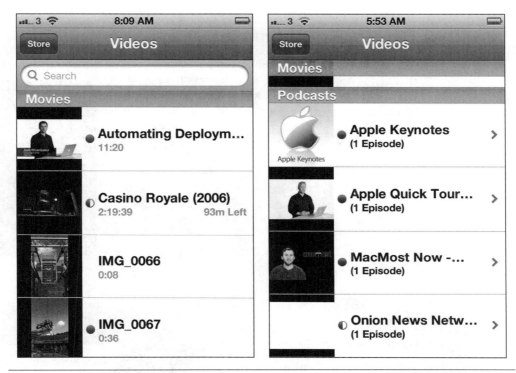

FIGURE 11-9   The Videos screen shows your list of movies (left) and your list of video podcasts (right).

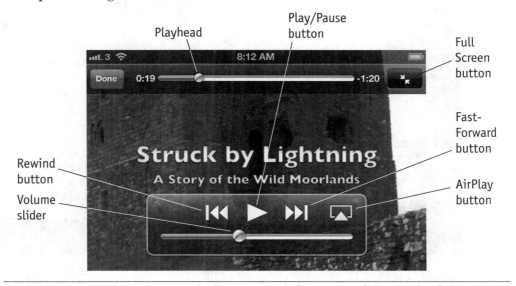

FIGURE 11-10   The onscreen playback controls let you easily control video playback on your iPhone.

How to... Play Videos from Your iPhone on Your TV

To play videos from your iPhone on your TV, you need a suitable cable. Look first at the Apple Composite AV Cable and the Apple Component AV Cable on the Apple Store (http://store.apple.com) and establish which one your TV needs. Then decide between buying the Apple version of the cable or a third-party equivalent.

When you have the cable, connect it to your iPhone's Dock Connector port and to the appropriate inputs on your TV. You can then play videos on the TV by starting playback. Your iPhone tells you that the output is going to the TV, as shown here. If the TV isn't showing the video, you'll need to fiddle with the AV buttons to make sure it's using the right input.

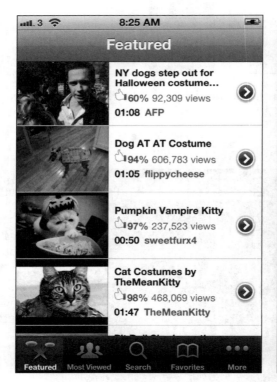
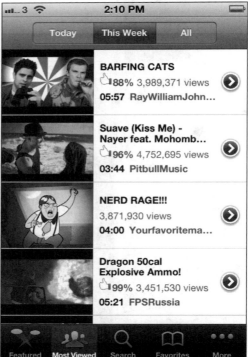

FIGURE 11-11 The YouTube app normally starts you off at the Featured screen (left). To find out which videos are popular, tap the Most Viewed button at the bottom of the screen (right), and then tap the Today tab, the This Week tab (shown here), or the All tab.

Find Videos on YouTube You Want to Watch

You can find videos on YouTube in any of these ways:

- **Featured list**   Scroll up or down the list, and tap any video that tickles your fancy.
- **Most Viewed list**   Tap the Most Viewed button at the bottom of the screen to display the Most Viewed screen. You can then tap the Today tab, the This Week tab, or the All tab at the top, and find out which videos have been popular. The right screen in Figure 11-11 shows the This Week tab.
- **Search**   To search for a video using keywords, tap the Search button at the bottom of the screen to display the Search screen (shown on the left in Figure 11-12), type your search terms, and then tap the Search button. In the results list (shown on the right in Figure 11-12), tap the video you want to view.
- **Favorites**   When you find a video you like, you can mark it as a favorite. You can then go back to it quickly by tapping the Favorites button to display the Favorites screen (shown on the left in Figure 11-13), and then tapping the video's button.

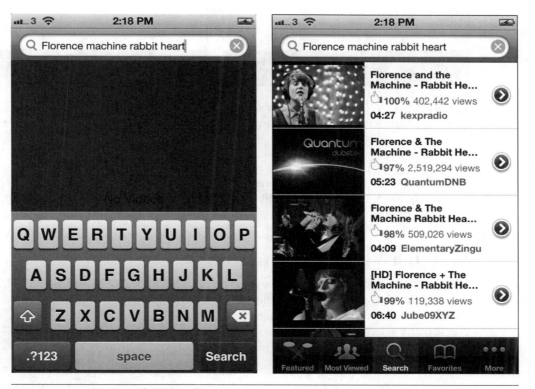

FIGURE 11-12   Use the Search screen to search quickly for videos. Type your search terms and tap the Search button (left), and then tap a video on the results list (right).

FIGURE 11-13 Use the Favorites screen (left) to return quickly to videos you like. Use the More screen (right) to browse YouTube by other means, such as your history.

- **More** Tap the More button to display the More screen (shown on the right in Figure 11-13), and then tap the button by which you want to browse. For example, tap the History button to revisit your browsing history and find a video you want to see again.

Watch a Video on YouTube

When you've found a video you want to watch, tap it. Your iPhone starts playing the video in landscape orientation, as shown here.

Tap anywhere on the screen to display the playback controls, shown marked in Figure 11-14. You can then take the following actions:

- Control playback using the Rewind button, Play/Pause button, and Fast-Forward button.

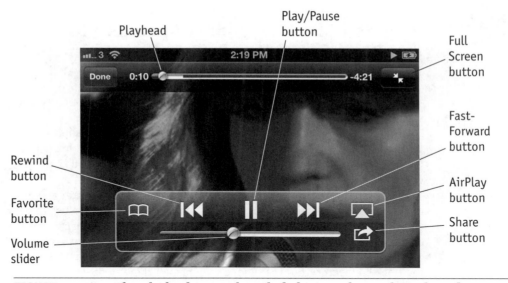

FIGURE 11-14   The playback controls include buttons for marking the video as a favorite, playing it via AirPlay, and sharing it.

- Scrub quickly through the video by dragging the Playhead left or right.
- Mark the video as a favorite by tapping the Favorite button.
- Change the volume by dragging the volume slider left or right.
- Expand the video to full screen by tapping the Full Screen button.
- Turn on AirPlay by tapping the AirPlay button and then tapping the button for the target device, as shown here. (The AirPlay button appears only if an AirPlay target device is within striking distance.)
- Share the video by tapping the Share button and then tapping the Add To Favorites button, the Mail Link To This Video button, or the Tweet button, as needed.

When the video finishes, tap the Done button. The YouTube app then displays the More Info button, which shows information about the video and provides links to more videos you may want to check out.

Use Your iPhone as Your Home Stereo

Earphones or headphones are great when you're the only one listening, but often you'll want to spread your music wider. In this section, we'll look at how you can play

Did You
Know?

Why You Should Connect Speakers to the Dock Connector Port Rather Than the Headphone Port

When you connect external speakers to your iPhone, you have a choice of ports: the headphone port or the Dock Connector port.

If possible, use the Dock Connector port rather than the headphone port. You can use it either directly with a speaker or cable that has a Dock Connector or indirectly, by connecting the iPhone to a dock and then connecting the speakers to the line-out port on the dock.

The Dock Connector port delivers a standard volume and better audio quality than the headphone port, so it's a much better choice. Most speakers designed specifically for use with the iPhone have a Dock Connector that enables them to receive audio at line-out quality and a constant volume.

When you need to connect speakers to the headphone port rather than the Dock Connector, turn the iPhone's volume all the way down at first. The headphone port puts out up to 60 milliwatts (mW) altogether—30 mW per channel—and can deliver a high enough signal to cause distortion or damage to an input that's expecting a standard line-out volume. After you make the connection, start playing audio and turn the iPhone's volume up gradually until you get a suitable level on the input.

music from your iPhone through external speakers or through your home stereo. In the next section, we'll consider the best ways to use your iPhone with your car stereo.

Equip Your iPhone with Speakers

The simplest way to get a decent volume of sound from your iPhone is to connect it to a pair of powered speakers (speakers that include their own amplifier). You can buy speakers designed especially for the iPhone, which use the Dock Connector port for high-quality output. But you can also get good sound using your iPhone with any powered speakers that accept input via a miniplug connector (the size of connector used for the iPhone's headphones).

Speakers designed for the iPhone tend to be smaller and more stylish than general-purpose speakers, but also considerably more expensive.

To get the highest sound quality possible from your iPhone, together with a consistent volume, use a dock or the Dock Connector port rather than the headphone port. Various dock models are available, from the utilitarian to the decorative. Connect the dock's line-out port to the speakers or receiver, and you're in business any time you've docked the iPhone. Similarly, most speakers designed for the iPhone include a Dock Connector, both to get the best sound quality from the iPhone and to be able to charge it.

Connect Your iPhone to a Stereo

If you already have a stereo that produces good-quality sound, you can play songs from your iPhone through the stereo. There are three main ways of doing this:

- Connect the iPhone directly to the stereo with a cable, either via the iPhone's headphone port or (better) via the Dock Connector port. You can use either a dock that provides a line-out feed or a cable that connects the Dock Connector port directly to your stereo.
- Use a radio transmitter to send the music from your iPhone to your radio, which plays it.
- Use your computer to play the music from your iPhone through an AirPort Express wireless access point that's connected to your stereo.

Connect Your iPhone to a Stereo with a Cable

The most direct way to connect your iPhone to a stereo system is with a cable. For a typical receiver, you'll need a cable that has a miniplug at one end and two RCA plugs at the other end. Figure 11-15 shows an example of an iPhone connected to a stereo via the amplifier.

 Some receivers and boom boxes use a single stereo miniplug input rather than two RCA ports. To connect your iPhone to such devices, you'll need a stereo miniplug-to-miniplug cable. Make sure the cable is stereo, because mono miniplug-to-miniplug cables are common. A stereo cable has two bands around the miniplug (as on most headphones), whereas a mono cable has only one band.

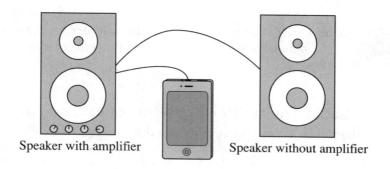

Speaker with amplifier   Speaker without amplifier

FIGURE 11-15   A miniplug-to-RCA-plugs cable is the most direct way of connecting an iPhone to your stereo system.

If you have a high-quality receiver and speakers, get a high-quality cable to connect your iPhone to them. After the amount you've presumably spent on your iPhone and stereo, it'd be a mistake to degrade the signal between them by sparing a few bucks on the cable.

You can find various home-audio connection kits that contain a variety of cables likely to cover your needs. These kits are usually a safe buy, but unless your needs are peculiar, you'll end up with one or more cables you don't need. So if you do know which cables you need, make sure a kit offers a cost savings before buying it instead of the individual cables.

Connect your iPhone to your receiver as follows:

1. Connect the miniplug to your iPhone's headphone port. If you have a dock, connect the miniplug to the dock's line-out port instead, because this gives a consistent volume and better sound quality than the headphone port.
2. If you're using the headphone port, turn down the volume on the iPhone all the way.
3. Whichever port you're using, turn down the volume on the amplifier as well.
4. Connect the RCA plugs to the left and right ports of one of the inputs on your amplifier or boom box—for example, the AUX input or the Cassette input (if you're not using a cassette deck).

Don't connect the iPhone to the Phono input on your amplifier. The Phono input is built with a higher sensitivity to make up for the weak output of a record player. Putting a full-strength signal into the Phono input will probably blow it.

5. Start the music playing. If you're using the headphone port, turn up the volume a little.
6. Turn up the volume on the receiver so that you can hear the music.
7. Increase the volume on the two controls in tandem until you reach a satisfactory sound level.

Too low a level of output from your iPhone may produce noise as your amplifier boosts the signal. Too high a level of output from your iPhone may cause distortion.

Use a Radio Transmitter Between Your iPhone and a Stereo

If you don't want to connect your iPhone directly to your stereo system, you can use a radio transmitter to send the audio from your iPhone to the radio on your stereo.

The sound you get from this arrangement typically will be lower in quality than the sound from a wired connection, but it should be at least as good as listening to a conventional radio station in stereo. If that's good enough for you, a radio transmitter can be a neat solution to playing music from your iPhone throughout your house.

Using a radio transmitter has another advantage: You can play the music on several radios at the same time, giving yourself music throughout your dwelling without complex and expensive rewiring.

Play Audio to an AirPort Express

If you have an AirPort Express (a wireless access point that Apple makes), you can use it not only to network your home but also to play music from your computer or iPhone through your stereo system.

To play music through an AirPort Express, first set it up like this:

1. Connect the AirPort Express to the receiver via a cable. The line-out port on the AirPort Express combines an analog port and an optical output, so you can connect the AirPort Express to the receiver in either of two ways:
   - Connect an optical cable to the AirPort Express's line-out socket and to an optical digital-audio input port on the receiver. If the receiver has an optical input, use this arrangement to get the best sound quality possible.
   - Connect an analog audio cable to the AirPort Express's line-out socket and to the RCA ports on your receiver.
2. If your network has a wired portion, connect the Ethernet port on the AirPort Express to the switch or hub using an Ethernet cable. If you have a DSL that you will share through the AirPort Express, connect the DSL via the Ethernet cable.
3. Plug the AirPort Express into an electric socket.

You can now play music from your iPhone by tapping the AirPlay icon, the icon showing a solid triangle superimposed on a hollow rectangle, as shown in the lower-right corner of the left screen in Figure 11-16. In the AirPlay dialog box that opens (shown on the right in Figure 11-16), tap the AirPort Express button.

When you need to switch back to the iPhone's speakers, tap the AirPlay icon again, and this time tap the iPhone button.

Use Your iPhone as Your Car Stereo

You can connect your iPhone to a car stereo in any of the following ways:

- Get a car with a built-in iPhone connection or add an after-market iPhone-integration device.
- Use a cassette adapter to connect the iPhone to the car's cassette player.
- Use a radio-frequency device to play the iPhone's output through the car's radio.
- Wire the iPhone directly to the car stereo and use it as an auxiliary input device.

Each of these methods has its pros and cons. The following sections tell you what you need to know to choose the best option for your car stereo.

FIGURE 11-16 Tap the AirPlay icon (the triangle and rectangle in the lower-right corner of the left screen) to display the AirPlay dialog box (right), and then tap the AirPort Express button.

Use a Built-in iPhone Connection

At this writing, Apple claims that more than 90 percent of new cars sold in the United States have an option for connecting an iPhone or iPod. (See the list at www.apple.com/ipod/car-integration.) So if you're in the market for a new car, add iPhone connectivity to your list of criteria. Similarly, if you're buying a used car that's only a few years old, you may be able to get iPhone connectivity built in.

If your car doesn't have its own means of integrating an iPhone, look for a third-party solution. Some adapters not only let you play back music from the iPhone through the car's stereo and control it using the stereo system's controls, but also let you display the song information from the iPhone on the stereo's display, making it easier to see what you're listening to.

Use a Cassette Adapter with Your iPhone

If the car stereo has a cassette player, your easiest option is to use a cassette adapter to play audio from your iPhone through the cassette deck. You can buy such adapters for between $10 and $20 from most electronics stores or from an iPhone specialist.

The adapter is shaped like a cassette and uses a playback head to input analog audio via the head that normally reads the tape as it passes. A wire runs from the adapter to the iPhone.

A cassette adapter can be an easy and inexpensive solution, but it's far from perfect. The main problem is that the audio quality tends to be poor, because the means of transferring the audio to the cassette player's mechanism is less than optimal. But if your car is noisy, you may find that road noise obscures most of the defects in audio quality.

If the cassette player's playback head is dirty from playing cassettes, audio quality will be that much worse. To keep the audio quality as high as possible, clean the cassette player regularly using a cleaning cassette.

 If you use a cassette adapter in an extreme climate, try to make sure you don't bake it or freeze it by leaving it in the car.

Use a Radio Transmitter with Your iPhone

If the car stereo doesn't have a cassette deck, your easiest option for playing music from your iPhone may be to get a radio transmitter. This device plugs into the iPhone and broadcasts a signal on an FM frequency to which you then tune your radio to play the music. Better radio transmitters offer a choice of frequencies to allow you easy access to both your iPhone and your favorite radio stations.

Radio transmitters can deliver reasonable audio quality. If possible, try before you buy by asking for a demonstration in the store (take a portable radio with you, if necessary).

The main advantages of these devices are that they're relatively inexpensive (usually between $15 and $50) and they're easy to use. They also have the advantage that you can put your iPhone out of sight (for example, in the glove compartment—provided it's not too hot) without any telltale wires to help the light-fingered locate it.

On the downside, most of these devices need batteries (others can run off the 12-volt accessory outlet or cigarette-lighter socket), and less expensive units tend not to deliver the highest sound quality. The range of these devices is minimal, but at close quarters, other radios nearby may be able to pick up the signal—which could be embarrassing, entertaining, or irrelevant, depending on the circumstances. If you use the radio transmitter in an area where the airwaves are busy, you may need to keep switching the frequency to avoid having the transmitter swamped by the full-strength radio stations.

If you decide to get a radio transmitter, you'll need to choose between getting a model designed specifically for the iPhone and getting one that works with any audio source. Radio transmitters designed for the iPhone typically mount on the iPhone, making them a neater solution than general-purpose ones that dangle from the headphone socket. Radio transmitters designed for use with iPhones in cars often mount on the accessory outlet or dash and secure the device as well as transmitting its sound.

How to... Find a Suitable Frequency for a Radio Transmitter

In most areas, the airwaves are busy these days—so to get good reception on your car's radio from your iPhone's radio transmitter, you need to pick a suitable frequency. To do so, follow these steps:

1. With the iPhone's radio transmitter turned off, turn on your car radio.
2. Tune the car radio to a frequency on which you get only static, and for which the frequencies one step up and one step down give only static as well. For example, if you're thinking of using the 91.3 frequency, make sure that 91.1 and 91.5 give only static as well.
3. Tune the radio transmitter to the frequency you've chosen, and see if it works. If not, identify and test another frequency.

This method may sound obvious, but what many people do is pick a frequency on the radio transmitter, tune the radio to it—and then be disappointed by the results.

Tip A radio-frequency adapter works with radios other than car radios, so you can use one to play music through your stereo system (or someone else's). You may also want to connect a radio-frequency adapter to a PC or Mac and use it to broadcast audio to a portable radio. This is a great way of getting streaming radio from the Internet to play on a conventional radio.

Wire Your iPhone Directly to a Car Stereo

If neither the cassette adapter nor the radio-frequency adapter provides a suitable solution, or if you simply want the best audio quality you can get, connect your iPhone directly to your car stereo. How easily you can do this depends on how the stereo is designed:

- If your car stereo has a miniplug input built in, get a miniplug-to-miniplug cable, and you'll be in business.
- If your stereo is built to take multiple inputs—for example, a CD player (or changer) and an auxiliary input—you may be able to simply run a wire from unused existing connectors. Plug your iPhone into the other end, press the correct buttons, and you'll be ready to rock-and-roll down the freeway.
- If no unused connectors are available, you or your local friendly electronics technician may need to get busy with a soldering iron.

If you're buying a new car stereo, look for iPhone integration or at least an auxiliary input that you can use with your iPhone.

12

Make the Most of the Built-in Apps

HOW TO...

- Manage your notifications with Notification Center
- Keep on top of your tasks with Reminders
- Use the Weather app
- Track stock prices with Stocks
- Perform simple or advanced calculations with Calculator
- Find yourself or get directions with Maps
- Use the Clock app for world clocks, alarms, timing, and countdowns
- Take notes with the Notes app
- Make audio recordings with the Voice Memos app

Even before you add any of the half-million apps available from the App Store, your iPhone is well equipped to handle everyday tasks with the impressive set of apps that comes built in. You've met many of these apps already: Safari, Mail, Messages, and several others. In this chapter, you'll meet the other key apps and learn how to use them: Notification Center, Reminders, Weather, Stocks, Calculator, Maps, Clock, Notes, and Voice Memos.

Notification Center

When your iPhone receives input that you might want to know about immediately, it displays a notification for you. For example, when a text message arrives, your iPhone displays a notification.

If your iPhone is locked, the notification appears as a dialog box on the lock screen, as shown on the left in Figure 12-1. If your iPhone is unlocked, the notification appears as a bar at the top of the screen for a few seconds, as shown on the right in Figure 12-1, and then disappears.

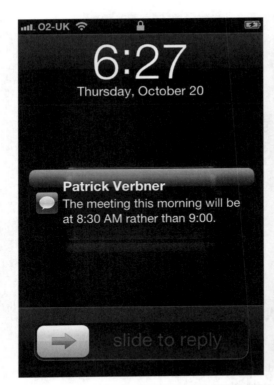

FIGURE 12-1 When locked, your iPhone displays a dialog box containing the notification (left). When unlocked, your iPhone displays the notification briefly on a bar at the top of the screen.

From the lock screen, you can slide the unlock slider to the right to unlock your iPhone and go directly to the notification in its app. When your iPhone is unlocked, you can tap the notification bar to display the notification in its app.

If you're not quick enough to catch the notification bar, tap at the top of the screen and swipe down to open Notification Center (shown in Figure 12-2). From here, you can tap a notification to display it in its app. For example, tap an instant message in the Messages category to open the Messages app and display the message.

 Tapping the button for a missed call in the Phone category in Notification Center returns the call rather than displaying information about it.

When you deal with a notification, Notification Center removes it from the list. You can also tap the × button at the right end of a notification category such as Phone or Messages to remove all the items from that category.

FIGURE 12-2   Notification Center puts all your notifications in one handy place, together with the weather forecast and a stock ticker. Tap an item to jump to it in its app.

To close Notification Center, tap the handle (the three horizontal bars) at the bottom of the screen—or anywhere along the bottom of the screen—and swipe up the screen.

Reminders

Your iPhone's Reminders app is a great way to track what you need to do when or where. You can set reminders for items by either time or by location. For example:

- **Time reminder**   You can set a reminder for 6 P.M. today reminding you to get the dog to take you for a run.
- **Location reminder**   You can set a reminder for whenever you arrive in Las Vegas, reminding you not to play the slots.

Reminders connects to the calendar accounts you sync with your iPhone, so any changes you make on your iPhone carry through to your computer and to any other iOS device you use (for example, an iPad).

In this section, we'll first open the Reminders app and look at its interface. We'll then get you set up with the lists of reminders you need. After that, we'll go through creating reminders and working with them.

Open the Reminders App

To start working with reminders, open the Reminders app by tapping the Reminders icon on the Home screen. At first, you'll see the main Reminders screen, which can show the reminders either as a list (as shown on the left in Figure 12-3) or by date (as shown on the right in Figure 12-3). To switch from list to date or vice versa, you tap the Date button or the List button at the top.

Set Up Your Lists of Reminders

What you'll probably want to do first in the Reminders app is set up your lists of reminders. For example, instead of having a single list called Reminders, you can

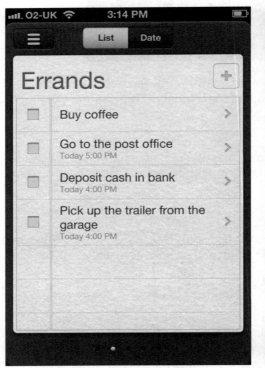

FIGURE 12-3 The Reminders app can display your reminders either as a list (left) or by date (right).

create a list called Work and a list called Personal. Keeping your reminders in different lists lets you view only your work-related reminders or only your personal reminders separately. You could also create a separate reminders list for Shopping, Errands, or a similar category—or as many other lists as you find helpful.

To set up your lists of reminders, follow these steps:

1. Tap the List button at the top of the screen if it's not currently selected.
2. Tap the View And Edit Lists button (the button with the three horizontal bars) at the upper-left corner of the screen to display the Lists screen (shown on the left in Figure 12-4).
3. Tap the Create New List button (shown on the right in Figure 12-4) to display the onscreen keyboard.
4. Type the name for the list, and then tap the Done button.

 If you want to rename the Reminders list, tap it on the Lists screen with Edit mode on. The onscreen keyboard appears, and you can type the new name. Tap the Done button when you finish.

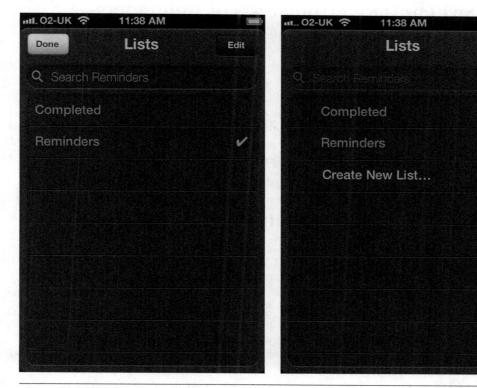

FIGURE 12-4 Use the Lists screen (left) to set up the Reminders app with the lists for keeping your reminders. To create a new list, tap the Edit button, and then tap the Create New List button (right).

5. Create other lists as needed by repeating steps 3 and 4.

 You can delete an existing list—but be warned that doing so also deletes all the reminders it contains. If you do need to delete an existing list, tap the round red Delete button that appears to its left on the Lists screen in Edit mode, and then tap the rectangular Delete button that appears to its right. In the confirmation dialog box that warns you this action will delete all the reminders in the list, tap the Delete button.

6. To rearrange your lists into a different order, tap a handle (the icon with three horizontal lines) to the right of a list's name and drag it up or down.
7. When you finish changing your lists, tap the Done button in the upper-right corner of the screen.

Tap the Done button in the upper-left corner of the screen to go back to the Reminders list.

Switch Among Your Lists of Reminders

You can switch among your lists of reminders in two ways:

- With the List button selected on the main Reminders screen, swipe your finger left to display the previous list or right to display the next list. The dots at the bottom of the screen show how many lists you have, and the white dot shows the current list. The leftmost list is the Completed list.
- Tap the View And Edit Lists button (the button with the three horizontal bars) at the upper-left corner of the screen to display the Lists screen. Tap the list's name, placing a check mark next to it. Then tap the Done button to return to the Reminders list.

Create and Use Reminders

To create a reminder, follow these steps:

1. Tap the New (+) button in the upper-right corner of the white page on the Reminders screen. Reminders starts a new reminder on the next free line on the page, as shown on the left in Figure 12-5.
2. Type the text of the reminder, and then tap the Return button. The Reminders app moves the insertion point to the next line.
3. Tap the new reminder's button to display the Details screen, shown on the right in Figure 12-5.
4. If you need to tie the reminder to a time or location (or both), follow these steps:

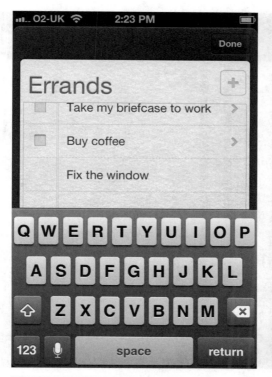

FIGURE 12-5   Type the name of the reminder, and then tap the Return button to enter it (left). Next, tap the new reminder's button to display the Details screen (right), where you can set the reminder's timing or location and other details.

a. Tap the Remind Me button to display the Remind Me screen, shown here.

b. To use a date and time for the reminder, tap the On A Day switch and move it to the On position. Reminders displays a date and time button below the On A Day button. Tap this date and time button to display the date and time spin wheels (shown on the left in Figure 12-6), and then select the date and time.

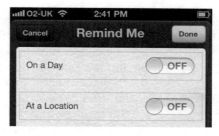

c. To use a location for the reminder, tap the At A Location switch and move it to the On position. Reminders displays the Current Location button, the When I Leave button, and the When I Arrive button below the At A Location button, as shown on the right in Figure 12-6. To choose a different location, tap the Current Location button, pick the location on the Location screen, and then tap the Remind Me button to go back to the Remind Me

FIGURE 12-6 For a time reminder, set the On A Day switch on the Remind Me screen to the On position and choose the date and time (left). For a location reminder, set the At A Location switch to the On position, specify the location, and then choose the When I Leave button or the When I Arrive button (right).

screen. Then tap the When I Leave button or the When I Arrive button, as needed, placing a check mark to the right of your choice.

5. Tap the Done button to return to the Details screen.
6. To make the reminder repeat, tap the Repeat button, tap the appropriate button on the Repeat screen (shown on the left in Figure 12-7), and then tap the Done button.
7. To set the reminder's priority, assign it to a different list, or add notes, tap the Show More button. Reminders displays an extra section of the Details screen, as shown on the right in Figure 12-7.
8. To set the reminder's priority, tap the Priority button. On the Priority screen, tap the Low button, the Medium button, or the High button instead of the default None button, and then tap the Done button.
9. To assign the reminder to a different list than the one you're working in, tap the List button, tap the appropriate list on the List screen, and then tap the Done button.

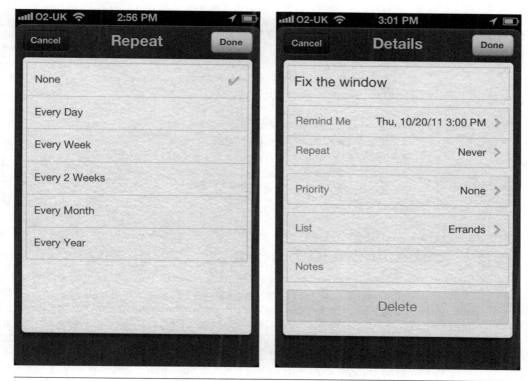

FIGURE 12-7   On the Repeat screen (left), you can set a reminder to repeat every day, every week, or at a longer interval. Tap the Show More button on the Details screen to display the Priority button, List button, and Notes button (right).

10. To add notes to the reminder, tap the Notes button, type the text on the onscreen keyboard, and then tap the Done button.
11. When you finish editing the reminder, tap the Done button.

Delete a Reminder

To delete a reminder, tap it to display its Details screen, tap the Delete button, and then tap the Delete button in the confirmation dialog box.

Weather

To find out how the weather's going to be, consult the Weather app by tapping the Weather icon on the Home screen. You can customize Weather with the cities you're interested in, turn local weather tracking on and off, and have Siri check the weather for you.

Tell Siri to...

Create Reminders for You

Siri is a great way to create reminders quickly and easily without having to fumble with the onscreen keyboard. Here are examples of what you can say to tell Siri to create a reminder:

- "Remind me to phone Shauna in half an hour."
- "Remind me to call Pete when I get to work."
- "Remind me to take my vitamins at eight A.M. tomorrow."
- "Remind me to start working on the relocation project at six this evening."
- "Remember to take my briefcase to work."

Use the Forecast Screen

At first, the Weather app displays the forecast screen. You can switch the Weather app between showing the next week's forecast (as shown on the left in Figure 12-8) and the current day's hourly forecast by tapping anywhere in the box except for the Y! button or the *i* button. With the hourly forecast displayed (as shown on the right in Figure 12-8), scroll down to see the forecast for other hours. Tap anywhere in the box (except for those buttons) to switch back to the week's forecast.

The dots at the bottom of the screen show how many cities the Weather app is set to show. You can scroll left and right to see other cities. If you look closely, you'll see that the leftmost dot is actually the location arrow, showing that the iPhone is giving you the weather based on your location. More on this in a moment.

Set Up Your List of Cities

To make the most of the Weather app, you need to customize the list of cities. You can also turn tracking of local weather on and off, and switch between Fahrenheit and Celsius.

To choose settings for the Weather app, follow these steps:

1. Tap the *i* button in the lower-right corner of the forecast screen to display the Weather screen (shown on the left in Figure 12-9).
2. If you want to turn off the local weather, tap the Local Weather switch and move it to the Off position.
3. Tap the Add (+) button in the upper-left corner to display the Type The City, State, Or ZIP Code screen (shown on the right in Figure 12-9).
4. Start typing the location—the city name, the ZIP code (if you know it), or the state. The screen shows matching locations.
5. Tap the correct location. The Weather app adds it to the Weather screen.
6. Remove any city you don't need by tapping the round red Delete button to

FIGURE 12-8   At first, the Weather app displays the daily forecast for the next week (left). Tap anywhere on the screen except for the Y! button or the *i* button to switch to the hourly forecast (right); tap again to switch back.

its left, and then tapping the rectangular Delete button that appears to its right. For example, if you don't care whether the sun is shining on Apple's headquarters at 1 Infinite Loop, remove Cupertino from the list of cities.

7. Drag the remaining cities into your preferred order by tapping a handle (the three horizontal lines on the right side of a city's button) and dragging up or down.

8. To switch from Fahrenheit to Celsius, or vice versa, tap the °C button or the °F button at the bottom of the screen.

9. When you finish choosing settings for the Weather app, tap the Done button to return to the forecast screen.

Stocks

If you own or trade stocks—or merely follow them out of academic interest—your iPhone's Stocks app enables you to keep track of important stocks and markets at any moment of the day so that you know whether you need to take action.

FIGURE 12-9 On the Weather screen (left), tap the Add (+) button to display the Type The City, State, Or ZIP Code screen (right). Type the location, and then tap the right place in the list of matches.

Tell Siri to...

Get Weather Information for You

Siri is a great way to get information about the weather, as she will give you helpful responses to a wide range of questions. Here are examples of the questions you can ask Siri about the weather:

- "How's the weather looking for Atlanta tomorrow?"
- "Is it going to rain in Oakland tonight?"
- "What's the high in Mexico City this weekend?"
- "Am I going to need an umbrella in Warsaw, Poland, tomorrow?"
- "Is it windy in Boston at the moment?"

Set Up the Stocks App with the Stocks You Want to Track

Your first move is to set up the Stocks app with the stocks you want to track. Tap the Stocks icon on the Home screen, and you'll see the default set of markets and companies in the app: typically, the Dow Jones Index, the NASDAQ, the Standard & Poor 500 (S&P 500), Apple (AAPL), Google (GOOG), Yahoo! (YHOO), the Footsie 100 (FTSE 100), the Deutsche Aktien Index (DAX—the German Stock Index), the Hang Seng Index (HSI) in Hong Kong, and the Footsie All Share Index (FTAS). The left screen in Figure 12-10 shows the part of this motley crew that fits in the Stocks screen at once.

To change the set of markets and companies, follow these steps:

1. Tap the *i* button in the lower-right corner of the screen to display the Stocks screen (shown on the right in Figure 12-10).
2. To add a stock to the Stocks screen, follow these steps:

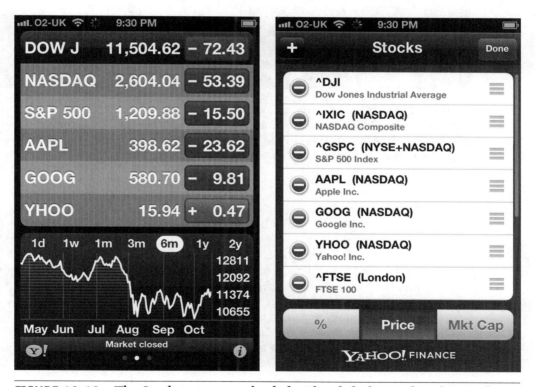

FIGURE 12-10   The Stocks app comes loaded with a default set of markets and companies (left). To customize the set, tap the *i* button in the lower-right corner of the screen, and then work on the Stocks screen (right).

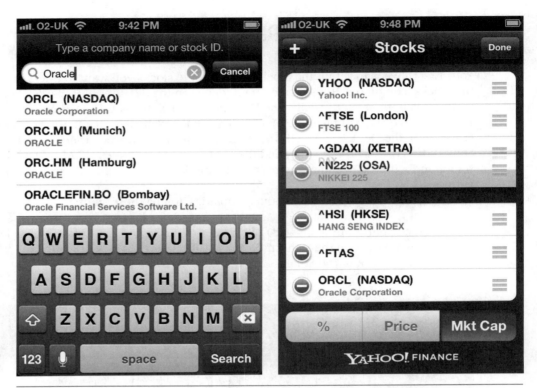

FIGURE 12-11 On the Type A Company Name Or Stock ID screen (left), type either an identifiable part of the name or the stock's ID code, and then tap the correct match. After setting up the list of stocks, drag them into your preferred order by using the handles on the right side (right).

- **a.** Tap the Add (+) button to display the Type A Company Name Or Stock ID screen (shown on the left in Figure 12-11 after a search for Oracle Corporation).
- **b.** If you know the stock's ID code, type it—for example, type the code **MSFT** for Microsoft Corporation. Otherwise, type a distinctive part of the company's name—for example, type **Oracle** for Oracle Corporation.
- **c.** In the list of matches that the Stocks app displays, tap the stock you want to add. The Stocks app adds the stock to the Stocks screen.
3. To remove a stock from the Stocks screen, follow these steps:
  - **a.** Tap the round red Delete button to the left of a stock's name.
  - **b.** Tap the rectangular red Delete button that the Stocks app displays to the right of the stock's name.
4. Rearrange the stocks in the list into your preferred order. To move a stock, tap the three-line handle to its right on the Stocks screen, and then drag the stock up or down the order, as shown on the right in Figure 12-11.

Tell Siri to...

Check Stocks

Siri is great for checking stocks quickly so that you can decide whether to double down, hold, fold, or fall to the floor gibbering prayers for a Powerball win.

To tell Siri to check stocks, use phrasing like this:

- "How's Apple doing today?"
- "How's Google's PE ratio doing?"
- "Where did the NASDAQ close today?"
- "What's happening with the Nikkei Index today?"
- "How are the markets looking today?"

5. When you finish rearranging the stocks, tap the Done button to fix your choices in stone (for now, anyway). The Stocks app then displays the list of companies and their current status.

View Your Stocks in the Stocks App

After setting up the stocks you want to watch in the Stocks app, you can quickly check how your stocks are doing by viewing the main screen.

Display the Market Capitalization, Percentage Change, or Value Change

You can tap any button in the right column to switch the display among the market capitalization (the company's total value; shown on the left in Figure 12-12), the percentage change (shown on the right in Figure 12-12), and the value change (not shown—but for example, –23.62 or +0.47).

Display the Details for a Stock

To display the details for a stock, tap the stock's name in the list. The area at the bottom of the screen displays the latest information. For example, tap the AAPL item in the list to display the latest information on Apple's stock.

There are three screens of information, which you can switch among by scrolling left or right or tapping the three dots at the bottom of the screen. As with the Home screen, the white dot shows which of the three screens you're viewing.

- **Statistics**   The first screen shows the stock's statistics—the opening price, high price, price/earnings ratio (P/E), and so on. The left screen in Figure 12-13 shows an example of this screen.
- **Stock Price Chart**   The second screen shows the stock's price, as you see in the right screen in Figure 12-13. Tap the button for the chart you want: 1d (one day),

FIGURE 12-12 Tap a button in the right column to switch the display among the company's market capitalization (left), the percentage change (right), and the value change.

1w (one week), 1m (one month), 3m (three months), 6m (six months), 1y (one year), or 2y (two years).

- **News** The third screen shows the latest news headlines related to the company. You can scroll down the list to see further headlines. Tap a headline to open the story in Safari.

Note Tap the Y! button in the lower-left corner of the Stocks screen to look up the current company in Yahoo! Finance in Safari.

View a Stock Price Chart in Detail

To view the current stock price chart in detail, turn your iPhone to landscape orientation. Your iPhone displays the chart full-screen, as shown here. You can then tap the button for the chart you want: 1d (one day), 1w (one week), 1m (one

FIGURE 12-13   Use the Statistics screen (left) to focus on the stock's details. Use the Stock Price Chart screen (right) to track the stock's movement over time. Tap a button at the top of the chart to choose the period you want to see.

month), 3m (three months), 6m (six months), 1y (one year), or 2y (two years).

To see a particular value, tap the stock's line on the chart, as shown here. You can then slide your finger left or right to see the value change.

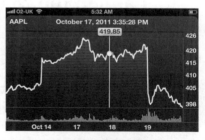

To see how the stock's price changed between two times, tap with two fingers at the beginning and end points, as shown next.

You can then scroll left or right to view another stock's chart. When you finish viewing stock charts, turn your iPhone back to portrait orientation to display the list of stocks again.

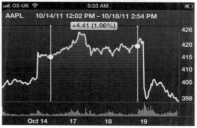

Calculator

Your iPhone's Calculator app (shown here) puts an easy-to-use calculator in the palm of your hand, always ready for quick calculations. You'll find the Calculator app in the Utilities folder by default. If you use Calculator frequently, drag its icon out of the Utilities folder to the Home screen so that you can launch it more easily.

Like a standard calculator, the Calculator app has a memory, which you manipulate using the M buttons: Press M+ to add the current number to the memory, M– to subtract the current number from the memory, MR to recall the current number, and MC to clear the memory.

When you need more calculating power, turn your iPhone to a landscape position. Calculator switches automatically to its Advanced mode (shown here), which includes mathematical and trigonometric functions.

Maps

When you need to find out where you are or how in the name of Loki you get to where you're supposed to be, turn to your iPhone's Maps app. Maps can help you find your present location, learn where somewhere else is, and get from point A to point B without losing your patience or your hair.

Launch the Maps App

To launch the Maps app, tap the Maps icon on your iPhone's Home screen. Maps at first displays a large-scale map, as shown in the left screen in Figure 12-14.

If your iPhone displays the Maps Would Like To Use Your Current Location dialog box, tap the OK button. If you tap the Don't Allow button, Maps won't be able to determine where you are.

Find Out Where You Are

To find your current location, tap the Location button (the arrowhead button) in the lower-left corner of the screen. Maps turns the Location button blue to indicate it's on, and then displays a map showing your location, with a blue dot at the center of a GPS homing circle, as shown on the right in Figure 12-14.

Perform Calculations for You

The Calculator app is easy to use when you have both hands free, but often it's quicker to have Siri run calculations for you. Siri can put mathematical calculations, currency conversions, temperature conversions, and other useful calculations through the Wolfram Alpha search engine and other sources.

Here are examples of the calculations you can ask Siri to perform:

- "What is the square root of 225?"
- "What is 15 percent of $92?"
- "How many British pounds is $300?"
- "How many days are there until the New Year?"
- "How much taller is Mount Everest than K2?"

The following illustrations shows a couple of examples of what Siri returns.

If what you see doesn't give you the information you need, you can zoom in and out or move the map as needed:

- **Zoom in**   Place your thumb and finger together on the screen, and then pinch out to zoom in as far as needed. Alternatively, double-tap the screen to zoom in using standard increments.
- **Zoom out**   Place your thumb and forefinger apart on the screen, and then pinch them together to zoom out as far as necessary. Alternatively, double-tap the screen with two fingers to zoom out in standard increments.
- **Move the map**   Tap the screen and drag the map in the direction you want to move what's displayed. For example, if you want to see the area to the east of what you're currently seeing, tap the screen and drag the map to the left.

FIGURE 12-14 Maps displays a large-scale map at first (left). Tap the Location button in the lower-left corner of the screen to display your current location (right).

View Different Types of Maps

At first, the Maps app typically displays the Standard map, which displays roads, cities and other settlements, and shaded areas indicating lakes, forests, parks, and so on. But Maps can also display a Satellite map—satellite photos, as shown on the left in Figure 12-15—and a Hybrid map that overlays the Standard map's roads and names on the Satellite map, as shown on the right in Figure 12-15.

To change the map displayed, tap the Options button, the page-curling icon in the lower-right corner of the Maps screen. The map rolls up to reveal a control screen, as shown in Figure 12-16. Tap the button for the map type you want to view, and then tap either the curled-up part of the map or the Options button again to uncurl the map.

View Traffic Status on the Roads

To view traffic status on the roads the map is showing, tap the Options button in the

FIGURE 12-15 The Satellite map (left) shows satellite pictures of the landscape. The Hybrid map (right) overlays roads and names on the Satellite map.

lower-right corner to curl the map up, and then tap the Show Traffic button. Tap the curled-up part of the map, or tap the Options button again, to uncurl the map.

The traffic appears as colored lines on the map, following traffic-signal coloring: green lines indicate traffic moving freely, yellow lines show slower traffic, and red lines show stationary traffic or gridlock. Figure 12-17 shows the same part of downtown San Francisco with (left) and without (right) the traffic lines. (Take my word that most of the colored lines are red.)

When you want to turn traffic off again, tap the Options button to curl the map up, tap the Hide Traffic button (if only it worked in real life!), and then tap the curled-up part of the map to uncurl it.

Search for a Place

To search for a place in the Maps app, follow these steps:

FIGURE 12-16   Tap the Options button, the page-curling icon in the lower-right corner of the Maps screen, to roll the map up, revealing the control screen. You can then choose the type of map you want to view, turn the display of traffic on or off, drop a pin on the map, or print the map.

1. Tap the Search button at the bottom of the screen to display the Search box at the top.
2. Tap in the Search box, and then type your search term, as shown on the left in Figure 12-18.
3. Tap the Search button to search for the term.
4. If the Maps app displays a list of possible matches, tap the correct one to display it on the map. If the Maps app finds only one convincing match, it displays the appropriate map and drops a pin on the place, as shown on the right in Figure 12-18.

Use Street View

The Maps app gives you access to Google's Street View feature, which has a giant database of pictures of streets and roads in the United States, Mexico, parts of Canada,

FIGURE 12-17   Turn on the Show Traffic option to display traffic lines (left) superimposed on the map (right).

most of Europe, the parts of Australia that have roads, New Zealand, South Africa, Japan, and the sexier parts of Brazil.

To use Street View, you need to have a pin on the map. These are the three main ways of getting a pin in a suitable place:

- **Search**   If you have already searched for (and found) a place, you may have a pin you can use already.
- **Existing contact**   If you want to see where a contact lives, tap the Contacts button at the right end of the Address box to display the Contacts list, and then tap the contact's name.
- **Drop a new pin**   If you don't have a pin or a contact, follow these steps:
    1. Line up the place you want to view in the center of the Maps screen.
    2. Tap the Options button to curl the map up, as shown on the left in Figure 12-19.
    3. Tap the Drop Pin button. Maps flattens the map and drops a pin right in the middle, as shown on the right in Figure 12-19. Being a taciturn geographical

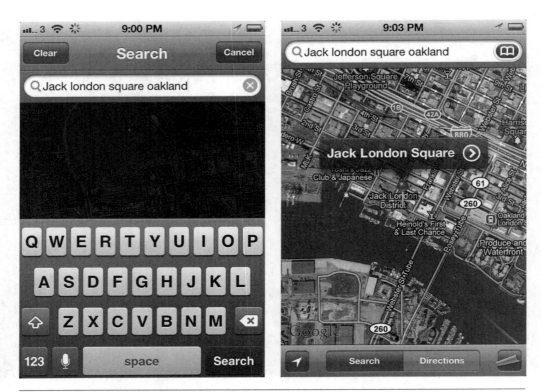

FIGURE 12-18 Type your search term in the Search box at the top of the Search screen (left), and then tap the Search button.

type and not imbued with the fires of artistic creation, Maps names the pin Dropped Pin.

4. If the pin isn't exactly where you want it, tap and hold the pinhead until it pops up. Still holding the pin, drag it to the right place, and then release it.

Once you've got a pin where you want it, tap the orange button (which contains a white figure) at the left end of the pin's label to enter Street View (shown here).

In Street View, swipe left or right to pan around you. Swipe down to view the sky, or swipe up to really view the street.

To move, tap a white arrow on the road.

To exit Street View, tap the screen to display a control bar at the top, and then tap the Done button. Maps displays the map from which you went through the Street View portal.

FIGURE 12-19   Tap the Drop Pin button (left) to drop a pin in the center of the screen (right), giving yourself access to Street View. Tap the orange button containing a figure at the left end of the pin to enter Street View.

Note   To get rid of a pin you've dropped, tap the pin to display its label. Tap the > button to display the Info screen, and then tap the Remove Pin button.

Get Directions from One Place to Another

To get directions from one place to another, follow these steps:

1. Tap the Directions button at the bottom of the screen. The Maps app displays the Directions controls at the top of the screen, as you see on the left in Figure 12-20.
2. In the bar across the top of the screen, tap your means of travel: car (the default), public transit, or on foot.
3. Tap in the Start box and enter your starting location. If you want to use your current location, and Maps has already entered Current Location, you're all set.

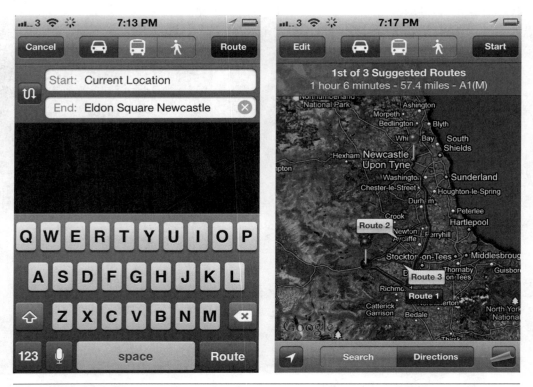

FIGURE 12-20 Enter your start location and current location at the top of the Directions screen (left), choose your means of transit, and then tap the Route button. Maps then returns one or more suggested routes (right).

4. Tap in the End box and enter your destination.

Tip If you need to swap the start location and end location, tap the S-arrow button to the left of the Start box and End box.

5. Tap the Route button—either the one at the upper-right corner of the screen or the one at the lower-right corner of the keyboard—to get the directions. The right screen in Figure 12-20 shows an example of a route.

Note If Maps shows two or more suggested routes, it displays Route 1 first. To view another route, tap the Route 2 button, the Route 3 button, and so on.

6. Tap the Start button to view the first direction. The left screen in Figure 12-21 shows the first direction for the sample route. You can then tap the right-arrow button to show the next instruction (shown in the right screen in Figure 12-21), and so follow along the route.

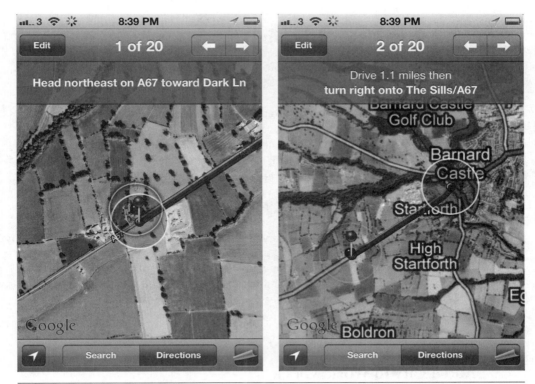

FIGURE 12-21   Tap the Start button to display the first direction (left), and then tap the right-arrow button to display the next direction (right).

Clock

Your iPhone's Clock app has four main features:

- World Clock
- Alarm
- Stopwatch
- Timer

We'll look at each of these features in turn.

Set Your World Clocks

The World Clock feature lets you see the time in as many locations as you need. So if you work with people in different time zones, or if you're planning to travel to places in different time zones, you can set a clock showing the time in each place you need to track.

Give You Directions

When you're on the move, Siri is a great way of getting directions. Here are examples of ways you can ask Siri for Maps information:

- "Where in the name of tarnation are we now?"
- "How's the traffic in Albuquerque?"
- "How do I get to Jack London Square from here?"
- "Tell me how to get back home from here."
- "Give me directions to that horrible dentist."
- "Find me a good Mexican restaurant in Emeryville, California."
- "Can you find a Peet's Coffee in Sacramento?"

As you can see, Siri gives you lots of flexibility—and if you say something Siri doesn't understand, you can always try again.

There's one big restriction you should know about when asking Siri for directions: Siri can give you directions only starting from your current location, not directions from one other place to a second other place. (For such directions, use Maps manually, as discussed in the main text.)

Add a City to World Clock

To add a city to World Clock, follow these steps:

1. Tap the World Clock button at the bottom of the screen to display the World Clock screen (shown on the left in Figure 12-22) if it's not already displayed.

> **Note** A dark clock face on the World Clock screen indicates that it is between 6 P.M. and 6 A.M. in that time zone. A white clock face indicates that it is between 6 A.M. and 6 P.M. These hours don't correspond exactly to night and day, but they give you a rough idea of whether it's day or night in each time zone.

2. Tap the Add (+) button in the upper-right corner to display the Search For A City To Add To World Clock screen (shown on the right in Figure 12-22 after performing a search).
3. Start typing the city's name in the Search box. Your iPhone displays matching results.
4. Tap the city you want to add. The city then appears on the World Clock screen.

Rearrange Your Cities or Remove a City from World Clock

To rearrange your cities in World Clock or to remove a city, follow these steps:

FIGURE 12-22   Tap the Add (+) button on the World Clock screen (left) to display the Search For A City To Add To World Clock screen (right). After finding the city you want, tap its button to add it to the World Clock screen.

1. On the World Clock screen, tap the Edit button. The Clock app switches to Edit mode, in which it displays a round Delete button (a red circle with a white bar across it) to the left of each clock and a movement handle (three horizontal gray bars) to the right of each clock.
2. To move a city, tap its movement handle and drag it up or down, as shown on the left in Figure 12-23.
3. To remove a city, tap its round Delete button, and then tap the rectangular Delete button that the Clock app displays to the right of the city (shown on the right in Figure 12-23).
4. When you finish rearranging or removing cities, tap the Done button to turn off Edit mode.

Set Alarms

Before you lull yourself to sleep, you may also want to set an alarm to blast yourself awake. Or you may simply want to set an alarm for a mustn't-miss appointment. You

FIGURE 12-23 Tap the Edit button on the World Clock screen to switch to Edit mode. You can then rearrange the cities by dragging the handle to the right of a city (left), or delete a city by tapping the round Delete button to its left and then tapping the rectangular Delete button (right).

can set as many alarms as you need on your iPhone, and you can choose exactly the right sound for each.

Set an Alarm

To set an alarm on your iPhone, follow these steps in the Clock app:

1. Tap the Alarm button at the bottom of the screen to display the Alarm screen (shown on the left in Figure 12-24).
2. Tap the Add (+) button in the upper-right corner of the screen to display the Add Alarm screen (shown on the right in Figure 12-24).
3. If you want to repeat the alarm, tap the Repeat button, and then choose the day or days on the Repeat screen—for example, Every Monday, Every Tuesday, Every Wednesday, Every Thursday, and Every Friday for a workweek alarm. The left screen in Figure 12-25 shows the Repeat screen. Tap the Back button after making your choice.

FIGURE 12-24   From the Alarm screen (left), you can quickly set one or more alarms on your iPhone by tapping the Add (+) button and working on the Add Alarm screen (right). The clock icon to the left of the battery icon indicates that an alarm is set.

4. Tap the Sound button to display the Sound screen (shown on the right in Figure 12-25), and then tap the sound you want. Again, tap the Back button.
5. Tap the Snooze switch and move it to the On position or the Off position to choose whether to allow snoozing.
6. If you want to change the name of the alarm, tap the Label button, type the name for the alarm, and then tap the Done button.
7. Use the spin wheels to set the time for the alarm.
8. Tap the Save button. The alarm appears on the Alarm page, with a switch for turning it on or off. When the alarm is on, a clock icon appears to the left of the battery icon.

Edit or Delete an Alarm

You can quickly change an alarm by editing it. And when you no longer need an alarm, you can easily delete it.

To edit or delete an alarm, tap the Edit button on the Alarm screen. Your iPhone displays a round red Delete button to the left of each alarm and a > icon to the right

FIGURE 12-25 On the Repeat screen (left), tap each day on which you want the alarm to repeat. On the Sound screen (right), tap the sound you want your iPhone to disturb you with.

Tell Siri to... Set, Edit, or Delete Alarms

Here's how to tell Siri to set, edit, and delete alarms for you:

- "Set an alarm for seven A.M. tomorrow."
- "Delete my seven A.M. alarm."
- "Wake me up in an hour."
- "Move my seven A.M. alarm to six A.M."
- "Change my seven-thirty alarm to six-thirty A.M."
- "Turn off my seven A.M. alarm."
- "Delete my seven A.M. alarm."
- "Cancel my seven A.M. alarm."

Siri can set alarms only for the next 24 hours. This is to protect you from setting alarms far enough in the future for you to forget about them. If you ask Siri to set an alarm for farther in the future, Siri offers to set a reminder instead.

Similarly, Siri can't set alarms for specific days.

of each (as shown here), indicating that each alarm is a button you can tap.

You can then edit or delete an alarm:

- **Edit an alarm** Tap an alarm's button to display the Edit Alarm screen, on which you can change any of the settings for the alarm. Tap the Save button when you finish.
- **Delete an alarm** Tap the round red button to the left of the alarm, and then tap the rectangular Delete button that appears to its right.

Tap the Done button when you're done messing with your alarms.

Time Events with the Stopwatch

When you need to time an event, tap the Stopwatch button at the bottom of the Clock screen to display the Stopwatch screen (shown on the left in Figure 12-26). You can then use the Stopwatch just as you would a physical stopwatch:

- Tap the Start button to start timing.

Siri can't manage the Stopwatch for you.

- Tap the Lap button to record a lap time, as shown on the right in Figure 12-26.
- Tap the Stop button to stop the Stopwatch.
- Tap the Reset button to reset the Stopwatch.

If you're planning to use the Stopwatch app to time your workout, check out the Nike + iPod app to see if it can do the job instead. Once you add a compatible sensor to your shoe, the Nike + iPod app can track your steps, calculate your speed, blast you to greater efforts with music and a Power Song, and generally keep you entertained while you make yourself suffer.

Use the Countdown Timer

When you need to count down a specific period of time, set the Timer like this:

1. Tap the Timer button on the Clock screen to display the Timer screen (shown on the left in Figure 12-27).
2. Spin the dials to set the countdown time.
3. Tap the When Timer Ends button to display the When Timer Ends screen, tap the sound you want, and then tap the Set button.

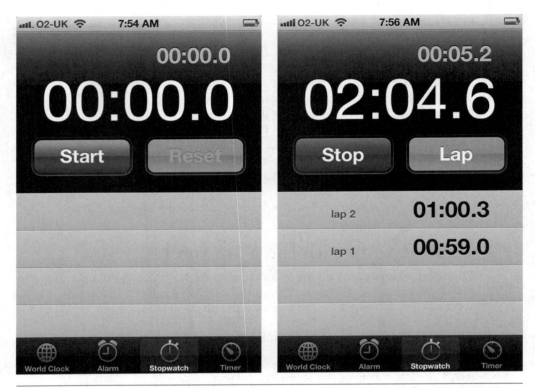

FIGURE 12-26 The Stopwatch has an easy-to-use interface including lap timing.

 At the very bottom of the When Timer Ends screen, you'll find a button called Sleep iPod. Tap this button to make your iPhone stop playing music (or video) when the timer stops. This setting is great for using your iPhone to play music while you go to sleep.

4. Tap the Start button to start the Timer running.

While the Timer is running (as shown on the right in Figure 12-27), you can tap the Pause button to pause the Timer (and then tap the Resume button to resume it) or tap the Cancel button to cancel the Timer. You can also change the sound by tapping the When Timer Ends button, tapping the new sound on the When Timer Ends screen, and then tapping the Set button.

Notes

Your iPhone's Notes app is a great tool for making text notes. In this section, we'll go quickly through taking notes with the Notes app, and then make sure you're using

FIGURE 12-27 On the Timer screen (left), spin the dials to set the countdown time, choose the sound, and then tap the Start button. While the Timer is running (right), you can change the sound, cancel the Timer, or pause the Timer.

Tell Siri to...

Set the Timer for You

Siri can set the Timer for you. This tends to be much quicker and easier than setting the Timer manually.

Here's how to tell Siri to control the Timer:

- "Set the Timer for twenty minutes."
- "Pause the Timer" or "Stop the Timer."
- "Cancel the Timer" or "Reset the Timer." (Or "Cancel that wretched Timer," if you like.)
- "Resume the Timer."
- "Change the Timer to thirty minutes."

the right account for Notes. Finally, I'll show you how to choose Notes' settings—all two of them.

Launch the Notes App

To launch the Notes app, tap the Notes icon on the Home screen. Notes at first displays the list of notes, with the most recently edited note at the top, as shown on the left in Figure 12-28.

To open an existing note, tap it. The note's contents appear, as shown on the right in Figure 12-28. To move from note to note, tap the left arrow button or the right arrow button at the bottom of the screen.

Navigate from One Notes Account to Another

When you have set up multiple accounts for Notes, the Notes screen displays the Accounts button in the upper-left corner, as you see in the left screen in Figure 12-29.

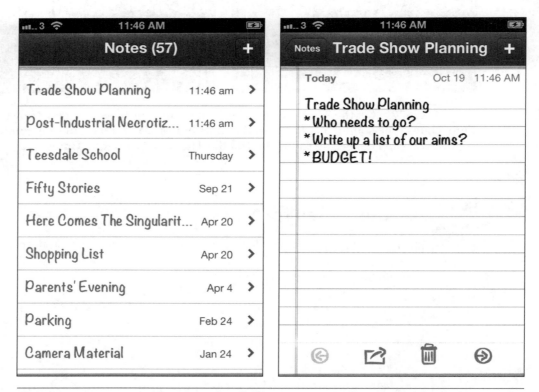

FIGURE 12-28 From the Notes list (left), you can tap the New (+) button to create a new note or tap an existing note to open it (right).

Tap this button to display the Accounts screen (shown on the right in Figure 12-29). You can then tap the account whose notes you want to view, or tap the All Notes button to view all your notes in a single list.

Create a New Note

To create a new note, tap the New (+) button on the Notes screen. The Notes app creates a new note called provisionally New Note, as you see on the left in Figure 12-30, and displays the keyboard.

You can then enter the text of the note by typing on the virtual keyboard, as shown on the right in Figure 12-30. Or you can enter text using Siri (see the upcoming Siri sidebar). After you enter the first line, the Notes app saves the note under that name.

When you finish entering text in the note, tap the Done button to hide the keyboard.

Tap the Notes button when you want to return from your new note to the notes list.

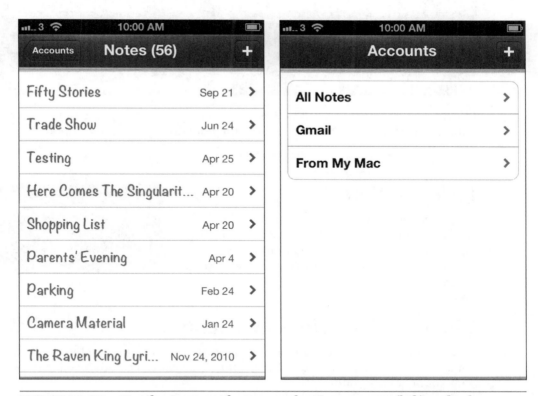

FIGURE 12-29 Tap the Accounts button on the Notes screen (left) to display the Accounts screen (right). You can then tap either the All Notes button or the account whose notes you want to work with.

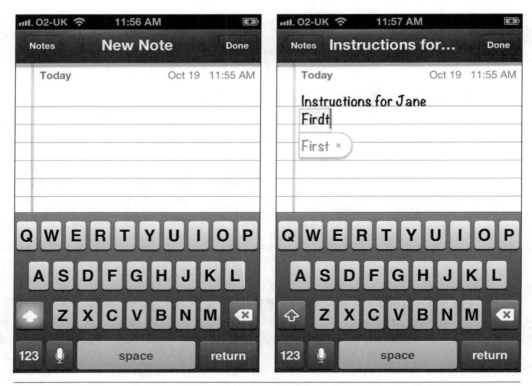

FIGURE 12-30 At first, each new note is called simply New Note (left). After you enter the first line, the Notes app saves the note under that name (right).

Delete a Note

To delete a note, open it in the Notes app, and then tap the Delete button (the button with the Trash icon) at the bottom of the screen. In the Delete Note dialog box that appears (shown here), tap the Delete Note button.

Choose Which Notes Accounts You Use

Your iPhone can sync notes from one or more accounts that you set up in Mail, Contacts, Calendars preferences. For example, you can sync notes from your Mac and from your Gmail account.

To choose which account you're using for syncing notes, follow these steps:

Take Notes

When you need to take a note quickly, call on Siri to take it for you.
To get Siri started creating a note, say something like

- "Note that Sam needs to take his sneakers to camp."
- "Take a note that Sam needs new sneakers."
- "Write a note saying that the assembly is at ten o'clock on Sunday."
- "Create a note saying that Siri is kind of cool."

In passing, one command to avoid saying is "Write me a note." This
phrasing causes Siri to create a note saying "me a," which doesn't get you far.
Tap the note that Siri creates to open it in the Notes app. You can then use
Siri to dictate text as usual:

1. Tap inside the note to position the insertion point where you want to add text.
   The Notes app displays the onscreen keyboard.
2. Tap the Siri button (the microphone button) on the keyboard to launch Siri.
3. Speak the text you want to input. If you need a new paragraph, say "New
   paragraph."
4. Tap the Done button. Siri plays a *bong* noise at you, processes your input, and
   types in the text.

1. Press the Home button to display the Home screen unless you're already there.
2. Tap the Settings icon to display the Settings screen.
3. Scroll down to the third box.
4. Tap the Mail, Contacts, Calendars button to display the Mail, Contacts,
   Calendars screen.

There's no easy way to move a note from one Notes account to another. Usually,
it's easiest to copy the note in one account, switch to the other account, and then
paste the copied material into a new note.

Choose Settings for Notes

The Notes app has just two settings, but it's worth taking a moment to make sure
they're set the way you prefer. Follow these steps:

1. Press the Home button to display the Home screen unless you're already there.
2. Tap the Settings icon to display the Settings screen.
3. Scroll down to the bottom of the third box.

4. Tap the Notes button to display the Notes screen (shown on the left in Figure 12-31).
5. In the Font box, tap the font you want to use. At this writing, the choices are Noteworthy, Helvetica, or Marker Felt.
6. If the Default Account button doesn't show the account you want to put new notes in by default, tap the Default Account button. On the Default Account screen (shown on the right in Figure 12-31), tap the account you want to use, placing a check mark next to it. Then tap the Notes button to go back to the Notes screen.
7. Tap the Settings button to display the Settings screen.

Voice Memos

Your iPhone's built-in microphone can make decent-quality recordings using the Voice Memos app. This can be a terrific way of taking down information quickly and accurately.

FIGURE 12-31 Choose your font for the Notes app on the Notes screen in Settings (left) and your default account for new notes on the Default Account screen (right).

If you need to make high-quality recordings with your iPhone, buy a third-party microphone. You can get either a model that plugs into the headphone socket or one that plugs into the Dock Connector port. If you go for a Dock Connector model, double-check that it's compatible with your iPhone. The iPhone 4S and iPhone 4 require a digital input through the Dock Connector port rather than the analog input that some mikes designed for iPods provide. For most third-party microphones, you'll need to use a third-party app, such as FiRe (Field Recorder).

You'll find the Voice Memos app in the Utilities folder by default. If you use Voice Memos frequently, drag the app's icon out of the Utilities folder and put it directly on the Home screen.

Record a Voice Memo

Voice Memos has a straightforward interface, as you can see on the left in Figure 12-32. Tap the Record button to the left of the VU meter to start recording, as shown on the right in Figure 12-32.

You can pause the recording by tapping the Pause button, and resume it by tapping the Record button again. When you're ready to stop the recording, tap the Stop button.

Listen to Your Voice Memos

To reach the voice memos you've recorded, tap the button to the right of the VU meter. Your iPhone displays the Voice Memos screen, as shown on the left in Figure 12-33.

From here, you can play a memo by tapping it and then tapping the Play button that appears. If you decide not to keep the memo, tap the Delete button, and then tap the Delete Voice Memo button in the confirmation dialog box that opens.

Trim a Voice Memo

When you record a voice memo, it's easy to include silence, mumblings, or blather at the beginning or end. The Voice Memos app lets you trim off this fat, leaving just the meat of the memo.

To trim a voice memo, follow these steps:

1. On the Voice Memos screen, tap the voice memo's > button to display its Info screen (shown on the right in Figure 12-33).
2. Tap the Trim Memo button to display the Trim Voice Memo dialog box.
3. Tap the Play button to play the voice memo. Note roughly where you want to trim the beginning, the end, or both.

FIGURE 12-32 Use the Voice Memos app (left) to record voice memos or other audio notes. When a recording is running (right), tap the Pause button to pause it, or the Stop button to stop it.

4. Tap the trimming handle at the beginning or the end of the voice memo and drag it to the point at which you want to trim the memo. This illustration shows the end trimming handle being dragged.
5. Play the memo again and make sure the trimming has the effect you want.
6. Tap the Trim Voice Memo button.

Label a Voice Memo

The Voice Memos app automatically names each voice memo with its date and time. It calls the name a "label," for reasons known only to Apple. To give a voice memo the name you want, you can either assign a preset label or create a custom label.

To label a voice memo, follow these steps:

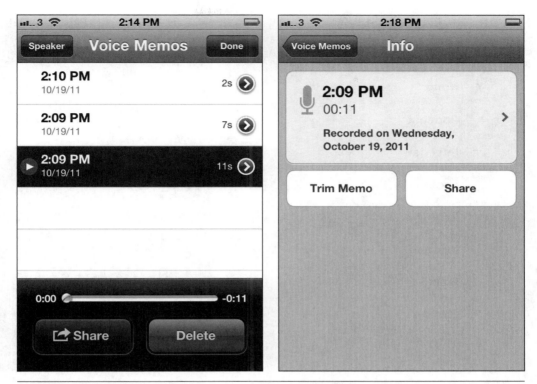

FIGURE 12-33   On the Voice Memos screen (left), tap the memo you want to play, and then tap its Play button. To see a memo's details, tap its > button, displaying the Info screen (right).

1. On the Voice Memos screen, tap the voice memo's > button to display its Info screen.
2. Tap the big button that shows the voice memo's recording time, duration, and date to display the Label screen (shown on the left in Figure 12-34).
3. Apply the label:
    - To apply a preset label, tap it, and then tap the Info button to return to the Info screen.
    - To create a custom label, tap the Custom button, type the label on the Custom screen (shown on the right in Figure 12-34), and then tap the Done button.

Share a Voice Memo via E-Mail or Instant Messaging

To share a voice memo with others, tap the voice memo on the Voice Memos screen, and then tap the Share button. You can also tap the Share button on the Info screen for the voice memo.

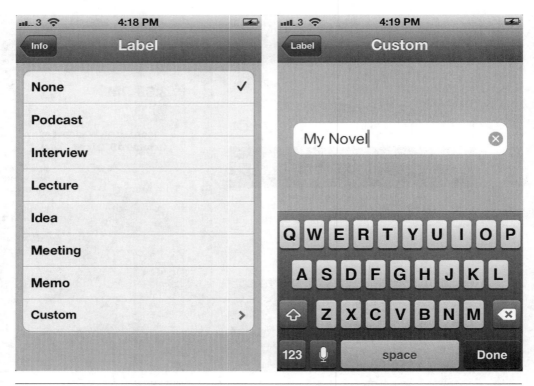

FIGURE 12-34 On the Label screen (left), tap the label you want to assign to the voice memo. To assign a custom label, tap the Custom button, type the label on the Custom screen (right), and then tap the Done button.

In the Share Voice Memo Using dialog box (shown here), tap the Email button or the Message button, as appropriate. Your iPhone starts a new e-mail message in the Mail app or a new MMS message in the Messages app, with the voice memo file attached. You can then address the message, type any explanatory text needed, and send the message as usual.

13

Create a Great Audio and Video Library for the iPhone and iTunes

HOW TO...

- Buy and download songs, videos, and more online
- Manage your music and video library with iTunes
- Create video files that work with your iPhone
- Recover your songs and videos from your iPhone

In this chapter, I'll show you how to create a great audio and video library that you can enjoy both on your iPhone and on your computer using iTunes. We'll cover how to buy and download songs online, how to manage your music and video library with iTunes, and how to create video files that work with your iPhone. We'll also look quickly at how to recover your songs and videos from your iPhone if your iTunes library gets corrupted.

Buy and Download Songs, Videos, and More Online

Instead of creating song files by ripping your own CDs as discussed in Chapter 2, you can buy songs online. You can also buy videos, movies, audio books, and other content.

In this section, we'll first look at how to buy songs and other items from the iTunes Store by using a computer. Next, we'll go over how to buy items from the iTunes Wi-Fi Store using your iPhone. After that, we'll consider other music stores you may want to try.

Buy Songs, Videos, and Movies from the iTunes Store

So far, the iTunes Store is one of the largest and most successful attempts to sell music online. The iTunes Store is far from perfect, and it still lacks many songs that users would like to be able to buy, but it already provides a great service and is growing rapidly. At this writing, the iTunes Store is available to iTunes users on Windows and the Mac.

Here's the deal with the iTunes Store:

- Most songs cost $0.69, $0.99, or $1.29.
- Most albums cost $9.99. Some CDs are available only as "partial CDs," which typically means that you can't buy the songs you're most likely to want. Extra-long songs (for example, those 13-minute jam sessions used to max out a CD) are sometimes available for purchase only with an entire CD.
- Most video items cost $1.99 or more, but you can also buy them in bulk and save. For example, you might buy a whole season of *Mad Men*.
- You can listen to a preview of any song to make sure it's what you want. Most previews are 90 seconds, unless the song is shorter than that or the record company has dug in its heels and insisted on 30 seconds. After you buy a song, you download it to your music library.
- You can burn songs to CD an unlimited number of times, although you can burn any given playlist only seven times without changing it or re-creating it under another name.
- The songs you buy are encoded in the AAC format (discussed in the section "Configure iTunes for the Audio Quality You Want," later in this chapter). Most videos and movies you buy are in the MPEG-4 video format and are protected with digital rights management (DRM).
- You can play the songs you buy on any number of iPhones (or iPods, or iPads) that you synchronize with your PC or Mac. You may also be able to play the songs on other music players that can use the AAC format (for example, some mobile phones other than iPhones can play AAC files).
- You can play the DRM-protected items you buy on up to five computers at once. These computers are said to be "authorized." You can change which computers are authorized for the items bought on a particular iTunes Store account.
- You can download any item you buy from the iTunes Store again if necessary, and you can share the items among all the devices linked to your iTunes Store account. For example, if you buy a song on your computer, you can download it to your iPhone and iPad as well.
- You can rent a movie and watch it on your computer, iPhone, iPod, iPad, or Apple TV. You can watch a rented movie on only one device at a time. So when you transfer a rented movie from your computer to one of the other devices mentioned above, it disappears from the iTunes library on your computer.

Know the Disadvantages of Buying from the iTunes Store

As of October 2011, the iTunes Store offers more than 20 million songs and has sold more than 16 billion songs altogether.

For customers, it's great to be able to find songs easily, buy them almost instantly for reasonable prices, and use them in enough of the ways we're used to (play the songs on a computer; play them on an iPhone, iPod, or iPad; or burn them to disc). For the record companies, the appeal is a still largely untapped market that can provide a revenue stream at minimal cost (no physical media are involved) and with an acceptably small potential for abuse.

Before you buy from the iTunes Store, though, be aware of these disadvantages:

- Even though the AAC format provides relatively high audio quality, the songs sold by the iTunes Store are significantly lower quality than CD-quality audio. Test a few songs through headphones or high-end speakers to make sure you're happy with the quality you're getting.
- When you buy a CD, you own it. You can't necessarily do what you want with the music—not legally, anyway. But you can play it as often as you want on whichever player, lend it to a friend, sell it to someone else, and so on. By contrast, when you buy a song from the iTunes Store, you're not allowed to lend it to other people, or to sell it.

As well as songs, the iTunes Store sells video files and movies. As with songs, the convenience of buying via download is wonderful, but there are still disadvantages:

- Even the high-definition format provides lower quality than a high-definition DVD.
- You buy not a tangible object but a license to use the file. You can't resell the file—in fact, you can't even give it to someone else.
- If the video or movie file is protected by DRM (as most are), Apple can change your rights to use it, or simply stop you from playing it.

Set Up an Account with the iTunes Store

To use the iTunes Store, you need a PC or a Mac running iTunes as well as an Apple ID or an AOL screen name. You can get an Apple ID by setting up an account with Apple's iCloud service or an account on the iTunes Store.

 If you already have an account with Apple's MobileMe service, you've already got an Apple ID. But Apple has announced that it will close MobileMe on June 30, 2012, so it is no longer selling MobileMe accounts. By that date, all MobileMe users will need to migrate to the iCloud service or lose access to their MobileMe content.

To get started with the iTunes Store, open it in iTunes. If you want to be able to keep your music playing while you browse the iTunes Store, double-click the iTunes

Store item in the Source list to open a separate window showing the iTunes Store. If you prefer to work in the main iTunes window, simply click the iTunes Store item in the Source list in iTunes.

iTunes accesses the iTunes Store and displays its home page. Figure 13-1 shows an example on the Mac, using a separate window.

To sign in or to create an account, click the Sign In button. iTunes displays the Sign In To Download From The iTunes Store dialog box (see Figure 13-2).

If you have an Apple ID, type it in the Apple ID text box, type your password in the Password text box, and click the Sign In button. Likewise, if you have an AOL screen name, select the AOL option button, type your screen name and password, and click the Sign In button.

 Remember that your Apple ID is the full e-mail address, including the domain—not just the first part of the address. For example, if your Apple ID is an iCloud address, enter **yourname@me.com** rather than just **yourname**.

The first time you sign in to the iTunes Store, iTunes displays a dialog box (shown in the next illustration) pointing out that your Apple ID or AOL screen name hasn't been used with the iTunes Store and suggesting that you review your account information:

FIGURE 13-1 The iTunes Store home page provides quick access to the songs, videos, and other items available. You can display the iTunes Store either in a separate window, as shown here, or in the main iTunes window.

Sign In to download from the iTunes Store
To create an Apple Account, click Create New Account

[Create New Account]

If you have an Apple Account (from the iTunes Store or MobileMe, for example),
enter your Apple ID and password. Otherwise, if you are an AOL member, enter
your AOL screen name and password.

○ 🍎 Apple ID:
jane_apfelfresser@me.co| Example: steve@me.com
Password:
○ **AOL.** ••••••   [Forgot Password?]

(?)   [Cancel] [Sign In]

FIGURE 13-2 From the Sign In dialog box, you can sign in to an existing account or create a new account.

This AOL screen name has not yet been used with the iTunes Store.

Please review your account information.

[Cancel] (Review)

Click the Review button to review your account information. (This is a compulsory step. Clicking the Cancel button doesn't skip the review process, as you might hope—instead, it cancels the creation of your account.)

To create a new account, click the Create New Account button and then click the Continue button on the Welcome To The iTunes Store page. The subsequent screens then walk you through the process of creating an account. You have to provide your credit card details and billing address. Beyond this, you get a little homily on what you may and may not legally do with the items you download, and you must agree to the terms of service of the iTunes Store.

Understand the Terms of Service

Almost no one ever reads the details of software licenses, which is why the software companies have been able to establish as normal the sales model in which you buy not software itself but a limited license to use it, and you have no recourse if it corrupts your data or reduces your computer to a pitiful puddle of silicon and steel. But you'd do well to read the terms and conditions of the iTunes Store before you buy music from it, because you should understand what you're getting into.

The iTunes window doesn't give you the greatest view of the terms of service. To get a better view, click the Printable Version link at the very bottom of the scroll box or direct your browser to www.apple.com/legal/itunes/us/service.html.

The following are the key points of the terms of service:

- You can play DRM-protected items that you download on five Apple-authorized devices—computers, iPhones, iPads, or iPods—at any time. You can authorize and deauthorize computers, so you can (for example) transfer your DRM-protected items from your old computer to a new computer you buy.
- You can use, export, copy, and burn songs for "personal, noncommercial use." Burning and exporting are an "accommodation" to you and don't "constitute a grant, waiver, or other limitation of any rights of the copyright owners." If you think that your being allowed to burn what would otherwise be illegal copies must limit the copyright owners' rights, I'd say you're right logically but wrong legally.
- You're not allowed to burn videos. Period.
- You agree not to violate the Usage Rules imposed by the agreement.
- You agree that Apple may disclose your registration data and account information to "law enforcement authorities, government officials, and/or a third party, as Apple believes is reasonably necessary or appropriate to enforce and/or verify compliance with any part of this Agreement." The implication is that if a copyright holder claims that you're infringing their copyright, Apple may disclose your details without your knowledge, let alone your agreement. This seems to mean that, say, Sony Music or the RIAA can get the details of your e-mail address, physical address, credit card, and listening habits by claiming a suspicion of copyright violation.
- Apple and its licensors can remove or prevent you from accessing "products, content, or other materials."
- Apple reserves the right to modify the Agreement at any time. If you continue using the iTunes Store, you're deemed to have accepted whatever additional terms Apple imposes.
- Apple can terminate your account for your failing to "comply with any of the provisions" in the Agreement—or for your being suspected of such failure. Terminating your account prevents you from buying any more songs and videos immediately, but you might be able to set up another account. More seriously, termination may prevent you from playing songs and videos you've already bought—for example, if you need to authorize a computer to play them.

Configure iTunes Store Settings

By default, iTunes displays a Store category in the Source list with an iTunes Store item and the Ping social-networking item. After you buy one or more items from the iTunes store, the Purchased item appears as well. If you buy items on an iPhone, iPad, or iPod touch, a Purchased On *Device* item appears too—for example, Purchased On Jane's iPhone.

To control how the iTunes Store works on your computer, follow these steps:

1. Display the iTunes dialog box or the Preferences dialog box:
   - In Windows, choose Edit | Preferences or press CTRL-COMMA or CTRL-Y to display the iTunes dialog box.
   - On the Mac, choose iTunes | Preferences or press ⌘-COMMA or ⌘-Y to display the Preferences dialog box.
2. Click the Parental tab to display the Parental preferences. Figure 13-3 shows the Parental tab on the Mac.
3. In the Disable area, select the iTunes Store check box if you want to remove the iTunes Store item from the Store category in the Source list. Select the Allow Access To iTunes U check box if you want to leave iTunes U's educational content enabled.

If you want to prevent anyone else from reenabling the iTunes Store, click the lock icon and then go through User Account Control for the iTunes Parental Controls Operation (on Windows 7 or Windows Vista) or authenticate yourself (on the Mac).

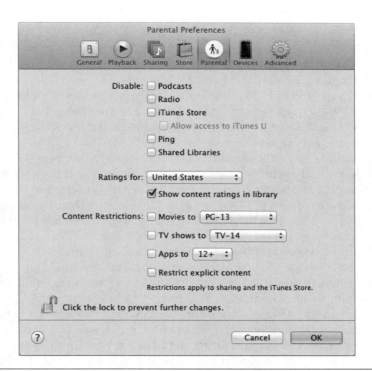

FIGURE 13-3 The Parental tab of the iTunes dialog box or Preferences dialog box lets you disable the iTunes Store or restrict the content it displays.

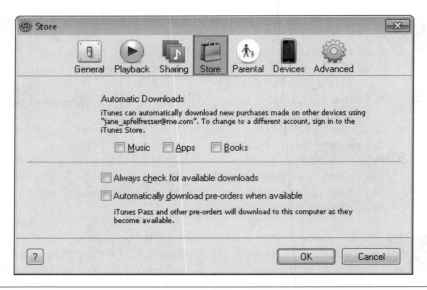

FIGURE 13-4 Configure the settings on the Store tab of the iTunes dialog box or the Preferences dialog box to control which items iTunes downloads automatically.

4. Also in the Disable area, select the Ping check box if you want to turn off the Ping social-networking feature.
5. If you didn't disable the iTunes Store, choose content ratings and restrictions:
   • Select your country in the Ratings For drop-down list.
   • Select the Show Content Ratings In Library check box if you want iTunes to display content ratings.
6. In the Content Restrictions area, choose whether to restrict movies, TV shows, apps, and explicit content. For example, to restrict movies to the PG rating, select the Movies To check box, and then choose PG in the drop-down list.
7. Click the Store tab (Windows) or Store button (Mac) to display the Store tab. Figure 13-4 shows the Store tab on Windows. The Store tab on the Mac has the same controls.
8. In the Automatic Downloads area, select the check box for each item—the Music check box, the Apps check box, and the Books check box—you want iTunes to download automatically to this computer when you've purchased it from another computer, or iPhone, iPod touch, or iPad.
9. Select the Always Check For Available Downloads check box if you want iTunes to look for new items you've purchased but not yet downloaded. Clear this check box if you prefer to check for new items manually—for example, because you need to run your downloads when your Internet connection isn't busy.
10. Select the Automatically Download Pre-Orders When Available check box if you want iTunes to automatically download content you've bought using prepurchase

features such as iTunes Pass (a kind of season ticket for items that come in episodes).

11. Click the OK button to apply your choices and close the dialog box.

Find the Songs, Videos, Movies, and Books You Want

You can find songs, videos, movies, and books in the iTunes Store in several ways that will seem familiar if you've used other online stores:

- You can meander through the interface looking for items by clicking links from the home page.
- You can browse by genre, subgenre, artist, and album. Click the Browse button, click the Browse link in the Quick Links area on the home page, choose View | Column Browser | Show Column Browser, or press CTRL-B (Windows) or ⌘-B (Mac) to display the column browser at the top of the iTunes Store (see Figure 13-5).
- You can search for specific items either by using the Search Store box or by clicking the Power Search link (in the Quick Links box on the right of the home page) and using the Power Search page to specify multiple criteria. Figure 13-6 shows the Power Search page with some results found. You can sort the search results by a column heading by clicking it. Click the column heading again to reverse the sort order.

FIGURE 13-5   Use the column browser to browse through the iTunes Store's offerings.

FIGURE 13-6 Use the Power Search feature to search for songs by song title, artist, album, genre, and composer.

Double-click a song's or video's listing to start the preview playing. To view the trailer for a movie, click the View Trailer button.

Navigate the iTunes Store

To navigate from page to page in the iTunes Store, click the buttons in the toolbar. Alternatively, use these keyboard shortcuts:

- In Windows, press CTRL-[to return to the previous page and CTRL-] to go to the next page.
- On the Mac, press ⌘-[to return to the previous page and ⌘-] to go to the next page.

Buy an Item from the iTunes Store

To buy an item from the iTunes Store, simply click its Buy button.

If you're not currently signed in, iTunes displays the Sign In To Download From The iTunes Store dialog box, as shown next.

How to... Understand A******s, "Explicit," and "Clean"

The iTunes Store censors supposedly offensive words to help minimize offense:

- Songs or videos deemed to have potentially offensive lyrics are marked EXPLICIT in the Name column. Where a sanitized version is available, it's marked CLEAN in the Name column. Some of the supposedly explicit items contain words no more offensive than "love." Some supposedly explicit songs are instrumentals.
- Strangely, other songs and videos that contain words that are offensive to most people aren't flagged as being explicit. So if you worry about what you and yours hear, don't trust the iTunes Store ratings too far.
- Any word deemed offensive is censored with asterisks (**), at least in theory. (In practice, some words sneak through.) When searching, use the real word rather than censoring it yourself.

Type your ID and password, and then click the Sign In button. iTunes then displays a confirmation message box like this:

Click the Buy button to make the purchase. Select the Please Don't Ask Me About Buying Songs Again check box if you don't want to have to confirm your purchases in the future. Leave this check box cleared if you're feeling the credit crunch and want to rein in your impulse buying.

iTunes then downloads the song or video to your library and adds an entry for it to your Purchased playlist.

Listen to Songs or Watch Videos You've Purchased

When you download a song or video from the iTunes Store, iTunes adds it to the playlist named Purchased in the Source list. When you click the Purchased playlist, iTunes automatically displays a message box to explain what the playlist is. Select the Do Not Show This Message Again check box before dismissing this message box, because otherwise it will soon endanger your sanity.

The Purchased playlist is there to provide a quick-and-easy way to get to all the items you buy. Otherwise, if you purchase items on impulse without keeping a list, they might vanish into your huge media library.

To delete the entry for an item in the Purchased playlist, right-click it (or CTRL-click it on the Mac) and then click the Delete item on the context menu. Alternatively, click the item to select it, and then press DELETE. iTunes deletes the entry from the playlist but doesn't delete the file.

 You can drag items that you haven't purchased to the Purchased playlist as well.

Restart a Failed Download

If a download fails, you may see an error message that invites you to try again later. If this happens, iTunes terminates the download but doesn't roll back the purchase.

To restart a failed download, choose Store | Check For Available Downloads. If you're not currently signed in, type your password in the Enter Account Name And Password dialog box, and then click the Check button. iTunes attempts to restart the failed download and also checks for any other items (such as new podcast episodes or items you've preordered) that are lined up for downloading to your computer.

Review What You've Purchased from the iTunes Store

To see what you've purchased from the iTunes Store, follow these steps:

1. Click the Account button (the button that displays your account name), enter your password, and click the View Account button to display the Account Information screen.
2. In the Purchase History area, click the See All button to display details of all the items you've purchased.
3. Click the arrow to the left of an order date to display details of the purchases on that date.

4. Click the Done button when you've finished examining your purchases. iTunes returns you to your Account Information page.

Authorize and Deauthorize Computers for the iTunes Store

As mentioned earlier in this chapter, when you buy a DRM-protected item from the iTunes Store, you're allowed to play it on up to five different computers at a time. iTunes implements this limitation through a form of license that Apple calls *authorization*. iTunes tracks which computers are authorized to play items you've purchased and stops you from playing the items when you're out of authorizations.

iTunes also uses authorization for its Home Sharing feature, to make sure you're not sharing items with other people. (The reason for this limitation is that most songs, videos, and other media items are protected by copyright.)

If you then want to play items you've purchased on another computer, you need to *deauthorize* one of the authorized computers so as to free up an authorization for use on the extra computer. You may also need to specifically deauthorize a computer to prevent it from playing the items you've bought. For example, if you sell or give away your Mac, you probably want to deauthorize it. You might also need to deauthorize a computer if you're planning to rebuild it.

Your computer must be connected to the Internet to authorize and deauthorize computers.

To authorize a computer to use the iTunes Store, follow these steps:

1. Choose Store | Authorize This Computer to display the Authorize This Computer dialog box, shown here.

You can also trigger an authorization request by setting up Home Sharing on an unauthorized computer or by trying to play a DRM-protected item purchased from the iTunes Store and stored on another computer—for example, when you access a purchased item in a shared library.

2. Type your Apple ID and password.
3. Click the Authorize button. iTunes checks in with the servers, and then displays the Computer Authorization Was Successful message box (shown here) if all is well. The message box shows how many of your available authorizations you've used so far.

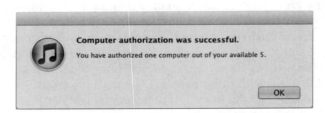

To deauthorize a computer so that it can no longer play the items you've purchased from the iTunes Store, follow these steps:

1. Choose Store | Deauthorize This Computer to display the Deauthorize This Computer dialog box, shown here.

2. Type your Apple ID and password, and then click the Deauthorize button. iTunes deauthorizes the computer and displays a message box to tell you it has done so, as shown here.

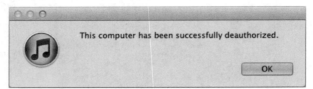

Buy Music from the iTunes Wi-Fi Store

Using your iPhone, you can buy songs and albums over the air from the iTunes Wi-Fi Store. You can connect to the iTunes Wi-Fi Store either via a wireless network—for

How to... Deauthorize a Computer You Can't Currently Access

The procedure you've just seen for deauthorizing a computer is easy—but you must be able to access the computer. If you've already parted with the computer, or if the computer has stopped working, this gives you a problem.

The solution is to deauthorize *all* your computers at once, and then reauthorize those you want to be able to use. You're only allowed to do this once a year.

To deauthorize all your computers, follow these steps:

1. Click the Account button (the button that displays your account name), then enter your password and click the View Account button to display the Account Information window.
2. Click the Deauthorize All button. iTunes displays a confirmation dialog box, as shown here.

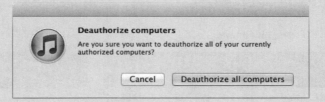

3. Click the Deauthorize All Computers button. iTunes deauthorizes all the computers, and then displays a message box to let you know it has done so.

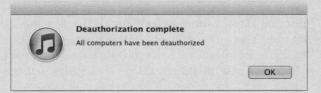

4. Click the OK button, and then click the Home button to return to the iTunes Store home screen.

example, your home wireless network or a wireless hotspot—or via the cellular network.

When you buy an item from the iTunes Wi-Fi Store, your iPhone downloads it, and you can play it immediately. The next time you synchronize your iPhone with your computer, iTunes copies the item, and you can then play it in iTunes as well.

To use the iTunes Wi-Fi Store, follow these steps:

FIGURE 13-7   The results of a successful search on the iTunes Wi-Fi Store (left) and previewing a song (right).

1. Press the Home button to display the Home screen.
2. Tap the iTunes icon to display the iTunes Wi-Fi Store.
3. Tap the buttons onscreen to navigate to the song or item you want. For example:
   - Tap the Featured button to view the songs that the iTunes Wi-Fi Store is featuring.
   - Tap the Top Tens button to display a list of Top Tens in different categories— for example, Pop, Alternative, or Rock. Tap the Top Ten item you want to view.
   - To search, tap the Search button, tap the Search box to bring up the onscreen keyboard, and then type your search term. The iTunes Wi-Fi Store searches as you type, so you usually needn't tap the Search button to start the search. The left screen in Figure 13-7 shows the results of a successful search.
   - Tap one of the buttons at the top of the screen, such as New Releases, What's Hot, or Genres, to display a list of songs.
4. When you've found a song or item you're interested in, tap it to start playing its preview. If what starts playing is unbearable, tap the Stop button at the left of the item's listing (shown on the right in Figure 13-7) to end the torment.

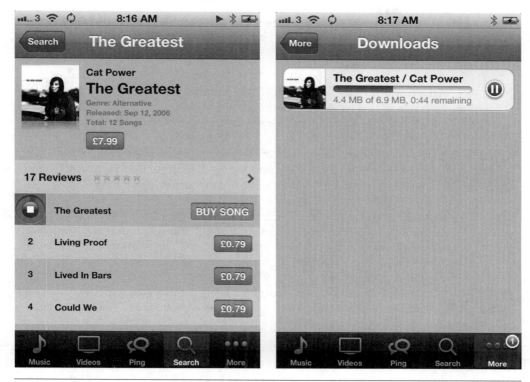

FIGURE 13-8   Tap the Buy Song button to buy a song (left), and use the Downloads screen to see how your downloads are coming along (right).

5. To buy a song or other item, tap its price. The price changes to a Buy Song button, as shown on the left screen in Figure 13-8.
6. Tap the Buy Now button. The iTunes Wi-Fi Store adds the song to your Downloads list and prompts you for your password.
7. Type the password, and then tap the OK button. Your iPhone starts downloading the song.
8. To see the progress of your downloads, tap the More button, then tap the Downloads button and look at the Downloads screen (shown on the right in Figure 13-8).
9. Once the download is finished, you can tap the Purchased button on the Downloads screen to jump straight to the Purchased playlist and play the downloaded item.

To transfer your purchases from your iPhone to your iTunes library, connect the device to your PC, and then choose File | Transfer Purchases From *iPhone*, where *iPhone* is the name you've given your iPhone.

Buy Music from Other Online Music Stores

As well as the iTunes Store, you can buy music from many other online stores. Here are four that you may want to try:

- **Amazon.com** Amazon.com (www.amazon.com) sells songs in the MP3 format, with most encoded at the 256-Kbps bitrate. Most songs cost $0.69, $0.99, or $1.29 apiece, but there are special deals on many whole albums.

 To promote their music and concerts, many artists make some of their songs available online. Usually the best way to find these is to start at the artist's online presence—for example, their website or Facebook page.

- **eMusic** eMusic (www.emusic.com) offers more than 8 million songs in MP3 format for download. eMusic offers various pricing plans, including yearly subscriptions. Each plan has a free 14-day trial, but you must provide valid credit card details. You download the songs using eMusic's software.

 Sites such as Pandora (www.pandora.com), Spotify (www.spotify.com), and Musicovery (www.musicovery.com) can be a great way of finding interesting music.

- **Rhapsody** Rhapsody (http://mp3.rhapsody.com) is a service that provides unlimited streaming access to several million songs. You can buy songs and put them on a variety of devices, including your iPhone. Rhapsody provides a good way to listen to a wide variety of music for a fixed fee.
- **Napster** Napster 2.0 (www.napster.com) offers more than 15 million songs at this writing. Napster 2.0 has nothing to do with the pioneering file-sharing application Napster except the name and logo. Napster sells songs in MP3 format and also provides an iPhone app for playing music straight from the iPhone. At this writing, Napster has been acquired by Rhapsody, which plans to integrate Napster with Rhapsody.

 You can also find high-quality MP3 files for download on sites hosted in Russia and other former Eastern Bloc countries. These sites typically offer a wide selection of music at very low prices. At this writing, the legal position of these sites is not clear. While these sites insist they are operating legally, most Western legal experts disagree. Music industry bodies, such as the RIAA, are actively trying to close down these sites.

 To promote their music and concerts, many artists make some of their songs available online. Usually the best place to look is the artist's website or Facebook page.

Manage Your Music and Video Library with iTunes

In Chapter 2, you learned how to start creating your library by copying music from your CDs and importing your existing music files. This is a great way to put songs on your iPhone quickly, but to get the most enjoyment out of your music, you may well want to customize iTunes' settings rather than use the defaults.

You may also want to do things with AAC files and MP3 files that iTunes doesn't support. For example, you may receive (or acquire) files in formats the iPhone can't handle, so you'll need to convert the files before you can use them on your iPhone. You may want to trim intros or outros off audio files, split files into smaller files, or retag batches of files in ways iTunes can't handle. Last, you may want to record streaming audio to your hard disk.

Choose Where to Store Your Library

Because your library can contain dozens—or even hundreds—of gigabytes of files, you must store it in a suitable location if you choose to keep all your files in it.

By default, iTunes stores your library in a folder named iTunes Media. This folder, the library folder, contains several folders:

- **Audiobooks**   This folder contains any audiobooks you've downloaded.
- **Books**   This folder contains any books you've downloaded.
- **iTunes U**   This folder contains any iTunes U podcasts you've downloaded.
- **Mobile Applications**   This folder contains apps you've downloaded from the App Store.
- **Movies**   This folder contains your movies, in subfolders named with the movie names.
- **Music**   This folder contains your songs, in subfolders named after the artists.
- **Podcasts**   This folder contains the podcasts you've downloaded, in subfolders named with the podcast names.
- **Ringtones**   This folder contains the ringtones you've bought or created.
- **TV Shows**   This folder contains the TV shows you've downloaded, in subfolders named with the show names.

 Instead of keeping all your song files in your library, you can store references to where the files are located in other folders. Doing so enables you to minimize the size of your library. But for maximum flexibility and to make sure you can access all the tracks in your library all the time, keeping all your song files in your library folder is best—if you can do so.

To change the location of your library from now on, follow these steps:

1. Display the iTunes dialog box or the Preferences dialog box:
   - In Windows, choose Edit | Preferences or press CTRL-COMMA or CTRL-Y to display the iTunes dialog box.
   - On the Mac, choose iTunes | Preferences or press ⌘-COMMA or ⌘-Y to display the Preferences dialog box.
2. Click the Advanced tab to display its contents. Figure 13-9 shows the Advanced tab of the iTunes dialog box in Windows.
3. Click the Change button to display the Change iTunes Media Folder Location dialog box.
4. Navigate to the folder that will contain your library, select the folder, and then click the Select Folder button (Windows 7), OK button (Windows Vista), Open button (Windows XP), or Choose button (Mac). iTunes returns you to the iTunes dialog box or Preferences dialog box.
5. Click the OK button to close the iTunes dialog box or the Preferences dialog box. iTunes displays a message box as it updates your iTunes library, as shown next.

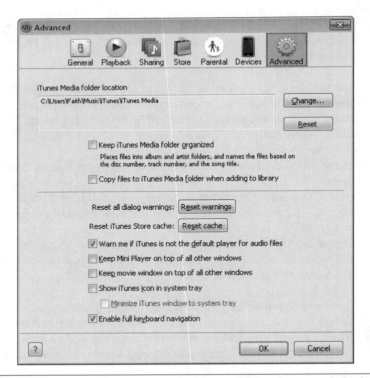

FIGURE 13-9 You may need to move your library folder from its default location to a folder that has more disk space available. To move your library folder, click the Change button, and then select the new folder in the Change iTunes Media Folder Location dialog box.

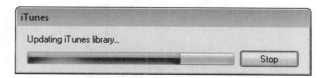

6. If iTunes prompts you to decide whether to let iTunes move and rename the files in your new iTunes Media folder, as shown here, click the Yes button.

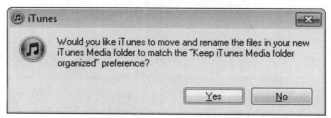

To reset your library folder to its default location, click the Reset button on the Advanced tab of the iTunes dialog box or the Preferences dialog box. On Windows, the default location is the \Music\iTunes\iTunes Media folder in your user folder. On the Mac, the default folder is the ~/Music/iTunes Media folder, where ~ represents your Home folder.

When you change the location of your library like this, iTunes doesn't actually move the files that are already in your library. To move the files, make sure the new folder contains enough space, and then follow these steps:

1. Display the iTunes dialog box or the Preferences dialog box again:
   - In Windows, choose Edit | Preferences or press CTRL-COMMA or CTRL-Y to display the iTunes dialog box.
   - On the Mac, choose iTunes | Preferences or press ⌘-COMMA or ⌘-Y to display the Preferences dialog box.
2. Click the Advanced tab to display its contents.
3. Select the Keep iTunes Media Folder Organized check box.
4. Select the Copy Files To iTunes Media Folder When Adding To Library check box.
5. Click the OK button to close the iTunes dialog box or the Preferences dialog box.
6. Choose File | Library | Organize Library to display the Organize Library dialog box (shown next).

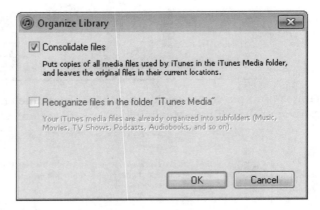

7. Select the Consolidate Files check box.
8. Click the OK button. iTunes copies the files, showing you its progress (as shown here) until it has finished.

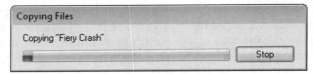

Configure iTunes for the Audio Quality You Want

Before you rip and encode your entire CD collection, check that the settings in iTunes are suitable for your needs.

iTunes' default is to encode to AAC files in stereo at a bitrate of 256 Kbps. This is a fair choice for defaults, but you may well want to change them; see the nearby sidebar titled "Choose the Best Audio Format for Your Needs" for advice. Spend some time choosing the right settings for ripping and encoding so that you don't waste time ripping your CDs more than once.

 The *bitrate* is a setting that specifies the amount of data that the encoder keeps.

First, decide which music format and audio quality you want. Then choose the appropriate settings in iTunes.

Check or Change Your Importing Settings

To check or change the importing settings, follow these steps:

1. Display the iTunes dialog box or the Preferences dialog box:
   - In Windows, choose Edit | Preferences or press CTRL-COMMA or CTRL-Y to display the iTunes dialog box.

How to... Choose the Best Audio Format for Your Needs

iTunes can encode audio in five formats:

- **AAC**   Advanced Audio Coding is a compressed audio format that gives a good balance between compressing the music to a manageable file size and retaining good audio quality. You can adjust this balance by choosing a suitable bitrate at which to encode the music to AAC. Generally speaking, AAC gives the best balance between small file size and high audio quality if you want to play your songs on your iPhone and your computer using iTunes.
- **MP3**   MP3 (the file format for MPEG-1 Layer 3) is a compressed audio format that gives good quality, but somewhat less than AAC at the same bitrates. As with AAC, you can choose the bitrate at which to encode the music. MP3 is the best format to use if you want to play your songs on your iPhone, on your computer using iTunes, and on other players that can't play the AAC format.
- **Apple Lossless Encoding**   Apple Lossless Encoding is a compressed audio format that gives full audio quality. This is the best format to use if you want to be sure that you're hearing your music at full quality, without any audio information removed. The disadvantage to Apple Lossless Encoding is that it gives less compression than AAC and MP3.
- **WAV**   WAV files contain uncompressed audio in the PCM (pulse-code modulation) format. WAV files are widely used on Windows, but they have a large file size (because they aren't compressed) and they have no containers for tag information, so they're not good for the iPhone or iTunes.
- **AIFF**   Like WAV files, AIFF files contain uncompressed audio in the PCM format. AIFF files are widely used on Mac OS X, but because they have the same shortcomings as WAV files—large file size and no containers for tag information—they're not good for iTunes or for the iPhone.

You'll notice that AAC, MP3, and Apple Lossless Encoding are compressed audio formats, whereas WAV and AIFF are not compressed. AAC and MP3 use *lossy* compression, compression in which some data about the audio is lost in the interest of compressing the audio to a smaller file size. Apple Lossless Encoding, as its name suggests, is mathematically lossless, so although the resulting file is smaller than the uncompressed file, it contains all the audio data that the uncompressed file contains.

If you're creating audio files to enjoy on your iPhone and in iTunes, AAC is usually the best format to use. The iTunes Plus default setting, which encodes at 256 Kbps, works well for general use, but if you want your music to sound as good as possible, crank the bitrate all the way up to 320 Kbps (the maximum). We'll look at how to do this shortly.

- On the Mac, choose iTunes | Preferences or press ⌘-COMMA or ⌘-Y to display the Preferences dialog box.

2. Click the General tab if it's not already displayed.

3. In the When You Insert A CD drop-down list, choose what you want iTunes to do when you insert a CD: Show CD, Begin Playing, Ask To Import CD, Import CD, or Import CD And Eject.

   - Show CD, Import CD, and Import CD And Eject all involve looking up the song names on the Internet (unless you've already played the CD and thus caused iTunes to look up the names before), so iTunes will need to use your Internet connection.
   - Avoid the Import CD And Eject setting unless your computer's optical drive can always open (or eject a CD) safely without hitting anything.

4. Click the Import Settings button to display the Import Settings dialog box. Figure 13-10 shows the Import Settings dialog box on iTunes for the Mac. The Import Settings dialog box on iTunes for Windows has the same controls.

5. In the Import Using drop-down list, choose the encoder for the file format you want:

   - The default setting is AAC Encoder, which creates compressed files in AAC format. AAC files combine high audio quality with compact size, making AAC a good format for both iTunes and the iPhone.
   - The other setting you're likely to want to try is MP3 Encoder, which creates compressed files in the MP3 format. MP3 files have marginally lower audio quality than AAC files for the same file size, but you can use MP3 files with a wider variety of software applications and hardware players.

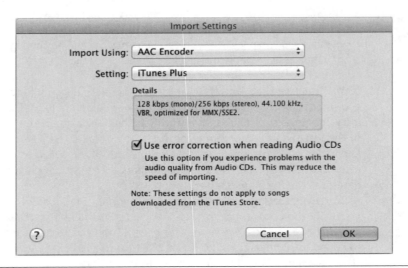

FIGURE 13-10 Configure your audio quality settings in the Import Settings dialog box.

How to... Choose an Appropriate Compression Rate, Bitrate, and Stereo Settings

To get suitable audio quality, you must use an appropriate compression rate for the audio files you encode with iTunes.

iTunes' default settings are to encode AAC files in stereo at the 256-Kbps bitrate using automatic sample-rate detection. iTunes calls those settings iTunes Plus, and they deliver great results for most purposes. If you need to create smaller song files with acceptable quality, choose High Quality (128 Kbps) instead. For podcasts, choose the Spoken Podcast setting to create smaller files with lower quality. Alternatively, you can specify custom AAC settings for the files you create. With AAC you can change the bitrate, the sample rate, and the channels.

iTunes' MP3 Encoder gives you more flexibility. The default settings for MP3 are to encode MP3 files in stereo at the 160-Kbps bitrate, using CBR and automatic sample-rate detection. iTunes calls those settings High Quality, and they deliver results almost as good as the High Quality settings with the AAC Encoder, although they produce significantly larger files because the bitrate is higher.

For encoding MP3 files, iTunes also offers preset settings for Good Quality (128 Kbps) and Higher Quality (192 Kbps). Beyond these choices, you can choose the Custom setting and specify exactly the settings you want: bitrates from 16 Kbps to 320 Kbps, CBR or VBR, sample rate, channels, the stereo mode, whether to use Smart Encoding Adjustments, and whether to filter frequencies lower than 10 Hz.

If possible, invest a few days in choosing a compression rate for your library. Choosing the wrong compression rate can cost you disk space (if you record at too high a bitrate), audio quality (too low a bitrate), and the time it takes to rip your entire collection again at the bitrate you prefer.

Pick a representative selection of the types of music you plan to listen to using your computer and iPhone. Encode several copies of each test track at different bitrates, and then listen to them over several days to see which provides the best balance of file size and audio quality. Make sure some of the songs test the different aspects of music that are important to you. For example, if your musical tastes lean to female vocalists, listen to plenty of those types of songs. If you prefer bass-heavy, bludgeoning rock, listen to that. If you go for classical music as well, add that to the mix. You may need to use different compression rates for different types of music to achieve satisfactory results and keep the file size down.

- Apple Lossless Encoding files have full audio quality but a relatively large file size. They're good for iTunes, but their size means you can't fit as many songs on your iPhone.
- AIFF files and WAV files are uncompressed audio files, so they have full audio quality (and are widely playable, as noted earlier) but take up a huge amount of space. You'll seldom need to use either of these formats.

6. In the Setting drop-down list, choose the setting you want to use:
   - For the AAC Encoder, the Setting drop-down list offers the settings High Quality (128 Kbps), iTunes Plus (which uses the 256-Kbps bitrate), Spoken Podcast, and Custom. When you select Custom, iTunes displays the AAC Encoder dialog box so you can specify custom settings. See the next section, "Choose Custom Encoding Settings for AAC or MP3," for a discussion of these options.
   - For the MP3 Encoder, the Setting drop-down list offers the settings Good Quality (128 Kbps), High Quality (160 Kbps), Higher Quality (192 Kbps), and Custom. When you select Custom, iTunes displays the MP3 Encoder dialog box so you can specify custom settings. See the next section, "Choose Custom Encoding Settings for AAC or MP3," for a discussion of these options.
   - The Apple Lossless Encoder has no configurable settings. (The Setting drop-down list offers only the Automatic setting.)
   - For the AIFF Encoder and the WAV Encoder, the Setting drop-down list offers the settings Automatic and Custom. When you select Custom, iTunes displays the AIFF Encoder dialog box or the WAV Encoder dialog box (as appropriate) so you can specify custom settings.

7. Select the Use Error Correction When Reading Audio CDs check box if you want to turn on the error-correction feature. Usually, you need error correction only if you get clicks or skips in your imported files without it, but you may want to turn it on anyway to avoid problems. Using error correction slows down the ripping process somewhat, but, unless you're ripping a huge pile of CDs in a hurry, usually not enough to worry about.

8. Click the OK button to close the Import Settings dialog box.

9. Click the OK button to close the iTunes dialog box or Preferences dialog box.

Choose Custom Encoding Settings for AAC or MP3

As well as the presets, both the AAC Encoder and the MP3 Encoder have a Custom item that you can choose to display a dialog box containing settings for adjusting the encoder. Figure 13-11 shows the AAC Encoder dialog box and the MP3 Encoder dialog box.

As you can see in Figure 13-11, most of the settings in the two dialog boxes are the same:

- **Stereo Bit Rate** In this drop-down list, choose the bitrate. You can use from 16 Kbps to 320 Kbps. The higher the bitrate, the better the audio quality. 128 Kbps provides acceptable audio quality to most people for songs. Bitrates below this are suitable only for spoken audio.

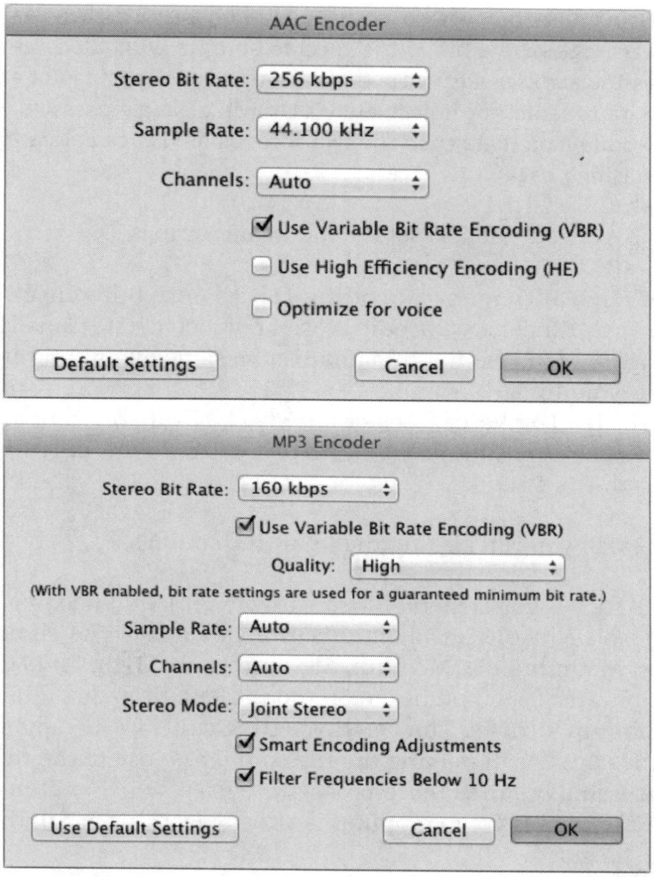

FIGURE 13-11   Use the AAC Encoder dialog box (top) and MP3 Encoder dialog box (bottom) to adjust the encoders to produce exactly the audio files you need.

- **Sample Rate**   In this drop-down list, it's normally best to choose the Auto setting. Alternatively, choose 44.100 kHz, which is the sample rate for CD-quality audio.
- **Channels**   In this drop-down list, select Auto, Stereo, or Mono, as appropriate. In most cases, Auto (the default setting) is the best bet, because it makes iTunes choose stereo or mono as appropriate to the sound source. But you may occasionally need to produce mono files from stereo sources.
- **Use Variable Bit Rate Encoding (VBR)**   If you want to use VBR encoding rather than Constant Bit Rate (CBR) encoding, select the Use Variable Bit Rate Encoding (VBR) check box.

Using VBR improves the audio quality of your files. Whereas CBR simply records each part of the file at the specified bitrate, VBR allocates space more intelligently as the audio needs it. For example, a complex passage of a song will require more data to represent it accurately than will a simple passage, which in turn will require more data than the two seconds of silence before the massed guitars come crashing back in.

For AAC, you can also set the following settings:

- **Use High Efficiency Encoding (HE)**   Select this check box if you want to use the High Efficiency Encoding format, which creates smaller files. Audiophiles disagree as to whether it maintains the same quality; try it for yourself and see what you think.
- **Optimize For Voice**   Select this check box if you want to optimize the encoding for voice instead of music. Normally, you'd do this only for podcasts and other spoken-word audio.

For MP3, you can also set the following settings:

- **Quality**   If you select the Use Variable Bit Rate Encoding (VBR) check box, choose a suitable setting in this drop-down list. The choices are Lowest, Low, Medium Low, Medium, Medium High, High, and Highest. iTunes uses the bitrates specified in the Stereo Bit Rate drop-down list as the guaranteed minimum bitrates. The Quality setting controls the amount of processing iTunes applies to making the file sound as close to the original as possible. More processing requires more processor cycles, which will make your computer work harder. If your computer is already working at full throttle, encoding will take longer.
- **Stereo Mode**   In this drop-down list, choose Normal Stereo or Joint Stereo. Use normal stereo for bitrates above 128 Kbps and joint stereo for 128 Kbps or lower bitrates. If you select Mono in the Channels drop-down list, the Stereo Mode drop-down list becomes unavailable because its options don't apply to mono.
- **Smart Encoding Adjustments**   Select this check box if you want iTunes to tweak your custom settings to improve them if you've chosen an inappropriate combination.
- **Filter Frequencies Below 10 Hz**   Select this check box if you want iTunes to filter out sounds below 10 Hz. These are infrasound and are of interest only to animals such as elephants, so filtering them out makes sense for humans.

 To restore iTunes to using its default settings for encoding AAC files or MP3 files, click the Default Settings button in the AAC Encoder dialog box or the Use Default Settings button in the MP3 Encoder dialog box.

When you've finished choosing encoding settings, click the OK button to close the AAC Encoder dialog box or MP3 Encoder dialog box.

Convert Other File Types to Formats an iPhone Can Play

Your iPhone can play AAC files, MP3 files (including files in the Audible audiobook format), Apple Lossless Encoding files, AIFF files, and WAV files. These common formats should take care of all your regular listening in iTunes and on your iPhone.

But if you receive files from other people, or download audio from the Internet, you'll encounter many other digital audio formats. This section describes a couple of utilities for converting files from other formats to ones the iPhone can use.

Convert a Song from AAC to MP3 (or Vice Versa)

Sometimes, you may need to convert a song from the format in which you imported it, or (more likely) in which you bought it, to a different format. For example, you may need to convert a song in AAC format to MP3 so that you can use it on an MP3 player that can't play AAC files.

 Don't convert a song from one lossily compressed format to another unless you must. The resulting file will have not only any defects present in the original file but also other defects introduced by the lossy compression on the new format.

 If the AAC file is a protected song you bought from the iTunes Store, you cannot convert it directly. Instead, you must burn it to a CD, and then rip that CD to the format you need.

To convert a song from one compressed format to another, follow these steps:

1. In iTunes, display the Advanced menu and see which format is listed in the Create Version command (for example, Create AAC Version or Create MP3 Version). If this is the format you want, you're all set, but you might want to double-check the settings used for the format.

 You can also right-click a file (or CTRL-click on the Mac) and look at the Create Version item on the shortcut menu.

2. Display the iTunes dialog box or the Preferences dialog box:
   • In Windows, choose Edit | Preferences or press CTRL-COMMA or CTRL-Y to display the iTunes dialog box.
   • On the Mac, choose iTunes | Preferences or press ⌘-COMMA or ⌘-Y to display the Preferences dialog box.
3. Click the General tab to display its contents.
4. Click the Import Settings button to display the Import Settings dialog box.

5. In the Import Using drop-down list, select the encoder you want to use. For example, choose MP3 Encoder if you want to convert an existing file to an MP3 file; choose AAC Encoder if you want to create an AAC file; or choose Apple Lossless Encoder if you want to create an Apple Lossless Encoding file.

Unless the song file is currently in WAV or AIFF format, it's usually not worth converting it to Apple Lossless Encoding, because the source file is not high enough quality to benefit from Apple Lossless Encoding's advantages over AAC or MP3.

6. If necessary, use the Setting drop-down list to specify the details of the format. (See "Check or Change Your Importing Settings" earlier in this chapter for details.)
7. Click the OK button to close the Import Settings dialog box.
8. Click the OK button to close the iTunes dialog box or the Preferences dialog box.
9. In your library, select the song or songs you want to convert.
10. Choose Advanced | Create *Format* Version. (The Create Version item on the Advanced menu changes to reflect the encoder you chose in Step 5.) iTunes converts the file or files, saves it or them in the folder that contains the original file or files, and adds it or them to your library.

Because iTunes automatically applies tag information to converted files, you may find it hard to tell in iTunes which file is in AAC format and which is in MP3 format. The easiest way to find out is to issue a Get Info command for the song (for example, right-click or CTRL-click the song and choose Get Info from the shortcut menu) and check the Kind readout on the Summary tab of the Item Information dialog box.

After converting the song or songs to the other format, remember to restore your normal import setting in the Import Settings dialog box before you import any more songs from CD.

Convert WMA Files to MP3 or AAC

If you buy music from any of the online music stores that focus on Windows rather than on the Mac, the songs may be in WMA format. WMA is the stores' preferred format for selling online music because it offers DRM features for protecting the music against being stolen. Similarly, if you have ripped CDs using Windows Media Player on Windows, you may have created WMA files.

In iTunes for Windows, you can convert a WMA file to your current importing format (as set in the Import Settings dialog box) by dragging the file to your library or by using either the File | Add File To Library or the File | Add Folder To Library command. iTunes for the Mac doesn't have this capability—but if you have access to a PC running Windows, you can then copy or transfer the converted files to the Mac.

To convert WMA files on Mac OS X, you need to use a third-party converter. At this writing, the best free choice is the free version of Switch (www.nch.com.au/switch/). There's also a paid version of Switch that has more features.

If you buy WMA files protected with DRM, you'll be limited in what you can do with them. In most cases, you'll be restricted to playing the songs with Windows Media Player (which is one of the underpinnings of the WMA DRM scheme), which won't let you convert the songs directly to another format. But most online music stores allow you to burn the songs you buy to CD. In this case, you can convert the WMA files to MP3 files or AAC files by burning them to CD and then use iTunes to rip and encode the CD as usual.

Convert FLAC Files or Ogg Vorbis Files to iTunes- and iPhone-Friendly Files

Free Lossless Audio Codec (FLAC) is a file format that's popular with audiophiles because it produces full-quality files. Ogg Vorbis is an open-source compressed format comparable to MP3. Neither iTunes nor your iPhone can play FLAC files or Ogg Vorbis files, so you need to convert them.

- **Windows**   Use a tool such as Total Audio Converter (www.coolutils.com).
- **Mac OS X**   Use the X Lossless Decoder (XLD; http://tmkk.pv.land.to/xld/index_e.html) or a similar tool to decode the files to Apple Lossless Encoding, AAC, or MP3.

Trim Audio Files to Get Rid of Intros and Outros You Don't Like

If you don't like the intro of a particular song, you can tell iTunes to suppress it by setting the Start Time option on the Options tab of the Item Information dialog box to the point where you want the song to start playing. Similarly, you can suppress an outro by using the Stop Time option, also on the Options tab.

You can also use these options to trim an audio file. Follow these steps:

1. In iTunes, right-click (or CTRL-click on the Mac) the song you want to shorten, and then choose Get Info from the shortcut menu to display the Item Information dialog box. (This dialog box's title bar shows the song name, not the words "Item Information.")

 If you've recorded songs that have empty audio at the beginning or end (or both), use this technique to remove the empty audio.

2. Click the Options tab to display its contents.

3. Set the Start Time, Stop Time, or both, as needed.

4. Click the OK button to close the Item Information dialog box.

5. Right-click (or CTRL-click on the Mac) the song, and then choose Create *Format* Version, where *Format* is the import format you've chosen in the Import Settings dialog box—for example, Create AAC Version.

6. iTunes creates a shorter version of the song. It's a good idea to rename the song immediately to avoid confusing it with the source file. Alternatively, delete the source file if you no longer want to keep it.

You can even use this trick to split a song file into two or more different files. For example, to create two files, work out where the division needs to fall. Create the first file by setting the Stop Time to this time and then performing the conversion. Return to the source file, set the Start Time to the dividing time, and then perform the conversion again.

Tag Your Compressed Files with the Correct Information for Sorting

The best thing about compressed audio formats such as AAC, MP3, and Apple Lossless Encoding—apart from their being compressed and still giving high-quality audio—is that each file format can store a full set of tag information about the song the file contains. The tag information lets you sort, organize, and search for songs on iTunes. The iPhone needs correct artist, album, and track name information in tags to be able to organize your AAC files and MP3 files correctly. If a song lacks this minimum of information, iTunes doesn't transfer it to the iPhone.

You can force iTunes to load untagged songs on an iPhone by assigning them to a playlist and loading the playlist. But in most cases it's best to tag all the songs in your library—or at least tag as many as is practicable.

You can tag your song files using any tool you choose, but you'll probably want to use iTunes much of the time, because it provides solid if basic features for tagging one or more files at once manually. But if your library contains many untagged or mistagged files, you may need a heavier-duty application. This section shows you how to tag most effectively in iTunes.

If you need more powerful tagging features than iTunes offers, try Tag&Rename ($29.95; www.softpointer.com/tr.htm; trial version available) for Windows or Media Rage ($29.95; www.chaoticsoftware.com; trial version available) for Mac OS X.

The easiest way to add tag information to an AAC file or MP3 file is by downloading the information from CDDB (the CD Database) when you rip the CD. But sometimes you'll need to enter (or change) tag information manually to make

How to... Tag Song Files After Encoding When Offline

Even if you rip CDs when your computer has no Internet connection, you can usually apply the CD information to the song files once you've reestablished an Internet connection. To do so, select the album or the songs in your library and then choose Advanced | Get Track Names. If the CD's details are in CDDB, iTunes should then be able to download the information.

If you imported the songs by using software other than iTunes, or if you imported the songs using iTunes on another computer and then copied them to this computer, iTunes objects with the "iTunes cannot get CD track names" dialog box shown here. In this case, you'll need to either reimport the songs on this computer or tag the songs manually.

> iTunes cannot get CD track names for songs that were not imported using iTunes.
>
> To allow iTunes to look for CD track names for this song, import the song again using iTunes.
>
> OK

iTunes sort the files correctly—for example, when the CDDB data is wrong or not available, or for existing song files created with software other than iTunes, such as song files you've created yourself.

Note Often, MP3 files distributed illegally on the Internet lack tag information or include incorrect tags. That said, officially tagged files aren't always as accurate as they might be—so if you want your files to be as easy to find and manipulate as possible, it's worth spending some time checking the tags and improving them as necessary.

If you need to change the tag information for a whole CD's worth of songs, proceed as follows:

1. In iTunes, select all the song files you want to affect.
2. Right-click (or CTRL-click on the Mac) the selection and choose Get Info from the shortcut menu to display the Multiple Item Information dialog box. Alternatively, choose File | Get Info or press CTRL-I (Windows) or ⌘-I (Mac). Figure 13-12 shows the Windows version of the Multiple Item Information dialog box with the Info tab at the front.

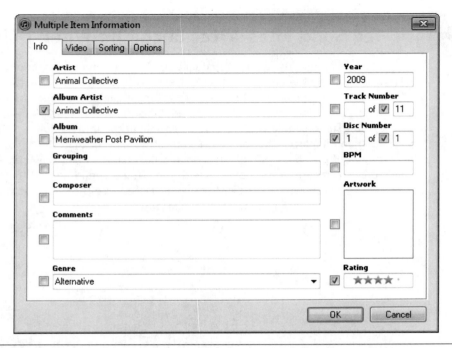

FIGURE 13-12 Use the Multiple Item Information dialog box to enter common tag information for all the songs on a CD or album at once.

By default, when you issue a Get Info command with multiple songs selected, iTunes displays a dialog box to check that you want to edit the information for multiple songs. Click the Yes button to proceed; click the Cancel button to cancel. If you frequently want to edit tag information for multiple songs, select the Do Not Ask Me Again check box in the confirmation dialog box to turn off confirmations in the future.

3. Enter as much common information as you can: the artist, year, album, total number of tracks, disc number, composer, comments, and so on. If you have the artwork for the CD available, drag it to the Artwork well on the Info tab.
4. Click the OK button to close the dialog box and apply the information to the songs.
5. Click the first song to clear the current selection. Right-click (or CTRL-click on the Mac) the song and choose Get Info from the shortcut menu to display the Item Information dialog box for the song. Click the Info tab to display it if iTunes doesn't display it automatically. Figure 13-13 shows the Windows version of the Item Information dialog box. On Windows, the Item Information dialog box shows "iTunes" in its title bar. On the Mac, the song's title appears in the title bar of the dialog box.

FIGURE 13-13   Use the Item Information dialog box (whose title bar shows "iTunes" on Windows and the song's name on the Mac) to add song-specific information.

6. Add any song-specific information here: the song name, the track number, and so on.
7. If you need to change the song's relative volume, equalizer preset, rating, start time, or stop time, work on the Options tab.
8. If you want to add lyrics to the song (either by typing them in or by pasting them from a lyrics site), work on the Lyrics tab.
9. Click the Previous button or the Next button to display the information for the previous song or next song.
10. Click the OK button to close the Item Information dialog box when you've finished adding song information.

Save Audio Streams to Disk So You Can Listen to Them Later

If you enjoy listening to Internet radio, you may want to record it so that you can play it back later. iTunes doesn't let you save streaming audio to disk because recording streaming audio without specific permission typically violates copyright. So you need to use either a hardware solution or a third-party application to record streams.

Save Audio Streams to Disk Using Hardware

To solve the problem via hardware, use a standard audio cable to pipe the output from your computer's sound card to its line-in socket. You can then record the audio stream as you would any other external input by using an audio-recording application such as Audacity (free; http://audacity.sourceforge.net/).

The only problem with using a standard audio cable is that you won't be able to hear via external speakers the audio stream you're recording. To solve this problem, get a stereo Y-connector. Connect one of the outputs to your external speakers and the other to your line-in socket. Converting the audio from digital to analog and then back to digital like this degrades its quality, but unless you're listening to the highest-bitrate Internet radio stations around, you'll most likely find the quality you lose to be a fair trade-off for the convenience you gain.

Save Audio Streams to Disk Using Software

To solve the problem via software, get an application that can record the audio stream directly.

At this writing, the best program for Windows is Total Recorder (www.highcriteria.com). Total Recorder comes in three editions: Standard, Professional, and Developer. Start by downloading the evaluation version to make sure that Total Recorder works with your PC and provides the features you need.

Here are three applications for the Mac:

- **RadioLover (www.bitcartel.com/radiolover)** RadioLover lets you record one or more radio streams at once.
- **Audio Hijack Pro (www.rogueamoeba.com/audiohijackpro)** Audio Hijack Pro lets you record the audio output from any application. You can set timers to record the items you want.
- **Radioshift (www.rogueamoeba.com/radioshift)** Radioshift lets you record Internet radio streams.

Create Video Files That Work with the iPhone

Apple's iTunes Store provides a wide selection of video content, including TV series and full-length movies, and you can buy or download video in iPhone-compatible formats from various other sites online. But if you enjoy watching video on your iPhone, you'll almost certainly want to put your own video content on it. You may also want to rip files from your own DVDs so that you can watch them on your iPhone.

Create iPhone-Friendly Video Files from Your Digital Video Camera

If you make your own movies with a digital video camera, you can easily put them on your iPhone. Use an application such as Windows Movie Maker (Windows) or iMovie (Mac) to capture the video from your digital video camera and turn it into a home movie.

Video formats are confusing at best—but the iPhone and iTunes make the process of getting suitable video files as easy as possible. The iPhone can play videos in the MP4 format up to 2.5 Mbps (megabits per second) or the H.264 format up to 1080p. Programs designed to create video files suitable for the iPhone typically give you a choice between the MP4 format and the H.264 format. As a point of reference, VHS video quality is around 2 Mbps, while DVD is about 8 Mbps.

Create iPhone-Friendly Video Files Using Windows Live Movie Maker or Windows Movie Maker

Unlike the last few versions of Windows, Windows 7 doesn't include Windows Movie Maker, the Windows program for editing videos. But you can download the nearest equivalent, Windows Live Movie Maker, from the Windows Live website (http://explore.live.com/windows-live-movie-maker?os=other).

What You Can and Can't Legally Do with Other People's Video Content

Before you start putting your videos and DVDs on your iPhone, it's a good idea to know the bare essentials about copyright and decryption:

- If you created the video (for example, it's a home video or DVD), you hold the copyright to it, and you can do what you want with it—put it on your iPhone, release it worldwide, or whatever. The only exceptions are if what you recorded is subject to someone else's copyright or if you're infringing on your subjects' rights (for example, to privacy).
- If someone has supplied you with a legally created video file that you can put on your iPhone, you're fine doing so. For example, if you download a video from the iTunes Store, you don't need to worry about legalities.
- If you own a copy of a commercial DVD, you need permission to rip (extract) it from the DVD and convert it to a format the iPhone can play. Even decrypting the DVD in an unauthorized way (such as creating a file rather than simply playing the DVD) is technically illegal.

When you install Windows Live Movie Maker, the Windows Live Essentials installer encourages you to install all the Windows Live Essentials programs—Messenger, Photo Gallery, Mail, Writer, Family Safety, and several others. If you don't want the full set, click the Choose The Programs You Want To Install button on the What Do You Want To Install? screen, and then select only the programs you actually want.

Windows Live Movie Maker can't export video files in an iPhone-friendly format, so what you need to do is export the video file in the WMV format, and then convert it using another application, such as Full Video Converter Free (discussed later in this chapter).

Similarly, the versions of Windows Movie Maker included with Windows Vista and Windows XP can't export video files in an iPhone-friendly format, so what you need to do is export the video file in a standard format (such as AVI) that you can then convert using another application.

Create a WMV File from Windows Live Movie Maker   To create a WMV file from Windows Live Movie Maker, open the project and follow these steps:

1. Choose File | Save Movie to display the Save Movie panel. The tab I'm calling "File" here is the unnamed tab at the left end of the Ribbon.
2. In the Common Settings section, click For Computer. The Save Movie dialog box opens.
3. Type the name for the movie, choose the folder, and then click the Save button.

Now that you've created a WMV file, use a converter program such as Full Video Converter Free (discussed later in this chapter) to convert it to a format that the iPhone can play.

Create an AVI File from Windows Movie Maker on Windows Vista   To save a movie as an AVI file from Windows Movie Maker on Windows Vista, follow these steps:

1. With your movie open in Windows Movie Maker, choose File | Publish Movie (or press CTRL-P) to launch the Publish Movie Wizard. The Wizard displays the Where Do You Want To Publish Your Movie? screen.
2. Select the This Computer item in the list box, and then click the Next button. The Wizard displays the Name The Movie You Are Publishing screen.
3. Type the name for the movie, choose the folder in which to store it, and then click the Next button. The Wizard displays the Choose The Settings For Your Movie screen (see Figure 13-14).
4. Select the More Settings option button, and then select the DV-AVI item in the drop-down list.

 The DV-AVI item appears as DV-AVI (NTSC) or DV-AVI (PAL), depending on whether you've chosen the NTSC option button or the PAL option button on the Advanced tab of the Options dialog box. NTSC is the video format used in most of North America; PAL's stronghold is Europe.

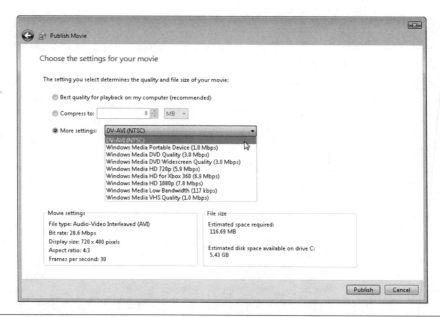

FIGURE 13-14   On the Choose The Settings For Your Movie screen, select the More Settings option button, and then pick the DV-AVI item in the drop-down list.

5. Click the Publish button to export the movie in this format. When Windows Movie Maker finishes exporting the file, it displays the Your Movie Has Been Published screen.
6. Clear the Play Movie When I Click Finish check box if you don't want to watch the movie immediately in Windows Media Player. Often, it's a good idea to check that the movie has come out okay.
7. Click the Finish button.

Now that you've created an AVI file, use a converter program such as Full Video Converter Free (discussed later in this chapter) to convert it to a format that works on the iPhone.

Create an AVI File from Windows Movie Maker on Windows XP   To save a movie as an AVI file from Windows Movie Maker on Windows XP, follow these steps:

1. Choose File | Save Movie File to launch the Save Movie Wizard. The Wizard displays its Movie Location screen.
2. Select the My Computer item, and then click the Next button. The Wizard displays the Saved Movie File screen.
3. Enter the name and choose the folder for the movie, and then click the Next button. The Wizard displays the Movie Setting screen (shown in Figure 13-15 with options selected).

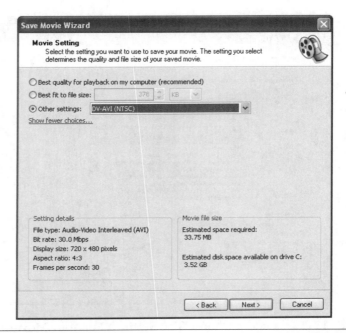

FIGURE 13-15 Click the Show More Choices link to make the Other Settings option button available, then select the Other Settings option button and pick the DV-AVI item from the drop-down list.

4. Click the Show More Choices link to display the Best Fit To File Size option button and the Other Settings option button.
5. Select the Other Settings option button, and then select the DV-AVI item in the drop-down list.

 The DV-AVI item appears as DV-AVI (NTSC) or DV-AVI (PAL), depending on whether you've chosen the NTSC option button or the PAL option button on the Advanced tab of the Options dialog box.

6. Click the Next button to save the movie in this format. The Wizard displays the Completing The Save Movie Wizard screen.
7. Clear the Play Movie When I Click Finish check box if you don't want to test the movie immediately in Windows Media Player. Usually, it's a good idea to make sure the movie has come out right.
8. Click the Finish button.

Now that you've created an AVI file, use a converter program such as Full Video Converter Free (discussed later in this chapter) to convert it to a format that works on the iPhone.

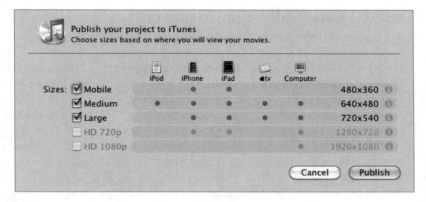

FIGURE 13-16   On the Publish Your Project To iTunes sheet in iMovie, choose which sizes of file you want to create—for example, Medium for the iPhone.

Create iPhone-Compatible Video Files Using iMovie

To use iMovie to create video files that will play on the iPhone, follow these steps:

1. With the movie open in iMovie, choose Share | iTunes to display the Publish Your Project To iTunes sheet (see Figure 13-16).
2. In the Sizes area, select the check box for each size you want to create. The dots show the devices for which that size is suitable. For example, if you want to play the video files on an iPhone classic, select the Medium check box.
3. Click the Publish button, and then wait while iMovie creates the compressed file or files and adds it or them to iTunes. iMovie then automatically displays iTunes.
4. Click the Movies item in the Source list, and you'll see the movies you just created. Double-click a file to play it, or simply drag it to the iPhone to load it immediately.

Create iPhone-Friendly Video Files from Your Existing Video Files

If you have existing video files (for example, files in the AVI format or QuickTime movies), you can convert them to iPhone format in a couple of ways. The easiest way is by using the capabilities built into iTunes—but unfortunately, these work only for some video files. The harder way is by using QuickTime Pro, which can convert files from most known formats but which costs $30.

On Windows, you can also use third-party converter programs, such as Full Video Converter Free, discussed later in this chapter.

Create iPhone Video Files Using iTunes

To create a video file for the iPhone using iTunes, follow these steps:

1. Add the video file to your iTunes library in either of these ways:
   - Open iTunes if it's not running. Open a Windows Explorer window (Windows) or a Finder window (Mac) to the folder that contains the video file. Arrange the windows so that you can see both the file and iTunes. Drag the file to the Library item in iTunes.
   - In iTunes, choose File | Add To Library, use the Add To Library dialog box to select the file, and then click the Open button (Windows) or the Choose button (Mac).
2. Select the movie in the iTunes window, and then choose Advanced | Create iPhone Or iPod Version.

If the Create iPhone Or iPod Version command isn't available for the file, or if iTunes gives you an error message, you'll know that iTunes can't convert the file.

Create iPhone-Friendly Video Files Using QuickTime

QuickTime, Apple's multimedia software for Mac OS X and Windows, comes in two versions: QuickTime Player (the free version) and QuickTime Pro, which costs $29.99.

Create iPhone-Friendly Video Files Using QuickTime Player on the Mac On Mac OS X, QuickTime Player is included in a standard installation of the operating system; and if you've somehow managed to uninstall it, it'll automatically install itself again if you install iTunes. The Mac version of QuickTime Player includes file conversions, which you can access by using the Share menu. For example, follow these steps:

1. Open QuickTime Player from Launchpad, the Dock, or the Applications folder.
2. Choose File | Open File, select the file in the Open dialog box, and then click the Open button.
3. Choose Share | iTunes to display the Save Your Movie To iTunes dialog box (see Figure 13-17).
4. Select the iPhone & iPod option button.
5. Click the Share button. QuickTime converts the file.

Create iPhone-Friendly Video Files Using QuickTime Pro on Windows On Windows, you install QuickTime Player when you install iTunes, because QuickTime provides much of the multimedia functionality for iTunes. The "Player" name isn't entirely accurate, because QuickTime provides encoding services as well as decoding services to iTunes—but QuickTime Player on the PC doesn't allow you to create most formats of video files until you buy QuickTime Pro.

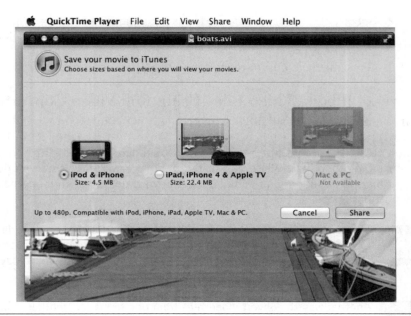

FIGURE 13-17   On the Mac, you can use QuickTime Player to convert video files to formats suitable for the iPhone.

 QuickTime Pro for Windows gets rave reviews from some users but wretched reviews from others. If you are thinking of buying QuickTime Pro for Windows, read the latest reviews for it at the Apple Store (http://store.apple.com) first.

QuickTime Player for Windows is a crippled version of QuickTime Pro, so when you buy QuickTime Pro from the Apple Store, all you get is a registration code to unlock the hidden functionality. To apply the registration code, choose Edit | Preferences | Register In Windows to display the Register tab of the QuickTime Settings dialog box.

 When you register QuickTime Pro, you must enter your registration name in the Registered To text box in exactly the same format as Apple has decided to use it. For example, if you've used the name John P. Smith to register QuickTime Pro, and Apple has decided to address the registration to *Mr. John P. Smith*, you must use **Mr. John P. Smith** as the registration name. If you try to use **John P. Smith**, registration fails, even if this is exactly the way you gave your name when registering.

To create an iPhone-friendly video file from QuickTime Pro, follow these steps:

1. Open the file in QuickTime Pro, and then choose File | Export to display the Save Exported File As dialog box.

2. Specify the filename and folder as usual, and then choose Movie To iPhone in the Export drop-down list. Leave the Default Settings item selected in the Use drop-down list.
3. Click the Save button to start exporting the video file.

Create iPhone Video Files Using Full Video Converter Free

If you have video files that you can't convert with iTunes on Windows, use a file conversion program such as Full Video Converter Free (see Figure 13-18). You can download this program from the CNET Download.com site (http://download.cnet.com) and other sites. When you install the program, make sure you decline any extra options such as adding a toolbar, changing your default search engine, or changing your home page.

 You can find various other free programs online for converting video files. If you're looking for such programs, check carefully that what you're about to download is actually free rather than a crippled version that requires you to pay before you can convert files.

 Another way to convert video files from one format to another—on either Windows or the Mac—is to use an online file conversion tool such as Zamzar (www.zamzar.com). For low volumes of files, the conversion is free (though it may take a while), but you must provide a valid e-mail address. For higher volumes of files or higher priority, you can sign up for a paid account.

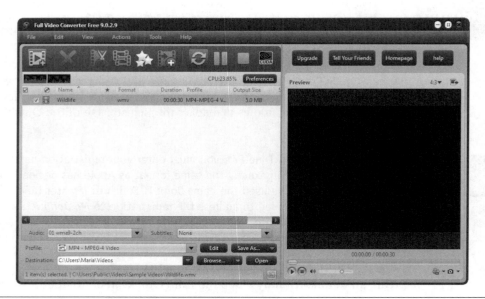

FIGURE 13-18 Full Video Converter Free lets you convert various types of videos to iPhone-friendly formats.

Create iPhone Video Files Using HandBrake on the Mac

If you have video files that you can't convert with iTunes on the Mac, try using the free conversion program HandBrake (http://handbrake.fr). Download HandBrake, install it to your Applications folder, run it from there, and then follow these steps:

1. Click the Source button on the toolbar to display an Open dialog box.

 HandBrake can also rip DVDs, provided you have a third-party decryption utility installed. See the end of the chapter for details.

2. Click the file you want, and then click the Open button. HandBrake shows the details of the file.
3. In the Title drop-down list, choose which title—which of the recorded items in the file—you want. Most files have only one title, so the choice is easy; DVDs have various titles.
4. If the file is broken up into chapters (sections), choose which ones you want. Pick the first in the Chapters drop-down list and the last in the Through drop-down list—for example, Chapters 1 through 4.
5. In the Destination area, change the name and path for the converted file if necessary.
6. If the Presets drawer isn't displayed on the right side of the window, click the Toggle Presets button on the toolbar to display it. Figure 13-19 shows the HandBrake window with the Presets drawer displayed.
7. In the Presets drawer, choose the iPhone 4 preset.
8. If necessary, change further settings. (Press ⌘-? to display the HandBrake User Guide for instructions.)
9. Click the Start button on the toolbar to start encoding the file.

Create Video Files from Your DVDs

If you have DVDs, you'll probably want to put them on your iPhone so that you can watch them without a DVD player. This section gives you an overview of how to create suitable files, first on Windows, and then on the Mac.

 Because ripping commercial DVDs without specific permission is a violation of copyright law, there are no DVD ripping programs from major companies. You can find commercial programs, shareware programs, and freeware programs on the Internet—but keep your wits firmly about you, as some programs are a threat to your computer through being poorly programmed, while others include unwanted components such as adware or spyware. Always read reviews of any DVD ripper you're considering before you download and install it—and certainly before you pay for it. As usual on the Internet, if something seems too good to be true, it most likely *is* too good to be true.

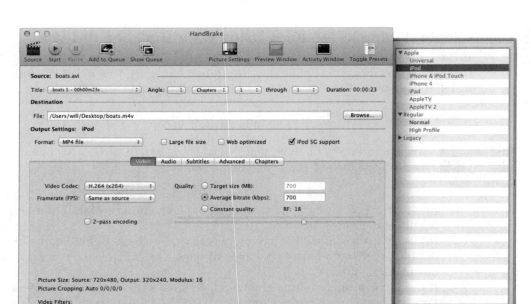

FIGURE 13-19 The Presets drawer on the right side of the HandBrake window lets you instantly choose video settings for the iPhone.

Before you start ripping, make sure that your discs don't contain computer-friendly versions of their contents. At this writing, some Blu-Ray discs include such versions, which are licensed for you to load on your computer and your lifestyle devices (such as your iPhone).

Rip DVDs on Windows

Here are two solutions for decrypting and ripping DVDs on Windows:

- **DVD43 and DVD Shrink** DVD43 is a free DVD-decryption utility that you can download from the links on the DVD43 and DVD43 Plug-in – Download Sites page (www.dvd43.com). DVD43 opens the DVD for ripping but doesn't rip the content from the DVD. To rip, use a program such as DVD Shrink ($28.95; www.official-dvdshrink.org).
- **AnyDVD and CloneDVD Mobile** AnyDVD from SlySoft (around $55 per year; www.slysoft.com) is a decryption utility that works with CloneDVD Mobile (around $45 per year; also from SlySoft). By using these two programs together, you can rip DVDs to formats that work on the iPhone. SlySoft offers 21-day trial versions of these programs.

Rip DVDs on the Mac

The best tool for ripping DVDs on the Mac is HandBrake, which you met earlier in this chapter. To rip DVDs with HandBrake, you must install VLC, a DVD- and video-playing application (free; www.videolan.org). This is because HandBrake uses VLC's DVD-decryption capabilities; without VLC, HandBrake cannot decrypt DVDs.

Once you've installed VLC, simply run HandBrake, click the Source button, click the DVD in the Source list, and then click the Open button. HandBrake scans the DVD. You can then choose which "title" (which of the recorded tracks on the DVD) to rip, and which chapters from it. The chapters are the bookmarks on the DVD—for example, if you press the Next button on your remote, your DVD player skips to the start of the next chapter.

Recover Your Songs and Videos from Your iPhone

As you know, you can copy all or part of your library onto your iPhone almost effortlessly by choosing suitable synchronization settings and then synchronizing the iPhone.

When you sync your iPhone with your computer, any songs and videos on your iPhone are also in your library on your computer, so you don't need to transfer the songs and videos from your iPhone to your computer. But if you have a computer

---

How to... Prevent the Mac OS X DVD Player from Running Automatically When You Insert a DVD

When you insert a movie DVD, Mac OS X automatically launches DVD Player, switches it to full screen, and starts the movie playing. This behavior is great for when you want to watch a movie, but not so great when you want to rip it.

To prevent DVD Player from running automatically when you insert a DVD, follow these steps:

1. Choose Apple | System Preferences to open System Preferences.
2. In the Hardware section, click the CDs & DVDs item.
3. In the When You Insert A Video DVD drop-down list, you can choose Ignore if you want to be able to choose freely which application to use each time. If you always want to use the same application, choose Open Other Application, use the resulting Open dialog box to select the application, and then click the Choose button.
4. Choose System Preferences | Quit System Preferences or press ⌘-Q to close System Preferences.

disaster, or if your computer is stolen, you may need to recover the songs and videos from your iPhone to your new or repaired computer.

 When you sync your iPhone with iCloud rather than with a computer, you store a copy of your songs and videos online. You can then sync them to another iPhone, iPad, or iPod touch as needed. The main limitation is that you may need to pay for the iTunes Match feature or for additional storage space on iCloud to store all your files.

To recover songs and videos from your iPhone, you need a utility that can read the iPhone's file system. To help you avoid losing your music and videos, iPhone enthusiasts have developed some great utilities for transferring files from the iPhone's hidden music and video storage to a computer.

 To avoid losing data, you should back up all your valuable data, including any songs and videos that you can't easily recover by other means (such as ripping your CDs again), especially the songs and videos you've bought from the iTunes Store or other online stores. But the amount of data—and, in particular, the size of many people's libraries—makes backup difficult, requiring either an external hard drive or multiple DVDs.

At this writing, several utilities are available for copying your music and videos from your iPhone to your computer. The best utility for both Windows and the Mac is DiskAid from DigiDNA ($24.90; www.digidna.net; trial version available). DiskAid (see Figure 13-20) reads your iPhone's library database and displays its contents so that you can easily copy them back to a computer.

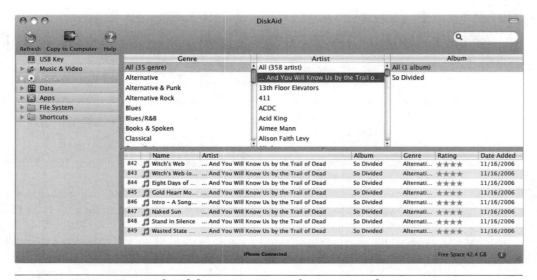

FIGURE 13-20 Use DiskAid from DigiDNA when you need to copy your songs and videos from your iPhone back to a computer.

Share Items and Access Shared Items

Listening to your own music collection is great, but it's often even better to be able to share your music with your friends or family—and to enjoy as much of their music as you can stand. In this section, we'll look at how to share your music in two ways:

- Share your own music with your other computers using iTunes' Home Sharing feature
- Share your music with other iTunes users on your network and play the music they're sharing

You can also share other file types that iTunes supports—for example, videos—but we'll concentrate on music here.

Share Your Library with Your Other Computers

iTunes' Home Sharing feature makes it easy to share your library among your computers. You can use up to five computers.

The big difference between Home Sharing and iTunes' library sharing is that Home Sharing enables you to copy songs from one computer to another. Regular sharing lets another computer play your shared songs but not copy the files to that computer.

To use Home Sharing, you set up each of the computers to use the same Apple ID. Using the same Apple ID is the mechanism for making sure that you're not violating copyright by giving copyrighted content to other people. If you don't have an Apple ID yet, you can create one from the Home Sharing screen.

To set up Home Sharing, follow these steps:

1. In the Source list, see if the Shared category is expanded, showing its contents. If not, expand it by holding the mouse pointer over the Shared heading and then clicking the word Show when it appears.
2. Click the Home Sharing item to display its contents.
3. Type your Apple ID in the Apple ID box.

If you don't yet have an Apple ID, click the Need An Apple ID? link, and then follow through the process of signing up for one. Once you're armed with your Apple ID, go back to the Home Sharing screen.

4. Type your password in the Password box.
5. Click the Create Home Share button. iTunes checks in with the iTunes servers and sets up the account.

If iTunes displays a dialog box saying that Home Sharing could not be activated because this computer is not authorized for the iTunes account associated with the Apple ID you provided, click the Authorize button.

6. When the Home Sharing screen displays the message that Home Sharing is now on, click the Done button. iTunes then removes the Home Sharing item from the Shared category in the Source list, and you have access to the libraries of the other computers on which you've set up Home Sharing.

Copy Files Using Home Sharing

After setting up Home Sharing, you can quickly copy files from one installation of iTunes to another. To do so, follow these steps:

1. In the Source list, make sure the Shared category is expanded, showing its contents. If the Shared category is collapsed, expand it by holding the mouse pointer over the Shared heading and then clicking the word Show when it appears.
2. Click the Home Sharing library whose contents you want to see. The library's contents appear in the main part of the iTunes window, and you can browse them as usual (see Figure 13-21). For example, choose View | Column Browser | Show Column Browser to display the column browser so that you can browse by genres, artists, albums, or whichever other items you prefer.

 The Home Sharing libraries appear in the Shared category with a Home Sharing icon next to them. The Home Sharing icon shows a house containing a musical note.

How to... **Deal with the "You Cannot Authorize More Than 5 Computers" Message**

If iTunes displays the message "You cannot authorize more than 5 computers" (shown here) when you try to set up Home Sharing on one of your computers, you must deauthorize one of your currently authorized computers in order to use this one. See the section "Authorize and Deauthorize Computers for the iTunes Store, earlier in this chapter, for instructions.

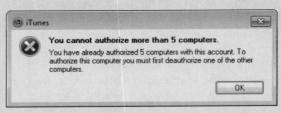

FIGURE 13-21   You can browse a Home Sharing library using the same techniques as for browsing your own library.

3. In the Show drop-down list at the bottom, choose which items to display:
   - **All Items**   This is the default setting. Use it when you want to get an overview of what the library contains.
   - **Items Not In My Library**   Use this setting to display only the items you may want to copy to your library.
4. Select the items you want to import to your library. If you've switched to the Items Not In My Library view, you may want to choose Edit | Select All (or press CTRL-A on Windows or ⌘-A on the Mac) to select everything.
5. Click the Import button. iTunes imports the files.

Share Your Library with Other Local iTunes Users

You can share either your entire library or selected playlists with other users on your network. You can share most items, including MP3 files, AAC files, Apple Lossless Encoding files, AIFF files, WAV files, and links to radio stations. You can't share Audible files or QuickTime sound files.

 Technically, iTunes' sharing is limited to computers on the same TCP/IP subnet as your computer is on. (A *subnet* is a logical division of a network.) A home network typically uses a single subnet, so your computer can "see" all the other computers

How to...

Make Home Sharing Automatically Import New Purchases from Your Other Computers

You can set Home Sharing to automatically import your new purchases from the iTunes Store to your computer. So if you buy a song on your laptop computer, you can have iTunes automatically import it to your desktop computer as well.

To set Home Sharing to automatically import new purchases, follow these steps:

1. In the Source list, click a Home Sharing library to display its contents and the Home Sharing control bar.
2. Click the Settings button to display the Home Sharing Settings dialog box (shown here).
3. Select the Music check box, the Movies check box, the TV Shows check box, the Books check box, and the Apps check box, as needed.
4. Click the OK button to close the Home Sharing Settings dialog box.

on the network. But if your computer connects to a medium-sized network, and you're unable to find a computer that you know is connected to the same network somewhere, it may be on a different subnet.

At this writing, you can share your library with up to five other computers per day, and your computer can be one of up to five computers accessing the shared library on another computer on any given day.

The shared library remains on the computer that's sharing it, and when a participating computer goes to play a song or other item, that item is streamed across the network. This means that the item isn't copied from the computer that's sharing it to the computer that's playing it in a way that leaves a usable file on the playing computer.

When a computer goes offline or is shut down, library items it has been sharing stop being available to other users. Participating computers can play the shared items but can't do anything else with them; for example, they can't burn shared songs to CD or DVD, download them to an iPod or iPhone, or copy them to their own libraries.

To share some or all of your library, follow these steps:

1. Display the iTunes dialog box or the Preferences dialog box:
   - In Windows, choose Edit | Preferences or press CTRL-COMMA or CTRL-Y to display the iTunes dialog box.

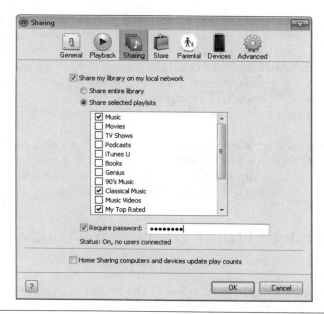

FIGURE 13-22   On the Sharing tab of the iTunes dialog box or the Preferences dialog box, choose whether to share part or all of your library.

- On the Mac, choose iTunes | Preferences or press ⌘-COMMA or ⌘-Y to display the Preferences dialog box.

2. Click the Sharing tab to display it. Figure 13-22 shows the Sharing tab of the iTunes dialog box with settings chosen.

3. Select the Share My Library On My Local Network check box. (This check box is cleared by default.) By default, iTunes then selects the Share Entire Library option button. If you want to share only some playlists, select the Share Selected Playlists option button. Then, in the list box, select the check box for each playlist you want to share.

4. By default, your shared library items are available to any other user on the network. To restrict access to people with whom you share a password, select the Require Password check box, and then enter a strong (unguessable) password in the text box.

If there are many computers on your network, use a password on your shared music to help avoid running up against the five-users-per-day limit. If your network has only a few computers, you may not need a password to avoid reaching this limit.

5. Select the Home Sharing Computers And Devices Update Play Counts check box if you want iTunes to update the play count for a song whenever any computer plays it, not just this computer.

6. Click the General tab to display its contents. In the Library Name text box near the top of the dialog box, set the name that other users trying to access your library will see. The default name is *username*'s Library, where *username* is your username—for example, Anna Connor's Library. You might choose to enter a more descriptive name, especially if your computer is part of a well-populated network (for example, in a dorm).

7. Click the OK button to apply your choices and close the dialog box.

 When you set iTunes to share your library, iTunes displays a message reminding you that "Sharing music is for personal use only"—in other words, remember not to violate copyright law. Select the Do Not Show This Message Again check box if you want to prevent this message from appearing again.

Disconnect Other Users from Your Shared Library

To disconnect other users from your shared library, follow these steps:

1. Display the iTunes dialog box or the Preferences dialog box:
   - In Windows, choose Edit | Preferences or press CTRL-COMMA or CTRL-Y to display the iTunes dialog box.
   - On the Mac, choose iTunes | Preferences or press ⌘-COMMA or ⌘-Y to display the Preferences dialog box.
2. Click the Sharing tab to display it.
3. Clear the Share My Library On My Local Network check box.
4. Click the OK button. If any other user is connected to your shared library, iTunes displays this dialog box to warn you:

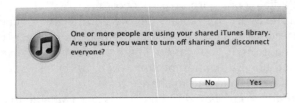

5. Click the Yes button or the No button, as appropriate. If you click the Yes button, anyone playing an item from the library will be cut off abruptly without notice.

 Home Sharing remains active even when you've turned off library sharing.

FIGURE 13-23   Computers sharing libraries appear in the iTunes Source list, allowing you to quickly browse the songs and other items that are being shared.

Access and Play Another Local iTunes User's Shared Library

iTunes automatically detects shared libraries when you launch the program while your computer is connected to a network. If iTunes finds shared libraries or playlists, it displays them in the Source list. Click a shared library to display its contents. Figure 13-23 shows an example of browsing the music shared by another computer.

If a shared library has a password, iTunes displays the Shared Library Password dialog box.

Type the password, and then click the OK button to access the library. Select the Remember Password check box before clicking the OK button if you want iTunes to save the password to speed up future access to the library.

Tip Double-click the entry for a shared library in the Source list to open a separate window that shows its contents.

When you've finished using a shared library, disconnect it by taking one of these actions:

- Click the Eject icon next to the library in the Source list.
- Click the library in the Source list, and then press CTRL-E (Windows) or ⌘-E (Mac).
- Click the library in the Source list, and then choose Controls | Disconnect *Library* from the shortcut menu (where *Library* is the name of the shared library).
- Right-click the library in the Source list (or CTRL-click on the Mac), and then choose Disconnect from the shortcut menu.

Access a Shared Library from Your iPhone

To access your network's shared libraries from your iPhone, follow these steps:

1. Open the Music app.
2. Tap the More button on the toolbar to display the More screen.
3. Tap the Shared button to display the Shared screen.
4. Tap the shared library you want to view. Your iPhone displays its contents, and you can browse and play its songs.

14

Use Your iPhone for File Backup, Storage, and Transfer

HOW TO...

- Decide whether or not to use your iPhone as an external drive
- Transfer files to your iPhone using iTunes File Sharing
- Use a third-party program to put other files on your iPhone

As well as providing you with communications, entertainment, and apps to work or play anywhere, your iPhone has plenty of space to carry your most important files so that they're always with you. This chapter shows you how to turn your iPhone into an external drive for backup, portable storage, and file transfer.

As you've probably noticed, iTunes includes a feature called File Sharing that enables you to put files into your iPhone's file system, where the apps you use can access them. In this chapter, we'll look at how File Sharing works and how you use it.

But transferring files via File Sharing ties the files to particular apps, so File Sharing isn't the right tool when you simply want to copy a large number of files to or from your iPhone. For that, you need a third-party program instead, as you'll see in this chapter.

 One external-drive feature this chapter *doesn't* show you is how to transfer files from an iPhone's library onto your computer. Chapter 13 covers this subject.

Decide Whether to Use Your iPhone as an External Drive

Here's why you may want to use your iPhone as an external drive:

- *It provides a great combination of portability and high capacity.* You can get smaller portable-storage devices (for example, USB keys, CompactFlash drives, SmartMedia cards, and Memory Sticks), but they're an extra expense and an extra device to carry with you. Assuming you always carry your iPhone, you can keep your files with you at all times.
- *You can take all your documents with you.* For example, you could take home that large PowerPoint presentation you need to review to prepare for the meeting tomorrow. You can even put several gigabytes of video files on your iPhone if you need to take them with you (for example, to a studio for editing) or transfer them to another computer.
- *You can use your iPhone for backup.* If you keep your vital documents down to a size you can easily fit on your iPhone (and still have plenty of room left for songs, videos, photos, and all the other files you need on it), you can quickly back up the documents and take the backup with you wherever you go.
- *You can use your iPhone for security.* By keeping your documents on your iPhone rather than on your computer, and by keeping your iPhone with you, you can prevent other people from accessing your documents.

The disadvantages to using your iPhone as an external drive are straightforward:

- Whatever space you use on your iPhone for storing other files isn't available for music, video, photos, or apps.
- If you lose or break your iPhone, any files stored only on it will be gone forever.

Transfer Files to Your iPhone Using iTunes' File Sharing

iTunes includes a feature called File Sharing that enables you to transfer files to and from your iPhone. This section shows you how to use File Sharing—after making sure you know how it works and what its limitations are.

First, we'll take a quick diversion and discuss how the iPhone's file system handles files. You need to understand this to make sense of File Sharing and why you will probably have to get a third-party program to put files freely on your iPhone.

Understand How the iPhone's File System Handles Files

On your PC or Mac, you can largely put files where you want. For example, on the PC, you can open a Windows Explorer window, navigate to most any folder in the file system, and paste files there. Similarly, on the Mac, you can open a Finder window, navigate to the folder you choose, and paste files there. Or you can use the Save As dialog box in a program or application to store a file in such a folder.

Both Windows and Mac OS X discourage you from storing your documents among the system files, but if you're determined enough, they don't prevent you from doing so. Putting the documents in unsuitable places may bring awkward consequences, such as the wrong people being able to access them, but the operating systems let you bring those consequences upon yourself.

The iPhone's operating system, iOS, is more restrictive. It strictly limits the areas of the file system that you can access—and it does the same for the iPhone's apps. Within its file system, iOS gives each app a separate storage area for documents: its own document silo. iOS largely confines each app to its own silo and prevents it from accessing any other silos. This security measure both protects against malware and prevents one app from stomping another app's data files.

For example, if you have the Pages app on your iPhone, you can use File Sharing to transfer a Pages document from your Mac to your iPhone. Once the Pages document is on your iPhone, you can launch Pages and then open the document. But you can't open the document in another app, because it's stored in Pages' silo.

The exception is apps that can receive incoming files, such as Mail and Safari. These apps can provide those files to other apps. For example, if you receive a Word document attached to an e-mail message on your iPhone, you can choose to open that document in Pages or another app that can handle Word documents. Mail makes the document available to Pages or the app you choose.

Use File Sharing to Transfer Files to and from Your iPhone

To transfer documents to and from your iPhone by using File Sharing, follow these steps:

1. Connect your iPhone to the computer as usual.
2. If the computer doesn't automatically launch or activate iTunes, launch or activate iTunes yourself.
3. In the Source list, click the entry for your iPhone to display its control screens.
4. Click the Apps tab to display its contents.
5. Scroll down to the File Sharing area (see Figure 14-1).
6. In the Apps list, click the app to which you want to transfer the files. The list of files for that app appears in the Documents pane to the right.
7. To add documents to the app, follow these steps:
   a. Click the Add button to display the iTunes dialog box (on Windows) or the Choose A File: iTunes dialog box (on the Mac).
   b. Navigate to and select the document or documents you want to add.
   c. Click the OK button (on Windows) or the Choose button (on the Mac).
8. To copy documents from the app to the computer, follow these steps:
   a. Click the Save To button to display the iTunes dialog box (on Windows) or the Choose A File: iTunes dialog box (on the Mac).
   b. Navigate to the folder in which you want to save the document.

FIGURE 14-1 The File Sharing area on the Apps tab in the iTunes control screen for an iPhone lists the apps that can transfer files. Click an app to see its files.

    c. Click the Select Folder button (on Windows) or the Choose button (on the Mac).

9. Click the Sync button to run the synchronization.

File transfers generally run pretty quickly, as USB 2.0 can handle up to 480 megabits per second (Mbps)—but if you're transferring many large files, it'll take a while.

Find a Suitable Program for Putting Other Files on Your iPhone

As you saw in the previous section, iTunes' File Sharing feature lets you put one or more files in a particular app's storage silo on your iPhone, or transfer files from your iPhone to your PC or Mac. But it doesn't give you full-on access to the file system.

If you've used an iPod (other than the iPod touch), you probably know that you can select a check box in iTunes to switch the iPod to "disk mode," making it show up in your PC's or Mac's file system as a removable drive. With disk mode on, you can transfer files to the iPod using Windows Explorer (on Windows) or the Finder (on the Mac), just as you can with any other removable drive.

At this writing, Apple doesn't provide a way to put an iPhone into disk mode so that you can transfer files to it. So instead you need to use a third-party program that lets you use your iPhone as an external drive. This section shows you three such programs: DiskAid, Air Sharing, and PhoneView. You can find others on the Web or in the App Store (which you can access via iTunes on your computer or via the App Store application on your iPhone).

DiskAid (Windows and Mac OS X)

DiskAid from DigiDNA ($9.90; www.digidna.net/diskaid) is a utility that lets you mount your iPhone as an external disk. Figure 14-2 shows DiskAid at work on a Mac.

DiskAid's toolbar buttons let you easily create folders, copy items to and from the device, and delete items from the device. But you can also simply drag files and folders from a Windows Explorer window or a Finder window to the DiskAid window to add them to the iPhone.

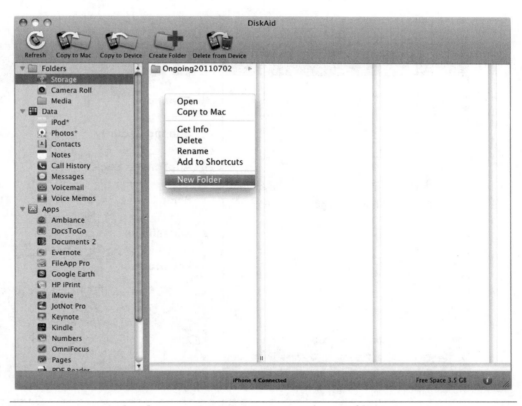

FIGURE 14-2   DiskAid gives you access to your iPhone's file system.

Air Sharing (Windows and Mac OS X)

Air Sharing from Avatron Software (www.avatron.com), which you can buy from the App Store for $6.99, lets you access your iPhone across a wireless network connection rather than the USB connection that most other programs require. Not having to connect the device to your computer is an advantage, but you get slower file transfers than via USB, and your iPhone doesn't get to recharge while you're using Air Sharing.

If Air Sharing suits you, you may want to upgrade to the Universal version ($9.99), which includes a wider variety of file operations (such as creating new folders and zipping and unzipping files), the ability to mount remote file servers (such as iCloud and Dropbox), and the ability to print to certain printers.

Set Up Air Sharing on Your iPhone

After downloading Air Sharing and installing it on your iPhone by synchronizing with iTunes, set up Air Sharing so that your computer can connect to it. Follow these steps:

1. On your iPhone, launch Air Sharing by tapping its icon on the Home screen. The My Documents screen appears, as shown on the left in Figure 14-3.

FIGURE 14-3 Tap the wrench icon in the lower-right corner of the My Documents screen (left) to display the Settings screen (right).

2. Tap the wrench icon in the lower-right corner to display the Settings screen (shown on the right in Figure 14-3).
3. Tap the Sharing button to display the Sharing screen (shown on the left in Figure 14-4).
4. Move the Enabled switch to the On position.
5. Tap the Settings button to return to the Settings screen.
6. Tap the Sharing Security button to display the Sharing Security screen (shown on the right in Figure 14-4).

 This section shows you how to implement a reasonable level of security on your iPhone for sharing. Air Sharing can provide not only password-free access but also public access to your iPhone, but neither is a good idea.

7. Move the Require Password switch to the On position.
8. Type the username and password you will use for the connection.
9. Move the Public Access switch to the Off position.

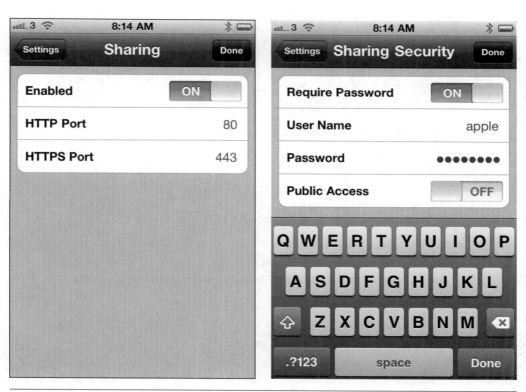

FIGURE 14-4   Turn on sharing by setting the Enabled switch on the Sharing screen (left) to the On position. On the Sharing Security screen (right), move the Require Password switch to the On position, and then enter the username and password for connecting.

10. Tap the Settings button to return to the Settings screen. Look at the readout at the bottom giving the Bonjour addresses and IP addresses of your iPhone, and note the address you need—the non-https IP address for Windows, and the non-https Bonjour address for Mac OS X.
11. Tap the Done button to return to the My Documents screen.

Now that you've set up Air Sharing on your iPhone, you can connect to Air Sharing from your PC or Mac, as discussed next.

Connect to Air Sharing on Your iPhone from a PC

To connect to Air Sharing on your iPhone from a PC, follow these steps:

1. Choose Start | Computer to open a Computer window.
2. Click the Map Network Drive button on the toolbar to display the Map Network Drive dialog box (see Figure 14-5).
3. In the Drive drop-down list, choose the drive letter you want to map to your iPhone.
4. In the Folder text box, type **http://** and the IP address shown for your iPhone—for example, **http://10.0.0.36**.

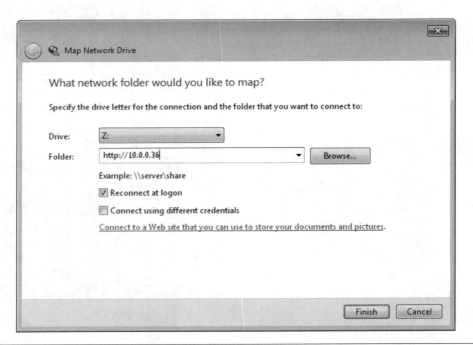

FIGURE 14-5 In the Map Network Drive dialog box, choose the drive letter to use, and then enter your iPhone's address in the Folder field.

5. Select the Reconnect At Logon check box if you want Windows to automatically reconnect the drive each time you log on. Unless you plan to run Air Sharing on your iPhone all the time, you're usually better off clearing this check box and establishing the connection manually when you need it.
6. Click the Finish button. Windows attempts to connect to your iPhone.
7. If you have set a username and password on Air Sharing, Windows prompts you to enter them, as shown here.

8. Type your username and password.
9. Select the Remember My Credentials check box if you want Windows to store the username and password for future use. If you're using your own PC, this is usually a good idea.
10. Click the OK button. Windows establishes the connection to your iPhone and displays a Windows Explorer window showing its contents (see Figure 14-6).

You can now work with your iPhone's file system using standard Windows Explorer techniques. For example, to create a new folder, right-click in open space in the document area, choose New | Folder from the context menu, type the name to give the folder, and then press ENTER.

 You can connect to your iPhone from two or more computers at once. You can even use your iPhone as a kind of server for your network if you want.

When you finish using your iPhone from your PC, disconnect the network drive like this:

1. In the Windows Explorer window, click Computer in the address box to display the Computer window. Alternatively, choose Start | Computer to open a Computer window.
2. Right-click the drive representing your iPhone, and then click Disconnect on the context menu.

Connect to Air Sharing on Your iPhone from a Mac

To connect to Air Sharing on your iPhone from a Mac, follow these steps:

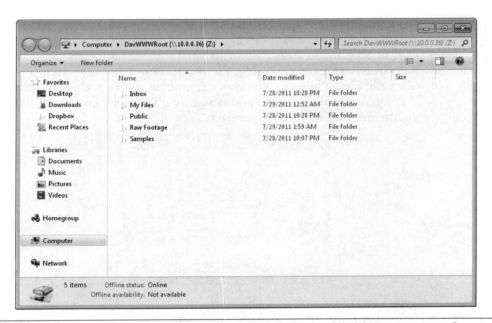

FIGURE 14-6 Windows opens a Windows Explorer window showing your iPhone's file system.

1. Click the desktop to activate the Finder.
2. Choose Go | Connect To Server or press ⌘-K to display the Connect To Server dialog box (shown here).

3. In the Server Address text box, type **http://** and the Bonjour address shown for your iPhone—for example, **http://iPhone.local**.

Instead of typing the Bonjour address, you can type the IP address shown for your iPhone. But given that your Mac is running Bonjour anyway, the Bonjour address is usually a better choice. This is because your iPhone's Bonjour address remains the same unless you change your iPhone's name, whereas if your iPhone gets its IP

How to... **Connect to Air Sharing from Windows XP**

If your PC is running Windows XP, you must have Service Pack 3 installed in order to connect to Air Sharing. If you're not sure which Service Pack your PC is running, click the Start button, right-click the My Computer icon, click Properties on the context menu, and then look at the System readout on the General tab of the System Properties dialog box.

There's also another complication: XP can't connect to the iPhone's shared directory. Instead, you must connect to a subdirectory—preferably the one you want to work in. If you use your iPhone mainly with a Windows XP PC, you'll probably want to set up your iPhone's file system with a subfolder that contains all your other folders.

Provided your PC has Service Pack 3 installed, connect like this:

1. Choose Start | My Computer to open a My Computer window.
2. Choose Tools | Map Network Drive to display the Map Network Drive dialog box.
3. In the Drive drop-down list, choose the drive letter you want to map.
4. In the Folder text box, type **http://**, the iPhone's IP address, a forward slash, and the name of a folder—for example, **http://10.0.0.36/Files**.
5. Click the Finish button.
6. If Windows XP displays a dialog box prompting you for your username and password, enter them, and click the OK button.

address from a DHCP server (as is the normal setup), your iPhone will typically get a different IP address each time it connects to the DHCP server.

4. Click the Add (+) button if you want to add your iPhone to your list of servers. This is a good idea if you plan to access your iPhone frequently using this Mac.
5. Click the Connect button. The Finder attempts to connect to your iPhone.
6. If you have set a username and password on Air Sharing, Mac OS X prompts you to enter them, as shown here.

7. Make sure the Registered User option button is selected.
8. Type your username and password.
9. Select the Remember This Password In My Keychain check box if you want your Mac to store the password for future use. When you're using your own Mac (as opposed to someone else's Mac), this is usually a good idea.
10. Click the Connect button. The Finder establishes the connection to your iPhone and displays your iPhone's contents in a Finder window.

You can now work with your iPhone's file system using the same techniques as for any other drive. For example, CTRL-click or right-click and then click New Folder on the context menu to create a new folder, as shown in Figure 14-7.

When you finish using your iPhone from the Mac, click the Disconnect button in the Finder window to disconnect the drive.

PhoneView (Mac OS X Only)

PhoneView (see Figure 14-8) from Ecamm Network (www.ecamm.com/mac/phoneview) lets you access your iPhone from your Mac. Ecamm provides a mostly functional trial edition, which gives you seven days to find out how well PhoneView suits your needs.

When you finish using PhoneView, quit it (for example, press ⌘-Q or choose PhoneView | Quit PhoneView). PhoneView closes its window and releases its grip on your iPhone's file system.

FIGURE 14-7   After connecting to your iPhone using Air Sharing, you can work with its file system using normal Finder techniques.

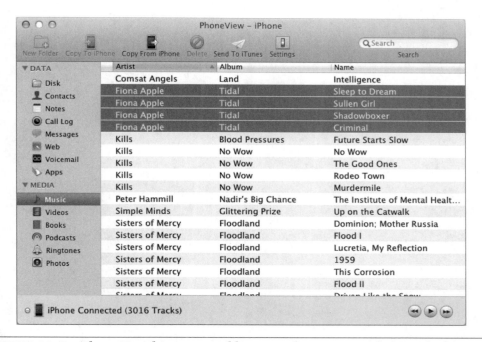

FIGURE 14-8   PhoneView lets you quickly access the contents of your iPhone to copy, add, or delete files.

PART IV

Use Your iPhone as a Work Tool

15

Connect to Your Company's Network via VPN

HOW TO...

- Get the information needed to connect to the VPN
- Set up a VPN on your iPhone by using a configuration profile
- Set up a VPN on your iPhone manually
- Connect to a VPN
- Disconnect from a VPN

If you use an iPhone for company business, you may need to connect the iPhone to your company's network so that you can grab your e-mail or Exchange data. When you're in the office, you'll probably connect via a wireless network, but when you're out of the office, you can connect across the Internet using a virtual private network, or VPN.

A VPN uses an insecure public network (such as the Internet) to connect securely to a secure private network (such as your company's network). A VPN acts as a secure "pipe" through the insecure Internet, providing a secure connection between your computer (in this case, your iPhone) and your company's VPN server.

Get the Information Needed to Connect to the VPN

To connect to a VPN, you need to know various pieces of configuration information, such as your username, the server's Internet address, and your password or other means of authentication. You also need to know which type of security to use: Layer 2 Tunneling Protocol (L2TP), Point-to-Point Tunneling Protocol (PPTP), or IP Security (IPSec).

Your company's network administrator will provide this information. The administrator may provide it as a written list, which you enter manually in your iPhone, as described a little later in this chapter. But it's easy to get one or more items wrong, so usually an administrator will use the iPhone Configuration Utility (a tool Apple provides for administering the iPhone, iPad, and iPod touch) to create a file called a *configuration profile* that you then install on your iPhone and that does the work for you. We'll start with this easier approach.

 If you're the administrator, you'll find the iPhone Configuration Utility here: www. apple.com/support/iphone/enterprise. There are versions for both Windows and Mac OS X.

Set Up a VPN by Using a Configuration Profile

To set up a VPN on your iPhone by using a configuration profile, all you need to do is get the configuration profile onto your iPhone. Normally, the administrator will either put the configuration profile on your iPhone directly by connecting it to his or her computer via USB or distribute the configuration profile in one of these ways:

- **Via e-mail** This is an easy way of distributing configuration profiles as long as the administrator knows your e-mail account. But if the configuration profile is for a corporate e-mail account as well as for the VPN, you'll need to use another e-mail account (because your iPhone won't yet be able to access your corporate account).
- **Via a website** The administrator can place the configuration profile on a website from which you can download it using your iPhone. Typically this will be an internal corporate website or at least a password-protected website, because the configuration profiles aren't encrypted.

Here's how to set up a VPN by installing a configuration profile you've received in an e-mail message or downloaded from a website:

1. Open the configuration profile:
   - If you've received the configuration profile in an e-mail message, as shown in the left screen in Figure 15-1, tap the configuration profile's button. Your iPhone then displays the Install Profile screen, as shown on the right in Figure 15-1.
   - If the configuration profile is posted on a web page, open that page in Safari, and then tap the profile's download link. Your iPhone then displays the Install Profile screen.
2. Look at the information on the Install Profile screen to make sure you want to install the profile. To see more information about the profile, tap the More Details button, which displays the profile's information screen (shown on the

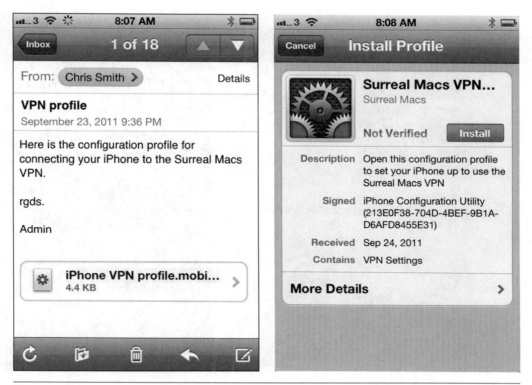

FIGURE 15-1   Tap the configuration profile's button in an e-mail message (left) to display the Install Profile screen (right).

left in Figure 15-2). Tap the Install Profile button in the upper-left corner to go back to the Install Profile screen.

3. Check the profile's status: Unsigned, Not Verified, or Verified. See the sidebar "What the Unsigned, Not Verified, and Verified Terms on the Install Profile Screen Mean" in Chapter 3 for an explanation of these terms and advice on how you should treat the profiles they mark.

4. Tap the Install button on the Install Profile screen to start installing the profile. You'll need to provide your username (as shown on the left in Figure 15-3), password (not shown), and shared secret (as shown on the right in Figure 15-3) to set up the VPN.

5. When the Profile Installed screen appears, tap the Done button. Your iPhone takes you back to where you started the installation—either the e-mail message containing the configuration profile or the web page from which you downloaded the profile.

You can now start using the VPN. Skip ahead to the section "Connect to a VPN," later in this chapter.

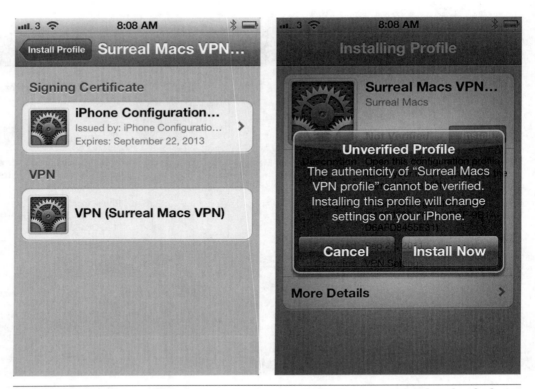

FIGURE 15-2 The profile's information screen (left) shows you the details of what the profile contains—in this case, the signing certificate and the VPN payload. When you tap the Install button on the Install Profile screen to install the profile, your iPhone makes sure you know that installing the profile will change settings on your iPhone (right).

Set Up a VPN Manually

If your administrator has supplied you with a list of configuration details for the VPN rather than with a configuration profile, you'll need to set it up the hard way. Because you have to type in all the details on your iPhone, this is somewhat laborious, but you need to do it only once for any connection. Follow these steps:

1. Press the Home button to reach the Home screen.
2. Tap the Settings icon to display the Settings screen.
3. Tap the General button to display the General screen.
4. Tap the Network button to display the Network screen (shown on the left in Figure 15-4).
5. Tap the VPN button to display the VPN screen (shown on the right in Figure 15-4).

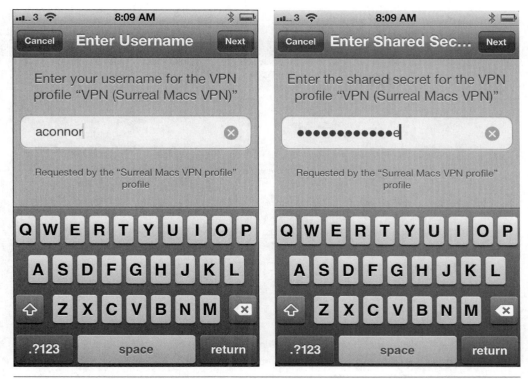

FIGURE 15-3   Your iPhone walks you through the process of setting up the VPN. You enter first your username on the Enter Username screen (left), next your password on the Enter Password screen (not shown), and then the VPN's shared secret on the Enter Shared Secret screen (right).

6. Tap the Add VPN Configuration button to display the Add Configuration screen, shown on the left in Figure 15-5.
7. Near the top of the screen, click the button for the security type the VPN uses: L2TP, PPTP, or IPSec. Your iPhone displays a list of the information required for the connection based on the security type you chose.
8. Type in the details for the VPN configuration on the screen:
   - **Description**   This is the name under which the VPN appears in the list of VPNs. Choose a descriptive name that suits you.
   - **Server**   Type the computer name (for example, macserver.surrealmacs.com) or IP address (for example, 216.248.2.88) of the VPN server.
   - **Account**   Type your login name for the VPN connection. Depending on your company's network, this may be the same as your regular login name, but in most cases it's different for security reasons.
   - **Password**   If the administrator has given you a password rather that a certificate (discussed next), you can enter it here and have your iPhone

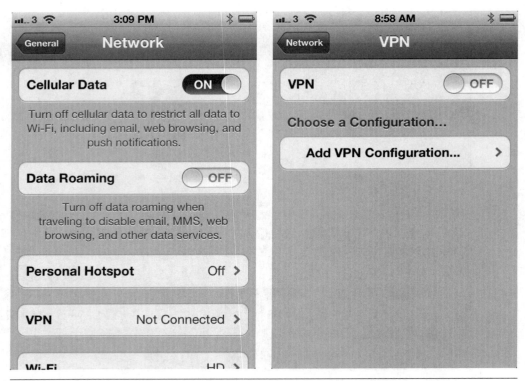

FIGURE 15-4 Tap the VPN button on the Network screen (left) to reach the VPN screen (right).

provide it for you each time you connect. For greater security, you can leave the password area blank and enter the password manually each time you connect. This prevents anyone else from connecting using your iPhone, but it's laborious, especially if your password uses letters, numbers, and symbols (as a strong password should).

Tip If you choose to store your VPN password in the connection, make sure you have secured your iPhone with a passcode as discussed in Chapter 4.

- **RSA SecurID** (PPTP and L2TP only) If the administrator provided you with an RSA SecurID token, move this switch to On to use it. Your iPhone then hides the Password field, because you don't need to use a password when you use the token.
- **Use Certificate** (IPSec only) If the administrator provided you with a configuration profile that installed a certificate for authenticating you on the connection, move this switch to On. To save you from temptation, the switch is available only when a certificate is installed.

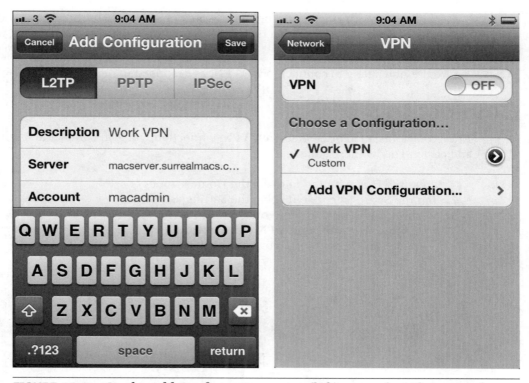

FIGURE 15-5   On the Add Configuration screen (left), enter the information for the connection. When you've saved the connection, move the slider on the VPN screen (right) to On to start the connection.

- **Secret**   (L2TP only) Type the preshared key, also called the *shared secret*, for the VPN. This preshared key is the same for all users of the VPN (unlike your account name and password, which are unique to you).
- **Group Name**   (IPSec only) Type the name of the group to which you belong for the VPN.
- **Send All Traffic**   (L2TP only) Leave this switch set to On (the default position) unless the administrator has told you to turn it off. When Send All Traffic is on, all your Internet connections go to the VPN server; when it is off, Internet connections to parts of the Internet other than the VPN go directly to those destinations.
- **Encryption Level**   (PPTP only) Leave this set to Auto to have your iPhone try 128-bit encryption (the strongest) first, then weaker 40-bit encryption, and then None. Choose Maximum if you know you must use 128-bit encryption only. Choose None only in desperate circumstances—no sane administrator will recommend it.

9. When you've finished entering the information, tap the Save button to save the connection. The VPN connection then appears on the VPN screen (as shown on the right in Figure 15-5).

You're now ready to connect to the VPN, as described in the next section.

Connect to a VPN

After you've installed or created your VPN connection, you can connect to it quickly and easily. Follow these steps:

1. Press the Home button to reach the Home screen.
2. Tap the Settings icon to display the Settings screen.
3. Start the VPN connection in one of these ways:
   - **If you have only one VPN connection** On the Settings screen (shown on the left in Figure 15-6), move the VPN switch to the On position.

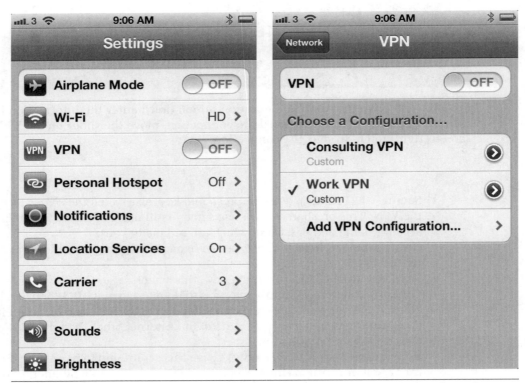

FIGURE 15-6 If you have a single VPN connection, you can turn it on from the Settings screen (left). If you have two or more connections, choose the connection on the VPN screen, and then turn it on.

- **If you have two or more VPN connections**   Tap the VPN button to display the VPN screen. In the Choose A Configuration list (shown on the right in Figure 15-6), make sure the correct VPN is selected; if not, tap the one you want, putting a check mark next to it. Then move the VPN switch to the On position.

If the administrator set you up to authenticate yourself with a password, and you chose not to store the password in the VPN connection, you'll be prompted for your password. Enter it, and your iPhone establishes the connection. The Status readout on the VPN screen shows the connection is active, and the VPN indicator also appears in the status bar as a reminder you're using the VPN (see the left screen in Figure 15-7). You can tap the Status readout to see the details of the connection (see the right screen in Figure 15-7), including your iPhone's IP address.

Once you've established the connection, you'll be able to work on the VPN. What exactly you'll be able to do depends on the permissions the administrator has

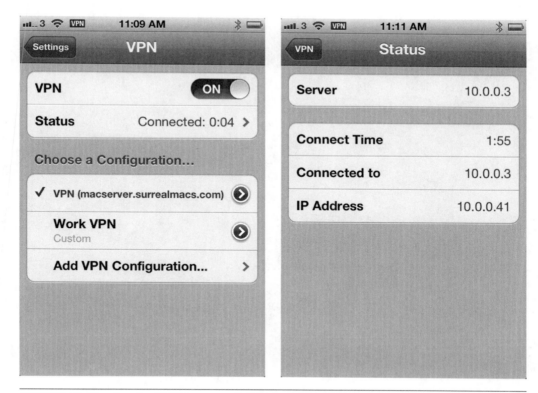

FIGURE 15-7   On the VPN screen (left), the Status readout shows the duration of the connection. You can see further details by tapping the Status button and looking at the Status screen (right). The VPN indicator appears on the status bar as long as the connection is open.

granted you, but you'll typically be able to access your e-mail and shared information resources.

Disconnect from a VPN

When you've finished using the VPN, close any files that you have been using, and then disconnect like this:

1. Press the Home button to reach the Home screen.
2. Tap the Settings icon to display the Settings screen.
3. If you have a single VPN set up, move the VPN switch on the Settings screen to the Off position. Otherwise, tap the VPN button to display the VPN screen, and then move the VPN switch on the VPN screen to the Off position.

16

Connect Your iPhone to Your Company's Exchange Server

HOW TO...

- Add an Exchange account by using a configuration profile
- Set up an Exchange account manually
- Choose which Exchange items to sync with your iPhone
- Troubleshoot iPhone connections to Exchange Server

If your company or organization runs Microsoft Exchange, you'll almost certainly want to connect your iPhone to Exchange so that you can use Exchange for e-mail, contact management, tasks, and calendaring. This chapter shows you how to connect your iPhone to Exchange.

To connect your iPhone, you set up an Exchange account either by installing a configuration profile that contains an Exchange ActiveSync payload of the account's details or by entering the Exchange account's details manually on your iPhone. Using a configuration profile is the smart and easy way to go, so we'll start there— but we'll also cover creating an Exchange account manually in case your Exchange administrator has decided you'll do things the hard way.

After that, we'll look at how you choose which Exchange items—Mail, Contacts, Calendars, or Reminders—to sync with your iPhone.

Finally, I'll give you some tips on troubleshooting connections between your iPhone and Exchange Server.

 Before we start, a quick word on the terms I'm using. "Exchange" refers to the overall technology, whose full name is "Microsoft Exchange." "Exchange Server" (with the capital *S* on "Server") is the server program, while "the Exchange server" (with the small *s*) is the particular server you're connecting to. (Many companies and organizations have several Exchange servers—or squadrons of them.) "Exchange ActiveSync" is an Exchange component used for syncing devices such as iPhones to Exchange.

Add an Exchange Account by Using a Configuration Profile

In most cases, the easiest way to set up an Exchange account on your iPhone is to install on the iPhone a configuration profile that contains the details of the Exchange account.

Normally, you'll get the configuration profile from your network's Exchange administrator. If the administrator is setting up your iPhone manually, he or she will put the configuration profile on your iPhone directly by connecting it to his or her computer via USB. If the administrator has already handed over the iPhone to you, or if it's your iPhone rather than one belonging to the company or organization, the administrator will distribute the configuration profile in one of these ways:

- **Via e-mail** This is an easy way of distributing configuration profiles as long as you have an e-mail account other than the Exchange account. If the administrator is trying to give you your main e-mail account via e-mail, you've got a chicken-and-egg situation that doesn't work out tidily.
- **Via a website** The administrator can place the configuration profile on a website from which you can download it using your iPhone. Typically this will be an internal corporate website or at least a password-protected website, because the configuration profiles aren't encrypted.

Here's how to set up an Exchange account by installing a configuration profile you've received in an e-mail message or downloaded from a website:

1. Open the configuration profile:
    - If you've received the configuration profile in an e-mail message, as shown in the left screen in Figure 16-1, tap the configuration profile's button. Your iPhone then displays the Install Profile screen, as shown on the right in Figure 16-1.
    - If the configuration profile is posted on a web page, open that page in Safari, and then tap the profile's download link. Your iPhone then displays the Install Profile screen (shown on the right in Figure 16-1).
2. Look at the information on the Install Profile screen to make sure you want to install the profile. To see more information about the profile, tap the More Details button, which displays the profile's information screen (shown on the left in Figure 16-2). Tap the Install Profile button in the upper-left corner to go back to the Install Profile screen.
3. Check the profile's status: Unsigned, Not Verified, or Verified. See the sidebar "What the Unsigned, Not Verified, and Verified Terms on the Install Profile Screen Mean" in Chapter 3 for an explanation of these terms and advice on how you should treat the profiles they mark.
4. Tap the Install button on the Install Profile screen to start installing the profile. Depending on how the administrator has set up the profile, you may need to enter your e-mail address and password to set up the account. The left screen

FIGURE 16-1   Tap the configuration profile's button in an e-mail message (left) to display the Install Profile screen (right).

in Figure 16-3 shows the Enter Email screen; the Enter Password screen (not shown) that appears next is equally straightforward.

5. Your iPhone displays the Exchange Account screen, on which you decide which items to sync with the iPhone. See the section "Choose Which Exchange Items to Sync with Your iPhone," later in this chapter, for details.

6. When the Profile Installed screen appears (as shown on the right in Figure 16-13), tap the Done button. Your iPhone takes you back to where you started the installation—either the e-mail message containing the configuration profile or the web page from which you downloaded the profile.

You can now start using the Exchange account.

Set Up an Exchange Account Manually

If your Exchange administrator doesn't provide a configuration profile for setting up Exchange on your iPhone, you'll need to set it up manually. Manual setup takes a few minutes, but it's not tricky as long as you have the right information.

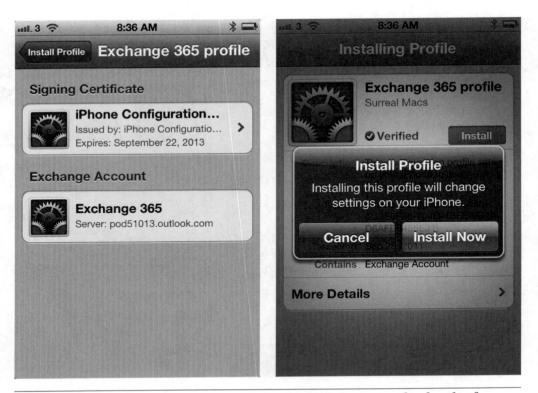

FIGURE 16-2 The profile's information screen (left) shows you the details of what the profile contains: here, the signing certificate and the Exchange Account payload. When you tap the Install button on the Install Profile screen to install the profile, your iPhone makes sure you know that installing the profile will change settings on your iPhone (right).

Here's the information you'll need:

- **E-mail address** For example, jsixpack@surrealpcs.com.
- **Username** For example, jsixpack.
- **Password** Some random burst of letters, numbers, and symbols.
- **Domain** For example, surrealpcs.com or corp.surrealpcs.com. You may not need to enter the domain—so you also need to know whether to enter it.
- **Server name or address** For example, exchange.surrealpcs.com or 215.12.191.14. Your iPhone may be able to locate the correct server without your entering it, but you should have this information to be sure you can set up the account.

To set up a connection to an Exchange server manually, follow these steps:

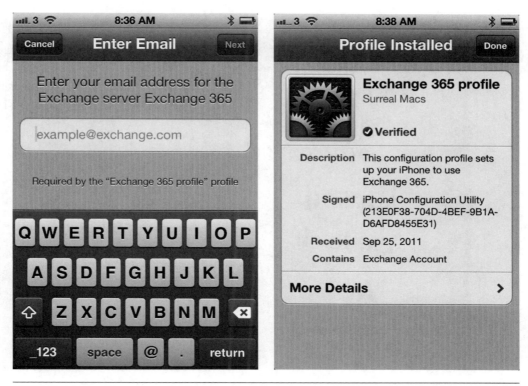

FIGURE 16-3   To set up the Exchange account, you may need to enter your e-mail address on the Enter Email screen (left), and then enter your password on the Enter Password screen (not shown). On the Profile Installed screen (right), tap the Done button to complete the installation.

1. Press the Home button to display the Home screen.
2. Tap the Settings icon to display the Settings screen.
3. Scroll down to the third box, and then tap the Mail, Contacts, Calendars button to display the Mail, Contacts, Calendars screen.
4. In the Accounts area, tap the Add Account button to display the Add Account screen (shown on the left in Figure 16-4).
5. Tap the Microsoft Exchange item to display the Exchange screen (shown on the right in Figure 16-4).
6. Type the e-mail address in the Email field.
7. If you log on to an Active Directory domain, type the domain in the Domain field. If you're not sure whether you log on to a domain, and you can't find an administrator to tell you, leave the Domain field blank.

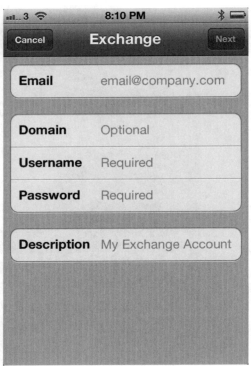

FIGURE 16-4   To start setting up an Exchange account manually, tap the Microsoft Exchange button on the Add Account screen (left). On the Exchange screen (right), enter the details of the Exchange account.

 In Exchange Server 2007 and Exchange Server 2010, the Autodiscover service normally enables you to locate the Exchange ActiveSync server without entering the domain name.

8. Type your username in the Username field.
9. Type your password in the Password field.
10. In the Description field, type the descriptive text you'd like your iPhone to display for the account. The iPhone enters "My Exchange Account" by default, but you may want to improve on this.
11. Tap the Next button. The iPhone displays the Verifying screen (as shown on the left in Figure 16-5) while it connects to the server and verifies the details of the account.

 Two things: First, finding the server and verifying the account may take several minutes. Second, if your iPhone can't locate the Exchange server, it displays the Exchange screen again, this time with the Server field added but blank. Type in the

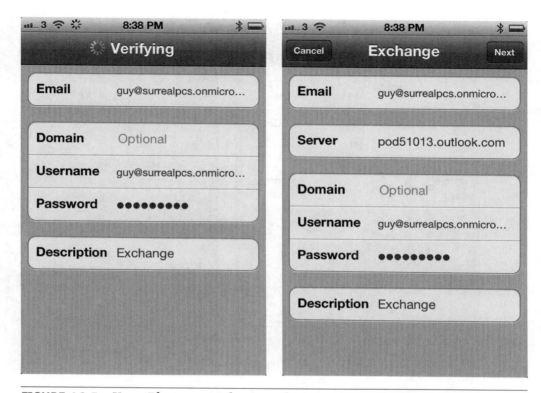

FIGURE 16-5 Your iPhone may take several minutes to verify the account information (left). When it has verified the information, the server name appears in the Server field (right).

server's address, and then tap the Next button. Armed with this vital information, your iPhone then tries the verification again.

12. When your iPhone has finished verifying the account, it displays the Exchange screen with the server name in the Server field (as shown on the right in Figure 16-5).
13. Tap the Next button. Your iPhone then displays the screen for choosing which features to use. The next section discusses how to make these choices.

Choose Which Exchange Items to Sync with Your iPhone

After you set up an Exchange account (either from a configuration profile or manually), your iPhone displays the screen for choosing which features to use (see the left screen in Figure 16-6).

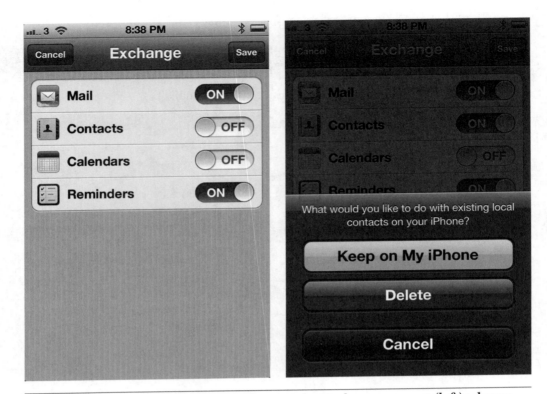

FIGURE 16-6   On the screen for configuring the Exchange account (left), choose which of the four features—Mail, Contacts, Calendars, and Reminders—to sync with your iPhone. If your iPhone prompts you to decide how to handle your existing local contacts (right) or calendars, tap the Keep On My iPhone button or the Delete button.

Use the Mail switch, Contacts switch, Calendars switch, and Reminders switch to choose which items to sync with your iPhone. In most cases, you'll want to sync all of them.

If your iPhone already contains contacts or calendars, it sets the Contacts switch or the Calendars switch to the Off position. When you move the switch to the On position, your iPhone displays a dialog box asking what you want to do with your existing contacts or calendars. The right screen in Figure 16-6 shows the contacts version of this dialog box; the calendars version is similar.

Tap the Keep On My iPhone button if you want to keep the contacts or calendars, and then tap the Keep On My iPhone button in the confirmation dialog box that warns that you risk duplicating entries. Otherwise, tap the Delete button to delete existing contacts or calendars, and then tap the Delete button in the confirmation dialog box that appears.

When you've finished choosing settings on this screen, tap the Save button. Your iPhone saves the account and then displays the Mail, Contacts, Calendars screen.

How to...   **Control Which Mail Days and Mail Folders Your iPhone Syncs with Exchange**

To make the most of Exchange e-mail on your iPhone, you'll want to sync your recent messages—but not so many of them that syncing takes all day. And you'll want to be able to choose which e-mail folders Exchange pushes out to your iPhone.

To reach these settings, tap the Exchange account on the Mail, Contacts, Calendars screen to display the configuration screen for the account (shown on the left in the next illustration). You can then tap the Mail Days To Sync button at the bottom to reach the Mail Days To Sync screen, which lets you choose among No Limit, 1 Day, 3 Days, 1 Week, 2 Weeks, and 1 Month. No Limit is usually not a good idea unless you manage your e-mail tightly.

To choose which e-mail folders Exchange pushes to your iPhone, tap the Mail Folders To Push button, and then work on the Mail Folders To Push screen (shown on the right in the next illustration). Tap to place a check mark next to a folder you want Exchange to push or to remove the check mark from a folder you want it to stop pushing.

Troubleshoot iPhone Connections to Exchange Server

This section tells you how to troubleshoot three problems that can occur when you're using your iPhone with Microsoft Exchange. We'll start with two problems connecting to the Exchange server, and then look at the primary cause of not being able to send or receive e-mail even though you've connected to Exchange.

Deal with the Message "The Account Cannot Be Verified"

If your iPhone can't find the Exchange ActiveSync server during setup, it adds the Server field to the Exchange Account screen so that you can enter the server name.

If you enter the server name, and then get the "The account cannot be verified" dialog box (shown in Figure 16-7), chances are you've got the wrong server name. Ask an administrator for the name of the Exchange ActiveSync server; most Exchange setups have various servers, so someone may have given you the wrong name.

 Make sure that your iPhone has a network connection—for example, use Safari to run through the odds on your favorite sports-betting site. Check also that the server is up.

If you're certain you've got the right server name, check the SSL setting—you may need to turn SSL off in order to connect. You'll find this setting at the bottom of the Account screen (shown on the right in Figure 16-7). To get to that screen from the Mail, Contacts, Calendars screen, tap the Exchange account's name, and then tap the Account button under the Exchange heading at the top.

 SSL is the abbreviation for Secure Sockets Layer, a technology for establishing a secure, encrypted connection between two computers across an insecure network.

Choose the Right Domain

To connect to the Exchange ActiveSync server, you may need to enter the correct domain when setting up the Exchange account—or you may need to leave the Domain field blank.

The best way to get the right domain is to ask an administrator. But if you can't reach an administrator who knows the right domain, and you need to set up the account anyway, first try leaving the Domain field blank. If the mail system is running Exchange Server 2007 or a later version, your iPhone should be able to pick up the server from the Autodiscover service.

If Autodiscover doesn't round up the Exchange server, and the Exchange system is provided by an external host, try the company's or organization's Internet domain name—for example, surrealpcs.com. And if that's no good, try the domain name without the suffix—for example, surrealpcs.

If you're still stuck at this point, you need to get in touch with an administrator who knows the details of the Exchange system.

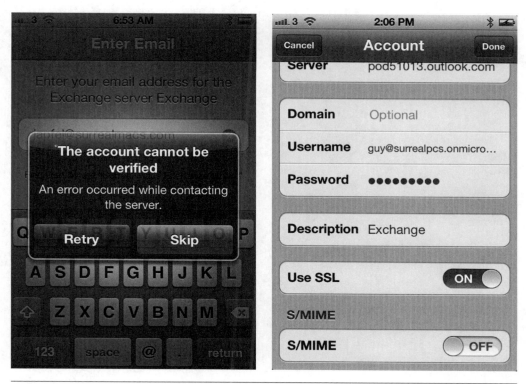

FIGURE 16-7   The message "The account cannot be verified" (left) usually means that your iPhone is trying to contact the wrong Exchange server. If you've got the right server, you may need to move the Use SSL switch to the Off position (right).

Solve the Inability to Send or Receive E-Mail When Connected to Exchange

If you've been able to set up the Exchange account okay, but you're unable to send or receive e-mail using Exchange, make sure that you've entered the correct name in the Domain field for the account. It's possible to set up the account even if the Domain field contains the wrong information—but the incorrect domain setting then prevents you from sending and receiving e-mail.

See the section "Choose the Right Domain" a couple of blocks north of here for advice on finding out which domain to use. To change the domain name, work on the Account screen (shown on the right in Figure 16-7).

17

Create, Edit, and Share Business Documents on Your iPhone

HOW TO...

- Understand how your iPhone's file system stores documents
- Create word-processing documents, spreadsheets, presentations, and PDFs
- Share documents with your PC or Mac

Whether hooked to your belt, snuggled in your pocket, or clenched in your non-dominant fist so that your dominant forefinger can caress its screen, your iPhone is always at hand when you need to turn your brilliant ideas and insights into forceful memos, incisive spreadsheets, and punchy presentations. All you need to create those documents is suitable apps.

In this chapter, we'll look quickly at your options for creating and editing business documents on your iPhone. We'll start with word-processing documents, move on to spreadsheets, and then visit presentations before examining apps for creating PDF files.

These apps are (with honorable exceptions) pretty easy to use, so I won't lecture you on their ins and outs. Instead, in the second half of the chapter, we'll explore trickier territory—how to share documents between your iPhone and your PC or Mac. You can copy documents using iTunes' File Sharing feature, shunt documents back and forth via e-mail, transfer documents by using third-party apps, or share documents using Apple's iWork.com site.

But first, there's something you need to understand about how the iPhone's operating system stores documents.

Understand How Your iPhone Stores Documents

As you know, Apple has made iTunes the preferred management tool for the iPhone, handling everything from initial setup to daily synchronization and updates. iTunes is also the main tool for adding most types of documents to your iPhone directly or deleting them from it.

The main exception to this is incoming photos and video, which iTunes doesn't handle. On the Mac, that's iPhoto's job—so if you use a Mac, iPhoto is the application you'll normally use to copy or remove photos, videos, or screen captures from your iPhone. On Windows, the iPhone's photo and video storage area shows up in Windows Explorer as a digital camera. You can then copy the photos to the PC's file system and enjoy them in whichever program you prefer.

> **Note** If you don't have iPhoto on your Mac, you can use Image Capture to copy photos and videos from your iPhone to your Mac.

Apart from this digital camera that Windows sees, the iPhone doesn't appear in Windows Explorer on Windows. On the Mac, Finder acts as if it's completely unaware of the iPhone's presence. This is to encourage you to use iTunes (and iPhoto or Image Capture on the Mac) to manage the device rather than trampling sensitive parts of the file system with a file browser such as Windows Explorer or Finder.

Within its file system, the iPhone's operating system, iOS, gives each app a separate storage area for documents. iOS largely confines each app to its own storage area and prevents it from accessing any other storage areas. But apps that can receive incoming files, such as Mail and Safari, can provide those files to other apps. For example, if you receive on your iPhone a Word document attached to an e-mail message, you can choose to open that document in Pages (if you have it installed) or another app that can handle Word documents. Mail makes the document available to Pages or the app you choose.

iOS doesn't give you a file browser that you can use to browse files and open them in their apps, let alone choose which app to open a particular file in. Instead, you open the app that can handle the document, then open the document from that app's document storage area. Or you use Mail to pick the app you want for opening a document stored in Mail, or use Safari to pick the app for a document you're downloading.

Similarly, when you need to copy a document from your iPhone to your computer, you can't just open a file browser window, find the document's file, and copy it to your computer's file system. Instead, you need to decide where you're going to send the document, and then export the file. You can copy the file to your computer using iTunes, send it via e-mail, or upload it to Apple's iWork.com sharing site.

That's the overview of transferring files back and forth. We'll look at the details later in this chapter.

Create Business Documents

In this section, we'll look quickly at the main apps for creating business documents on the iPhone: word-processing documents, spreadsheets, presentations, and PDF files.

Did You Know?

Your iPhone Includes Viewers for Major File Types

Your iPhone's operating system has built-in viewers for major file types, including these:

- PDF
- Word (both the .docx and .doc formats)
- Excel (both the .xlsx and .xls formats)
- PowerPoint (both the .pptx and .ppt formats)
- Rich-text format (RTF)
- Text documents
- HTML

Various apps that enable you to transfer files to or from your iPhone can display the documents using these viewers but cannot open the documents for editing. The viewers display the documents for viewing but don't provide full features. For example, if you open a PDF file for a second time, the viewer doesn't remember the last page you read the first time you opened it; and you can't follow internal links within a PDF file. But as far as straightforward reading goes, the viewers are pretty good.

Given that Microsoft Office not only dominates the Windows market for office documents but also has a hefty chunk of the Mac market, it's most likely you'll need to create your business documents in the Word, Excel, and PowerPoint formats—so we'll start there. Next, we'll cover creating documents in the Pages, Numbers, and Keynote formats used by the apps in Apple's iWork suite. Finally, we'll look at how to create PDF files.

Create Documents in the Microsoft Office File Formats

To create documents in the Microsoft Office file formats on your iPhone, you have four main choices:

- **Documents To Go**   The basic version of Documents To Go can create Word documents and Excel spreadsheets and view PowerPoint presentations and iWork files. The advanced version, Documents To Go Premium, adds creating and editing PowerPoint presentations to the list. Figure 17-1 shows Documents To Go opening (left) and at work on a Word document (right).
- **Quickoffice**   The basic version of Quickoffice can create Word documents and Excel spreadsheets. The pro version, Quickoffice Pro, can create and edit

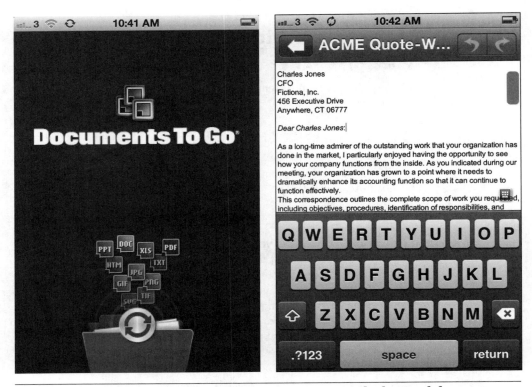

FIGURE 17-1   Documents To Go Premium can create and edit Word documents, Excel spreadsheets, and PowerPoint presentations.

PowerPoint presentations as well. Figure 17-2 shows Quickoffice Pro creating a presentation (left) and a spreadsheet (right).

- **Google Docs**   If you have an account with Google Docs (http://docs.google.com), you can log in using Safari or another web browser on your iPhone, and then create word-processing documents, spreadsheets, and presentations in it. The interface is clumsy because of the iPhone's screen being small, but if you have a sure touch, it's workable. The files you create remain online; you can't save them to your iPhone. Figure 17-3 shows the iPhone creating a presentation in Google Docs.

- **iWork**   Pages, Numbers, and Keynote (discussed in the next section) can export files in the corresponding Microsoft Office formats. For example, from Numbers, you can export a spreadsheet in the Microsoft Excel format. See the later sidebar "Convert Your iWork Files to the Microsoft Office Formats" for details.

 Documents To Go and Quickoffice are impressive apps, but they enable you to use only the most widely used formatting and objects (such as tables and shapes) when creating documents, spreadsheets, and presentations. Because of these

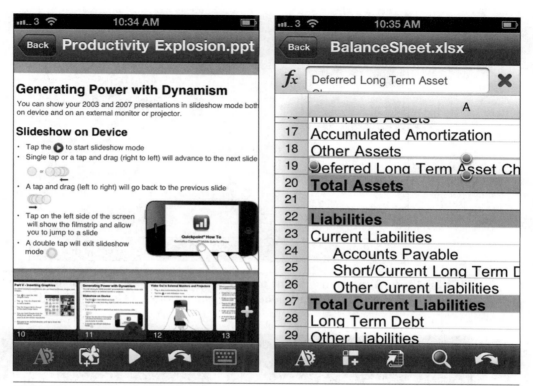

FIGURE 17-2 Quickoffice Pro can create Word documents, Excel spreadsheets, and PowerPoint presentations.

limitations, and because the iPhone's screen offers only a small area to work in, you will normally do best to finish your documents on a computer rather than on the iPhone.

Create Documents in the iWork File Formats

If you need to create documents in the iWork file formats on your iPhone, look no further than Apple's iWork apps. These apps are the iPhone versions of the full-scale Mac OS X applications:

- **Pages** Pages is an app for creating word-processing and layout documents. The left screen in Figure 17-4 shows Pages working on a document.
- **Numbers** Numbers is an app for creating spreadsheets. The right screen in Figure 17-4 shows a spreadsheet open in Numbers.
- **Keynote** Keynote is an app for creating and editing presentations. Figure 17-5 shows Keynote.

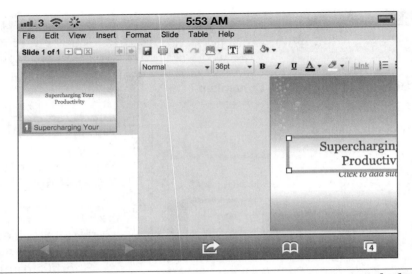

FIGURE 17-3 You can use Safari or another web browser to create and edit word-processing documents, spreadsheets, or presentations on Google Docs.

FIGURE 17-4 Use the Pages app (left) to create and edit word-processing documents on your iPhone or use the Numbers app (right) to create and edit spreadsheets.

FIGURE 17-5   Use the Keynote app to create and edit presentations on your iPhone. You can export presentations in Microsoft PowerPoint format if necessary.

How to... Convert Your iWork Files to the Microsoft Office Formats

The three iWork apps—Pages, Numbers, and Keynote—are great for working on the iPhone (and even better on the iPad, because it gives you so much more screen space). But if you or your colleagues use Microsoft Office on your computers, you'll need to convert the iWork files you create to their Office equivalents. To convert the files, you use the Share And Print feature in the iWork apps.

To convert a file using the Share And Print feature, follow these steps on your iPhone:

1. Open the app to which the document belongs. I'll use Pages for this example.
2. If the app launches with a document open other than the document you want to convert, tap the Documents button, the Spreadsheets button, or the Presentations button in the upper-left corner of the screen to go back to the Document Manager screen. This is the screen that shows the contents of the Documents folder, the Spreadsheets folder, or the Presentations folder.
3. Tap the document you want to convert. The app opens the document.
4. Tap the Tools button (the button with the wrench icon in the upper-right corner of the screen) to display the Tools screen (shown on the left in the next illustration).

(Continued)

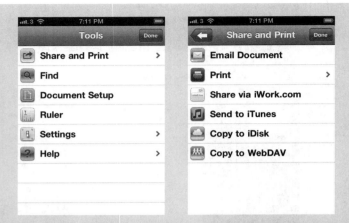

5. Tap the Share And Print button to display the Share And Print screen (shown on the right in the illustration).

6. Tap the Email Document button or the Send To iTunes button, as appropriate. Your iPhone displays a screen for choosing the format of the document. The left screen in the next illustration shows the Email Document screen, which Pages displays when you choose to e-mail a document. The Email Spreadsheet screen in Numbers, the Email Presentation screen in Keynote, and the Choose Format screen (for sending to iTunes) offer similar choices.

7. Tap the format to use for the exported file:
   - **Native format**   Tap the Pages button, the Numbers button, or the Keynote button to keep the document in its native format.
   - **PDF**   Tap the PDF button to create a Portable Document File format for viewing on any computer (but not for editing).
   - **Office format**   Tap the Word button (from Pages), the Excel button (from Numbers), or the PowerPoint button (from Numbers).

8. The app exports the file in the format you chose, and then displays the document again.

Create PDF Files

Creating documents, spreadsheets, or presentations is helpful, but sometimes you may need to create PDF files on your iPhone so that you can give your clients fully laid out documents that they can't change.

 If you're using Pages, Numbers, or Keynote, you can create a PDF by exporting the document. See the sidebar "Convert Your iWork Files to the Microsoft Office Formats" for details.

When you need to create PDFs, try these two apps:

- **Adobe CreatePDF**   CreatePDF from Adobe, the company behind the PDF file format, enables you to take a document from a file storage area and turn it into a PDF. CreatePDF is a little clumsy, because it doesn't have a file browser for picking the document from which to create the PDF: Instead, you have to start from the file storage area of the app the document is in, then use the Open In command to open it in CreatePDF, as shown on the left in Figure 17-6. But once you've picked the document, the conversion to PDF (shown on the right in Figure 17-6) runs smoothly.
- **Save2PDF**   Save2PDF is an app for creating and manipulating PDF files. Save2PDF's features include merging two or more PDF files into a single file and adding extra pages to an existing document. For example, if you have a PDF file that contains a standard contract, you can add to it an extra page that turns it into a customized version.

Share Documents with your PC or Mac

In this section, we'll look at how to share documents between your iPhone and your computer. We'll cover iTunes' File Sharing feature, look into transferring documents via e-mail, discuss three third-party apps that can transfer documents, and finally dig into sharing documents using Apple's iWork.com site.

Share Documents Using iTunes' File Sharing

If you use iTunes rather than iCloud to sync your iPhone, you can use iTunes' File Sharing feature to put documents on the iPhone from your computer or copy documents from your iPhone to your computer. This is the most direct way of shifting files from point A to point B.

To transfer documents by using File Sharing, follow these steps:

1. Connect your iPhone to the computer as usual.
2. If the computer doesn't automatically launch or activate iTunes, launch or activate iTunes yourself.

FIGURE 17-6 To create a PDF file using CreatePDF, you give the Open In command from the app that contains the source document, then tap CreatePDF on the Open In screen (left). CreatePDF then converts the file to a PDF (right).

3. In the Source list, click your iPhone's entry to display its control screens.
4. Click the Apps tab to display your iPhone's apps and files.
5. Scroll down to the File Sharing area (see Figure 17-7).
6. In the Apps list, click the app to which you want to transfer the files. The list of files for that app appears in the Pages Documents pane to the right.
7. To add documents to the app, follow these steps:
   a. Click the Add button to display the Open dialog box.
   b. Navigate to and select the document or documents you want to add.
   c. Click the OK button (on Windows) or the Open button (on the Mac).
8. To copy documents from the app to the computer, follow these steps:
   a. Click the file you want to save.
   b. Click the Save To button to display the iTunes dialog box (on Windows) or the Choose A File: iTunes dialog box (on the Mac).
   c. Navigate to the folder in which you want to save the document.
   d. Click the Select Folder button (on Windows) or the Open button (on the Mac).

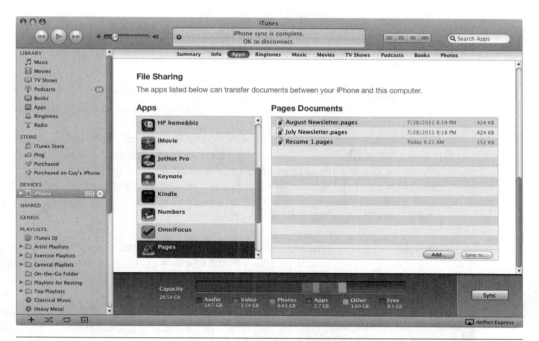

FIGURE 17-7   The File Sharing area on the Apps tab in the iTunes control screens for an iPhone lists the apps that can transfer files. Click an app to see its files.

File transfers generally run pretty quickly, as USB 2.0 can handle up to 480 megabits per second (Mbps)—but if you're transferring many large files, it'll take a while. (And if you're using a USB 1.x port, its 12-Mbps limit will make things much slower.)

Transfer Documents via E-Mail

When you need to get documents onto your iPhone quickly, you can simply e-mail them to an account on it. You can then open a document directly from the e-mail message into either one of the iPhone's viewers or into whichever app you want to use to work on the document.

E-mail may seem like a clumsy solution to document transfer, but it's quick and effective unless the document is too big to go through e-mail servers. E-mail is especially useful when the document is on somebody else's computer rather than the computer with which you normally sync your iPhone.

And you can use Mail to send a document back after you've edited it, or send it along to the next person who needs to deal with it.

Copy a Document from a Message to an App's Storage Area

To get a document out of an e-mail message and into an app's storage area, follow these steps:

1. In the message list, tap the message to display its contents.
2. Tap and hold the document's button in the message until Mail displays a menu (shown on the left in Figure 17-8).
3. If you want to open the basic viewer for the document, tap the Quick Look button; normally, though, you'll do better to open the document in an app. If you want to open the document in the default app (in this example, Pages), tap the Open In "*App*" button (where *App* is the app's name). Otherwise, tap the Open In button to display the Open In menu (shown on the right in Figure 17-8), and then tap the app you want to use.

That's the most efficient way to copy the document from the message and get it into the app. But what you'll probably want to do often is view the contents of the

FIGURE 17-8 Tap and hold a document's button in an e-mail message until the menu for opening the document appears (left). To use a different app, tap the Open In button to display the Open In menu (right), and then tap the app you want.

document so that you can decide which app to open it in. For example, if you receive a Word document on your iPhone, you may want to bring it into Pages so that you can use Pages' streamlined layout tools. But if you simply want to edit the document as a Word document, you'll do better to open the document in Documents To Go or a similar app that can maintain the Word document format.

View a Document and Decide Which App to Open It In

To view a document and then decide which app to open it in, follow these steps:

1. In the message list, tap the message to display its contents.
2. Tap the button for the attached document you want to open. Your iPhone displays the document in the viewer.
3. Tap the action button (the button with a curving arrow in the upper-right corner of the screen) to display the menu for opening the document in the default app, opening it in another app, or printing it. The left screen in Figure 17-9 shows a PDF document, for which iBooks is the default app.
4. If you want to use the default app, tap its button to open the document in it. Otherwise, tap the Open In button to display the list of apps that can open the document. The right screen in Figure 17-9 shows an example of this list.
5. Tap the app in which you want to open the document.

This approach leaves the document open in the viewer in Mail. So when you go back to Mail, tap the Message button to close the viewer and return to the message.

Delete the Document from Mail if Necessary

Once you've opened an attached document in another app, that app stores a copy of the document in its storage area. You can now delete the e-mail message and the attached document if necessary; the copy of the document that you've added to the other app's storage area remains unaffected.

If you attach a picture to an e-mail message, the recipient can save the picture to his iPhone's Photos storage area. But if you attach a music file or video file, the recipient can only play it in the viewer or add it to third-party apps that handle media file types, not add it to the iPhone's Music storage area.

Transfer Documents Using Third-Party Apps

If you need more direct or wider-ranging access to the iPhone's file system than iTunes provides, you'll need to use a third-party app instead. This section introduces you to three of the most widely useful apps at this writing: Air Sharing, FileApp Pro (with or without DiskAid), and Documents To Go.

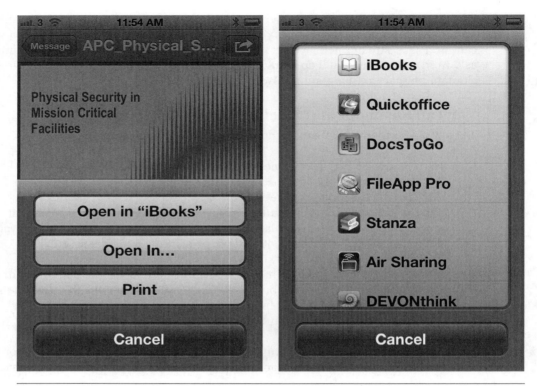

FIGURE 17-9 To copy a document from an e-mail message, open it in the viewer. From the action menu (left), you can open the document in its default app. To use another app, tap the Open In button, and then tap the app to use (right).

Transfer Documents Using Air Sharing

Air Sharing is an app for transferring documents to and from the iPhone and viewing them on the device. Air Sharing enables you to connect your computer to your iPhone via a wireless network connection and comes in three different versions:

- **Air Sharing** Air Sharing is the basic version of the app for the iPhone. You can mount the iPhone as a drive on a PC or Mac, transfer files both ways, and view or e-mail documents in the formats the iOS viewer supports. Figure 17-10 shows a Finder window displaying the contents of an iPhone mounted as a drive using Air Sharing.
- **Air Sharing Pro** Air Sharing Pro adds abilities such as connecting to a Windows PC running a companion program, mounting remote file systems, opening and creating Zip files, and downloading files from the Web.
- **Air Sharing HD** Air Sharing HD is the iPad version of Air Sharing Pro and provides similar features at the larger screen size.

FIGURE 17-10   With Air Sharing, you can mount an iPhone as a drive on your computer so that you can easily transfer files.

Transfer Documents Using FileApp Pro

Like Air Sharing, FileApp Pro is an app for transferring documents to and from your iPhone and for viewing documents on it. With FileApp Pro, you can connect to the iPhone either via the USB cable (which is good for speed) or via a wireless network connection (which is good for flexibility). To connect via USB, you need to either use iTunes's File Sharing feature or run the DiskAid program (from DigiDNA; www.digidna.net) on your PC or Mac.

The left image in Figure 17-11 shows the Sharing screen of FileApp Pro. The right image in Figure 17-11 shows the FileApp Pro interface for manipulating folders on the iPhone. You tap the USB button or the WIFI button to choose the means of sharing, then tap the button for the operating system you're using—Win 7, Win Vista, Win XP, or Mac OS X—to display instructions for connecting.

You can transfer documents by using the FileApp Pro entry in the File Sharing area of the Apps tab in iTunes, but if you want to transfer many files easily and choose the folders to put them in, it's worth getting DiskAid and installing it on your computer. Once you've set up sharing on the iPhone, you can connect via DiskAid and transfer files easily back and forth. Figure 17-12 shows DiskAid in action.

Apart from managing files, FileApp Pro also makes it easy to browse and view your files. You can use FileApp to create text documents, play audio and video, and even show slideshows of images.

FIGURE 17-11 FileApp Pro lets you choose between USB and Wi-Fi connections (left) and create and manipulate folders easily on your iPhone (right).

Tip DiskAid is a handy tool if you want to simply store files on your iPhone—for example, to transfer them from one computer to another—rather than open the files on the iPhone. With DiskAid, you can create your own folders on the iPhone, enabling you to use it as an external disk.

Transfer Documents Using Documents To Go

If you need to work extensively with Microsoft Office documents—for example, Word documents or Excel workbooks—you'll probably find the iWork apps too cumbersome. Instead of struggling with frustrating conversions, get a third-party program that can handle the main Office file formats without having to translate them.

As discussed earlier in this chapter, the main choices for creating and editing Microsoft Office documents directly on the iPhone are Documents To Go and Quickoffice. At this writing, Documents To Go seems the stronger of the two, especially as it has good features for transferring documents between your computer and your iPhone.

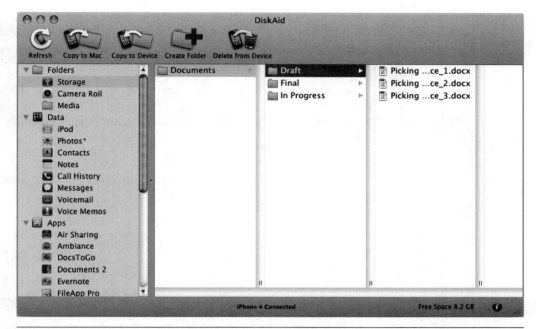

FIGURE 17-12   DiskAid is a companion program for FileApp Pro that makes it easy to transfer files to and from your iPhone. You can also use DiskAid on its own.

You can load documents into Documents To Go by using the Documents To Go entry in the File Sharing area of the Apps tab in iTunes, but for regular use, download the free companion desktop program that runs on your PC or Mac to synchronize documents with the iPhone. To get the program, go to the DataViz website (www. dataviz.com), click the iPhone link, and then click the Download button. Once you've installed the program, you go through a HotSync setup process to pair the iPhone with the desktop program. You can then use the desktop program to transfer files to and from the device (see Figure 17-13).

 Documents To Go Premium can access documents in an online storage account such as Google Docs, Box.net, Dropbox, or iDisk.

Share Documents Using iWork.com

Apple's iWork.com site is a means of sharing files you've created in the iWork applications, either on the iPhone (or iPod touch, or iPad) or on the Mac. From one of the iWork applications, you share the file to the iWork.com site so that other people can view it or download it.

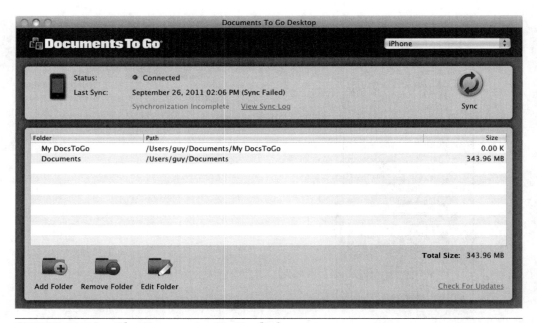

FIGURE 17-13 The Documents To Go desktop program runs on your computer and connects to the iPhone.

To use iWork.com, you sign up for it with an Apple ID. These are the three main ways to sign up:

- **iPhone** Use the Tools | Share And Print | Share Via iWork.com command from Pages, Numbers, or Keynote.
- **Computer** Steer your favorite web browser to the iWork website (www.iwork.com).
- **Mac** Give the Share | Share Via iWork.com command in Pages, Numbers, or Keynote.

Once you've signed up for iWork.com and verified your e-mail address by clicking the link the site e-mails to you, you can place files on the site. When you place a file on iWork.com, you choose who to share it with by sending e-mail invitations. You can send invitations to anyone who has an e-mail account, but each person needs to set up an iWork.com account before they can view the document you're sharing with them.

To use iWork.com to transfer and share files, follow these steps on your iPhone:

1. Open the app to which the document belongs—for example, Keynote.
2. If the app launches with a document open other than the document you want to share, tap the Documents button, the Spreadsheets button, or the

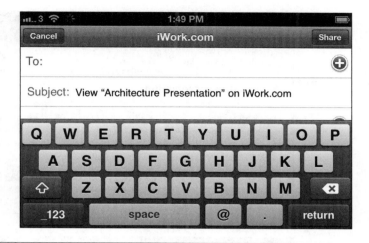

FIGURE 17-14 The iWork app automatically creates an e-mail message containing details of the document you're sharing on iWork.com. You choose the recipients, set options, and send the message.

Presentations button in the upper-left corner of the screen to go back to the Document Manager screen.

3. Tap the document you want to share. The app opens the document.
4. Tap the Tools button (the button with the wrench icon) in the upper-right corner to display the Tools screen.
5. Tap the Share And Print button to display the Share And Print screen.
6. Tap the Share Via iWork.com button. The app contacts iWork.com, and creates a new e-mail message containing details of the shared document. The message uses a default subject line such as View *"Document"* On iWork.com, where *Document* is the document's name. Figure 17-14 shows an example in Keynote.
7. Address the message and change the default subject line as needed.
8. Type any explanatory text the message needs to help the recipients understand why you're sharing this document with them.
9. Tap the i button to display the Sharing Options screen (shown in Figure 17-15).
10. If you need to change the document's name, tap the name button at the top. On the Name screen that appears, type the new name, and then tap the Sharing Options button to return to the Sharing Options screen.
11. In the Viewer Options area, choose restrictions on viewers as needed:
    - **Password** To protect the document with a password, tap the Password field, and then type the password.
    - **Allow Comments** Move this switch to the Off position if you don't want viewers to be able to add comments to the document.
12. In the Download Options area, use the On/Off switches to specify which formats the user can download the document in. Move both or all three

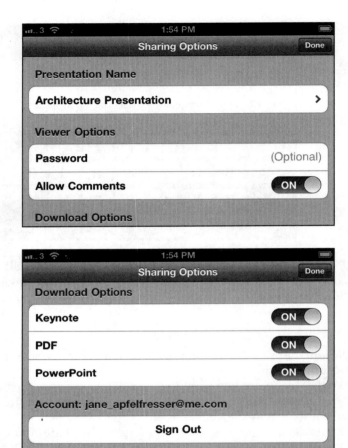

FIGURE 17-15 On the Sharing Options screen, choose whether to password-protect the document, whether to allow comments, and which download formats to offer.

switches to the Off position if you want people to be able only to view the document online, not download it.

13. When you've finished choosing sharing options, tap the Done button to return from the Sharing Options screen to the message.
14. Tap the Share button to send the message and upload the presentation.
15. When the app has finished uploading the presentation to iWork.com, tap the Done button.

PART V

Advanced Moves

18

Take Your iPhone to the Limit

HOW TO...

- Use multiple computers, multiple iPhones, or both
- Keep your iPhone running at full speed
- Share your iPhone's Internet connection using Personal Hotspot
- Create your own custom ringtones

In this chapter, we'll look at four advanced moves for the iPhone. We'll start by examining how to use an iPhone with multiple computers instead of a single computer, and how to use multiple iPhones with the same computer. We'll then go quickly through actions you can take to keep your iPhone running at full speed. After that, we'll look at how to share your iPhone's Internet connection with your computers or other devices by using the Personal Hotspot feature. Finally, I'll show you how to create your own custom ringtones from songs.

Use Multiple Computers, Multiple iPhones, or Both

Unless you set up your iPhone to sync with iCloud (as discussed in Chapter 1), you normally set it up to sync all its information with a single computer. In this section, we'll look at how you can sync different types of information to your iPhone from different computers, because this is often useful.

I'll also show you how to load media files onto the iPhone from multiple computers, which you may also want to do. Finally, I'll mention a few things to keep in mind when you sync multiple iPhones or other i-devices—iPads or iPods—with the same computer.

Understand What You Can and Can't Sync

Here's what you need to know about syncing your iPhone with multiple computers:

- The iPhone can sync only with a single iTunes library at a time. So if you sync your desktop's iTunes library with your iPhone, you can't then sync your laptop's iTunes library without wiping the desktop library from the iPhone.
- The iTunes library includes music, movies, TV shows, ringtones, podcasts, and books. To sync any of these items with the iTunes library of a computer other than your iPhone's home computer's iTunes library, you must wipe out the iPhone's existing library.
- Apps are separate, but you can sync only one computer's set of apps to an iPhone. This can be a different computer than the computer whose library you're syncing for music, movies, and so on. Syncing apps with another computer removes all the existing apps from the iPhone. (Not the built-in apps—you'd need a virtual bulldozer to shift those.)
- Photos are also separate from the iTunes library you're using for syncing music, but you can sync photos from only one computer with the iPhone. Syncing photos with another computer removes the existing photos (but not any photos or videos in the iPhone's Camera Roll).
- The items that appear on the Info tab of the iPhone's control screens—contact information, calendar information, mail accounts, bookmarks, and notes—are also handled separately from music. When you start to sync your iPhone's information items with another library, you can choose between merging the new information with the existing information and simply replacing the existing information.
- You can tell iTunes that you want to manage your iPhone's music and videos manually. After doing this, you can connect the iPhone to a computer other than its home computer and add music and videos to it from that computer. But if you switch your home computer's library back to automatic syncing, you'll lose any music and videos you've added from other computers.
- For copyright reasons, iTunes puts limitations on which music and video files you can copy from your iPhone to a computer. For example, you can't connect your iPhone to your friend's computer and copy all the songs from your iPhone to the computer. (Chapter 13 shows you ways to work around this limitation—for example, to recover your iTunes library after your computer crashes.)

Set Your iPhone to Sync Data from Multiple Computers

In this section, we'll look at how to set your iPhone to sync data from multiple computers rather than a single computer.

 When you set your iPhone to sync music or photos with another computer, the initial sync may take hours, because of the amount of data involved. By contrast, syncing information (contacts, calendars, and so on) usually takes only seconds, and syncing apps takes a few minutes, depending on how many apps there are and how chunky their developers have made them.

Sync All Your iPhone's Data with Its Current Computer

Before you start making changes, connect the iPhone to its current home computer and run a sync. This makes sure that you have a copy of the latest information from the iPhone on your computer in case you need it later.

Change the iTunes Library Your iPhone Is Syncing Music With

To change the iTunes library your iPhone is syncing music with, follow these steps:

1. Connect your iPhone to the computer that contains the music you want to sync.
2. Click the iPhone's entry in the Source list to display its control screens.
3. Click the Music tab to display its contents.
4. Select the Sync Music check box.
5. Use the controls to specify which music you want to sync. For example, either select the Entire Music Library option button to sync the whole library (assuming your iPhone has enough room for it), or select the Selected Playlists, Artists, Albums, And Genres option button, and then select the check box for each item you want to include.

 At this point, you can also choose sync settings for the other items that changing the music library will affect: ringtones, movies, TV shows, podcasts, and books.

6. Click the Apply button. iTunes displays a dialog box asking if you want to erase and sync the library, as shown here.

The iPhone "iPhone" is synced with another iTunes library. Do you want to erase this iPhone and sync with this iTunes library?

An iPhone can be synced with only one iTunes library at a time. Erasing and syncing replaces the contents of this iPhone with the contents of this iTunes library.

Cancel   Erase and Sync

7. Click the Erase And Sync button. iTunes replaces the existing library items on your iPhone with the items you chose from the new library.

Change the Computer Your iPhone Is Syncing Information With

To change the computer your iPhone is syncing contacts, calendars, mail accounts, and other information with, follow these steps:

1. Connect your iPhone to the computer that contains the information you want to sync.
2. Click the iPhone's entry in the Source list to display its control screens.
3. Click the Info tab to display its contents.
4. Select the appropriate check boxes. For example, on the Mac, select the Sync Address Book Contacts check box, the Sync iCal Calendars check box, and the Sync Mail Accounts check box; and select the Sync Safari Bookmarks check box and the Sync Notes check box in the Other box as needed.
5. Use the controls in each box to specify which items you want to sync. For example, select the check box for each mail account to sync in the Selected Mail Accounts list box.
6. Click the Apply button. iTunes displays a dialog box (shown here) that offers you the choice between replacing the information on the iPhone and merging the new information with the existing information.

7. Click the Replace Info button if you want to replace the information, or click the Merge Info button if you want to merge the old information and new information together.

Change the Computer Your iPhone Is Syncing Apps With

To change the computer your iPhone is syncing apps with, follow these steps:

1. Connect your iPhone to the computer that contains the apps you want to sync.
2. Click the iPhone's entry in the Source list to display its control screens.
3. Click the Apps tab to display its contents.
4. Select the Sync Apps check box.
5. In the list box, clear the check box for each app you want to sync. These check boxes are all selected by default.
6. Select the Automatically Sync New Apps check box if you want iTunes to automatically sync new apps with the iPhone. (This is usually helpful.)
7. Click the Apply button. iTunes displays a dialog box (shown next) to confirm that you want to replace all the iPhone's apps with the apps in this computer's iTunes library.

8. Click the Sync Apps button. iTunes syncs the apps.

Change the Computer Your iPhone Is Syncing Photos With

To change the computer your iPhone is syncing photos with, follow these steps:

1. Connect your iPhone to the computer that contains the photos you want to sync.
2. Click the iPhone's entry in the Source list to display its control screens.
3. Click the Photos tab to display its contents.
4. Select the Sync Photos From check box.
5. In the Sync Photos From drop-down list, choose the source of the photos. For example, choose the Pictures folder on Windows or iPhoto on Mac OS X.
6. Use the controls to specify which photos to sync. For example, select the All Photos, Albums, Events, And Faces option button if you want to sync all the photos (assuming they'll fit on your iPhone). Or select the Selected Albums, Events, And Faces, And Automatically Include option button, choose a suitable item in the drop-down list, and then select the check box for each album, event, and face you want to sync.
7. Click the Apply button. iTunes displays a dialog box (shown here) to confirm that you want to replace the synced photos on the iPhone.

8. Click the Replace Photos button. iTunes replaces the photos.

If you're using a Mac, you can use iPhoto or Image Capture to copy photos from your iPhone to your Mac. Use iPhoto when you want to gather your photos into Events, edit them, and manage them in iPhoto. Use Image Capture when you just want to get the photos (or screen captures, or saved images) from your iPhone into your Mac's file system.

Synchronize Several iPhones with the Same Computer

Instead of syncing your iPhone with several computers, as discussed in the previous section, you can sync multiple iPhones—or iPhones, iPods, and iPads—with the same computer. (Or you can both sync your iPhone with several computers and sync multiple iPhones with your computer.) Keep the following points in mind:

- Even if your computer has plenty of USB ports, it's best not to plug in more than one iPhone or other device at once. That way, neither you nor iTunes becomes confused, and synchronization can take place at full speed.
- Each iPhone, iPad, or iPod has a unique ID number that it communicates to your computer on connection, so your computer knows which device is connected to it. You can even give two or more devices the same name if you find such ambiguity amusing rather than confusing.
- You can configure different sync options for each device by connecting it and choosing options on its control screens in iTunes.

Load Your iPhone with Music and Video from Two or More Computers

As you read earlier in this chapter, you can synchronize your iPhone's music and video library with only one computer at a time—the device's home computer. You can change the home computer from one computer to another, and even from one platform (Mac or PC) to the other, but you can't actively synchronize your iPhone with more than one computer at once.

But you *can* load songs, videos, or other items onto your iPhone from computers other than the home computer. All the computers you use must have iTunes installed and configured, and you must configure your iPhone for manual updating on each computer involved—on the home computer as well as on each other computer. Otherwise, synchronizing the iPhone with the home computer after loading tracks from other computers will remove those tracks because they're not in the home computer's library.

Configure Your iPhone for Manual Updating

The first step in loading your iPhone from two or more computers is to configure it for manual updating. You'll need to do this on your iPhone's home computer first, and then on each of the other computers you plan to use.

To configure your iPhone for manual updating, follow these steps:

1. Connect your iPhone to your Mac or PC. Allow synchronization to take place. (If you need to override synchronization, see the sidebar "Temporarily Override Automatic Synchronization.")

Synchronize a Full—Different—Library onto Different iPhones from the Same Computer

Synchronizing two or more iPhones with the same computer works well enough provided that each user is happy using the same library or the same playlists (perhaps a different selection from the set of playlists). But if you want to synchronize the full library for each iPhone, yet have a different library on each, you need to take a different approach.

In most cases, the easiest solution is to have a separate user account for each separate user who uses an iPhone with the computer. Having separate user accounts is best in any case for keeping files and mail separate.

Place the music files that users will share in a folder that each user can access. In iTunes, make sure that the Copy Files To iTunes Media Folder When Adding To Library check box on the Advanced tab of the iTunes dialog box (in Windows) or the Preferences dialog box (on the Mac) is cleared so iTunes doesn't copy all the files into the music library.

If you have enough free space on your hard disk, you can set up your own libraries under your own user account and store all your music files in them. But unless your hard disk is truly gigantic, sharing most of the files from a central location is almost always preferable.

Another possibility is to start iTunes using a different library from within the same user account. To start iTunes using a different library:

- **Windows** Hold down SHIFT as you click the iTunes icon to start iTunes.
- **Mac** Hold down OPTION as you click the iTunes icon to start iTunes.

See the section "Use Multiple Libraries on the Same Computer" in Chapter 13 for more details on using multiple libraries.

2. Click the iPhone's entry in the Source list to display its control screens.
3. Select the Manually Manage Music And Videos check box.
4. Click the Apply button to apply the changes.

Note Even after you select the Manually Manage Music And Videos check box on the Summary tab of the iPhone's control screens, you can set the iPhone to sync music, movies, or both automatically. To sync music automatically, click the Music tab, select the Sync Music check box, and then select the Entire Music Library option button. To sync movies automatically, click the Movies tab, and then select the Sync Movies check box. Select the Automatically Include check box, and then choose All in the drop-down list.

Load Files onto an iPhone Manually

After you've configured an iPhone for manual updating, you can load files onto it manually by following these general steps:

1. Connect the iPhone to the computer that contains the files you want to load. The iPhone appears in the Source list in iTunes.
2. Drag song files from your iTunes library, or from a Windows Explorer window or a Finder window, and then drop them on the iPhone or on one of its playlists.
3. After loading all the songs you want from this computer, eject the iPhone by clicking the Eject button next to its name in the Source list.

You can then disconnect the iPhone from this computer, move it to the next computer, and then add more song files by using the same technique.

 From this point on, to add further song files to the iPhone from your home computer, you must add them manually. Don't synchronize the iPhone with its home computer, because synchronization will delete from the iPhone all the song files that do not appear in your library.

Keep Your iPhone Running at Full Speed

Apple has built the iPhone and its operating system to run as well as possible—and normally the iPhone can handle any challenge you throw at it. But if you find that your iPhone seems sluggish, try these three moves to get it back up to full speed.

These moves are in increasing order of seriousness. Use only as many as it takes to bring your iPhone up to speed again.

 If you've tuned up a Windows PC or a Mac, you're probably familiar with *virtual memory*—space on the hard drive (or SSD) that Windows or Mac OS X uses to supplement the physical memory (RAM). The iPhone's operating system doesn't

How to... **Temporarily Override Automatic Synchronization**

If an iPhone is configured for automatic synchronization, you can override this setting by holding down keys when you connect the iPhone:

- **Windows**   Hold down CTRL-SHIFT.
- **Mac**   Hold down ⌘-OPTION.

Release the keys when the iPhone appears in the Source list in iTunes.

use virtual memory, so you don't need to worry about keeping space free in the iPhone's storage area for the operating system to use as virtual memory.

Close Any Apps You're Not Using

The iPhone manages memory as smartly as possible, but the more apps you open, the more memory it needs to manipulate. So if your iPhone is running slowly after you've been using it for a while, try closing any apps you're no longer using.

To close one or more apps, follow these steps:

1. Press the Home button twice in quick succession to display the app-switching bar.
2. Tap and hold any app's icon on the app-switching bar until the icons start to jiggle, and a Close button—a red circle containing a white bar—appears at the upper-left corner of each icon.
3. Tap the Close button for each app you want to close. Scroll left or right to find further victims.
4. When you've finished closing apps, press the Home button to hide the app-switching bar again.

Restart Your iPhone

If your iPhone is still running slowly, restart it. Follow these steps:

1. Press and hold the Sleep/Wake button for several seconds until the Slide To Power Off slider appears.
2. Tap the slider and slide it across to the right.
3. Wait for your iPhone to power off.
4. Hold down the Sleep/Wake button for a couple of seconds until the Apple logo appears on the iPhone's screen, and then release it.

 Restarting the iPhone clears all the running processes out of its memory.

Reset Your iPhone's Settings

If restarting your iPhone doesn't get it back up to speed, you may need to reset its settings. Don't take this step lightly, because you will need to set all your custom settings again.

 Resetting all your iPhone's settings doesn't remove your content from the iPhone.

 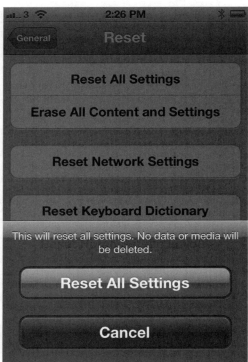

FIGURE 18-1 On the Reset screen (left), tap the Reset All Settings button. In the confirmation dialog box (right), tap the Reset All Settings button.

To reset your iPhone's settings, follow these steps:

1. Press the Home button to display the Home screen.
2. Tap the Settings icon to display the Settings screen.
3. Scroll down to the third box, and then tap the General button to display the General screen.
4. Scroll right down to the bottom, and then tap the Reset button to display the Reset screen (shown on the left in Figure 18-1).
5. Tap the Reset All Settings button. The iPhone displays a confirmation dialog box, as shown on the right in Figure 18-1.
6. Tap the Reset All Settings button.

On the Internet, you can find various apps for speeding up the iPhone—but they all require you to "jailbreak" the iPhone in order to use them, because they are not approved by Apple. Jailbreaking involves circumventing Apple's security measures designed to ensure that only approved software runs on the iPhone (see Chapter 6).

Share Your iPhone's Internet Connection with Personal Hotspot

Your iPhone not only can get a high-speed Internet connection through the cellular network, but can also share that connection with your computer or other devices. This capability is great for when you're on the road and need to get your computer online where no Wi-Fi connection is available. But you can also use it for home Internet access if your data plan is generous enough.

Sharing the iPhone's Internet connection used to be called Internet tethering, but iOS 5 changes the name to Personal Hotspot. You can connect up to five computers or other devices at a time using Personal Hotspot. You can connect a single computer via USB or connect multiple computers and devices via Wi-Fi or Bluetooth. In this section, we'll look at how to use USB and Wi-Fi, which are the two most useful connections.

 USB gives the fastest connection to Personal Hotspot—but it works for only one computer at a time. Wi-Fi gives good speeds and is the best choice for connecting multiple devices. Bluetooth gives slower speeds and requires pairing your iPhone with the computer or device, so it is best used only when you have no other means of connection.

Set Up Personal Hotspot

To set up Personal Hotspot on your iPhone, follow these steps:

1. Press the Home button to display the Home screen.
2. Tap the Settings icon to display the Settings screen.
3. Scroll down a little way, and then tap the General button to display the General screen.
4. Tap the Network button to display the Network screen.
5. Tap the Personal Hotspot button to display the Personal Hotspot screen (shown on the left in Figure 18-2).
6. Tap the Personal Hotspot switch and move it to the On position. The Personal Hotspot screen shows that the network is discoverable under the name you've given your iPhone.
7. Look at the default password on the right side of the Wi-Fi Password button. If you want to change it, tap the Wi-Fi Password button, and then type the new password on the Wi-Fi Password screen (shown on the right in Figure 18-2). Tap the Done button to return to the Personal Hotspot screen.
8. Tap the Network button to return to the Network screen.
9. Tap the General button to return to the General screen.
10. Tap the Settings button to return to the main Settings screen. You'll see that Personal Hotspot now appears on it under the Wi-Fi item, giving you quick access to the settings for turning Personal Hotspot on and off.

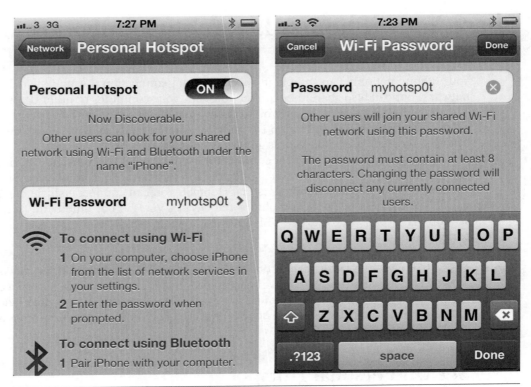

FIGURE 18-2 On the Personal Hotspot screen (left), move the Personal Hotspot switch to the On position, and then tap the Wi-Fi Password button to display the Wi-Fi Password screen (right). Type in the password you want to use, and then tap the Done button.

Now that you've turned on Personal Hotspot, you can connect your computers or devices to it.

Connect a Computer or Device to Personal Hotspot via Wi-Fi

To connect a computer or device to Personal Hotspot via Wi-Fi, you need only connect via Wi-Fi to the Personal Hotspot wireless network, just as you would connect to any other wireless network.

The Personal Hotspot wireless network has your iPhone's name and uses the password that appears on the Personal Hotspot screen.

Connect a Single Computer to Personal Hotspot via USB

Instead of connecting via Wi-Fi, you can connect a single computer to Personal Hotspot by using your iPhone's USB cable.

Connect a Windows PC to Personal Hotspot via USB

When you connect your iPhone via USB to a Windows PC, and Personal Hotspot is enabled on the iPhone, Windows automatically detects the iPhone's Internet connection as a new network connection. The first time this happens, Windows automatically installs the driver for the connection and displays the Driver Software Installation dialog box to let you know it has done so. Click the Close button to close the dialog box.

Next, Windows displays the Set Network Location dialog box (see Figure 18-3), asking you whether this new network is a Home Network, a Work Network, or a Public Network. Normally, you'll want to click the Home Network button here.

Windows then sets up the network. When it has done so, it displays another Set Network Location dialog box (see Figure 18-4) confirming the network location.

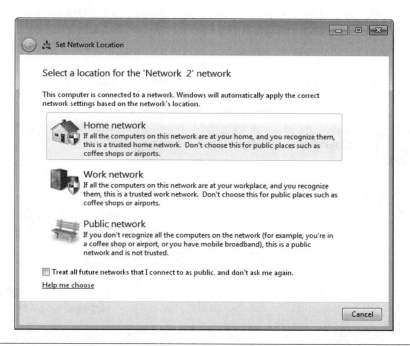

FIGURE 18-3 In the first Set Network Location dialog box, click the Home Network button to tell Windows that the Personal Hotspot network is safe to use.

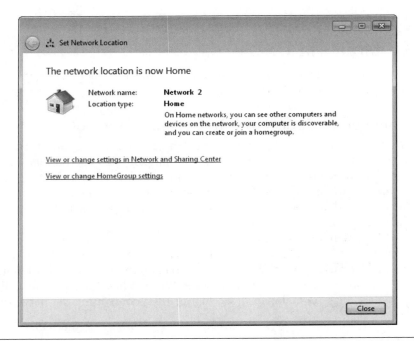

FIGURE 18-4 In the second Set Network Location dialog box, click the Close button. You can then start using the network.

Click the Close button to close the Set Network Location dialog box. The connection is now ready for you to use.

 An easy way to check that the Internet connection is working is to open Internet Explorer and see if it can load your home page.

Connect a Mac to Personal Hotspot via USB

When you connect your iPhone via USB to a Mac, and Personal Hotspot is enabled on the iPhone, the Mac automatically detects the iPhone's Internet connection as a new network connection. The first time this happens, Mac OS X automatically displays the Network preferences pane in System Preferences (see Figure 18-5) so that you can set up the network.

Click the iPhone USB interface in the left box, and then click the Apply button. Mac OS X assigns an IP address to the iPhone USB interface, and then displays the details (see Figure 18-6).

Press ⌘-Q or choose System Preferences | Quit System Preferences to quit System Preferences. You can now start using the Internet connection.

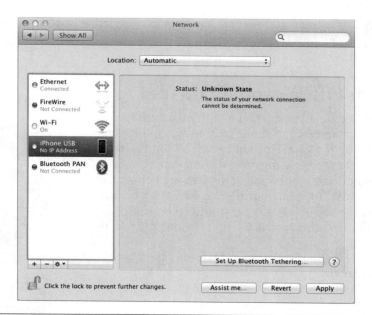

FIGURE 18-5   In the Network preferences pane in System Preferences, click the iPhone USB interface in the left box, and then click the Apply button.

FIGURE 18-6   Mac OS X assigns an IP address to the iPhone USB interface to enable your Mac to use the iPhone as a network connection.

If you want to check that the Internet connection is working, open Safari and see if your home page appears.

Turn Off Personal Hotspot

When Personal Hotspot is on with no computers or devices connected to it, the only way to tell it's on is that the Personal Hotspot switch on the Personal Hotspot screen is in the On Position.

When any computers or devices are connected to Personal Hotspot, your iPhone displays a blue bar across the top of the screen, as shown here.

To turn off Personal Hotspot, follow these steps:

1. Press the Home button to display the Home screen.
2. Tap the Settings icon to display the Settings screen.
3. Tap the Personal Hotspot button to display the Personal Hotspot screen.
4. Tap the Personal Hotspot switch and move it to the Off position.

Create Your Own Custom Ringtones

To make your iPhone sound unique and to give yourself a clear indication of when you receive phone calls, texts, voicemail, tweets, and so on, you can create custom ringtones and sync them to the iPhone.

Earlier versions of iTunes included a feature for making ringtones from songs bought from the iTunes Store. But Apple has removed this feature from iTunes 10, so you need to create your ringtones manually as described here.

To create a ringtone from a song, follow these steps:

1. Play the song and identify the part you want to use. This can be up to 30 seconds long. Note down the start time and end time.
2. Right-click or CTRL-click the song, and then click Get Info on the context menu to display the Item Information dialog box for the song. On Windows, this dialog box shows "iTunes" in its title bar; on the Mac, this dialog box shows the song's title rather than the words "Item Information."
3. Click the Options tab to bring it to the front of the Item Information dialog box (see Figure 18-7).

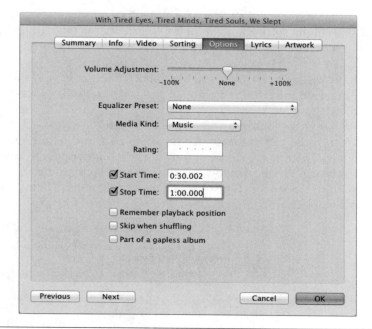

FIGURE 18-7 Use the Item Information dialog box (whose title bar shows the song's name in Mac OS X) to cut a ringtone out of a song.

4. Click in the Start Time box and enter the start time for the ringtone section— for example, 1:23.200. iTunes automatically selects the Start Time check box for you, so you don't need to select it manually.

When setting the Start Time value and Stop Time value, use a colon to separate the minutes and seconds but a period to separate the seconds and thousandths of seconds.

5. Click in the Stop Time box and enter the end time for the ringtone section. Again, iTunes automatically selects the Stop Time check box for you.
6. Click the OK button to close the Item Information dialog box.
7. Right-click or CTRL-click the song, and then click Create AAC Version on the context menu. iTunes creates a new song file containing just the section of the song you specified by using the Start Time value and Stop Time value.

If the command on the context menu is not Create AAC Version, you need to change the current encoder. Choose Edit | Preferences on Windows or iTunes | Preferences on the Mac to display the iTunes dialog box or the Preferences dialog box. On the General tab, click the Import Settings button. In the Import Settings dialog box, choose AAC Encoder in the Import Using drop-down list and iTunes Plus in the Setting drop-down list. Then click the OK button to close each dialog box in turn.

8. Right-click or CTRL-click the new, shorter song file, and then click Show In Finder on the context menu. iTunes opens a Finder window showing the song file.

9. Press RETURN to display an edit box around the song name.

10. Change the file extension from m4a to m4r, and then press RETURN to apply the change. The m4r extension indicates the file type for a ringtone.

11. Leave the Finder window open for the moment and go back to iTunes.

12. With the new song file still selected, choose Edit | Delete. iTunes displays a dialog box confirming you want to remove the file, as shown here.

13. Click the Remove button. iTunes displays a second dialog box asking if you want to move the file to the Trash, as shown here.

14. Click the Keep File button.

15. In the Finder window, click the ringtone file and drag it to the Library section of the Source list in the iTunes window.

16. You're almost done, but you've set the original song file to play only your ringtone section. Restore it to normality by following these substeps:
    a. Right-click or CTRL-click the original file in the iTunes window, and then choose Get Info to display the Item Information dialog box.
    b. If the Summary tab doesn't appear at the front, click it to bring it there.
    c. Clear the Start Time check box and the Stop Time check box.
    d. Click the OK button to close the Item Information dialog box.

17. Now click the Ringtones item in the Source list to display your ringtones. The file you created appears there, and you can start using it.

19

Troubleshoot Your iPhone

HOW TO...

- Understand what's in your iPhone
- Avoid things that may harm your iPhone
- Keep your iPhone's operating system up to date
- Carry, clean, and care for your iPhone—and avoid voiding the warranty
- Approach troubleshooting your iPhone
- Troubleshoot connection issues
- Deal with app crashes
- Restart, reset, or erase your iPhone
- Restore your iPhone

Apple designs and builds your iPhone to be as reliable as possible—after all, Apple would like to sell at least one iPhone to everyone in the world, and it would much prefer to be thwarted in this aim by economics or competition than by negative feedback.

But even so, iPhones go wrong sometimes. This chapter shows you what to do when your iPhone goes wrong.

We'll start by going over what your iPhone contains, and then briefly consider several things you should avoid because they're likely to make your iPhone temporarily or permanently unhappy. We'll then move on to how to keep your iPhone's operating system up to date, and how to carry, clean, and care for your favorite shiny toy.

After that, I'll show you how to troubleshoot connection issues between your iPhone and your computer; how to deal with app crashes; how to restart, reset, or erase your iPhone; and how to restore its software using iTunes. Along the way, you'll also learn how to drain the battery if your iPhone goes into a coma, and how to solve the problem of iTunes failing to transfer songs to your iPhone.

Chapter 20 explains how to troubleshoot iTunes.

Know What's in the iPhone

Much of the space behind the iPhone's touch screen is taken up by a large battery that can hold enough power for several days' standby, a day's worth of phone calls, or around 24 hours of audio playback.

Then there's the storage (for example, 16GB, 32GB, or 64GB of flash memory); the processor, wireless chips, and assorted circuitry; an amplifier and speaker; and a microphone, camera lens, and sensor. Compared to the touch screen and the battery, these items are surprisingly small.

Apart from these items, the iPhone also contains the following:

- **Antennas** The iPhone uses the antennas to connect to cell networks, Wi-Fi networks, Bluetooth, and GPS.
- **Ambient light sensor** The iPhone automatically changes the brightness of the screen to make it visible in current light conditions. You can turn off the light sensor and adjust the brightness manually.
- **Accelerometer and three-axis gyroscope** The accelerometer detects when you turn the iPhone and changes the display of supported programs to match the orientation. The gyroscope detects motion, the 3D attitude in which you're holding the iPhone (the iPhone's attitude, not yours—that's for passersby to critique), and the speed of rotation. For example, when browsing in Safari, when you turn the iPhone to landscape orientation, Safari changes the display of the current web page to landscape (which is normally better for browsing). When you rotate the iPhone in a game, the iPhone conveys that movement to the game, which reacts correspondingly.
- **SIM card** The SIM card lives in the slot at the side of the iPhone. You can take it out, but there's little reason to do so beyond curiosity unless you're planning to hack your iPhone with another SIM. (To open the SIM slot, push the SIM Eject tool that comes with the iPhone or a blunt object such as the end of a straightened paperclip into the little hole.)

Avoid Things That May Harm Your iPhone

This section discusses four items that are likely to make your iPhone unhappy: unexpected disconnections, fire and water (discussed together), and punishment. None of these should come as a surprise, and you should be able to avoid all of them most of the time.

Avoid Disconnecting Your iPhone at the Wrong Time

When you sync your iPhone, try to wait until syncing is complete before disconnecting it. Completing the sync enables the iPhone and iTunes to work out which files are supposed to be where and to resolve any conflicts or discrepancies.

 Disconnecting your iPhone at the wrong time may interrupt data transfer and corrupt files. In the worst case, you may need to restore your iPhone, losing any data on it that wasn't already on your computer (for example, files you have created on your iPhone since the last sync). But because Apple has been working to minimize problems caused by disconnection, you may be able to disconnect your iPhone at the wrong time without causing problems.

The easiest way to see if syncing is complete is to look at the iPhone's entry in the Source list in iTunes. If the round symbol on the right of the iPhone's entry shows two rotating arrows, syncing is underway. If the round symbol shows the Eject button, the sync is over, and the iPhone is ready for ejection.

 When your iPhone is connected to your computer via USB, the battery readout appears in the Source list between the iPhone's name and the round symbol. When your iPhone is connected via Wi-Fi, the battery readout doesn't appear.

The other way to see if syncing is still happening is to look at the iPhone's status bar. If the symbol with the two rotating arrows appears to the right of the carrier symbol and the Wi-Fi symbol (if the iPhone has a Wi-Fi connection), the sync is still running. If this symbol doesn't appear, the iPhone isn't syncing. Because your iPhone turns its screen off and locks it while syncing to save power, you may need to press the Home button or the Sleep/Wake button to illuminate the iPhone's screen so that you can see what's happening.

 If you have selected the Manually Manage Music And Videos check box for your iPhone, it's a good idea to eject your iPhone manually after each sync. The easiest way to eject it is to click the Eject button that appears next to it in the Source list in iTunes.

Avoid Fire and Water

Your iPhone has a wider range of operating temperatures than most humans, so if you keep it in your pocket or clipped to your belt, it will generally be at least as comfortable as you are.

Where your iPhone may run into trouble is if you leave it running in a confined space, such as the glove box of a car parked in the sun, that might reach searing temperatures. If you live somewhere sunny, take your iPhone with you when you get out of the car. I'm guessing you usually take your iPhone with you when you leave the car—but perhaps not when you park at the beach for a swim.

 If your iPhone gets much too hot or much too cold, don't use it. Give it time to return to a more normal temperature before trying to find out if it still works.

You can deal with excess heat by allowing it to dissipate, but water is trickier. You can see from the ports on the outside of your iPhone that your iPhone isn't waterproof. So unless you seal it in a fully waterproof case, don't expect to take it swimming or use it in the bath.

Avoid Physically Abusing Your iPhone

Apple has built your iPhone to be tough, so it will survive an impressive amount of rough handling. If you're interested in finding out how tough a particular model is without funding the experiment yourself, check out sites such as these:

- Ars Technica (http://arstechnica.com) performs real-world tests to destruction, such as dropping devices and seeing whether they work afterward.
- Will It Blend (www.willitblend.com) tests devices in a blender, which is entertaining if less practical. Will It Blend doesn't test the resulting debris to see if it works.

 Unless you need to be able to admire your iPhone's sleek casing and beautiful lines, protect it with a case. You can find any number of widely varied cases on sites such as the Apple Store (http://store.apple.com), Amazon (www.amazon. com), and eBay (www.ebay.com).

Keep Your iPhone's Operating System Up to Date

To get the best performance from your iPhone, it's a good idea to keep its operating system (or *firmware*) up to date. To do so, follow the instructions in this section to update your iPhone on its own (over the air), on Windows, or on Mac OS X.

Update Your iPhone over the Air

To update your iPhone using only the iPhone, follow these steps:

1. Press the Home button to display the Home screen.
2. Tap the Settings icon to display the Settings screen.

3. Scroll down to the third box, and then tap the General button to display the General screen.
4. Tap the Software Update button to display the Software Update screen. Software Update automatically checks for a new version.
5. If a new version is available, tap the button to download and install it.

 iPhone updates can involve transferring many megabytes of data. So when you're updating your iPhone, use a Wi-Fi network rather than a cellular connection unless you have an unlimited data plan and like to give it a good workout.

Update Your iPhone on Windows

iTunes is set to check automatically for updates for both itself and any iPhone you regularly connect to your PC, and it displays a message box such as that shown here if it finds an update. Click the Download And Install button to download the update and install it immediately, or click the Download Only button if you want to download the file and install it later at a time you choose.

 If you don't want iTunes to check for updates automatically, clear the Check For New Software Updates Automatically check box on the General tab of the iTunes dialog box.

Alternatively, you can check for updates manually. Follow these steps:

1. Connect your iPhone to your computer. The computer starts iTunes (if it's not running) or activates it (if it is running).
2. In iTunes, click your iPhone's entry in the Source list to display its control screens.
3. Click the Summary tab if it's not automatically displayed.
4. Click the Check For Update button.

When the update is complete, your iPhone appears in the Source list in iTunes.

Update Your iPhone on Mac OS X

You can get iPhone updates on Mac OS X in three ways:

- **iTunes** iTunes checks periodically for updates for both itself and any iPhone you sync with it. When it finds an update, iTunes displays a dialog box prompting you to download and install it, as shown here. Click the Download And Update button to download the update and install it immediately.

A new iPhone software version (5.0.1) is available for the iPhone "iPhone". Would you like to download it and update your iPhone now?

iTunes will verify the software update with Apple.

☐ Do not ask me again

Cancel   Download Only   Download and Update

Note If you don't want iTunes to check for updates automatically, clear the Check For New Software Updates Automatically check box on the General tab of the Preferences dialog box for iTunes.

- **Software Update** Choose Apple | Software Update to check for updates to Mac OS X and all Apple software. Mac OS X presents all updates to you in the Software Update dialog box. Click the Install button, and then enter your administrative password in the authentication dialog box. Mac OS X downloads the updates and installs them.

Alternatively, you can check for updates manually. Follow these steps:

1. Connect your iPhone to your computer. The computer starts iTunes (if it's not running) or activates it (if it is running).
2. In iTunes, click your iPhone's entry in the Source list to display your iPhone screens.
3. Click the Summary tab if it's not automatically displayed.
4. Click the Check For Update button, and then follow through the process of installing the update.

When the update is complete, your iPhone appears in the Source list in iTunes.

Carry, Clean, and Care for Your iPhone

Carrying and storing your iPhone safely is largely a matter of common sense:

- Use a case to protect your iPhone from scratches, dings, and falls. A wide variety of cases are available, from svelte-and-stretchy little numbers designed to hug your body during vigorous exercise, to armored cases apparently intended to

How to... ## Clean Your iPhone

To keep your iPhone looking its best, you'll probably need to clean it from time to time. Before doing so, unplug it to reduce the chance of short disagreements with the basic principles of electricity. Treat the Dock Connector port and headphone port with due care; neither is waterproof.

Various people recommend different cleaning products for cleaning iPhones. You'll find assorted recommendations on the Web—but unless you're sure the people know what they're talking about, proceed with great care. In particular, avoid any abrasive cleaner that may mar an iPhone's faceplate or its polished back and sides.

Unless you've dipped your iPhone in anything very unpleasant, you'll do best to start with Apple's recommendation: Simply dampen a soft, lint-free cloth (such as an eyeglass or camera-lens cloth) and wipe your iPhone gently with it.

But if you've scratched your iPhone, you may need to resort to heavier-duty cleaners. PodShop iDrops seems to have a good reputation; you can get it from Amazon.com and other online retailers, or directly from PodShop (http://podshop.com).

survive Vin Diesel movies, to waterproof cases good enough to take sailing, swimming, or even diving.

- If your iPhone spends time on your desk or another surface open to children, animals, or moving objects, use a dock or stand to keep it in place. A dock or stand should also make your iPhone easier to control with one hand. For example, if you connect your iPhone to your stereo via a cable, use a dock or stand to keep your iPhone upright so you can push its buttons with one hand.

Understand Your Warranty and Know Which Actions Void It

Like most electronics goods, your iPhone almost certainly came with a warranty. Unlike with most other electronics goods, your chances of needing to use that warranty are relatively high. This is because you're likely to use your iPhone extensively and carry it with you. After all, that's what it's designed for.

Even if you don't sit on your iPhone, rain or other water doesn't creep into it, and gravity doesn't dash it sharply against something unforgiving (such as the sidewalk), your iPhone may suffer from other problems—anything from critters or debris jamming the Dock Connector port, to its flash memory becoming faulty, its memory getting corrupted, or its operating system getting scrambled. Perhaps most likely of all is that the battery will lose its potency, either gradually or dramatically. If any of these misfortunes befalls your iPhone, you'll probably want to get it repaired under warranty—provided you haven't voided the warranty by treating your iPhone in a way that breaches its terms.

Your iPhone comes with a one-year warranty. To find details of whether your iPhone is under warranty, enter your iPhone's serial number and your country into Apple's Online Service Agent (https://selfsolve.apple.com).

Most of the warranty is pretty straightforward, but the following points are worth noting:

- Your iPhone isn't covered for damage by liquid. It contains two Liquid Contact Indicators to enable a technician to tell whether water has gone into the iPhone. One of the Liquid Contact Indicators is in the headphone port. The other is in the Dock Connector port. The Liquid Contact Indicators turn red when the iPhone gets wet.
- You have to make your claim within the warranty period, so if your iPhone fails a day short of a year after you bought it, you'll need to make your claim instantly. Do you know where your receipt is?
- If your iPhone is currently under warranty, you can buy an AppleCare package for it to extend its warranty to two years. Most extended warranties on electrical products are a waste of money, because the extended warranties largely duplicate your existing rights as a consumer to be sold a product that's functional and of merchantable quality. But given the attrition rate among hard-used iPhones, AppleCare may be a good idea.
- Apple can choose whether to repair your iPhone using either new or refurbished parts, exchange it for another device that's at least functionally equivalent but may be either new or rebuilt (and may contain used parts), or refund you the purchase price. Unless you have valuable data on your iPhone, the refund is a great option, because you'll be able to get a new iPhone—perhaps even a higher-capacity one.
- Apple takes no responsibility for getting back any data on your iPhone. This isn't surprising because Apple may need to reformat the memory or replace your iPhone altogether. But this means that you must back up your iPhone if it contains data you value that you don't have copies of elsewhere.

You can void your warranty more or less effortlessly in any of the following easily avoidable ways:

- Damage your iPhone deliberately.
- Open your iPhone or have someone other than Apple open it for you. The iPhone is designed to be opened only by trained technicians. The only reason to open an iPhone is to replace its battery or replace a component—and you shouldn't do that yourself unless your iPhone is out of warranty (and out of AppleCare, if you bought AppleCare for it). If you're tempted to replace a battery, make sure

you know what steps are involved. You can find detailed instructions online, especially in YouTube videos.

- Modify your iPhone. Modifications such as installing higher-capacity memory in an iPhone would necessarily involve opening it anyway, but external modifications can void your warranty, too. For example, if you choose to trepan your iPhone so as to screw a holder directly onto it, you would void your warranty. (You'd also stand a great chance of drilling into something sensitive inside the case.)

Approach Troubleshooting Your iPhone

When something goes wrong with your iPhone, take three deep breaths before you do anything. Then take another three deep breaths if you need them. Then try to work out what's wrong.

Remember that a calm and rational approach will always get you further than blind panic. This is easy to say (and if you're reading this when your iPhone is running smoothly, easy to nod your head at). But if you've just dropped your iPhone onto a hard surface from a great enough height for gravity to give it some acceleration, left it on the roof of your car so it fell off and landed in the perfect position for you to reverse over it, or gotten caught in an unexpectedly heavy rainfall, you'll probably be desperate to find out if your iPhone is alive or dead.

So take those three deep breaths. You may well *not* have ruined your iPhone forever—but if you take some heavy-duty troubleshooting actions without making sure they're necessary, you may lose some data that wasn't already lost or do some damage you'll have trouble repairing.

Things can go wrong with any of the following:

- Your iPhone's hardware—anything from the Dock Connector port or headphone port to the battery or the flash memory
- Your iPhone's software
- The cable you're using to connect your iPhone to your computer
- Your computer's USB port or USB controller
- iTunes

Given all these possibilities, be prepared to spend some time troubleshooting any problem.

Troubleshoot Connection Issues

If your computer (Mac or PC) doesn't react when you plug in your iPhone, any of several things might have gone wrong. Try the actions described in the following subsections.

Unplug Any Other Devices in the USB Chain

If there's another device plugged into your computer's USB controller, try unplugging it. The problem may be that the controller can't supply power to another unpowered device as well as to your iPhone.

If the connection uses a hub, disconnect the hub and try a direct connection.

 When checking the USB connection, disconnect any USB devices that aren't essential. For example, the mouse and keyboard are essential, so leave them—but disconnect your printer and scanner. If possible, eject and then disconnect any USB external drive you're using.

Check That the Cable Is Working

Make sure that the cable is firmly connected to your iPhone (or its dock) and to the USB port on your computer. If you normally use a dock or connecting stand for your iPhone, try the connection without it in case the dock or stand is causing the problem.

If you're not sure whether the cable is working, and you have an Apple USB Power Adapter, you can run a partial check by plugging the cable into your iPhone and the Apple USB Power Adapter, and then plugging the Apple USB Power Adapter into an electrical socket. If your iPhone starts charging, you'll know that at least the power-carrying wires on the cable are working. It's likely that the data-carrying wires are working as well.

Check That the USB Port on the Computer Is Working

In most cases, the easiest way to check is by plugging in another device that you know is working. For example, you might plug in a USB scanner or external DVD drive.

Deal with App Crashes

Normally, the programs on your iPhone just keep running: When you use the Home screen to switch to a different program, the program you were using before keeps running in the background, where you can't see it. When you go back to that program, you'll find it doing what it was doing before.

If a program stops responding, you can close it by "force-quitting" it—in other words, forcing it to quit. To force-quit a program, follow these steps:

1. Press the Home button twice in rapid succession to display the app-switching bar.
2. If the app you want to force-quit doesn't appear on the first screen displayed of the app-switching bar, scroll left or right until you can see it.

3. Tap and hold the app's icon on the app-switching bar until the icons start to jiggle and a Close button (a red circle with a horizontal white bar across it) appears at the upper-left corner of each icon, as shown here.

4. Tap the Close button for the app.
5. Press the Home button to stop the icons jiggling.

Restart, Reset, or Erase Your iPhone

Usually, you'll keep your iPhone running all the time so that you can receive incoming calls, texts, and e-mail messages even when you're not using any of its other functions. But if your iPhone gets seriously hung, so that it stops responding to the touch screen, you may need to restart it. If restarting doesn't work, you will need to reset it.

Restart Your iPhone

To restart your iPhone, follow these steps:

1. Hold down the Sleep/Wake button until the screen shows the message Slide To Power Off.
2. Slide your finger across the screen. The iPhone shuts down.
3. Wait a few seconds, and then press the Sleep/Wake button again. Hold the button down for a second or two until the Apple logo appears. The iPhone then starts.

Perform a Hardware Reset

If you're not able to restart your iPhone as described in the previous section, take the problem to the next level and perform a hardware reset. Hold down the Sleep/Wake button and the Home button together for around ten seconds until the Apple logo appears on the screen.

Perform a Software Reset

If performing a hardware reset (as described above) doesn't clear the problem, you may need to perform a software reset. This action resets the iPhone's settings but doesn't erase your data from it.

To perform a software reset, follow these steps:

1. Press the Home button to go to the Home screen unless you're already there.
2. Tap the Settings icon to display the Settings screen.
3. Scroll down to the third box, and then tap the General button to display the General screen.
4. Scroll down to the bottom and tap the Reset button to display the Reset screen (shown on the left in Figure 19-1).
5. Tap the Reset All Settings button, and then tap the Reset All Settings button in the confirmation dialog box (shown on the right in Figure 19-1.

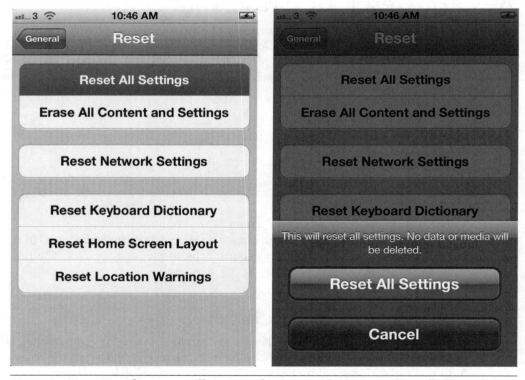

FIGURE 19-1 Tap the Reset All Settings button on the Reset screen (left), and then tap the Reset All Settings button in the confirmation dialog box (right).

Erase the Content and Settings on Your iPhone

If even the software reset doesn't fix the problem, try erasing all content and settings. Before you do so, remove any content you have created on your iPhone and not yet synced—assuming the iPhone is working well enough for you to do so. For example, send to yourself via e-mail any notes that you have written on your iPhone, or sync your iPhone to transfer any photos you have taken with its camera to your computer.

To erase the content and settings, follow these steps:

1. Press the Home button to display the Home screen unless you're already there.
2. Tap the Settings icon to display the Settings screen.
3. Scroll down to the third box, and then tap the General button to display the General screen.
4. Tap the Reset button to display the Reset screen.
5. Tap the Erase All Content And Settings button, and then tap the Erase iPhone button on the first confirmation screen.
6. Tap the Erase iPhone button on the second confirmation screen. (Erasure is such a serious move that the iPhone makes you confirm it twice.)

After erasing all content and settings, sync your iPhone to load the content and settings back onto it.

How to... **Drain Your iPhone's Battery**

If you can't reset your iPhone, its battery might have gotten into such a low state that it needs draining. This supposedly seldom happens—but the planets might have decided that you're due a bad day.

To drain the battery, disconnect your iPhone from its power source and leave it for 24 hours. Then try plugging your iPhone into a power source—either a USB socket on a computer or the Apple USB Power Adapter. After your iPhone has received power for a few seconds, perform a hardware reset by holding down the Sleep/Wake button and the Home button together for around ten seconds until the Apple logo appears on the screen.

If draining the battery and recharging it revives your iPhone, update your iPhone's software with the latest version to try to prevent the problem from occurring again. See the section "Keep Your iPhone's Operating System Up to Date," earlier in this chapter, for details on how to update the operating system.

Restore Your iPhone

If you've tried all the other troubleshooting actions described earlier in this chapter, and your iPhone is still acting hinky, you need to restore it. The process is the same for Windows and the Mac; this section shows screens from the Mac.

Restoring your iPhone wipes all the data off the device, resets the hardware, and reinstalls the software. Restoring your iPhone essentially returns it to the condition in which you bought it, except that the SIM remains activated. After restoring your iPhone, you sync it with iTunes again, and it picks up all the data from iTunes (and other programs, such as your address book) that it had before.

 Before restoring your iPhone, remove any content that you've created on it—for example, notes, photos, or screen captures—and not yet synced. Again, this assumes that your iPhone is functioning well enough for you to remove the content.

To restore your iPhone, follow these steps:

1. Connect your iPhone to your computer, and wait for it to appear in the Source list in iTunes.
2. Click your iPhone's entry in the Source list to display the iPhone screens.
3. Click the Summary tab if it's not already displayed.
4. Click the Restore button. iTunes displays a confirmation dialog box, as shown here, to make sure you know that you're about to erase all the data from the device.

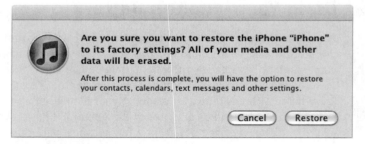

 If a new version of the iPhone software is available, iTunes prompts you to restore and update the device instead of merely restoring it. Click the Restore And Update button if you want to proceed; otherwise, click the Cancel button.

5. Click the Restore button to close the dialog box. iTunes wipes the device's contents, and then restores the software, showing you its progress while it works.
6. At the end of the restore process, iTunes restarts your iPhone. iTunes displays an information message box for ten seconds while it does so. Either click

FIGURE 19-2   After restoring your iPhone's system software, you will normally want to restore your data from backup. The alternative is to set up your iPhone as a new iPhone.

the OK button or allow the countdown timer to close the message box automatically.

7. After your iPhone restarts, it appears in the Source list in iTunes. Instead of the iPhone's regular tabbed screens, the Set Up Your iPhone screen appears (see Figure 19-2).

8. To restore your data, make sure the Restore From The Backup Of option button is selected, and verify that the correct iPhone appears in the drop-down list.

9. Click the Continue button. iTunes restores your data and then restarts the iPhone, displaying another countdown message box while it does so. Either click the OK button or allow the countdown timer to close the message box automatically.

10. After your iPhone appears in the Source list in iTunes following the restart, you can use it as normal.

Resolve the "SIM Card Is Not Installed" Error on an iPhone

If your iPhone shows you the message "The iPhone cannot be used with iTunes because the SIM card is not installed," have a look at the iPhone's SIM slot to make sure that it hasn't been popped out. Normally, opening the SIM slot requires human intervention, though not necessarily your own—for example, the iPhone seems to have an even greater attraction for children than for adults.

If the SIM slot is open, make sure the SIM is correctly aligned, and then push it back in. If the SIM slot seems fine, check the USB connection between your iPhone and your computer. This error can occur when the connection between the two is broken while iTunes is trying to access the iPhone—for example, if you bump the iPhone shortly after you put it in a dock.

Solve the Problem of Songs Not Being Transferred to Your iPhone

If songs you've added to your library aren't transferred to your iPhone even though you've synchronized successfully since adding the songs, there are two possibilities:

- First, check that you haven't configured your iPhone for partial synchronization or manual synchronization. For example, if you've chosen to synchronize only selected playlists, your iPhone won't synchronize new music files not included on those playlists.
- Second, check that the songs' tags include the artist's name and song name. Without these two items of information, iTunes doesn't transfer the songs to your iPhone, because your iPhone's interface won't be able to display the songs to you. You can force iTunes to transfer song files that lack artist and song name tags by adding the song files to a playlist, but in the long run, you'll benefit from tagging all your song files correctly.

20

Troubleshoot iTunes

In the previous chapter, you learned how to troubleshoot problems that occur with your iPhone itself. But that's only the first part of the equation. In this chapter, I'll show you how to troubleshoot problems that occur with iTunes.

We'll start by looking at problems that occur on Windows. These range from iTunes refusing to start, through iTunes refusing to play certain files even though they're in the AAC file format, to iTunes complaining that it isn't your default player when it does consent to start.

After that, we'll look at problems that occur on the Mac. These include iTunes objecting that your iPhone is linked to another iTunes library, claiming that you don't have enough access privileges when you try to import songs, and running you flat out of disk space when you try to consolidate your library.

Toward the end of the chapter, I'll show you how to troubleshoot the problems that arise most frequently with iTunes' Home Sharing feature. These problems occur equally on Windows and the Mac, so we'll deal with both operating systems together.

 Before trying to solve iPhone-related problems in this chapter, make sure you've taken care of any connection issues as discussed in Chapter 19.

Troubleshoot iTunes on Windows

This section shows you how to troubleshoot the problems you're most likely to encounter when running iTunes on Windows.

iTunes Won't Start on Windows

If iTunes displays the Cannot Open iTunes dialog box saying that you can't open iTunes because another user currently has it open, it means that Windows is using Fast Switching and that someone else is logged on under another account and has iTunes open. The following illustration shows the Cannot Open iTunes dialog box on Windows 7, but this dialog box also appears on Windows Vista and Windows XP.

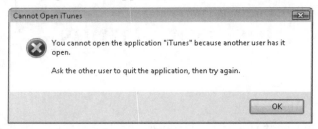

Click the OK button to dismiss the dialog box. If you know the other user's password, or if you know they have no password, switch to their account, close iTunes, and then switch back to your own account.

If you don't know the other user's password and you have a Standard user account (Windows 7 or Windows Vista) or a Limited user account (Windows XP), you'll need to get them to log on and close iTunes for you.

If you have an Administrator account, you can use Task Manager to close iTunes. Follow these steps:

1. Right-click the taskbar, and then choose Task Manager from the shortcut menu to open Task Manager.
2. Click the Processes tab to display its contents. At first, as shown on the left in Figure 20-1, Task Manager shows only the processes running for your user session of Windows, not for other users' sessions.
3. Display processes for all users:
   - **Windows 7 or Windows Vista**   Click the Show Processes From All Users button. You may then need to go through User Account Control for the Windows Task Manager feature. Task Manager replaces the Show Processes From All Users button with the Show Processes From All Users check box (which it selects), and then adds the other users' processes to the list.
   - **Windows XP**   Select the Show Processes From All Users check box.
4. Select the iTunes.exe process in the Image Name column, as shown on the right in Figure 20-1. (If the list isn't sorted by the Image Name column, click the Image Name header to sort it that way.)
5. Click the End Process button. Task Manager displays the dialog box shown next, confirming that you want to end the process.

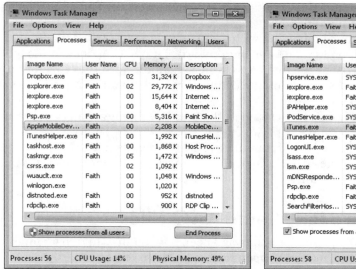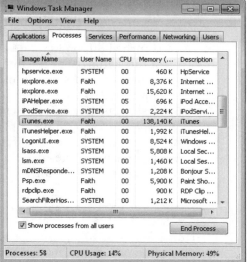

FIGURE 20-1   If someone else is running iTunes on a Windows 7 or Windows Vista computer that uses Fast User Switching, you may need to use Task Manager to close iTunes before you can use it.

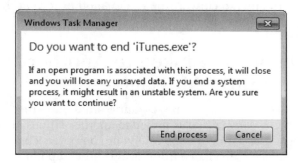

6. Click the End Process button. Task Manager closes the instance of iTunes in the other user's session.
7. Click the Close button (the × button) to close Task Manager.

You can now start iTunes as normal.

iTunes Doesn't Recognize Your iPhone

If your iPhone doesn't appear in the Source list in iTunes, take as many of the following steps as necessary to make it appear there:

1. Check that your iPhone is okay. If you find it won't turn on at all, you'll know iTunes isn't guilty this time.
2. Check that your iPhone knows it's connected to your PC. If the iPhone's screen is turned off, press the Home button to turn it on. Then look at the left end of the status bar at the top to see if the sync indicator—the circle of turning arrows—appears. If not, fix the connection so that your iPhone knows it's connected to the computer.
3. Reset your iPhone as discussed in the previous chapter, and then see if it appears in the Source list.
4. Restart iTunes, and see if it notices your iPhone this time.
5. If restarting iTunes doesn't make it recognize your iPhone, restart Windows, and then restart iTunes.

iTunes Won't Play Some AAC Files

iTunes and AAC go together like pizza and beer, but you may find that iTunes can't play some AAC files. This can happen for either of two reasons:

- You're trying to play a protected AAC file in a shared library or playlist, and your computer isn't authorized to play the file. In this case, iTunes skips the protected file.
- The AAC file was created by an application other than iTunes that uses a different AAC standard. The AAC file then isn't compatible with iTunes. To play the file, use the application that created the file, or another application that can play the file, to convert the file to another format that iTunes supports—for example, MP3 or WAV.

The iPhone "Is Linked to Another iTunes Library" Message

If, when you connect the iPhone to your computer, iTunes displays a message such as "The iPhone '*iPhone_name*' is linked to another iTunes library," chances are that you've plugged the wrong iPhone into your computer. The dialog box also offers to change this device's allegiance from its current computer to this PC. Click the No button and check which iPhone this is before synchronizing it.

 For details about moving an iPhone from one computer to another, see the section "Change the Computer to Which the iPhone Is Linked" in Chapter 18.

iTunes Runs You Out of Hard-Disk Space on Windows

As you saw earlier in the book, when you add files to your library, you can choose how to add them:

- Copy the files to your library folder
- Leave the files in their current folders and add references to your library that indicate where the files are located

Adding all the files to your library means you have all the files available in one place. This can be good, especially if your computer is a laptop and you want to be able to access your music and videos when it's not connected to your external drives or network drives. But if you have a large library, it may not all fit on your laptop's hard disk. In this case, adding references enables you to add the files to your library without taking up extra space.

If your files are stored on your hard drive in folders other than your library folder, you have three choices:

- You can issue the File | Library | Organize Library command, and then select the Consolidate Files check box, to make iTunes copy the files to your library folder, doubling the amount of space they take up. In almost all cases, this is the worst possible choice to make. (Rarely, you might want redundant copies of your files in your library so you can experiment with them.)
- You can have iTunes store references to the files rather than copies of them. If you also have files in your library folder, this is the easiest solution. To do this, clear the Copy Files To iTunes Media Folder When Adding To Library check box on the Advanced tab in the iTunes dialog box in Windows.
- You can move your library to the folder that contains your files. This is the easiest solution if your library is empty.

If you choose to consolidate your library, and there's not enough space on your hard disk, you'll see the following message box. "IBM_PRELOAD" is the name of the hard disk on the computer.

Clearly, this *isn't* okay, but iTunes doesn't let you cancel the operation. Don't let iTunes pack your hard disk as full of files as it can, because that may make Windows crash. Quit iTunes by pressing ALT-F4 or choosing File | Exit. If iTunes doesn't respond, right-click the taskbar and choose Task Manager to display Windows Task Manager. On the Applications tab, select the iTunes entry, and then click the End Task button. If Windows double-checks that you want to end the task, confirm the decision.

Once you've done this, you may need to remove the files you've just copied to your library from the folder. You can do this by using the Date Created information about the files and folders, because Windows treats the copy made by the consolidation as a new file.

To find the files and folders, search for them. The process differs on Windows 7, Windows Vista, and Windows XP, so follow the instructions in the next sections for the OS you're using.

Search for the New Files and Folders on Windows 7

To search for the new files and folders on Windows 7, follow these steps:

1. Choose Start | Computer to open a Computer window.
2. Click in the Search box in the upper-right corner of the window to place the insertion point there.
3. Type **datecreated:** (including the colon) to start a search filter based on the Created attribute of the folders. Windows opens the Select A Date Or Date Range panel.
4. In the Select A Date Or Date Range panel, double-click today's date. Windows returns a list of the folders created today (see Figure 20-2).
5. Select the folders created by the consolidation, and then press SHIFT-DELETE to delete them without adding them to the Recycle Bin (because you're out of space).

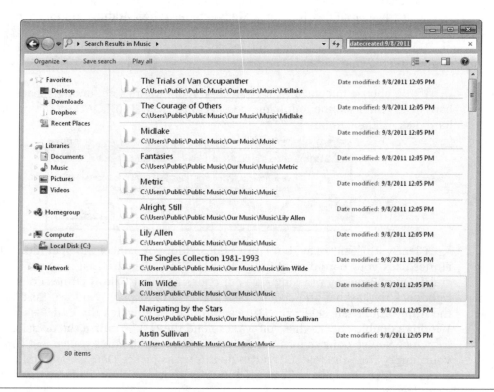

FIGURE 20-2   Use the datecreated: search term to search for items created today.

Search for the New Files and Folders on Windows Vista

To search for the new files and folders on Windows Vista, follow these steps:

1. Choose Start | Search to display a Search Results window.
2. Click the Advanced Search link at the right end of the toolbar to display the Advanced Search options.
3. In the Location drop-down list, click the Choose Search Location item to display the Choose Search Locations dialog box.
4. In the Change Selected Locations box, navigate to the folder that contains your iTunes Media folder. For example, if your iTunes Media folder is in its default location, follow these steps:
   a. Click the triangle next to your username to expand its contents.

> **Note**   If you're not sure where your iTunes Media folder is, switch to iTunes, press CTRL-COMMA, and look at the iTunes Media Folder Location box on the Advanced tab in the iTunes dialog box.

   b. Click the triangle next to the Media folder to expand its contents.
   c. Click the triangle next to the iTunes folder to expand its contents.
   d. Click the iTunes Media folder to select its check box. Windows adds the folder to the Summary Of Selected Locations list box.
5. Click the OK button to close the Choose Search Locations dialog box and enter the folder you chose in the Location drop-down list in the Search Results window.
6. On the line below the Location drop-down list, set up the condition Date Created (in the first drop-down list), Is (in the second drop-down list), and today's date (in the third drop-down list).
7. Click the Search button. Windows searches and returns a list of the files and folders created.
8. If the Search Results window is using any view other than Details view, choose Views | Details to switch to Details view.
9. Display the Date Created column by taking the following steps:
   a. Right-click an existing column heading, and then choose More from the shortcut menu to display the Choose Details dialog box.
   b. Select the Date Created check box.
   c. Click the OK button to close the Choose Details dialog box.
10. Click the Date Created column heading twice to make Windows Explorer sort the files by reverse date. This way, the files created most recently appear at the top of the list.
11. Check the Date Created column to identify the files created during the consolidation, and then delete them without putting them in the Recycle Bin. (For example, select the files and press SHIFT-DELETE.)
12. Click the Close button (the × button) to close the Search Results window.

After deleting the files (or as many of them as possible), you'll need to remove the references from iTunes and add them again from their preconsolidating location before iTunes can play them. When iTunes discovers that it can't find a file where it's supposed to be, it displays an exclamation point in the first column. Delete the entries with exclamation points and then add them to your library again.

Search for the New Files and Folders on Windows XP

To search for the new files and folders on Windows XP, follow these steps:

1. Choose Start | Search to display a Search Results window.
2. On the What Do You Want To Search For? screen, click the Pictures, Music, Or Video link. (If Search Companion displays the Search By Any Or All Of The Criteria Below screen instead of the What Do You Want To Search For? screen, click the Other Search Options link to display the What Do You Want To Search For? screen. Then click the Pictures, Music, or Video link.)
3. On the resulting screen, select the Music check box and the Video check box in the "Search For All Files Of A Certain Type, Or Search By Type And Name" area.
4. Click the Use Advanced Search Options link to display the remainder of the Search Companion pane.
5. Display the Look In drop-down list, select the Browse item to display the Browse For Folder dialog box, select your iTunes Media folder, and then click the OK button.

 If you're not sure where your iTunes Media folder is, switch to iTunes, press CTRL-COMMA, and look at the iTunes Media Folder Location box on the General subtab of the Advanced tab in the iTunes dialog box.

6. Click the When Was It Modified? heading to display its controls and then select the Specify Dates option button. Select the Created Date item in the drop-down list and then specify today's date in the From drop-down list and the To drop-down list. (The easiest way to specify the date is to open the From drop-down list and select the Today item. Windows XP then enters it in the To text box as well.)
7. Click the Search button to start the search for files created in the specified time frame.
8. If the Search Results window is using any view other than Details view, choose View | Details to switch to Details view.
9. Click the Date Created column heading twice to make Windows Explorer sort the files by reverse date. This way, the files created most recently appear at the top of the list.
10. Check the Date Created column to identify the files created during the consolidation, and then delete them without putting them in the Recycle Bin. (For example, select the files and press SHIFT-DELETE.)

After deleting the files (or as many of them as possible), you'll need to remove the references from iTunes and add them again from their preconsolidating location before iTunes can play them. When iTunes discovers that it can't find a file where it's supposed to be, it displays an exclamation point in the first column. Delete the entries with exclamation points and then add them to your library again.

"iTunes Has Detected That It Is Not the Default Player" Message on Startup

When you start iTunes, you may see the dialog box shown next, telling you that "iTunes has detected that it is not the default player for audio files" and inviting you to go to the Default Programs control panel to fix the problem.

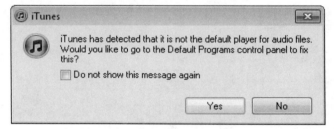

This dialog box doesn't indicate a problem as most people understand the word, but having it appear each time you start iTunes grows old fast, so you'll probably either want to suppress the dialog box or deal with the problem.

What's happened is that some other audio player has grabbed the associations for one or more of the audio file types that iTunes can play. For example, Windows Media Player may have taken the association for the MP3 file type. In this case, if you double-click an MP3 file in a Windows Explorer window, the file will play in Windows Media Player rather than in iTunes.

If you've set up your file associations deliberately to use different programs, simply select the Do Not Show This Message Again check box, and then click the No button. iTunes will drop the matter and not bug you again.

If you want to reassign the file associations to iTunes, click the Yes button. iTunes opens the Set Program Associations window (see Figure 20-3), which shows you the available associations and the programs to which they are assigned.

Select the check box for each file type you want to associate with iTunes, and then click the Save button.

Troubleshoot iTunes on the Mac

This section shows you how to troubleshoot a handful of problems that you may run into when running iTunes on the Mac.

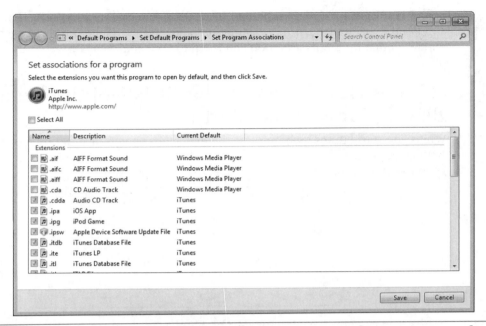

FIGURE 20-3 You can use the Set Program Associations window to reassign audio file associations to iTunes after other programs have grabbed them.

The iPhone "Is Linked to Another iTunes Library" Message

If, when you connect the iPhone to your computer, iTunes displays a message such as "The iPhone '*iPhone_name*' is linked to another iTunes library," chances are that you've plugged the wrong iPhone into your computer. The dialog box also offers to change this device's allegiance from its current computer to this Mac. Click the No button and check which iPhone this is before synchronizing it.

Eject a "Lost" CD

Sometimes Mac OS X seems to lose track of a CD (or DVD) after attempting to eject it. It's as if the eject mechanism fails to get a grip on the CD and push it out, but the commands get executed anyway, so that Mac OS X believes it has ejected the CD even though the CD is still in the drive.

When this happens, you probably won't be able to eject the disc by issuing another Eject command from iTunes, but it's worth trying that first. If that doesn't work, use Disk Utility to eject the disc. Follow these steps:

1. Press ⌘-SHIFT-U or choose Go | Utilities from the Finder menu to display the Utilities folder.
2. Double-click the Disk Utility item to run it.
3. Select the icon for the CD drive or the CD itself in the list box.
4. Click the Eject button.
5. Press ⌘-Q or choose Disk Utility | Quit Disk Utility to quit Disk Utility.

If that doesn't work, you may need to force your Mac to recognize the drive. If it's a hot-pluggable external drive (for example, FireWire or USB), try unplugging the drive, waiting a minute, and then plugging it back in. If the drive is an internal drive, you may need to restart your Mac to force it to recognize the drive.

If the disc is still stuck in your Mac's internal optical drive, follow as many of these steps as necessary to eject it:

1. Restart your Mac. If it's too hung to restart by conventional means, press the Reset button (if it has one) or press ⌘-CTRL-POWER. At the system startup sound, hold down the mouse button until your Mac finishes booting. This action may eject the disc.
2. Restart your Mac again. As before, if the Mac is too hung to restart by conventional means, press the Reset button or press ⌘-CTRL-POWER. At the system startup sound, hold down ⌘-OPTION-O-F to boot to the Open Firmware mode.
3. Type **eject cd** and press RETURN. If all is well, the CD drive will open. If not, you may see the message "read of block0 failed. can't OPEN the EJECT device." Either way, type **mac-boot** and press RETURN to reboot your Mac.

If Open Firmware mode won't fix the problem, you'll need to take your Mac to a service shop.

"You Do Not Have Enough Access Privileges" When Importing Songs

The following error occurs when you've moved the iTunes Media folder to a shared location and the user doesn't have Write permission to it.

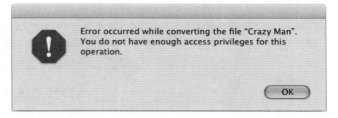

Error occurred while converting the file "Crazy Man". You do not have enough access privileges for this operation.

OK

To fix this problem, an administrator needs to assign Write permission for the iTunes Media folder to whoever received this error.

Audio Stops When iTunes Starts Playing Another Song

Sometimes iTunes has been playing audio just fine—but when it starts playing another song, the audio just stops.

The lack of sound suggests that there's something wrong with the song file, but usually there isn't. Simply double-click the song to restart it, and all should be well.

If you can't already see the song, press ⌘-L or choose View | Go To Current Song to display it. Then double-click the song.

If restarting the song doesn't start the audio again, restart iTunes.

iTunes Runs You Out of Hard-Disk Space on the Mac

As you saw earlier in the book, when you add files to your library, iTunes can copy the files to your library folder. Adding all the files to your library means you have all the files available in one place. This can be good when (for example) you want your MacBook's hard disk to contain copies of all the song and video files stored on network drives so you can enjoy them when your computer isn't connected to the network. But it can take more disk space than is free on your Mac's hard disk.

If your files are stored on your hard drive in folders other than your library folder, you have three choices:

- You can choose File | Library | Organize Library, select the Consolidate Files check box, and then click the OK button to cause iTunes to copy the files to your library. This doubles the amount of space the files take up and is usually the worst choice. (Rarely, you might want redundant copies of your files in your library so you can experiment with them.)
- You can have iTunes store references to the files rather than copies of them. If you also have files in your library folder, this is the easiest solution. To do this, clear the Copy Files To iTunes Media Folder When Adding To Library check box on the Advanced tab in the Preferences dialog box.
- You can move your library to the folder that contains your files. This is the easiest solution if your library is empty.

If you choose to consolidate your library, and your Mac doesn't have enough disk space, iTunes displays this message box to alert you to the problem.

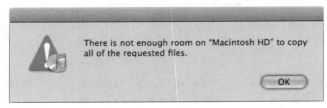

Click the OK button to dismiss this message box—iTunes gives you no other choice. Worse, when you click the OK button, iTunes goes ahead and tries to copy all the files anyway.

This is a bad idea, so stop the copying process as soon as you can. To do so, quit iTunes by pressing ⌘-Q or choosing iTunes | Quit iTunes. If you can't quit iTunes gently, force quit it: OPTION-click the iTunes icon in the Dock, and then choose Force Quit from the shortcut menu. (Failing that, press ⌘-OPTION-ESC to display the Force Quit dialog box, click the entry for iTunes, and then click the Force Quit button.)

Once you've done this, remove the files you've just copied to your library from the folder. Unfortunately, Mac OS X maintains the Date Created information from the original files on the copies made by the consolidation, so you can't search for the files by date created on the Mac the way you can on Windows.

Your best bet is to search by date created to identify the folders that iTunes has just created in your library folder so that you can delete them and their contents. This approach will get all of the consolidated songs and videos that iTunes put into new folders, but it will miss any songs and videos that were consolidated into folders that already existed in your library.

For example, if the song file I Love That Girl.m4a is already stored in your library with correct tags, your library will contain a John Hiatt/Dirty Jeans & Mudslide Hymns folder. If you then consolidate your library so that other songs from that album are copied, the files will go straight into the existing folder, and your search will miss it. The date-modified attribute of the Dirty Jeans & Mudslide Hymns folder will change to the date of the consolidation, but you'll need to drill down into each modified folder to find the song files that were added.

To search for the new folders, follow these steps:

1. Open a Finder window to the folder that contains your iTunes Media folder. For example, in Column view, click the Finder icon on the Dock, click the Music item in the Sidebar, click the iTunes folder, and then click the iTunes Media folder.

 If you're not sure which folder the iTunes Media folder is in, look on the Advanced tab in iTunes' Preferences dialog box.

2. Press ⌘-F or choose File | Find to display the Search bar, and then click the iTunes Media button on it to tell Mac OS X to search in that folder.
3. In the top search line, set up this condition: Kind: Folders.
4. In the second search line, set up this condition: Created Date Is Today. Mac OS X searches for folders created today and displays a list of them.
5. Sort the folders by date created, identify those created during the consolidation by the time on the date, and then delete them.
6. Verify that the Trash contains no other files you care about, and then empty the Trash to get rid of the surplus files.

After deleting the files (or as many of them as possible), you'll need to remove the references from iTunes and add them again from their preconsolidating location before iTunes can play them. When iTunes discovers that it can't find a file where it's supposed to be, it displays an exclamation point in the first column. Delete the files with exclamation points and then add them to your library again.

Troubleshoot Problems with Home Sharing on Windows and the Mac

Home Sharing is a great feature, and you'll probably want to make the most of it. So it's doubly frustrating when Home Sharing won't work. To help you get Home Sharing working, this section explains how to solve a handful of the problems and apparent problems that crop up most frequently with Home Sharing.

Home Sharing Isn't Available in iTunes 8 or Earlier

Apple introduced Home Sharing in iTunes 9, so if you have an earlier version of iTunes, you need to upgrade.

Usually, you'll do best to get the latest version of iTunes, which you can find on the Apple website (www.apple.com/itunes/download). The only exception is if your computer's operating system doesn't support the latest version of iTunes. In this case, get the latest version the operating system can handle.

Home Sharing Computers Can't See Each Other on the Network

If your Home Sharing computers can't see each other's songs and other items on the network, first make sure that the computers are connected to the same network. In a home setup, this is usually clear enough, unless you've deliberately divided the network into different *subnets* (logical sections) to keep your loved ones away from your mission-critical files. But if you're dealing with a bigger network, such as a dorm network, it may be divided into different subnets, in which computers on each subnet can see only other computers on that subnet.

Second, make sure that iTunes on each computer is set to use the same Apple ID. If you've set up two (or more) Apple IDs, and you're using different ones for different computers, you'll need to standardize on a single Apple ID for Home Sharing.

If the computers are on the same network and using the same Apple ID, check whether the computers can see other shared items—for example, printers or shared folders of files. If they can, most likely the router is set to suppress *multicasting*, a feature that sends data packets to several computers at once across the network. Home Sharing requires multicasting to be turned on, but some routers turn it off by default to help avoid too much traffic bouncing around the network and overwhelming it.

How to... **Deal with Occasional Glitches in Home Sharing**

Once you've gotten Home Sharing working, it usually works consistently. But if you find Home Sharing is acting hinky, try these four basic moves to get it working again. Start at the beginning, and stop when the problems disappear.

- **Restart iTunes** Begin by restarting iTunes on each of the computers you're using.
- **Restart your wireless network connections** If your computers are using wireless network connections, drop each connection, and then reestablish it. For example, on Mac OS X, click the Wi-Fi menu or AirPort menu on the menu bar, and then click Turn Wi-Fi Off or Turn AirPort Off. Click the menu again, and then click Turn Wi-Fi On or Turn AirPort On.
- **Restart your PC or Mac** This move is tedious, but it clears up many problems.
- **Restart your router** This move is even more tedious, because it takes down your Internet connection—but it often solves problems with Home Sharing.

If this seems to be the case, log in to your router's configuration utility or web-based configuration screens and look for an option for turning on multicasting. Routers use different terms for this, and the configuration tools hide it in different locations, so you'll need to use your initiative. For example, some Linksys routers have a Filter Multicast check box, which you can find in the Security | Firewall area.

The Home Sharing Item Disappears from the Source List When You Set Up Home Sharing

This isn't actually a problem—it's just that the way the iTunes user interface works is a bit confusing.

Before you set up Home Sharing on a computer, the Home Sharing item appears in the Source list in iTunes. This item gives you access to the controls for setting up Home Sharing. But as soon as you finish setting up Home Sharing on that computer, the Home Sharing item disappears from the Source list. Instead, you see whichever Home Sharing libraries are available, each showing a house icon to indicate that it's Home Sharing rather than plain old sharing. This is normal.

Home Sharing Transfers Duplicate Files

When transferring files, Home Sharing doesn't check if your library already contains copies of the files you're transferring. So if the files you tell Home Sharing to transfer include files your library already contains, you'll get duplicate files.

To avoid this problem, open the Show drop-down list and choose Items Not In My Library rather than All Items. iTunes then displays only those items in the shared library that your library doesn't contain.

 Use the File | Display Duplicates command to identify duplicate files within your library.

Home Sharing Doesn't Transfer Playlists and Ratings

Some people expect Home Sharing to transfer playlists and ratings from one computer to another. But this is simply something Home Sharing doesn't do.

 If you want to copy or move your playlists and ratings from one computer to another, you need to export your library from the source computer (the computer that currently contains it) and then import it to the destination computer. Before you import the library on the destination computer, use Home Sharing to make sure that the destination computer's library contains all the files that the source computer's library contains.

Index